HANDBOOK ON THE ECONOMICS OF THE MEDIA

Handbook on the Economics of the Media

Edited by

Robert G. Picard

Reuters Institute, University of Oxford, UK

Steven S. Wildman

Michigan State University, USA

Edward Elgar
PUBLISHING

Cheltenham, UK • Northampton, MA, USA

Published by
Edward Elgar Publishing Limited
The Lypiatts
15 Lansdown Road
Cheltenham
Glos GL50 2JA
UK

Edward Elgar Publishing, Inc.
William Pratt House
9 Dewey Court
Northampton
Massachusetts 01060
USA

A catalogue record for this book
is available from the British Library

Library of Congress Control Number: 2014952137

This book is available electronically in the **Elgar**online
Economics subject collection
DOI 10.4337/ 9780857938893

MIX
Paper from
responsible sources
FSC® C013056

ISBN 978 0 85793 888 6 (cased)
ISBN 978 0 85793 889 3 (eBook)

Typeset by Columns Design XML Ltd, Reading
Printed and bound in Great Britain by T.J. International Ltd, Padstow

Contents

PART III ECONOMICS AND POLICY

Contributors

Nodir Adilov is Associate Professor and Chair of the Economics Department at Indiana-Purdue University, Fort Wayne. Adilov's peer-reviewed work has been published in a variety of journals, including *Economic Inquiry*, *International Journal of Industrial Organization*, *Economics Letters*, and *Information Economics and Policy*, among many others. Adilov's published output is wide-ranging, covering strategic bargaining, merger analysis, environmental issues, copyrights, monetary policy, and a pioneering economic model of peer-to-peer file sharing. Adilov is currently the co-editor of the *Journal of Media Economics*.

Peter J. Alexander is a Senior Economist at the Federal Communications Commission in Washington, DC. His research has been published in a variety of journals, including the *Journal of Economic Behavior and Organization*, *Economics Letters*, *American Sociological Review*, and the *Review of Industrial Organization*. Alexander's published output covers strategic bargaining, merger analysis, peer-to-peer file sharing, technological change, and the economics of culture-based industries, among other topics.

Patrick Barwise is Emeritus Professor of Management and Marketing at London Business School, a visiting fellow at the Reuters Institute, University of Oxford, and Chairman of Which?, the UK's leading consumer organization. He joined LBS in 1976 after an early career at IBM and has published widely on management, marketing, and media. His interest in the media focuses on audience behaviour, revenue, and related policy implications, mainly in the context of television and new media. His book, *Simply Better: Winning and Keeping Customers by Delivering What Matters Most*, co-authored with Professor Seán Meehan (IMD, Lausanne), won the American Marketing Association's 2005 Berry-AMA Book Prize and has been translated into seven other languages. Their second book, *Beyond the Familiar: Long-Term Growth through Customer Focus and Innovation*, was published in 2011.

Benjamin J. Bates is a Professor in the School of Journalism and Electronic Media, and adjunct professor in the School of Information Sciences, at the University of Tennessee. He received his PhD from the University of Michigan. His research examines how social, political, and economic factors influence the evolution and utilization of media and information systems and markets.

Tom Björkroth is Senior Research Officer at the Finnish Competition and Consumer Authority. He holds a doctorate degree in Political Science (Economics) from the Åbo Akademi University and a MA degree in EC Competition Law from King's College, London. His research interests include, but are not constrained to, industrial organization and its application in competition law. He is a member of the board of the National Consumer Research Centre.

Edward Castronova is Professor of Telecommunications at Indiana University, Research Professor, Deutsches Institut für Wirtschaftsforschung, Berlin, Fellow at the Center for Governance, UCLA, and Research Fellow, CESifo, University of Munich. He holds a PhD in Economics from the University of Wisconsin-Madison. Professor Castronova specializes in the study of games, technology, and society. Notable works include *Synthetic Worlds: The Business and Culture of Online Games* (Chicago, 2005), *Exodus to the Virtual World* (Palgrave, 2007), *Virtual Economies: Analysis and Design* (with Vili Lehdonvirta, MIT, in press), and *Wildcat Currency: The Virtual Transformation of the Economy* (Yale, in press). He is a member of the editorial boards of *Game Studies*, *Games and Culture*, and *Journal of Virtual and Personal Learning Environments*.

Brendan Cunningham is Professor of Economics at the United States Naval Academy. He received an MA and PhD in economics from Columbia University and was previously employed by Hartwick College and the US Federal Trade Commission. He has been editor of the *Journal of Media Economics* and his work has been published in journals including the *Journal of Law and Economics*, *Information Economics and Policy*, and *Review of Economic Research on Copyright Issues*.

Anthony Dukes is an Associate Professor of Marketing in the Marshall School of Business, University of Southern California. He received a PhD in economics from the University of Pittsburgh. His research focuses on the economics of marketing strategies, particularly as it applies to pricing, retail channels, and commercial media and has appeared in the *Journal of Marketing Research*, *Marketing Science*, *Management Science*, and other leading academic journals. He currently serves as Associate Editor of *Marketing Science* and *Quantitative Marketing and Economics* and on the editorial review board of the *Journal of Marketing* and *Marketing Science*.

Jean J. Gabszewicz is a Professor Emeritus at the Catholic University of Louvain. He has contributed to various fields of economic theory:

industrial organization, mathematical economics, game theory, international economics and media economics. His recent work also deals with network economics and two-sided markets.

Nick Geidner is an Assistant Professor of Journalism in the School of Journalism and Electronic Media at the University of Tennessee. He received his PhD from Ohio State University and his research examines how changes in the journalism industry affect the functioning of American democracy.

Lisa George is Associate Professor of Economics at Hunter College, City University of New York. She received her doctoral in applied economics from the Wharton School, University of Pennsylvania and was previously on the faculty of Michigan State University. George is editor of the journal *Information Economics and Policy*.

Mikko Grönlund is Research Manager of the BID Business and Innovation Development at the University of Turku. He holds a MSc in Economics from Turku School of Economics and Business Administration. Mr Grönlund has more than 15 years of experience as a researcher and has extensive experience in the field development of creative and media industries and businesses, their structure, operations and markets. He has conducted numerous studies in the field of media and creative industries commissioned by institutions such as the European Commission, Finnish ministries of communication, culture, education and labour, industry federations, and media industry firms. He is also author of several publications in the field of media and creative industries.

Sung Wook Ji is Assistant Professor in the Department of Radio, Television, and Digital Media at Southern Illinois University, Carbondale. He holds a PhD from the Department of Telecommunications at Indiana University, Bloomington. His primary research interests center on the interdisciplinary intersections of mass communication, economics, and media policy. He is particularly interested in the social and economic impact of new media technologies on the media industry, and how these technologies are shaping the media industries and society. His research has been published in *Journal of Media Economics*, *The Information Society*, *Review of Industrial Organization* and *Telecommunications Policy*.

Charlie Karlsson is Professor of the Economics of Technological Change at Jönköping International Business School; Professor of Industrial Economics and Organization at Blekinge Institute of Technology, Sweden; Research Professor, Institute for Economic Research, Halle (Saale); and Associate Professor ("docent") in Regional Planning at the

Royal Institute of Technology, Stockholm. Charlie Karlsson was the president of the European Regional Science Association (ERSA) from 2009 to 2014. He has published articles in *Papers in Regional Science*, *Entrepreneurship and Regional Development*, *Regional Studies*, *Environment and Planning A*, *Growth and Change*, *The Annals of Regional Science*, *Annales D'Économie et de Statistique, Italian Journal of Regional Science, Industry and Innovation*, *Research Policy* and *Small Business Economics*, contributed with chapters in a large number of edited books, and served as editor for more than 20 books published by Springer, Edward Elgar, Routledge, Cambridge University Press and Oxford University Press.

Hans Jarle Kind is Professor in Industrial Organization at NHH, the Norwegian School of Economics. Kind received his PhD in 1999. The topic of his thesis was international trade and location of economic activity (economic geography). His research interests include telecommunications and media economics, management science, channel relationships, and competition policy. He is Research Director at SNF, Institute for Research in Economics and Business Administration, and has headed several projects on the economics of two-sided markets. He has published in leading academic journals such as *Management Science*, *Journal of Public Economics, Marketing Science, and Journal of International Economics.*

Isaac Knowles is a doctoral candidate in the Department of Telecommunications at Indiana University Bloomington. He specializes in virtual economics and game behavior using approaches from econometrics, machine learning, and data mining. He received an MSc in economics from Louisiana State University and has been employed in the game industry.

Sang Yup Lee is a research associate with the Creative Future Research Laboratory and has a PhD in Media and Information Studies from Michigan State University. His research focuses on economic and social aspects of information and communication technology (ICT) industries. His research primarily examines how an individual forms relationships with others and interacts with them on the Web, and how online relationships and interactions influence an individual psychologically and economically. He is also interested in studying strategic behaviors between ICT firms and how those strategic behaviors influence consumers in the industry.

Jonathan D. Levy is the Deputy Chief Economist at the Federal Communications Commission in Washington, DC, and a senior economist in the Commission's Office of Strategic Planning and Policy

Analysis. His primary activities are analysis of competition in broadcasting and multichannel video programming distribution markets, and review of proposed changes in government regulation of the mass media. Dr Levy has played a significant role in the Commission's review of broadcast ownership rules and digital television transition issues. Prior to joining the FCC in 1980, he taught economics at the University of Wisconsin-Milwaukee. He holds a PhD in economics from Yale University. In 1993, Dr Levy was a Fulbright Senior Scholar in the School of Humanities at the University of Technology Sydney.

Agostino Manduchi is an Assistant Professor of Economics at Jönköping International Business School and an affiliated researcher in the Media Management and Transformation Centre. He received a BS in Economics and Banking from the University of Siena, Italy, and a PhD in Economics and Finance from Columbia Business School, New York. His current research interests include the economics of information in general and media economics. He has published in the *Journal of Economic Theory*, the *Journal of Economics* and the *Journal of Media Economics*.

Jarle Møen is Professor of Applied Econometrics at NHH, the Norwegian School of Economics. Møen received his PhD in 2002 and has been Visiting Fellow at Harvard University and guest researcher at the NBER Productivity group. His research interests include innovation, knowledge spillovers, policy evaluation, firm subsidies and business taxation. He is a member of the executive board of the Research Council of Norway and has published in leading academic journals such as *Management Science*, *Journal of the European Economic Association* and *Journal of Labor Economics*.

Robert G. Picard is Director of Research at the Reuters Institute in the Department of Politics and International Relations at the University of Oxford, Hamrin Professor of Media Economics at Jönköping International Business School, research fellow at Green Templeton College (Oxford), and a fellow of the Royal Society of Arts. A specialist in media economics and policy, he is the author and editor of 29 books, including *The Economics and Financing of Media Companies* and *Media Clusters: Spatial Agglomeration and Content Capabilities*. He has been editor of the *Journal of Media Business Studies* and the *Journal of Media Economics*. Picard received his PhD from the University of Missouri, Columbia, and has been a fellow at the Shorenstein Center at the John F. Kennedy School of Government at Harvard University. He has consulted and carried out assignments for governments in North America, Europe,

Africa, and Asia and for international organizations including the European Commission, UNESCO, and the World Intellectual Property Organization. He has been a consultant for leading media companies worldwide.

Joana Resende is an Assistant Professor at the University of Porto and an associate researcher at CefUP. She obtained a joint PhD-degree from Université Catholique de Louvain and UP. She is part of the Scientific Committees of the Master in Multimedia, and the PhD in Digital Media at the UP. Her research interests lie in industrial organization and media economics. Her research is mainly focused on network formation games and the dynamics of price competition in network industries. Her recent work also covers topics such as two-sided markets, "freemium" business models and targeted advertising strategies.

Travis Ross has a PhD in Telecommunications and Cognitive Science from Indiana University. His research focuses on the forces that shape antisocial and prosocial behavior in online societies and the psychology of motivation. He has worked on a number of projects that used virtual worlds or games to study social behavior and has written extensively about using virtual worlds as laboratories for social science experimentation.

Philippe Rouchy is an Assistant Professor in the Department of Industrial Economics at Blekinge Institute of Technology, Sweden. He graduated with a PhD in sociology from both the University of Nice Sophia-Antipolis, France and the University of Manchester, UK. His research interest lies in technological change, the ICT impact on innovation, and regional development.

Nathalie Sonnac is Professor of Information and Communication at l'université Panthéon-Assas and Director of l'Institut français de presse. She is the author of *Économie de la presse*, *Culture Web, L'Industrie des médias à l'ère numérique*, and *L'Auteur au temps du numérique*. Her research has been published in *Economica*, *Revue d'économie industrielle*, and *Les Cahiers du Journalisme*.

Ruth Towse has been Professor of Economics of Creative Industries at Bournemouth University since 2007, where she is Co-Director for Economics at CIPPM (the Centre for Intellectual Property Policy and Management) and CREATe Fellow in Cultural Economics (University of Glasgow). She specializes in cultural economics and the economics of copyright. She has published widely on both fields in academic journals and books and has also edited several collections of papers and original contributions, including *A Textbook of Cultural Economics* (Cambridge

University Press, 2010). With Christian Handke, she edited *Handbook of the Digital Creative Economy* (Edward Elgar Publishing, 2013).

David Waterman is Professor in the Department of Telecommunications at Indiana University. In addition to numerous journal articles and book chapters, he is author of *Hollywood's Road to Riches* (2005, Harvard University Press) and co-author of *Vertical Integration in Cable Television* (1997; MIT Press, with Andrew Weiss). Professor Waterman has presented his research in testimony before the US Congress, and has served as a consultant to the Federal Communications Commission, the US Department of Justice, and other government agencies. He served as a Principal Editor, and later Coordinating Editor of *Information Economics and Policy*. He is a past Organizing Committee Chair and member of the Board of Directors of TPRC.

Steven S. Wildman is the James H. Quello Professor of Telecommunication Studies and former Chief Economist of the US Federal Communications Commission. He was previously director of the Program in Telecommunications Science, Management and Policy at Northwestern University and Assistant Professor of Economics at University of California, Los Angeles. He holds a PhD in economics from Stanford University and a BA in economics from Wabash College. Wildman has been editor of the *Journal of Media Economics* and is an author or editor of *International Trade in Films and Television Programs*, *Electronic Services Networks: A Business and Public Policy Challenge*, *Video Economics*, *Making Universal Service Policy: Enhancing the Process Through Multidisciplinary Evaluation*, and *Rethinking Rights and Regulations: Institutional Responses to New Communications Technologies*.

Yi-Xi Zhu is a doctoral candidate in Economics at the School of Economics and Management at Southeast University, Nanjing, and was a visiting research scholar at the University of Tennessee during the 2012/2013 academic year. Her research interests focus on the role of policy in promoting competition between Chinese broadcasting, cable (wired multichannel video and broadband), and telecommunication markets.

Introduction

Robert G. Picard and Steven S. Wildman

The economics of media are often misunderstood and mischaracterized because media involve complicated and multifaceted economic factors and industry dynamics. The interactions of these factors create complex decision-making environments not easily explained by single economic theories and principles. This challenge is compounded because some observers mistakenly approach all media as if their economic characteristics are similar and that comparable structures, opportunities, constraints, incentives, and disincentives are involved when choices are made.

Media encompass both commercial and non-commercial enterprises and involve complicated value creation and business models not found in many other industries. Some produce physical products; others do not. Some media are durable; some are ephemeral. Some operate in simple markets; some in multi-sided markets. Some media combine service, manufacturing, and retail activities not found in other media. Some face significant social demands and public intervention; others are closer to markets. These differences require considerable media industry understanding and specificity when studying media industries and behaviors.

One cannot assert media exceptionalism and repudiate economic theory and analyses when trying to understand media economics, however. Economic theory and analysis are central to understanding media industries and their behaviors, but the context and assumptions must encompass some characteristics and interactions that are unique to media.

This handbook explores the divergent economic features of media and their infrastructures to help provide readers a sophisticated understanding of the factors and issues and their influences on companies, audiences, and regulators. An extraordinary group of economic scholars from the academy and government explore and explain how underlying factors such as multi-sided platforms, advertising, and industry structure influence media, the unique economic factors affecting print, broadcast, and broadband-based media, and how the economics of media influences policy making. Each contribution introduces readers to the specific topic, reviews the literature of its development, explores critiques of the approach, and provides understanding of application of the knowledge and its implications.

The handbook is intended to be used by scholars, practitioners, and regulators seeking significant understanding of the topics. It assumes and builds upon fundamental comprehension of economics and the business of media. The handbook is divided into three sections focusing on influential factors and practices, application to specific media platforms, and economics and policy.

In the first section, Jean Gabszewicz, Joana Resende, and Nathalie Sonnac reveal how multi-sided platform operations influence choices and the operations of media. Sung Wook Ji and David Waterman explore how company and industry structure combine with technology to influence the operations of media. Steven S. Wildman and Sang Yup Lee explain how the globalized nature of media influences trade in media products. Charlie Karlsson and Philippe Rouchy investigate why and how media clusters are forming worldwide to support media operations. Anthony Dukes and Agostino Manduchi demonstrate the economics of advertising and the effects of advertising pricing.

These initial entries lay the foundation for focused explorations of the economics of specific media and media infrastructures in the second section. Robert G. Picard details the economics of print media and, together with Patrick Barwise, explicates the economics of broadcast media. Benjamin J. Bates, Nick Geidner, and Yi-Xi Zhu explain the economics of broadband telecommunications and its economic implications. Nodir Adilov, Peter J. Alexander, and Brendan Cunningham explore the economic factors and relations in peer-to-peer file sharing. Isaac Knowles, Edward Castronova, and Travis Ross explore virtual economies in the game industry and their implications. Lisa George exposes how digital technologies are altering the economics of media.

The final section of the handbook places attention on economic factors in regulatory aspects of media. Jonathan D. Levy explains how economic analysis is used in policy making and regulation. Tom Björkroth and Mikko Grönlund demonstrate the fundamental importance of economic analysis to competition law. Ruth Towse explores the economic bases and effects of copyright and Hans Jarle Kind and Jarle Møen explore the impact of taxation and subsidies on the economics of media.

The breadth and depth of the handbook are intended to provide readers crucial knowledge that develops understanding of the economic factors, issues, and contexts involved in various media and media practices. It is meant to expand the knowledge of readers and to serve as a valuable reference book that will be continue to be consulted for years to come.

PART I

INFLUENTIAL FACTORS AND PRACTICES

1. Media as multi-sided platforms

Jean J. Gabszewicz, Joana Resende and Nathalie Sonnac

Media are among the most influential institutions in modern societies. Media outlets – press, TV, Internet, radio, cinema – have become the leading players in the production and diffusion of information.[1] Universal access to information, knowledge and pluralism of opinions are fundamental vectors for promoting a democratic and free society.

However, the production of information is costly and the survival of media outlets crucially depends on the possibility of financing their activities. To avoid overloading consumers with all the costs of information production and promote as much as possible a universal access to information, media outlets have long relied[2] on the combination of circulation/subscription revenues and advertising revenues (sometimes complemented by public subsidies[3]) to finance their activities.

The conventional business model used by media firms exploits their role as platforms of interaction between two categories of users: audiences (consumers) and advertisers. Exchanges arising in media markets often generate cross network externalities (between advertisers and consumers, and vice versa), producing interactions between the demand for advertising and the demand for media content. Accordingly, traditional media outlets naturally appear as two-sided platforms.

In light of all changes carried by the digital disruption and the convergence phenomenon, the frontiers of media markets are going through a process of deep transformation. The cost of information provision and diffusion has become much lower and the speed of information exchange has enormously increased. This process has immensely expanded the possibilities to create value. Conventional media are now "coopeting"[4] with a variety of new media outlets, predominantly based on the existence of Internet (e.g. online press, online TV, social networks, news aggregators, blogs, and many others). In this context, new important players, like telecommunication companies or "Internet giants" (Apple, Google, Amazon) are consolidating their positions in the media markets. In particular, telecommunications companies see their activity no longer restricted to the provision of telephone or Internet connections. Nowadays these companies present themselves as service providers who integrate several activities in the value chain of media markets (connection, provision of content services[5] and, even, production of media content).

Given all the striking changes that are presently taking place in the media markets, the firms involved in these markets are rethinking their business model. New approaches to the market are being designed and media firms are embracing the model of multi-sided platforms, relying on multiple interaction channels (such as press, social networks, blogs, applications for smartphones, TV, radio, cinema, content distribution online platforms) and serving multiple categories of agents, such as Internet service providers, different categories of content producers, advertisers, and consumers, who also produce content.

In this chapter, we highlight the role of media as multi-sided platforms, in the context of both traditional and new media. Surprisingly, the economic aspects of the theory of media markets have escaped the attention of economists for a long time. The theoretical foundations of the field of media economics, formally modelling media markets as two-sided platforms, have only been set up in the late nineties, even if various interesting contributions have already been made before the expansion of the literature on two-sided markets (e.g. Corden, 1953; Owen et al., 1974; Picard, 1989; Owen and Wildman, 1992; Albarran, 1996, among others). Some of the pioneering theoretical approaches to media markets as two-sided platforms include the works by Sonnac (2000, 2002), Gabszewicz et al. (1999, 2001, 2002) and Anderson and Coate (2005). At the same time, the fast development of the general theory of two-sided markets (for example Rochet and Tirole, 2003; Armstrong, 2005; Caillaud and Jullien, 2003) has played an important role in promoting the field of media economics, and has provided a systematic and unified framework for the analysis of traditional media markets.

In the last decade, the theoretical literature investigating the economics of media platforms has grown immensely. In particular, in the field of Economics, scholars have been very interested in *(i)* studying the specific interactions occurring in media markets due to cross network externalities, as described, for example, by Gabszewicz et al. (1999), Sonnac (2000), Ferrando et al. (2008), Resende (2008) or Anderson et al. (2012); *(ii)* analyzing the optimal price structure in media markets and the behavior of advertising and circulation/subscription revenues, as in the works by Peitz and Valletti (2008), Manduchi and Picard (2009) or Reisinger (2012); *(iii)* investigating the nature of competition in media markets and its effects on the provision of quality and diversity (as in Gabszewicz et al., 2001 or Dukes and Gal-Or, 2003); *(iv)* exploring the profit-maximizing and the socially optimal price structure (advertising rates *vis-à-vis* subscription fees) and the resulting content allocation between advertising and media content, as in Anderson and Coate (2005); *(v)* designing an appropriate regulatory framework for media markets (among others, Yoo, 2002; de Bijl and Peitz, 2010; Economides and Tag, 2012).

In light of the recent developments of the sector, the scope of cross network externalities became wider and wider, and the field of media economics now intersects with the fields of economics of information (Shapiro and Varian, 1999; Gensollen, 1998), economics of networks (Jackson, 2008; Page and Wooders, 2009, 2010), economics of telecommunications (Laffont and Tirole, 2000) and economics of the Internet (Illing and Peitz, 2006; Peitz and Waldfogel, 2012).

This chapter focuses only on the economic aspects of media viewed as multi-sided platforms. We start by describing the specific economic features of media markets, namely the specific nature of the "commodity" information and the role of network externalities. Then, we characterize the business model of conventional and new media outlets, and describe the main challenges arising in the media markets as a result of convergence and digital disruption.

1. TWO-SIDED PLATFORMS AND TRADITIONAL MEDIA

1.1 Information: Specific Economic Features

Information can be conceived as a commodity with very specific features. First, information can be (at least partially) conceived as a public good. Following Samuelson (1964), rivalry and exclusion are the two essential characteristics distinguishing public and private goods. Public goods are said to be non-rival (consumption by one agent does not preclude consumption by other agents) and non-exclusive (consumers cannot be excluded from the market through prices). Although the consumption of information may be excluded through prices (in that case, information is said to be a club good), its consumption is always non-rival. This specific feature of information may raise several issues such as the under-production of information or the issue of the aggregation of consumers' preferences over different contents.

Second, the technology behind the production of information often leads to very extensive economies of scale. The cost of producing the first copy tends to be very high but the marginal cost of bringing an extra copy to the market is almost zero. Since the vast majority of the costs are fixed, the conventional rule of pricing at the margin (setting the price equal to marginal cost) may lead to economic losses for the information producers (Sonnac, 2009).[6] Accordingly, media firms often rely on less conventional business models, which exploit additional sources of revenues (like advertising or public subsidies). The digital revolution has accentuated this problem even further: the cost of reproduction is now virtually zero, enhancing firms' difficulties in raising money from the distribution of media content only. In addition, piracy activities have become much easier. Together, these phenomena may reduce firms' incentives to invest in content production (and assure its quality). Hence, business models exclusively based on the sales of media content are being challenged more than ever before.

Finally, information also exhibits characteristics of an experience good (see Caves, 2002), meaning that its quality can only be ascertained after experimentation.[7] Consequently, the distribution of information often involves specific procedures of signalling and selection of contents (for example newspaper titles, journalists' reputation, media brands), increasing the weight of marketing and promotion expenditures (Sonnac, 2009).

1.2 The Business Model of Traditional Media

According to the recent literature on media economics, the basis of the business model of traditional media is explained by the theory of two-sided markets. Rochet and Tirole (2006) define two-sided markets as follows: *"Two-sided (or more generally multi-sided) markets are roughly defined as markets in which one or several platforms enable interactions between end-users, and try to get the two (or multiple) sides 'on board' by appropriately charging each side."* In two-sided markets, the interactions among end-users often engender network externalities. This type of externalities arises when the utility of an agent is enhanced by the number of agents participating in the same market (in the case of direct network externalities) or in a related market (in the case of indirect network externalities).[8] Due to non-internalized network externalities, the business models arising in two-sided markets have some idiosyncrasies. The platforms acting on those markets need to figure out how to bring both sides of the market on board and, as pointed out by Rochet and Tirole (2006), *"managers devote considerable time and resources to figure out which side should bear the pricing burden, and commonly end up making little money on one side (or even using this side as a loss-leader) and recouping their costs on the other side"*.

Traditional media constitute one of the sharpest examples of two-sided market structures. First, media outlets can be conceived as platforms of interaction between audiences ("eyeballs") and advertisers. Furthermore, the interaction between these two groups of agents often engenders cross network externalities. On the one hand, the eyeballs (the size and the composition of the audiences) have a positive effect on advertisers' payoffs. When firms rely on a mass advertising strategy (as it is often the case with traditional media), the larger the potential audience of a certain ad, the higher the expected profit generated by it. On the other hand, outcomes in the advertising market also have some influence on consumers' payoffs. However, in this case, the sign of the network externality is not as obvious as in the previous case. In many situations (for example TV or radio), advertisements are a nuisance for consumers, engendering a negative network externality (Dukes and Gal-Or, 2003; Anderson and Coate, 2005). In other situations, consumers may actually benefit from more advertising, as with classified advertisements and commercials in newspapers or ads in specialized magazines[9] (Kaiser, 2006; Kaiser and Wright, 2006; Gabszewicz et al., 2007; Ferrando et al., 2008; Resende, 2008; Kaiser and Song, 2009).

Due to the network externalities between audiences and advertisers, media outlets often face interdependent demands, meaning that the demand in each side of the market (by audiences and advertisers, respectively) depends on the number of agents participating in the other side of the market. This aspect of media markets is illustrated in Figure 1.1.

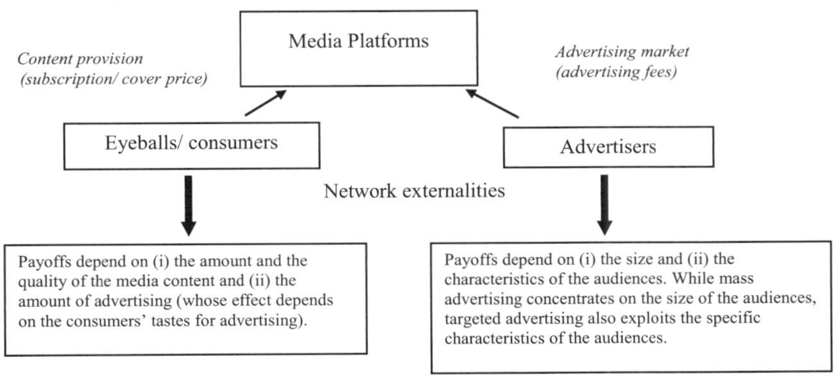

Figure 1.1 The business model of traditional media

In light of the intricate nature of network externalities arising in traditional media platforms, the design of an appropriate business model constitutes a complex task. In particular, media firms face three important challenges: *(i)* choosing an adequate pricing structure to assure their ability to reach the critical mass of eyeballs and advertisers;[10] *(ii)* choosing the profit maximizing advertising rates and subscription/cover prices; *(iii)* choosing the optimal mix of advertising/media content. These three challenges are obviously interrelated. For example, a TV channel may choose to include a considerable amount of advertising in its programming schedule. Considering that advertising is a nuisance to consumers, the subscription price charged on the viewers' side should be low enough: for example, it would be zero in the case of free-to-air TV. The pricing structure used by free-to-air TV channels is such that these outlets are entirely financed by advertising revenues (sometimes complemented by public subsidies). By charging a zero price on the viewers' side, the TV channel attracts more viewers, which should attract more advertisers (or, at least, allow the TV channel to increase its advertising rates). Of course, other business models are possible as well. In the case of pay-TV, channels usually devote less time to advertising, charging a positive subscription price on viewers. Thus, the pricing structure arising in this business model supposes two sources of revenues: subscription and advertising.

Due to the indirect network externalities arising in media markets, the pricing structure chosen by media platforms is certainly not neutral. The price level charged in one side of the market affects the profitability of the other side of the market and vice versa. As a result, the optimal pricing structure is often asymmetric (Rochet and Tirole, 2003, 2006; Armstrong, 2005; Caillaud and Jullien, 2003; Wauthy, 2008). To bring both sides of the market on board, one of the sides is often subsidized to enlarge the number of users joining the platform on that side of the market and, at the same time, stimulate the demand on the other side of the market (due to indirect network externalities).

Of course, the specific characteristics of the profit maximizing price structure will differ from market to market. The elasticity of demand in each side of the market (more precisely, the price elasticity of advertising demand and the price elasticity of the demand for content) and the ratio of advertisments to media content distributed by the media platform are two important determinants of the optimal pricing structure. The market structure (for example monopoly versus oligopoly) and the nature of strategic interaction are other important determinants of the equilibrium pricing structure.

In the following subsection, we present a simple economic model representing the business of traditional media. Despite its simplicity, the model allows us to characterize the optimal pricing structure and derive some implications regarding the impact of network externalities phenomena on the diversity of media contents.

1.3 A Formal Model of Traditional Media Markets

The interactions taking place in traditional media platforms can be formally modelled in light of the two-sided market theory. This section derives a simple illustrative model applied to the newspaper industry.[11] The model considers a simplified version of Gabszewicz et al. (2001) and it proceeds as follows.

Consider a duopoly newspaper industry in which two outlets participate in two interrelated markets: *(i)* the press market, in which the firms sell horizontally differentiated[12] newspapers to the readers; and *(ii)* the advertising market, in which the firms sell advertising space to advertisers. Horizontal differentiation is modelled *à la* Hotelling (1929). Readers have heterogeneous tastes regarding the content of the newspapers. The set of tastes is represented by the Hotelling line [0,1]. To each point in the interval corresponds a specific reader for whom that specification of the newspaper content would be the ideal one. The further existing newspapers are from the readers' ideal specification, the higher the disutility of this specific reader, which is given by $tx_i + p_i$, where p_i stands for the price of newspaper i, x_i denotes the distance between the content specification effectively selected by newspaper i and the reader's ideal specification. Finally, the parameter t measures the magnitude of horizontal differentiation. Concerning the positioning of the two newspapers on the Hotelling line, we assume that newspapers are located at the extreme of the line: one of the newspapers (say newspaper 1) is located at point 0, while the other (newspaper 2) is located at 1. To keep the analysis as simple as possible, we assume readers are neutral to advertising, which seems to be particularly suitable for offline press.[13] If readers were averse to advertising, readers' demand on the press market would incorporate the negative indirect network externality engendered by advertisers (Dukes and Gal-Or, 2003; Gabszewicz et al., 2004; Anderson and Coate, 2005). In contrast, if the newspapers' advertising content pleases readers, a positive network externality should be incorporated on readers' demand (Resende, 2008). In the context of neutral readers, the readers' demands for each newspaper are respectively given by:

$$D_1(p_1, p_2) = \frac{p_2 - p_1}{2t} + \frac{1}{2} \text{ and } D_2(p_1, p_2) = \frac{1}{2} - \frac{p_2 - p_1}{2t}.$$

In the advertising market, newspapers sell "eyeballs" to advertisers. Firms have different propensities to advertise while some firms are quite optimistic with respect to the advertising's effectiveness, others are rather pessimistic. The size (density) of the population of advertisers is equal to $4k$, corresponding to each existing propensity. Advertisers are price-takers and the continuum of firms is assumed to be uniformly distributed on the interval [0,1] according to firms' propensity to advertise (θ). When firms decide to advertise their products, they might either *(i)* buy an ad-insertion from only one of the existing newspapers (single-homing) or *(ii)* buy an ad-insertion from both of the newspapers (multi-homing). The advertisers' payoff when buying an ad-insertion in newspaper i is given by $\Theta D_i(p_1, p_2) - s_i$.

Considering that each newspaper is produced at a constant marginal cost equal to c > 0, the total profits of newspaper i can be written as $\pi(p_1, p_2) = (p_i - c)\, D(p_1, p_2) + s_i D_i^a(s_i, D_i(p_1, p_2))$, where s_i denotes the advertising rate charged by newspaper i and $D_i^a(s_i, D_i(p_1, p_2))$ stands for the demand for advertising in newspaper i, which depends not only on the advertising rates but also on the size of the newspaper's readership, given by $D_i(p_1, p_2)$. This last effect is caused by the cross network externalities of audiences over advertisers and it analytically shows the interdependence of demands arising in media markets.[14]

The timing of the interactions among newspapers, readers and advertisers is assumed to be as follows. In the first stage, newspapers strategically compete in prices on the press market. Afterwards, given the resulting newspapers' audiences, they sell the advertising space to advertisers, setting the price s_i. The subgame perfect Nash equilibrium of the above game is fully characterized by Gabszewicz et al. (2001).[15]

In the advertising market, they show that the equilibrium amount of advertising content is always equal to $4k(1/2)$ whatever the audience of the newspaper. All the effects of indirect network externalities on the advertising market are then conveyed by the equilibrium advertising rates, which are increasing on the size of the newspapers' audiences $s_i^* = D_i(p_1, p_2)/2$. Since, on the second stage, the newspapers are able to anticipate the effect of audiences on the price of advertising, newspapers' profits can be rewritten as $\pi(p_1, p_2) = (p_i + k - c)\, D_i(p_1, p_2)$. When both newspapers are active in the market, equilibrium subscription prices are obtained from the system of first order conditions: $\dfrac{\partial \pi_i(p_1, p_2)}{\partial p_i} = 0,\ i = 1,2.$

As shown by Gabszewicz et al. (2001), equilibrium prices are equal to $p_1^* = p_2^* = c - k + t$. Comparing these subscription prices with the ones that would arise if the newspapers were *not* involved in the advertising market, $p_1^* = p_2^* = c + t$, we observe that the participation of newspapers in the latter entails lower subscription fees on the press market. Accordingly, the optimal pricing structure in this market differs from the conventional rules, requiring the subsidization on the side of readers. The rationale for this divergence lies precisely on indirect network externalities. Since newspapers anticipate the positive effect of audiences on the advertising revenues (through higher advertising rates), they rely on a more aggressive pricing policy on the readers' side as a means of enhancing their audiences. The expressions obtained for the equilibrium price levels show that the discount on the readers' side is increasing on the size of the advertising market (eventually, if k is very large, the newspapers could even be sold at a price below the marginal cost).[16] Again this is driven by the interdependence between demands in the advertising and the press market. As the advertising market becomes larger (k increases), the marginal profitability of reaching an additional reader increases and, consequently, competition in the press market becomes tougher.

It is worth noting that the presentation of this simple model was mainly chosen with a pedagogic purpose. Of course, the model remains highly stylized, omitting some relevant features of the business model of traditional media. Other characteristics of the media markets can be easily accommodated in the model by relaxing the appropriate assumptions. The following subsections illustrate how this two-sided market model can be extended to analyze other key issues of traditional media markets (besides the optimal pricing structure) like (i) readers' attitudes towards advertising; (ii) the endogenous mechanisms favoring concentration in media markets; (iii) the impact of advertising markets on the diversity of media content; (iv) the impact of regulation on the diversity of media content; or (v) the effects of advertising on media bias.

1.4 Readers' Attitudes Towards Advertising

The basic model presented in the previous section assumes that readers' utility is unaffected by the amount of advertising displayed in the newspaper. However, advertising may be beneficial (or detrimental) to readers, generating a positive (negative) network externality and an additional source of demand interdependence. This possibility can be easily incorporated in the model, as in Ferrando et al. (2008). The authors extend the previous model to accommodate the possibility of having a proportion γ of readers who are "ad-avoiders" (negative network externality), while the remaining readers are "ad-lovers" (positive network externality).

The authors show that, when the model is extended to accommodate readers' tastes towards advertising, new equilibrium outcomes may arise. When the majority of readers dislike advertising, at least one of the newspapers may find it profitable to eliminate the advertising content, adopting a very different type of business model. When the majority of readers benefit with advertising and the intensity of the corresponding network externality is weak enough (i.e. the marginal utility delivered by an additional ad is sufficiently low), both newspapers remain active. The newspaper enjoying the largest audience is more expensive and it also charges higher advertising rates than the rival. When the intensity of the network externality advertising exerts on readers is very strong, there is only room for one newspaper in the market. This result illustrates how network externalities arising in media markets may engender endogenous mechanisms favoring concentrated market structures. This issue is analyzed in more detail in the following section.

1.5 Endogenous Concentration Mechanisms

Traditional media industries often present a substantial degree of concentration. Frequently, a relatively small number of media platforms serves a large fraction of the audiences and, simultaneously, attracts the vast majority of advertising revenues. For example, several studies have provided factual evidence pointing out the high concentration levels observed in the press industry: for example Rosse (1967); George and Waldfogel (2003); and Genesove (2004).

One unquestionable source of concentration in traditional media markets is the extent and relevance of economies of scale in the production of media contents (recall that in these markets costs are mostly fixed and the marginal production costs are very low). However, this supply side mechanism may not be the only determinant favoring concentration in the media markets. In particular, the demand interdependence caused by network externalities may lead to a "circulation spiral" that favors newspapers with larger audiences. Note that this circulation spiral mechanism does not necessarily require readers to be ad-lovers. As pointed out by Furhoff (1973) newspapers with narrower audiences may simply find it difficult to match the quality standards of economically stronger newspapers (see Resende, 2008 for a more detailed analysis of this argument). Then, the amount of advertising has a positive (though indirect) externality over readers.

Gustafsson (1978) described the mechanisms underlying the circulation spiral as follows:

> The larger of the two competing newspapers is favored by a process of mutual reinforcement between circulation and advertising, as a larger circulation attracts advertisements, which in turn attracts more advertising and more readers. In contrast, the smaller of two competing newspapers is caught in a vicious circle; its circulation has less appeal for advertisers, and it loses readers. (p. 1)

The results of Ferrando et al. (2008) illustrate the circulation spiral effect in a static set-up. When the majority of readers are ad-lovers and their marginal benefit from advertising is strong enough, the cross network externalities arising in the media market reinforce each other, leading to the eviction of the smaller newspaper. However, it should be noticed that the circulation spiral mechanism is intrinsically dynamic. Not only are demands interdependent across the two sides of the market, they also tend to yield inter-temporal interdependence (see Garcia and Resende, 2011 for a survey on the dynamic aspects of network externalities). Gabszewicz et al. (2007) provide a dynamic extension of the basic model used in this chapter. They compute the equilibrium trajectories of the newspapers' market shares, showing that eventually the minority newspaper may indeed be evicted from the market when the network externality over readers is large enough. Amir et al. (2014) also raise the problem of minority's survival in two-sided markets. When we apply their model to the specific case of media markets, it would predict that the degree of concentration of media markets depends on the relative strength of network externalities over readers *vis-à-vis* the network externalities over advertisers.

1.6 Diversity of Media Content

Another extremely important question in the context of media markets refers to the promotion of diversity of media content. The diversity and pluralism of content is considered to be essential to society. Media are key vehicles in the diffusion of information and cultural principles, shaping the values and beliefs of societies themselves (for example, the European Commission has endorsed several initiatives to discuss and promote media pluralism in the European Union[17]).

When governments aim at promoting content diversity and pluralism of ideas, a first important question is to know whether less concentrated market structures always lead to more diversity. In other words, is it the case that an increase in the number of media voices always entails more diversity of content? Steiner (1952) was one of the first to analyze this question. He considered the competition between two radio or TV channels, comparing (i) the case in which they are owned by independent firms and (ii) the case in which a monopoly firm owns the two channels. He concluded that competition might actually be harmful for diversity. The intuition behind this paradox lies on the specifics of the business model of traditional media, which often depends substantially on the advertising revenues (recall that media platforms may have to subsidize readers to attract more advertisers). Accordingly, when aiming at maximizing audiences, two independent media owners may choose to offer the same content (the one aligned with the tastes of the majority). In contrast, a monopoly media platform would prefer to specialize each channel on a different type of content, serving all the consumers in the market. Therefore, in the model of Steiner (1952), competition may be harmful for consumers. Evidently, this result is driven by the specific assumptions of the referred model.

Other studies dealing with the relation between competition and content duplication include Blank (1966), Greenberg and Barnett (1971), Levin (1971), Baxter (1974), Berry and Waldfogel (2001), George (2007), McDonald and Shu-Fang (2004), and Van der Wurff (2005).

Among the studies dealing with content diversity, it is worth mentioning the analysis by Gabszewicz et al. (2001). These authors study the problem of diversity of the political content of newspapers by extending the basic duopoly model presented in section 1.3. To this end, they introduce an extra stage in the beginning of the game. In this extra stage, newspapers are allowed to choose their positioning on the Hotelling line, which defines the political slant of the news dispatched by each newspaper. While in the standard Hotelling model, the maximum differentiation principle should prevail (see d'Aspremont et al., 1979), this might no longer be the case when the interactions between advertising and press markets are taken into consideration. Gabszewicz et al. (2001) find that in a newspaper industry with the characteristics described in section 1.3, the maximum differentiation only prevails if the unit value t attached by readers to the political differentiation of newspapers is high enough, and/or the dimension of the advertising market is relatively limited (k is small). When these conditions do not hold (the advertising market is large enough and/or the readers do not sufficiently value the political differentiation between the newspapers), minimum differentiation is the equilibrium choice of newspapers. In that case, newspapers provide news with similar political slant and the landscape of political opinions conveyed in the press can be qualified as "La pensée unique". This result is a reminiscence of the well-known median voter result (Downs, 1957).

Other authors have also highlighted the tendency towards "La pensée unique" due to the interdependent demands faced by traditional media platforms (even before the advent of the analytical models of two-sided markets). For example, Bagdikian (1992, 129–30) states:

> As mass advertising grew, the liberal and radical ideas – in editorials, in selection of news, and in investigative initiatives – became a problem. If a paper wished to attract maximum advertising, its explicit politics might create a disadvantage. To obtain more advertising it needed readers of all political persuasions … The answer in the news was a technique called "objectivity". The doctrine of "'objectivity" … has given American standard news a profoundly establishmentarian cast.

All the previous models emphasize that content diversity may be reduced due to media dependence on advertising revenues. However, this is not always necessarily the case. There are other models in which the interdependence of demands by audiences and advertisers does not preclude content diversity (Niven, 1999). McChesney (1987) also argues that newspaper publishers do not necessarily benefit from sensational events.

1.7 Diversity, Regulation and Programming

Given the crucial importance of media in the transmission of information, in the shaping of opinions and in the promotion of democracy, traditional media sectors in Europe have been highly regulated in the last decades. In the case of traditional media, the existing regulation aims to, among other things: restrict the amount of advertising displayed by the media platforms; and promote the diffusion of national content. In relation to the last aspect, regulators can define rules that force media platforms to display a certain amount of nationally produced content. For example, in France, TV channels must devote 60 per cent of their programming time to European content, among which 40 per cent should be of French origin.

Regarding the first objective, regulators often define a cap on the amount of advertising content of several media outlets.[18] The rationale for this measure lies on the theory that the quality of content may be reduced when media platforms are excessively exposed to the outcomes in advertising markets. This question has raised the attention of many scholars. Economists in particular have developed several models to investigate the role of advertising revenues on the quality of content. Relevant works include Spence and Owen (1977), Coase (1966), Beebe (1977), Cancian et al. (1995), Motta and Polo (1997), Berry and

Waldfogel (1999), Brown and Cave (1992), Owen and Wildman (1992), Dukes and Gal-Or (2003), Wright (1994), and Anderson and Coate (2005).

Gabszewicz et al. (1999) develop a two-sided market model to study the problem faced by a regulator who may impose quotas on the advertising shares of TV programming. They show that such quotas affect the structure of newspapers' revenues and in consequence also affect the characteristics of the media content integrating the programming schedules of the media platforms. They conclude that the imposition of quotas leads media platforms to deliver homogeneous media content (while they would prefer maximum differentiation if the quotas were not imposed).

1.8 Media Bias

The promotion of content diversity and pluralism of ideas is not the only concern of public authorities regulating media markets. The problem of media bias and its impact on the accuracy of information also constitutes a central question in the media economics literature (Gentzkow and Shapiro, 2006; Baron, 2006; Mullainathan and Shleifer, 2005; Stromberg, 2004; Ellman and Germano, 2009). The literature on media bias investigates what may drive media platforms to manipulate the information they distribute, either by slanting the content of their media, or by selecting some pieces of information to the detriment of others.

The literature has provided several justifications for the existence of media bias: *(i)* journalists' own incentives and beliefs (Baron, 2006), *(ii)* pressure from the government and other external entities (Besley and Prat, 2006; DellaVigna and Kaplan, 2007), *(iii)* the need to build reputation as a provider of accurate information (Gentzkow and Shapiro, 2006), and *(iv)* the fact that readers are pleased to confirm in the news their own views and beliefs about reality (Mullainathan and Shleifer, 2005).

A particularly relevant study is Ellman and Germano (2009), who analyze how the two-sided market structure of the media platforms may produce media bias. They take into consideration not only the relevance of advertising revenues on the business of traditional media, but also the fact that advertisers may be sensitive to the content dispatched by media platforms.[19] They conclude that "advertising can actually raise accuracy by increasing the intensity of competition for readers". If advertising is sufficiently large, the newspapers are fully accurate. This is no longer the case if advertisers are able to commit to withdraw advertising from media platforms that are too accurate in relation to certain topics.

2. DISRUPTIVE TECHNOLOGY AND CONVERGENCE

The digital revolution brought a paradigm change in media markets. Internet is a disruptive innovation in its capacity to generate value. First, it drove a technological innovation in the production of contents. It pushed the digital revolution, which not only affected content production itself – disrupting media and cultural industries – but also allowed for the appearance of new media supports, like tablets, computer screens, smartphones, and connected TVs. In addition to the technological revolution, a deep sociological change has been taking place. Modern societies are characterized by the universal access to the Internet, the accelerated penetration of new communication tools, new types of consumption behavior for new types of services, like video on demand or streaming, new types of content, like promotional videos and targeted advertising. These phenomena are on the basis of a non-stop increasing consumption of media content (mostly in digital format).

In this context, new categories of economic agents are becoming increasingly relevant to media markets: Internet providers and telecommunications companies, Internet giants (Google, Apple, Amazon), new platforms dedicated to the provision of specific streaming[20] services (for example Netflix, Hulu and Lovefilm), social networks (Facebook, LinkedIn). The arrival of these new operators is fostering the adoption of new business models, integrating the specific features of the Internet economy.[21]

The business model of two-sided markets, which used to be specific to media industries, has invaded the whole Web. Media companies have become multi-sided platforms as they constitute an interface for several kinds of interactions (content (self)-production, content consumption, target advertising, e-commerce) and they serve multiple groups of agents (not only advertisers and audiences). Traditional media are facing a challenging environment and they are struggling to accommodate their business models to the new players and the new phenomena brought by the Internet (see Osterwalder and Pigneur, 2010): audience fragmentation; piracy and free access to digital contents (see Belleflamme and Peitz, 2012 for a survey); viral networks; co-production of media content; (in)compatibility among platforms and the imposition of standards; reduction of (re) production and distribution costs; globalization of content distribution; and so on.

These new features of the media markets raise several exciting questions: how to charge for the distribution of media contents whose reproduction marginal cost is virtually zero? Can media platforms find alternatives to raise the money needed to subsidize consumers, despite audiences' fragmentation? What is the impact of the digital disruption on the diversity and the quality of contents? What is the optimal market structure?

In the second part of the chapter, we aim at providing a systematic characterization of media firms as multi-sided platforms, highlighting the main challenges currently arising in this market.

2.1 Information Networks, Disintermediation and Value Chain

In media markets, the old paradigm of industrial information economics has been replaced by the concept of information networks (Benckler, 2009). The advent of information networks results from *(i)* the major role played by information and cultural products on modern societies, together with *(ii)* a new communicational environment based on agents' interconnectivity sustained by new technologies with increasingly high computing capabilities.

In this subsection, we briefly analyze the effects of digital disruption on the production of information itself, stressing the role of information networks. Then, we identify the changes arising in the value chain of information consumption in the digital era.

Internet access (and broadband penetration) has increased enormously worldwide. More and more people are participating in media platforms, producing and diffusing information through the Web. This new trend has a strong impact on media markets. The information is consumed less vertically and it is no longer exclusively distributed through traditional media (nor even through media professionals). Multiple sources of information are now available and social networks are playing a very significant role. Consumers are now valuing more the recommendations made by experts or friends rather than the opinions of professional journalists in traditional media. Accordingly, the role of producers and consumers of media content becomes intermingled, with both of them intervening in the (co) production of contents. This gives rise to the user-generated content, so profuse on the Web through forums, blogs, wikis and other social networks (see Goyal, 2012 for an analysis of social networks in the digital era).

The new technologies and the rise of information networks have also brought deep changes to the information value chain. All traditional media (press, publishing, audiovisual, TV, cinema) have been affected by the transition to digital. The digital revolution has transformed each link in the value chain of information. Some activities have been removed, fostering "disintermediation" processes.[22] Consider, for example, the case of press. In this market, the production of a newspaper or a magazine used to require five actions: creation, edition, print, distribution and commercialization. With the digital revolution, several actions of the value chain can be easily "disintermediated". For example, the transition to digital has remarkably changed the journalists' working practices. Internet allows them to speak directly to their audiences, enabling them to publish content without going through the filter of the newspaper's editors.

While it is true that the growing connectivity in media markets has brought the disintermediation of some activities, it should also be noted that intermediation remains essential to the media markets, even if now it takes new forms. Considering the example of newspapers, we observe that editors start to find themselves in a completely different business ecosystem, facing the competition of platforms like Google News. These platforms are intermediaries themselves. They are involved in the aggregation, indexing, archiving, alerts, and so on, of information produced by the others. In a world where information abounds, the new "infomediaries"[23] are important players in gathering and selecting information.

2.2 Convergence, Vertical Integration and Exclusivity

One of the most important trends currently arising in media markets refers to the convergence among media, telecommunications and information industries (see, for example, Jenkins, 2001). In fact, the Internet and the whole industrial sector of information and communication can be viewed as an ecosystem based on four basic components. The first component consists in the equipment production. It includes the producers of equipment (Alcatel, Cisco), the cell and telephone manufacturers (Nokia, Motorola, Sony) and firms specialized in the production of electronic equipment (Microsoft, Apple, Dell, Samsung). The second component embodies network operators (France Telecom, Deutsch Telecom, ATT), mobile phone operators (Vodafone), Internet providers (Free, Orange), cable (Numericable, Time Warner) and satellite operators (Canal+France, BSkyB). The business firms operating in the third component are service providers, consisting in interconnected platforms centering their economic activity on intermediation. These platforms can be subdivided into three categories:[24] (i) exchange platforms, associated with electronic markets, like Amazon or PriceMinister, referencing sites and price comparison sites, whose objective is to interconnect agents in order to allow for direct or indirect commercial transactions; (ii) audience platforms, such as research engines (Google, Bing), portals (Yahoo, MSN), online websites of traditional media (radio, newspapers), online sales (eBay, Cdiscount), personal (Facebook, Flickr) or professional (LinkedIn, Viadeo) social networks, whose objective is to raise "audiences" and, eventually, sell them to advertisers; and (iii) exploitation platforms, like Windows Mac OS, Android or Linux, whose objective consists in providing generalized access to multiple applications. Finally, the last component, located upstream in the ecosystem, includes all the producers of digital content, embodying all existing editorial sectors (NBC, Canal plus) as well as all content produced by the consumers themselves (user-generated content, UGC) and invading the Web via websites like YouTube or Dailymotion.

Until the arrival of the digital revolution, the four components were clearly identified and fully separated (Curien, 2000; Barua et al., 1999). The convergence phenomenon that recently arose in the media markets resulted in the intersection of the industries of telecommunications, computer sciences and audiovisual. A given platform may now integrate several components of the ecosystem. Thus, the four components are no longer separated. Nowadays, the ecosystem is endowed with a global coherence in which R&D performed at the level of one component is diffused into the firms of the others (open innovation). Following the convergence phenomenon, the borders of traditional markets for content are now being redefined. This is, in particular, the case of the audiovisual market (Baranès and Encaoua, 2002; Vogel and Vogel, 2009; Sonnac, 2012).[25]

In light of the new configuration of the information ecosystem, media companies are no longer the exclusive providers of information and media content. Platforms with different characteristics are also playing a very important role, including telecom, ISPs (Internet Service Providers), Internet users (who also generate content), online social networks, equipment producers, and application developers. In the digital world, the media content available to consumers is immense and extremely diversified (Anderson, 2006). Also, the patterns of substitution among media platforms are now completely different (Motta and Polo, 1997). For example, twenty years ago, the substitutability between TV and cinema was relatively limited since the former could only broadcast movies much later than their release in the movie theaters. The reality is completely different nowadays. The introduction of VoD, "home cinema" and the appearance of TV channels specialized in cinema has considerably reduced the degree of differentiation between the two platforms.

Accordingly, traditional media platforms have been forced to revise their business models. At the moment, given the heterogeneity of media platforms (including traditional media, telecoms, application developers, equipment producers, ISPs, and cable firms) several business models co-exist in the ecosystem. In the next subsection, we identify the more prevalent business models currently adopted by media platforms. Regardless of the business model, the success of a platform depends on its capacity of raising communities of users and offering them tools and services to facilitate their virtual social interactions via certification and recommendation systems.

2.3 Business Models in the Digital Era

Earlier we showed how the business model of traditional media relied on the strategic interaction between audiences and advertisers. The network externalities underlying this strategic interaction often led to asymmetric price structures, with the audiences being subsidized by advertisers.

Following the digital disruption, new business models are arising in media markets. Given the complex typology of firms participating in these markets nowadays, several models have been developed. For example, Google relies on an open source ecosystem (Android) and makes money from advertising revenues. In contrast, Apple relies on a closed and proprietary ecosystem.

In addition, the arrival of telecoms and ISPs in media markets has introduced further complications. By providing access to the Internet, these platforms are in control of an input that is essential for network formation, and they want to charge media platforms on the Web for that.[26] In addition, these companies are often vertically integrated, being involved in the production and distribution of content themselves.

In the remainder of this section, we provide a non-exhaustive description of some business models currently adopted in media markets. We start by briefly describing the main ingredients of three business models frequently adopted by audience platforms: (i) free content; (ii) paid content; and (iii) freemium.

In the first model, firms deliver the media content for free (for example GoogleNews, Facebook, YouTube, Wikipedia). The business model is then financed by an alternative source of revenue, such as advertising, crowd-funding (Belleflamme et al., 2011) or cross-selling. The free content model is commonly adopted when the protection of content is very difficult, and/or media platforms need to expand their base of users to generate sufficiently strong network externalities.

In contrast, in the pay content model, audiences do not have access to free content. Even if firms may (or not) rely on additional sources of revenue, audiences must pay for access to information. This model is more common for media content whose protection is easy or inexpensive. It is also more common when media platforms already benefit from a sufficiently large base of users, meaning they already generate sufficiently strong network externalities.

Finally, the freemium model is based on a mixed strategy. It provides free access to a considerable amount of content but it charges a positive price for premium exclusive contents (for example editorial news, exclusive interviews, recent movies or TV series, and high resolution content). The freemium model uses free content to expand the base of users and generate network externalities. Once network externalities are launched, the media platforms may exploit their base of users to sell (at least to some users) higher-quality content at a positive price. The "freemium" model allows media platforms to price discriminate among consumers, without precluding media platforms to generate strong network externalities. Examples of media platforms relying on the freemium business model include Hulu, Deezer and Spotify.

Comparing the three business models, it becomes evident that they endorse a very different role for content revenues: while they are irrelevant to free content models, they can be vital to paid content models. Content pricing is indeed one of the most central aspects in the previous business models. When media platforms sell their content at a positive price, they may meet (at least) two types of problems. First, the fact that content is paid may deter some consumers from participating in the market, reducing the scope of network externalities and the attractiveness of the corresponding media platform. Second, given the characteristics of digital content (whose reproduction marginal cost is virtually zero), media platforms may face competition from piracy activities, P2P networks, and so on. To minimize the impact of these problems, media platforms may have to design new pricing schemes, and/or exploit other competitive dimensions such as versioning, bundling, cross-selling, crowd-funding, and advertising markets. When the protection of media content is feasible and relatively inexpensive (for example through DRM technologies), firms may also sign exclusivity contracts that give them the monopoly provision of certain media contents.

In the following subsections, we provide further details regarding the characterization of business models adopted by media platforms, starting with the issue of content pricing.

2.4 Content Pricing Schemes

Content pricing has become quite sophisticated in modern media markets. The media firms have a huge range of possibilities when it comes to choosing their pricing schedule. For example, they may either opt for a subscription based model (like Netflix) or for a transaction based model (like i-Tunes music). The former enhances the level of consumption of media content, while the latter might be able to attract a wider base of consumers (when the transaction fee is not combined with the payment of an access fee). In addition, media platforms may choose between adopting a uniform price strategy, in which all consumers pay a similar price (for example i-Tunes music) or, instead, adopting a price discrimination strategy. In the case of first-degree price discrimination, the consumers of information may pay different prices for the same content, reflecting differences in their willingness to pay for such content (Esteves and Resende, 2012). The adoption of this type of pricing strategy is very demanding since media platforms need to be informed about the specific preferences of their consumers. While that was extremely difficult in the case of traditional media (tailored to mass audiences), it has become easier in the context of some new media interactive platforms (such as social networks, online press, Hulu). As consumers interact through these platforms, they reveal information about their tastes and preferences, amplifying the range of possibilities to effectively implement price discrimination strategies (Esteves, 2010).[27]

When first-degree price discrimination is not possible, firms may opt for less sophisticated price discrimination strategies. These include second-degree price discrimination, in which media platforms propose a menu of contracts which specify the access to different types of content (quality and quantity) at different rates; and third-degree price discrimination, in which firms set different prices to different groups of consumers (for example according to their age, job, income and so on).

In the context of modern business models for media platforms, the sophisticated pricing rules described above are being complemented with additional strategic actions aimed at improving network externalities without hindering firms from extracting surplus from consumers with higher willingness to pay. These additional strategies include versioning, bundling, cross-selling, exclusive dealing and so on.

2.5 New Strategies

Versioning strategies refer to the possibility of offering differentiated variants of a given media content, such as base, premium or family packages. These strategies are often used as a price discrimination device. On the one hand, platforms use basic content to attract more consumers, boosting network externalities. On the other hand, they rely on more sophisticated contents to extract surplus from consumers with higher willingness to pay.

Bundling strategies[28] consist in promoting the joint sale of several different products. Examples of these strategies include channel bundles sold by TV cable companies, triple play contracts (Internet, telephone and TV) or quadruple play contracts (Internet, fixed and mobile phone, and TV) by telecom/ISP operators. Through bundling practices firms may get higher revenues due to the cross subsidization among the products in the bundle.[29]

Cross-selling strategies arise when media platforms use certain contents, which are freely distributed, as a device to sell other products to their audiences (or their networks). For example, a music distribution platform may allow the free download of music as a device to sell more tickets to concerts (Regner et al., 2009).

Finally, exclusive dealing arises when platforms have the exclusive right to distribute certain contents. There is a vast economics literature dealing with the effects of exclusive dealing (for example, Rasmusen et al., 1991; Bernheim and Whinston, 1998; Segal and Whinston, 2000). In the case of media markets, two effects of exclusive dealing have been stressed. On the one hand, exclusive dealings may reduce static efficiency by distorting competition in the market, slowing down the distribution of media content through new platforms and eventually increasing the prices charged to consumers (Nicita and Ramello, 2007). Harbord and Ottaviani (2001) show that exclusive dealings on premium content may imply higher prices and a loss of welfare for the consumer. On the other hand, the rents from exclusive content distribution may be crucial to promote investment in new content (and promote high quality standards). This is particularly relevant for premium content that is riskier, has greater entry barriers and often requires more investment than base content[30] (Gerardin, 2005).

When exclusivity contracts exist, differentiation becomes a key dimension of competition among media platforms.

2.6 New Dynamics in Advertising Markets

In the context of new media markets, interactivity and interconnectivity are two dominant features. The new possibilities offered by modern media platforms have also changed the advertising market considerably (see Anderson, 2012). Advertisers are no longer investing in mass advertising strategies, which were dominant in the context of traditional media. The new technologies not only allow advertisers to collect an incredible amount of data about their consumers but also allow them to send different messages to different consumers (Iyer et al., 2005; Brahim et al., 2010; Galeotti and Moraga-Gonzalez, 2008; Esteves and Resende,

2012). Accordingly, advertising strategies above the line are now being replaced by advertising below the line (for example targeted advertising, advertising through social networks, recommendations and reviewing platforms). By tailoring their advertisements to specific audiences, advertisers reduce wasteful advertising and, in addition, they gain an effective instrument to price discriminate among their consumers.

The possibility of targeting advertisements to specific groups also changes the business model of advertisers, and the nature of interactions between audiences and advertisers through media platforms.[31] These interactions become more complex since advertisers are no longer exclusively interested in the size of the platforms' audiences. They value the specific characteristics of the audience and they are mostly interested in exploiting local network externalities (network externalities arising within a certain category of consumers).

The new possibilities launched by advertising strategies below the line are challenging the traditional approach of media platforms to the advertising market. On the one hand, advertisements must be tailored to specific audiences and they must exploit as much as possible the connectivity among consumers (for example through recommendations systems). On the other hand, the role of consumers in the advertising messages becomes more active (interactivity) and the impact of advertising itself becomes more visible (for example, advertisers can control the number of consumers watching/reading their advertisements; or, they can control how many consumers engage in online commerce after being exposed to their advertisements). In light of all these recent trends, business models of media firms on the advertising market (for example advertising rates pricing, advertisements' characteristics and design) must be redesigned in order to be attractive to advertisers and, simultaneously, generate enough revenue for media platforms, especially the ones adopting free content business models.

2.7 Net Neutrality Debate

At the present moment, Internet is an essential input to access information and media contents. Therefore, ISPs are definitely very relevant players in the media markets. ISPs can themselves be conceived as two-sided platforms connecting Internet users and content providers.[32] The traditional approach to the Internet lies in the principle of "net neutrality", according to which all Internet traffic is treated equally and therefore ISPs must provide the same conditions to all Internet platforms. As Internet platforms become more and more relevant (and some of them attract an increasing amount of money, for example Google or Facebook), ISPs are becoming interested in discriminating among content providers, charging them for the provision of a network of potential users. The ISPs argue that Internet giants (such as Google) are receiving most of the benefits from the network externalities generated on the Web and, therefore, net neutrality is dampening ISPs' incentives to invest in broadband capacity and technological innovation. Whether the future design of the Internet will embody the net neutrality principle or not remains an open question. Both the Federal Communications Commission (FCC), in the USA, and the European Commission have promoted public debates on this issue, but neither the major players in the sector (ISPs, Internet giants, equipment producers, consumers' associations) nor scholars seem to have reached a consensus on this subject.[33]

3. CONCLUSION

In this chapter, our main objective was to characterize media firms as multi-sided platforms. In the first part, we have shown how traditional media, like TV, newspapers and radio, can constitute platforms of interaction between audiences and advertisers. Then, in the second part, we have concentrated on new media markets. Due to digital disruption and the convergence phenomenon, media markets have changed drastically. Traditional media are now facing the competition of new media platforms, mostly based on the Internet. The new firms participating in the media market can be viewed as multi-sided platforms, in which several agents interact: audiences, content producers (who might be information consumers themselves), advertisers, ISPs, equipment producers and so on.

In our characterization of the media markets, we have emphasized the major role played by network externalities. They take place when agents' choices are somehow influenced by the choices of other agents in the same or in another related market. For example, in the context of traditional media, network externalities arise due to the influence of audiences on advertisers' expected payoffs and vice versa. Traditional media have often pushed the network externalities that audiences exert on advertisers by fixing an asymmetric price structure in which audiences are (at least partially) subsidized (for example, radio, free-to-air TV, free press).

In the context of modern media platforms, the nature and extent of network externalities becomes much more complex. On the one hand, the interactions among audiences and advertisers remain present but the latter are interested in exploiting local networks through targeted advertising technologies and/or increasing the speed of diffusion of their messages through viral marketing strategies that rely on network connections built on media platforms. On the other hand, due to the diversity of agents interacting through media platforms, new forms of network externalities take place. For example, the virtual social interactions via user-generated content, certification and recommendation systems are on the basis of new types of network externalities among consumers themselves. In addition, the arrival of new players in the market (e.g. ISPs) has created new levels of network externalities. A first level refers to the service of Internet provision itself (platforms with a larger base of consumers may offer a better service since they have more resources to improve quality – indirect network externalities). Furthermore, when providing access to the Internet, ISPs also enable media platforms to benefit from their installed base of users. This induces network externalities among users, between users and advertisers, and also between media platforms and ISPs.

An additional level of network externalities now arising in media markets refers to the interaction between media platforms, equipment producers and software developers. For example, in the smartphones market, consumers' equipment choices affect the incentives of software developers: the latter will be interested in developing applications for equipment platforms with a larger installed base of consumers. However, when buying their equipment consumers also account for the expected number of applications that will be developed for each available smartphone. As a result, a new form of network externalities arises.

Due to the variety of players and the complexity of network externalities arising in modern media markets, the design of a unique optimal business model is impracticable. Accordingly, the literature on media economics has not yet developed a unified model to study strategic interaction in the new media platforms. For this reason, in the second part of the text, we tried to provide a non-exhaustive review of some models commonly adopted by media platforms. Understanding the basic ingredients of these models opens a new avenue of research for media economists. An important challenge is to develop an analytical framework that allows economists to study in a systematic way the interactions taking place in media markets. Given the characteristics of modern media markets, we believe that the foundations for this framework should accommodate the contributions of the literature on two-sided markets as well as the literature on network formation games.

We believe that the development of this analytical framework is crucial on at least two levels. First, it is important to understand (and measure) the pros and cons of alternative existing business models in the perspective of media platforms and consumers. Second, it is important to support regulatory authorities in the media sectors. Following digital disruption and convergence, media regulators are now faced with a very challenging ecosystem. Although the analysis of regulation of media markets is beyond the scope of the present chapter, we should note that many important questions remain open: in a world of network externalities, in which media platforms need to reach a critical mass of consumers, is competition always desirable? In the era of convergence, are firms' cooperation and agreements on standards always welfare improving? Should ISPs be able to charge media platforms and other content producers for enabling them to access audiences that they will sell to advertisers afterwards? How to deal with piracy? How to evaluate its impact on the incentives to produce new content? How to set up property rights over downloads and content delivered through streaming? How to regulate exclusivity contracts,[34] through which some ISPs or media platforms have the exclusive right to distribute certain content? Are they detrimental to consumers or do they promote innovation and quality?

This non-exhaustive list of questions is sufficient to illustrate the intricacy of regulatory activities in modern media markets. Media economists certainly have a lot to contribute to these open debates and we expect the literature on regulation of media multi-sided platforms to grow in the forthcoming years.

NOTES

1. The Arab Spring revolution illustrates how media and social networks can impact on democracy.
2. For example, already in 1836, the French newspaper *La Gazette* was relying on circulation and advertising revenues.
3. These subsidies are frequent, for example, in the case of public TV channels.
4. "Coopeting" means that they simultaneously compete and cooperate.
5. For example, paid TV channels and VoD.
6. This problem becomes even more evident in the case of new media based on the Internet, where the marginal cost of serving an additional consumer is often zero.
7. In some cases, even after being exposed to the information, consumers may experience difficulties in evaluating its quality (e.g. its accuracy). In that case, information can be classified as a credence good (see, e.g. Gabszewicz and Resende, 2012).
8. Following the seminal papers by Rohlfs (1974) and Katz and Shapiro (1985), a vast literature has studied the economic effects of network externalities (see Farrell and Klemperer, 2007 for a survey). Recent studies on this matter include, for example, Amir and Lazzati (2011).
9. For example, this is usually the case of ad insertions in fashion or car magazines.

10. The ability of reaching a critical mass of advertisers is more relevant in the case of ad-loving audiences. When advertising is a nuisance to consumers, the optimal pricing structure will obviously be different than in the case of ad-loving audiences (see Ferrando et al. 2008).
11. Note that our focus on the newspaper industry is merely pedagogical and the model could be easily extended to represent other traditional media, such as TV or radio.
12. This could be due to their different political slant (Gentzkow and Shapiro, 2006; Mullainathan and Shleifer, 2005; Ellman and Germano, 2009; Gabszewicz and Resende, 2012), or to different type of content (cultural versus entertainment content) or different regional scope.
13. See Kaiser (2006). This assumption was also used in other studies dealing with the newspaper market, e.g. Argentesi and Filistrucchi (2007).
14. Notice that if readers were not ad-neutral, there would be an extra channel of demand interdependence on the readers' side as well.
15. In fact, the model presented in this section is a simplified version of Gabszewicz et al. (2001). While they endogenize the choice of the newspapers' positioning on the Hotelling line, we assume here exogenous locations, with newspapers being located at the extreme of the Hotelling line.
16. It is possible to find real world examples sustaining this type of practices. For example, the offer of DVDs together with the newspaper.
17. See, e.g., the discussions and publications by the EU Media Futures Forum available at: http://ec.europa.eu/information_society/media_taskforce/pluralism/forum/index_en.htm
18. For example, France is one the countries with more restrictive regulation. On public TV channels it is forbidden to interrupt movies to display advertisements, while on private TV channels, movies can be interrupted at most once. The government also regulates the duration of advertising spots on French TV (maximum 6 minutes/hour).
19. For example, polluting firms may be skeptical about advertising in newspapers that are known for dispatching lots of news related to global warming and other environmental concerns.
20. Streaming can be viewed as a delivery method in which content is continuously delivered through the media platform without the need to download it.
21. Interconnectivity is perhaps the most important feature of the Internet, on the basis of free access requested by consumers (Bomsel, 2007), concentration due to network externalities, consumers' interaction, generalization of users' generated content, and increasing importance of recommendations systems.
22. See Gille (2009).
23. The term "infomediaries" combines the words "information" and "intermediaries". According to Rebillard and Smyrnaios (2010), infomediaries aim to (i) assist consumers in the management of information; and (ii) gather information about consumers and sell it to producers of goods and services.
24. See Evans and Schmalensee (2005).
25. For example, in France, LCI, a paid channel specialized on continuous information and news, has recently endured the rivalry of new free information channels (iTele and BFM) broadcast by digital terrestrial television. In light of this, the owners of LCI have requested permission to broadcast programs for free! This simple example illustrates that the traditional dichotomy has become null and void, making obsolete the traditional competitive analysis of the sector. On the audiovisual sector, the classical dichotomy between paid and free channels rested on the underlying business model (based on subscription revenues, for the first, and advertising revenues for the second), as well as on the type of content broadcast (with the first

proposing an unspecialized content supply while the second provided more specialized or thematic contents). The previous example illustrates that this dichotomy does not necessarily hold any more.
26. The possibility of remunerating ISPs for their role as network enablers gave rise to the "net neutrality debate". This debate is briefly characterized in subsection 2.7.
27. The information about consumers' tastes or preferences is not only useful to facilitate the adoption of price discrimination strategies. In some business models, media platforms sell this information to independent firms. In fact, this constitutes a frequent source of revenue in the context of free content models.
28. A vast literature has focused on the analysis of bundling practices. For more details on this subject see, for example, Armstrong and Vickers (2010).
29. Consider the following simple example. Suppose two groups, of S consumers each. In group 1 consumers' valuations for TV channels A and B are, respectively, 9 and 3. In group 2, the corresponding valuations are 10 and 2, instead. Considering null production costs and no-price discrimination, we observe that, when commercialized separately, channel A would be sold at 9, while channel 2 would be sold at 2, yielding a revenue of 22S for the firm. Instead, when the two channels are sold together, the firm can sell the bundle at 12, obtaining a revenue equal to 24S.
30. The producers of this type of content tend to offer exclusive long term contracts to media platforms. Buyers often try to negotiate the right to preempt second windows of distribution, in order to have the monopoly provision of the content.
31. Gal-Or and Gal-Or (2005) study the competitive effects of targeted advertising when a single media content distributor delivers advertising messages on the behalf of firms. Gal-Or et al. (2006) deal with the issue of imperfect advertising tailoring, studying to what extent an advertiser should allocate resources to increase the quality of its targeting.
32. Content providers are often multi-sided platforms themselves. They connect consumers with each other and in the case of audience platforms they also frequently connect consumers and advertisers.
33. For example, Economides and Tag (2012) conclude that the "overall effect of implementing network neutrality regulations can still be both positive and negative depending on parameter values". Bourreau et al. (2012) find that innovation in the discriminatory regime is higher than under network neutrality. Congestion in the network is also managed more effectively under a discriminatory regime. Brito et al. (2012) show that the impact of network neutrality on incentives to invest depends on the nature of the investment as well as on the ability of the ISP to freely allocate its capacity among content providers. They also conclude that the effects of the integration between ISPs and content providers under a discriminatory regime (i.e. no network neutrality) are ambiguous and they depend on the interaction with advertising markets. Jullien and Sand-Zantman (2012) argue that the "cost sharing between the network and content producers has two benefits: it raises efficiency for the paid content and reduces the price charged to consumers due to a waterbed effect."
34. For example, some ISPs have the exclusive right to broadcast the official TV channels of some soccer teams.

REFERENCES

Albarran, A.B. (1996), *Media Economics: Understanding Markets, Industries and Concepts*, Ames, Iowa: University Press.

Amir, R., Gabszewicz, J.J. and Resende, J. (2014), 'Thematic clubs and the supremacy of network externalities', *Journal of Public Economic Theory*, **16**(5): 706–729.

Amir, R. and Lazzati, N. (2011), 'Network effects, market structure and industry performance', *Journal of Economic Theory*, **146**, 2389–2419.

Anderson, C. (2006), *The Long Tail*, London: Random House.

Anderson, S. (2012), 'Advertising and the Internet', in Martin Peitz and Joel Waldfogel (eds), *The Oxford Handbook of the Digital Economy*, New York: Oxford University Press.

Anderson, S. and Coate, S. (2005), 'Market provision of broadcasting: a welfare analysis', *Review of Economic Studies*, **72**, 947–972.

Anderson, S., Foros, Ã., Kind, H. and Peitz, M. (2012), 'Media market concentration, advertising levels, and ad prices', *International Journal of Industrial Organization*, **30**(3), 321–325.

Argentesi, E. and Filistrucchi, L. (2007), 'Estimating market power in a two-sided market: the case of newspapers', *Journal of Applied Econometrics*, **22**(7), 1247–1266.

Armstrong, M. (2005), 'Competition in two-sided markets', *RAND Journal of Economics*, **37**(3), 668–691.

Armstrong, M. and Vickers, J. (2010), 'Competitive non-linear pricing and bundling', *Review of Economic Studies*, **77**(1), 30–60.

Bagdikian, B.H. (1992), *The Media Monopoly*, Beacon Press: Boston.

Baranès, E. and Encaoua, D. (2002), 'The relevant market for television: the French case', *Communications & Strategies*, **47** (3rd quarter), 63–86.

Baron, D. (2006), 'Persistent media bias', *Journal of Public Economics*, **90**(1–2), 1–36.

Barua, A., Pinnel, J., Shutter, J. and Whinston, A. (1999), *Measuring the Internet Economy: an Exploratory Study*, Center for Research in Electronic Commerce, University of Texas at Austin.

Baxter, W.F. (1974), 'Regulation and diversity in communications media', *The American Economic Review*, Papers and Proceedings of the Eighty-Sixth Annual Meeting of the American Economic Association, **64**(2), May, 392–399.

Beebe, J. (1977), 'Institutional structure and program choices in television markets', *Quarterly Journal of Economics*, **91**, 15–37.

Behringer, S. and Filistrucchi, L. (2009), 'Price wars in two-sided markets: the case of the UK quality newspapers', Working Papers 09-26, NET Institute.

Belleflamme, P., Lambert, T. and Schwienbacher, A. (2011), 'Crowdfunding: tapping the right crowd', mimeo, CORE Discussion Papers 2011–032.

Belleflamme, P. and Peitz, M. (2012), 'Digital piracy: theory', in Martin Peitz and Joel Waldfogel (eds), *The Oxford Handbook of the Digital Economy*, New York: Oxford University Press.

Benckler, I. (2009), *La richesse des réseaux. Marchés et libertés du partage social*, Presses universitaires de Lyon.

Benhamou, F. and Peltier, S. (2007), 'How should cultural diversity be measured? An application using the French publishing industry', *Journal of Cultural Economics*, April, 85–107.

Bernheim, B. and Whinston, M. (1998), 'Exclusive dealing', *Journal of Political Economy*, **106**, 64–103.

Berry, S. and Waldfogel, J. (1999), 'Free entry and social inefficiency in radio broadcasting', *Rand Journal of Economics*, **30**, 397–420.

Berry, S.T. and Waldfogel, J. (2001), 'Do mergers increase product variety? Evidence from radio broadcasting', *The Quarterly Journal of Economics*, **116**(3), August, 1009–1025.

Besley, A. and Prat, A. (2006), 'Handcuffs for the grabbing hand? Media capture and political accountability', *American Economic Review*, **96**(3), 720–736.

Blank, D.M. (1966), 'The quest for quantity and diversity in television programming', *The American Economic Review*, **5**(1/2), March, 448–456.

Bomsel, O. (2007), *Gratuit!*, Gallimard, Folio actuel.

Bourreau, M., Kouranti, F. and Valletti, T.M. (2012), 'Net neutrality with competing internet platforms', mimeo.

Brahim, N., Lahmandi-Ayed, R. and Laussel, D. (2010), 'Is targeted advertising always beneficial?', *International Journal of Industrial Organization*, **29**(6), 678–689.

Brito, D., Pereira, P. and Vareda, J. (2012), 'Network neutrality debate: investment and integration', mimeo.

Brown, A. and Cave, M. (1992), 'The economics of television regulation: a survey with application to Australia', *The Economic Record*, **68**, 377–394.

Caillaud, B. and Jullien, B. (2003), 'Chicken and egg: competing matchmakers', *Rand Journal of Economics*, **34**, 309–328.

Cancian, M., Bills, A. and Bergstrom, T. (1995), 'Hotelling location problems with directional constraints: an application to television news scheduling', *Journal of Industrial Economics*, **43**, 121–124.

Caves, R. (2002), *Creative Industries, Contracts between Arts and Commerce*, Harvard University Press.

Coase, R. (1966), 'The economics of broadcasting and government policy', *American Economic Review*, **56**, 440–447.

Corden, W.M. (1953), 'The maximisation of profit by a newspaper', *Review of Economic Studies*, **20**, 181–190.

Curien, N. (2000), *Economie des réseaux*, La Découverte: Repères.

D'Aspremont, C., Gabszewicz, J.J. and Thisse, J.F. (1979), 'On Hotelling's stability in competition', *Econometrica*, **47**(5), 1145–1150.

De Bijl, P. and Peitz, M. (2010), 'Regulatory legacy, VoIP adoption, and investment incentives', *Telecommunications Policy*, **34**(10), 596–605.

DellaVigna, S. and Kaplan, E. (2007), 'The Fox News effect: media bias and voting', *Quarterly Journal of Economics*, **122**, 1187–1234.

Downs, A. (1957), *An Economic Theory of Democracy*, New York: Harper.

Dukes, A. and Gal-Or, E. (2003), 'Minimum differentiation in commercial media markets', *Journal of Economics and Management Strategy*, **12**, 291–325.

Economides, N. and Tag, J. (2012), 'Network neutrality on the Internet: a two-sided market analysis', *Information, Economics and Policy*, **24**, 91–104.

Ellman, M. and Germano, F. (2009), 'What do the papers sell? A model of advertising and media bias', *Economic Journal*, **119**(537), 680–704.

Esteves, R.B. (2010), 'Pricing with customer recognition', *International Journal of Industrial Organization*, **28**(6), 669–681.

Esteves, R.B. and Resende, J. (2012), 'Competitive target advertising with price discrimination', mimeo.

Evans, D. and Schmalensee, R. (2005), 'The industrial organization of markets with two-sided platforms', Working Paper, MIT, Cambridge, NBER n°11603.

Farrell, J. and Klemperer, P. (2007), 'Coordination and lock-in: competition with switching costs and network effects,' in Armstrong, M. and Porter, R. (eds) *Handbook of Industrial Organization*, Vol. 3, Amsterdam: North-Holland.

Ferrando, J., Gabszewicz, J.J., Laussel, D. and Sonnac, N. (2008), 'Intermarket network externalities and competition: an application to media industries', *International Journal of Economic Theory*, **4**(3), 357–379.

Furhoff, L. (1973), 'Some reflections on newspaper concentration', *Scandinavian Economic History Review*, **21**, 1–27.

Gabszewicz, J.J., Laussel, D. and Sonnac, N. (1999), 'TV-broadcasting competition and advertising', *CORE Discussion Paper 2000/6*, Université catholique de Louvain and Lucarnes bleues n° 9972 CREST/LEI.

Gabszewicz, J.J., Laussel, D. and Sonnac, N. (2001), 'Press advertising and the ascent of the "Pensée unique"', *European Economic Review*, **45**, 645–651.

Gabszewicz, J.J., Laussel, D. and Sonnac, N. (2002), 'Press advertising and the political differentiation of newspapers', *Journal of Public Economic Theory*, **4**(3), 249–259.
Gabszewicz, J.J., Laussel, D. and Sonnac, N. (2004), 'Programming and advertising competition in the broadcasting industry', *Journal of Economics and Management Strategy*, **13**(4), Winter, 657–669.
Gabszewicz, J.J., Garela, P. and Sonnac, N. (2007), 'Newspapers' market shares and the theory of the circulation spiral', *Information Economics and Policy*, in J. Waldfogel (ed.), **19**, 405–441.
Gabszewicz, J.J. and Resende, J. (2012), 'Differentiated credence goods and price competition', *Information, Economics and Policy*, **24**(3-4): 277–287.
Gal-Or, E. and Gal-Or, M. (2005), 'Customized advertising on television', *Marketing Science*, 241–253.
Gal-Or, E., Gal-Or, M., May, J. and Spangler, W. (2006), 'Targeted advertising strategies on television', *Management Science*, 713–725.
Galeotti, A. and Moraga-Gonzalez, J.L. (2008), 'Segmentation, advertising and prices', *International Journal of Industrial Organization*, **26**(5), 1106–1119.
Garcia, F. and Resende, J. (2011), 'Dynamic games of network effects', in Peixoto, M.M., Pinto, A.A. and Rand, D.A. (eds), *Dynamics, Games and Science II, in Honor of Maurício Peixoto and David Rand*, Springer.
Genesove, D. (2004), 'Why are there so few (and fewer and fewer) two-newspaper towns?', mimeo.
Gensollen, M. (1998), 'The Internet: a new information economy?', *Communications et Stratégies*, **32**, 4th quarter, 197–227.
Gentzkow, M. and Shapiro, J.M. (2006), 'Media bias and reputation', *Journal of Political Economy*, **114**(2), 280–316.
George, L. (2007), 'What's fit to print: the effect of ownership concentration on product variety in daily newspaper markets', *Information, Economics and Policy*, **19**(3–4), 285–303.
George, L. and Waldfogel, L. (2003), 'Who affects whom in daily newspaper markets?', *Journal of Political Economy*, **111**(4), 765–784.
Gerardin, D. (2005), 'Access to content by new media platform: a review of the competition law problems', *European Law Review*, February, **30**(1), 68–94.
Gille, L. (2009), 'Vers de nouveaux modèles d'affaires et de chaînes de valeur', in Gille, L. (ed.), *Les dilemmes de l'économie numérique*, Vuibert.
Goyal, S. (2012), 'Social networks on the Web', in Martin Peitz and Joel Waldfogel (eds), *The Oxford Handbook of the Digital Economy*, New York: Oxford University Press.
Greenberg, E. and Barnett, H.J. (1971), 'TV program diversity – new evidence and old theories', *The American Economic Review*, Papers and Proceedings of the Eighty-Third Annual Meeting of the American Economic Association, **61**, 2, May, 89–93.
Gustafsson, K.E. (1978), 'The circulation spiral and the principle of household coverage', *The Scandinavian Economic History Review*, **XXVI**(1), 1–14.
Harbord, D. and Ottaviani, M. (2001), 'Contracts and competition in the pay-tv market', London Business School: Department of Economics, Working Paper no. DP 2001/5.
Hotelling, H. (1929), 'Stability in competition', *Economic Journal*, **39**, 41–57.
Illing, G. and Peitz, M. (2006), *Industrial Organization and the Digital Economy*, MIT Press.
Iyer, G., Soberman, D. and Villas-Boas, M. (2005), 'The targeting of advertising', *Marketing Science*, **24**, 461–476.
Jackson, M.O. (2008), *Social and Economic Networks*, New Jersey: Princeton Univeristy Press.
Jenkins, H. (2001), 'Convergence? I Diverge', *Digital Renaissance, Technology Review.*
Jullien, B. and Sand-Zantman, W. (2012), 'Congestion pricing and net neutrality', mimeo.

Kaiser, U. (2006), 'Magazine-readers: ad-lovers, ad-haters or ad-neutrals', Discussion Paper, Centre for Economic and Business Research, 2006–09.
Kaiser, U. and Song, M. (2009), 'Do media consumers really dislike advertising? An empirical assessment of the role of advertising in print media markets', *International Journal of Industrial Organization*, **27**(2), 292–301.
Kaiser, U. and Wright, J. (2006), 'Price structure in two-sided markets: evidence from the magazine industry', *International Journal of Industrial Organization*, **24**(1), 1–28.
Katz, M. and Shapiro, C. (1985), 'Network effects, competition and compatibility', *American Economic Review*, **75**(3), 424–440.
Laffont, J. and Tirole, J. (2000), *Competition in Telecommunications*, MIT Press.
Levin, H.J. (1971), 'Program duplication, diversity, and effective viewer choices: some empirical findings', *The American Economic Review*, Papers and Proceedings of the Eighty-Third Annual Meeting of the American Economic Association, **61**(2), May, 81–88.
Manduchi, A. and Picard, R. (2009), 'Circulations, revenues, and profits in a newspaper market with fixed advertising costs', *The Journal of Media Economics*, **22**(4), 211–238.
McChesney, F.S. (1987), 'Sensationalism, newspaper profits and the marginal value of Watergate', *Economic Inquiry*, **25**(1), 135–144.
McDonald, D.G. and Shu-Fang, L. (2004), 'The effect of new networks on U.S. television diversity', *The Journal of Media Economics*, **17**(2), 105–121.
Motta, M. and Polo, M. (1997), 'Concentration and public policies in the broadcasting industry: the future of television', *Economic Policy*, **12**(25), October, 293–334.
Mullainathan, S. and Shleifer, A. (2005), 'Market for news', *American Economic Review*, **95**(4), 1031–1053.
Nicita, A. and Ramello, G. (2007), 'Property, liability and market power: the antitrust side of copyright', *Review of Law & Economics*, **3**(3), 7.
Niven, D. (1999), 'Partisan bias in the media? A new test', *Social Science Quarterly*, 80, 847–858.
Osterwalder, A. and Pigneur, Y. (2010), *Business Model Generation*, Toronto: Flash Reproductions Ltd.
Owen, B. and Wildman, S. (1992), *Video Economics*, Cambridge, MA: Harvard University Press.
Owen, B., Beebe, M. and Manning, W.G. (1974), *Television Economics*, Lexington, MA: Lexington Books.
Page, F. and Wooders, M. (2009), 'Strategic basins of attraction, the path dominance core, and network formation games', *Games and Economic Behavior*, **66**(1), 462–487.
Page, F. and Wooders, M. (2010), 'Club networks with multiple memberships and noncooperative stability', *Games and Economic Behavior*, **70**(1), 12–20.
Peitz, M. and Valletti, T. (2008), 'Content and advertising in the media: pay-tv versus free-to-air', *International Journal of Industrial Organization*, **26**(4), 949–965.
Peitz, M. and Waldfogel, J. (2012), *The Oxford Handbook of the Digital Economy*, Oxford University Press.
Picard, R. (1989), *Media Economics: Concepts and Issues*, Newbury Park, CA: Sage.
Rasmusen, E.B., Ramseyer, J.M. and Wiley, J.S. Jr (1991), 'Naked exclusion', *American Economic Review*, **81**, 1137–1145.
Rebillard, F. and Smyrnaios, N. (2010), 'Les infomédiaires, au cœur de l'information en ligne', *Réseaux*, **160–161**, 165–194.
Regner, T., Barria, J., Pitt, J. and Neville, B. (2009), 'An artist life cycle model for digital media content: strategies for the Light Web and the Dark Web', *Electronic Commerce Research and Applications*, **8**, 334–342.
Reisinger, M. (2012), 'Platform competition for advertisers and users in media markets', *International Journal of Industrial Organization*, **30**(2), 243–252.

Resende, J. (2008), 'The economic advantage of being the voice of the majority', *The Journal of Media Economics*, **21**(3), 158–190.
Rochet, J.C. and Tirole, J. (2003), 'Platform competition in two-sided markets', *Journal of the European Economic Association*, **1**, 990–1023.
Rochet, J.C. and Tirole, J. (2006), 'Two-sided markets: a progress report', *The RAND Journal of Economics*, **35**(3), 645–667.
Rohlfs, J. (1974), 'A theory of interdependent demand for a communication service', *Bell Journal of Economics*, **5**, 16–37.
Rosse, J. (1967), 'Daily newspapers, monopolistic competition and economies of scale', *The American Economic Review*, **57**(2), 522–533.
Samuelson, P. (1964), 'Public goods and subscription TV: correction of the record', *Journal of Law and Economics*, **7**, October, 81–83.
Segal, I. and Whinston, M. (2000), 'Naked exclusion: comment', *American Economic Review*, **90**(1), 296–309.
Shapiro, C. and Varian, H.R. (1999), *Information Rules. A Strategic Guide to the Network Economy*, Boston, MA: Harvard Business School Press.
Sonnac, N. (2000), 'Readers' attitudes towards press advertising: are they ad-lovers or ad-averse?', *Journal of Media Economics*, **13**(4), 249–259.
Sonnac, N. (2002), 'Monopole télévisuel et publiphobie', *Recherches Economiques de Louvain*, **68**(4), 513–526.
Sonnac, N. (2009), 'L'économie de la presse: vers un nouveau modèle d'affaires', *Cahiers du journalisme*, **20** (automne), 22–43.
Sonnac, N. (2012), 'Médias audiovisuels et concurrence. Le cas de télévision payante', *Revue d'économie industrielle*, **137**, 1er trimestre, 109–129.
Spence, M. and Owen, B. (1977), 'Television programming, monopolistic competition and welfare', *Quarterly Journal of Economics*, **91**, 103–126.
Steiner, P. (1952), 'Program patterns and preferences, and the workability of competition in radio broadcasting', *Quarterly Journal of Economics*, **66**(2), 194–223.
Stromberg, D. (2004), 'Mass media competition, political competition, and public policy', *Review of Economic Studies*, **71**(1).
Van Der Wurff, R. (2005), 'Competition, concentration and diversity in European television markets', *Journal of Cultural Economics*, **29**, 249–275.
Vogel, L. and Vogel, J. (2009), 'Comment intégrer les notions de demande et d'élasticités pour définir le marché pertinent', *Concurrences*, **4**.
Wauthy, X. (2008), 'Concurrence et régulation sur les marchés de plate-forme: une introduction', *Reflets et perspectives*, **1** (XLVII), 37–52.
Wright, D.J. (1994), 'Television advertising regulation and program quality', *The Economic Record*, **70**(211), December, 361–367.
Yoo, C.S. (2002), 'Vertical integration and media regulation in the new economy', *Yale Journal on Regulation*, **19**(1), 171.

2. Vertical ownership, technology and programming content

Sung Wook Ji and David Waterman

In this chapter, we investigate two different economic determinants of the quantity and diversity of television programming. One is the effects of vertical integration between programming networks and content suppliers, or between those networks and retail level programming distributors (such as cable television systems) on the menus of programming available to consumers. The other is the effects over time of technological advances in the distribution and exhibition of television and video media programming. Although we consider theoretical developments in some instances, our primary focus is on empirical research.

We report on a considerable amount of empirical research that has investigated the effects of vertical integration on television programming menus. Much less systematic research, however, has investigated the effects of technological change on programming supply, and we rely primarily on descriptive data in that part of the chapter. As will also be apparent, however, the effects of technological change have undoubtedly been far more dramatic than those of vertical ownership.

We begin in Section 1 with a review and analysis of empirical research on the effects of vertical integration in the broadcast and cable television industries. We then turn in Section 2 to a more speculative consideration of how advances in technology since the 1970s have affected the supply of television programming. In the Section 3 conclusion, we consider the emerging role of Internet television distribution and draw links between vertical integration and technological change.

1. THE EFFECTS OF VERTICAL OWNERSHIP

There is a long history of policy concerns about vertical integration in television. From an economic perspective, these concerns involve potentially conflicting social objectives. First, we desire the benefits of efficiency; a large general literature in economics has established that economic efficiency is likely to be improved by vertical integration

(Perry, 1989; Joskow, 2005). In the media industries, this greater efficiency may translate into increased program supply and diversity, and/or lower prices for consumers. Vertical integration also, however, has potentially undesirable vertical foreclosure effects, and that has attracted much of the policy attention (Federal Communications Commission (FCC), 1993). In particular, unaffiliated programming might be excluded from the market, reducing competition in programming supply. This outcome not only threatens efficiency, but the broader social objective of having a wide diversity of programming content available to viewers.

Regulators have also been concerned that vertically integrated cable operators in bottleneck positions have the ability to restrict the development of new cable programming networks by discriminating against unaffiliated networks. Or they might withhold their popular "must have" programming networks from competing multi-channel video programming distributors (MVPDs) (FCC, 1993; FCC, 2012). We discuss this latter concern briefly in Section 3, but our primary focus is integration's direct effects on the program supply market.

We first consider research about the effects of vertical integration in the broadcast television industry, which is mostly concerned with ownership ties between program production and the major broadcast networks. We then turn to vertical integration in cable television, which has mostly involved ownership ties between cable program networks and cable TV system operators.

Vertical Integration in Broadcasting

The program supply industry

Several authors have established that television production itself has few economies of scale or natural barriers to entry (Owen et al., 1975; Owen and Wildman, 1992; Caves, 2005). Rental markets for the means of production, such as sound stages, cameras and other equipment, are well developed and talent is generally employed on a program-by-program contract basis. During a long period from 1970 to the early 1990s, the FCC's Financial Interest and Syndication ("fin-syn") rules discouraged vertical ownership ties between the major broadcast networks and prime-time program producers, thus providing something of a natural laboratory setting to investigate market structure of the program supply industry.[1] Descriptive data collected during this time by Owen et al. (1975) and Owen and Wildman (1992) showed that the individual production companies which supplied prime-time TV series programming to the major broadcast networks were very diverse in size, ranging from "independent" firms that produced only a single series in any given year, to companies such as the major film studios, which often supplied several. Market shares of the most successful suppliers rarely exceeded 20 percent and tended to fluctuate substantially from year to year. There was also considerable entry and exit, reflecting the inherently high risk in predicting which TV shows would be successful and which not. Thus, programming supply naturally tends to be competitive in nature with free entry and has not in itself created policy concerns. Those concerns have focused on ownership relationships between production suppliers and the gatekeepers to viewer access, the major broadcast networks.

The growth of vertical ties with broadcast networks

In about 1989, ownership ties between prime-time program production and the broadcast networks began growing, especially after 1993 (Einstein, 2002, 2004; Bielby and Bielby, 2003). In a study commissioned by the FCC, Goolsbee (2007) reported that 58.0 percent of prime-time shows appearing on the largest six broadcast networks from the 2000–01 to the 2004–05 seasons had vertical ownership ties to the network that exhibited the show. Of the remainder, 23.5 percent were shows owned by other networks and only 18.5 percent were "fully independent" shows. This pattern was fairly consistent across the networks.

Caves (2005) writes, however, that the growing vertical ownership ties in broadcasting did not fundamentally change the nature of production management by the networks. Very often, integrated programs were co-produced by a network's affiliated production company in collaboration with another unaffiliated producer. Production management by the networks was generally conducted on an arm's length, program-by-program basis. The writer, producer, and other creative roles remained essentially the same whatever the ownership ties.

Caves (2005) identifies several motivations for the growing integration after regulation fell away, mostly involving contracting efficiencies. First, no contracts between producers and the networks can ever be complete, leaving open the possibility of opportunistic behavior by the producer or the network to take advantage, for example, of unexpected changes in a show's audience reception. Networks also have an incentive to guide the production process and this cannot be effectively accomplished with contracts. Networks also desire to control decisions about program scheduling and series renewal that potentially can be adverse to the interests of a show's producer. Caves acknowledges (but minimizes) another incentive for integration identified by Owen et al. (1975) and Besen et al. (1984) in earlier arguments they had made for repeal of the fin-syn rules: efficient risk sharing by networks and independent producers.

The empirical effects of vertical integration in broadcasting

Presumably, consumers benefit from vertical contracting and risk sharing efficiencies achieved through ownership, but negative effects of vertical integration are also empirically plausible. Expressed most generally, the networks might in some way favor carriage of their vertically affiliated programs at the expense of unaffiliated programs – even though the latter are better programs. The unaffiliated programs would thus be foreclosed from the market to the extent that their producers have no comparably effective routes to reach viewers.

There have been only a few empirical studies of the effects of vertical integration between broadcast networks and their program suppliers. Guo and Caves (2001) found no overall indications that vertically affiliated shows had a better chance of renewal in subsequent seasons.[2] Barth (2003) reported slightly positive but inconclusive effects of vertical integration on chances for renewal by comparing the prime-time programming menus before and after the fin-syn rules. Using a sample of all 500 prime-time shows aired on the six national broadcast networks from 2000 to 2005, Goolsbee (2007) tested the hypothesis that major networks' vertically affiliated shows performed worse than "independently" produced shows in terms of their advertising revenues. He reported no significant differences in that comparison, although he notes that if vertical efficiencies were realized, one would expect this result.[3]

In summary, there is scant empirical evidence that vertical ownership ties between broadcast networks and program producers have significantly foreclosed unaffiliated producers from access to viewers. On the one hand, Goolsbee (2007) notes that the high frequency of vertical integration is by itself apparent evidence that the possibilities of independent producer entry into this market are limited. On the other hand, the preponderance of co-production and joint venture relationships suggests that the broadcast networks remain open to proposals for new shows coming from outside their corporate entity. Indeed, Caves (2005) argues, it is imperative given the highly uncertain nature of programming success that the networks remain open to new ideas – wherever they may come from. There is no persuasive evidence that vertical market relationships as they have evolved fail to accommodate that need.

As a whole, while the prime-time shows of the major broadcast networks still mostly command the largest television audiences in the US, time has not been on their side. Policy concerns about vertical foreclosure in broadcasting have faded along with their declining share of all television viewing, which fell from over 50 percent in the early 1970s to only 14 percent by the late 2000s (Papazian, 2009).

Vertical Integration in Cable Television

Parallel to the broadcasting case, policy concerns about vertical integration in cable television have also focused on its potential efficiency benefits to program supply vs. potentially negative market foreclosure effects. In the cable case, however, both policy and research, however, have been focused not on ownership of program production itself, but on vertical ties between cable programming networks and cable system operators. That is because, historically, cable television service has tended to be monopolized at the local level, creating a potential bottleneck between the suppliers of programming and consumers. If a cable system has an ownership interest in a given cable network, it may have an incentive to exclude an unaffiliated network with similar programming, thus foreclosing consumers from access to that programming. These concerns have been enhanced by the fact that many cable television systems are owned by multiple system operators (MSOs) whose combined systems have a significant national market share of all cable subscribers. In this case, a corporate decision not to carry an unaffiliated network could potentially drive it out of business, especially if it is a nascent network attempting to enter the market.

Several empirical studies have shown that a cable system that is vertically affiliated with cable programming networks has a tendency to favor those networks, and have also shown or suggested that integration leads to exclusion of similar unaffiliated programming. Empirical studies about this network carriage pattern include Waterman and Weiss (1996, 1997) and Chipty (2001), each of which found that cable systems which own their own channels (either basic or premium) are more likely to carry their own channels. Using a 1989 database of US cable systems, Waterman and Weiss (1996) found that cable systems having ownership ties to premium cable networks tended to offer their own affiliated networks more frequently, and unaffiliated rival networks less frequently. Based on 1991 data, Chipty (2001) showed that vertical integration between MSOs and premium cable networks led to the offering of fewer premium networks and fewer basic movie networks (which are rivals of the premium movie networks that they own). She also documented that cable systems having vertical ties with a certain basic channel (the TV shopping service, QVC) were less likely to offer a competing independent TV shopping channel (HSN). These basic effects of integration were confirmed by the subsequent empirical studies of Chen and Waterman (2007); GAO (2004); Goolsbee (2007); Ji (2012); Kang (2009); and Suzuki (2009).

These empirical findings suggest that vertical integration makes it less likely that non-vertically integrated, "independent" networks can survive in the marketplace. Exclusion of rival networks by vertically integrated cable systems might occur, however, for benign, efficiency-based reasons, and thus benefit consumers in other ways. Similar to the broadcasting case, for example, cable operators potentially realize contracting efficiencies, such as reduced risk of opportunistic behavior, by carrying a vertically affiliated network instead of a rival with similar programming. A more important benefit of vertical integration by cable operators may be a greater flow of financial resources back to the cable program supply industry, which could have the effect of increasing the supply of programming. While most empirical studies do not distinguish between efficiency and anti-competitive foreclosure motives, some authors have reported empirical evidence that vertical integration results in greater economic welfare by increasing the number of cable network subscribers (Chipty, 2001), by lowering cable prices (Ford and Jackson, 1997; Suzuki, 2009), or by providing more programming networks to subscribers (Suzuki, 2009).

The development of digital technologies has massively expanded the channel capacity of cable systems. That increased capacity might be expected to alleviate the practice of vertical market foreclosure because digital cable systems are able to offer a large number of channels regardless of any vertical ties with cable networks. Findings of Chen and Waterman (2007) and Ji (2012) also suggest that increased channel capacity attenuates the vertical foreclosure effect. Nevertheless, new forms of vertical favoritism were also identified by these later studies. That is, a cable system with vertical ties may discriminate against unaffiliated rival cable networks by positioning them on higher priced optional tiers, which usually have fewer subscribers than basic tiers, thus limiting the subscribership base of its rival.

Another major change in the cable industry has, of course, been the increase in competition resulting from the development of alternative video programming delivery systems. The most successful of these services has been DBS, which was first introduced in 1994 and quickly grew as an alternative to cable service (Parsons and Frieden, 1998; Parsons, 2003). By 2010, over 30 percent of the MVPD market, in terms of basic subscribers, was served by DBS systems. In his FCC commissioned study, Goolsbee (2007) considered the effects of cable system carriage of vertical affiliated programming. Using market-by-market carriage data for 12 nationally distributed networks having vertical ownership ties to cable systems, he found that these networks were significantly less likely to be carried by their vertically affiliated cable systems in geographic areas where there was higher DBS penetration. He interpreted these results to be evidence that vertical foreclosure effects are diminished by an increase in multi-channel competition.

In the mid-2000s, Internet Protocol TV (IPTV) transmission of multi-channel television was introduced by telephone service providers. As of 2012, IPTV accounted for about 9.9 percent of the approximately 100 million total MVPD subscribers (SNL Kagan Research, 2013). Although no study has to our knowledge empirically examined the effect of local competition resulting from the development of multi-channel IPTV, it is reasonable to speculate that this enhanced competition also may decrease vertical foreclosure effects in the cable market.

Finally, the historical trend of vertical integration in the cable TV industry has been generally downward since the mid-1990s. The percentage of national cable programming networks which have vertical ties with at least one multi-channel programming distributor declined from 53 percent in 1994 to 15 percent in 2006 (FCC, 1995, 2009).[4] This trend also limits our concerns with the foreclosure effects of vertical integration in cable television.

In sum, several empirical studies have shown or suggested that vertical integration between cable systems and cable networks may reduce programming diversity at the cable system level. In other ways, however, vertical integration may increase the supply of programming and thus benefit program diversity. Although the foreclosure effects of vertical integration in cable have been shown to persist in higher capacity digital systems, they have been attenuated at least somewhat, and the historical incidence of vertical integration in cable has declined.

2. TECHNOLOGY AND THE SUPPLY OF PROGRAMMING CONTENT

We have already seen that concerns about the effects of vertical integration in both broadcasting and cable television have been diminished by technology to the extent that alternative delivery systems give consumers other options, and in the cable television case because the incentives of vertically integrated system operators to foreclose unaffiliated programming appear to attenuate with higher channel capacity.

In this section, we provide further perspective on the concerns about vertical integration in the television industries by explicitly considering how technological advance in television distribution and exhibition systems have affected the supply of programming content.

The Economic Development of Television[5]

Since the 1970s, there has been remarkable growth in the variety of television programming available to most US TV households. Between 1970 and 2010, the percentage of households served by multi-channel delivery systems – first cable, then DBS from 1994 and telephone company IPTV from the mid-2000s – rose from 12 percent to 86 percent. As mentioned above, channel capacities of these MVPD systems also jumped dramatically as consumers converted, partly due to fiber optic cable and related hardware technologies, but especially due to a conversion from analog to digital transmission beginning in the mid-1990s. Digital programming tiers magnified cable system capacity as well as permitting HD transmission; DBS and IPTV were all digital from their launch. A wave of new network entry responded to digitization. In 2006, the FCC reported that there were 565 satellite-delivered national programming networks, although typically only a fraction of these have been available to a given household. According to one source, the average number of channels available to US TV households grew from 7 in 1970 to 72 in 2000 and 137 by 2011 (Papazian, 2009, 2012).

The overall economic effects of this technological transition on revenues of the US television industries are illustrated in Figure 2.1. Income from all sources (both advertising and direct consumer payment) for the entire television industry, including online TV, are shown.[6]

Over the four decade period, industry revenues grew steadily, nearly tripling in size as a proportion of total economic activity, continuing even as Internet broadband adoption grew from 3 percent in 2000 to 66 percent in 2010 (Pew Research Center, 2011). At the core of the revenue growth was the conversion from free ad-supported broadcasting to pay television. The growing consumer value of television services is further suggested by a one-third increase in TV viewing from about 43 hours per week per household in the "early 1970s," to nearly 58 hours in the "early 2010s" (Papazian, 2012). Meanwhile, digital technology also permitted more efficient price discrimination as multi-channel operators created more complex arrays of optional tiers, along with video-on-demand (VOD) programming options. Revenue from TV services offered by cable and DBS and then IPTV systems sharply increased after the mid-1990s. The average cable subscriber paid $52.37 for cable TV service in 2009, and higher value consumers were encouraged to pay far more (FCC, 2011a).

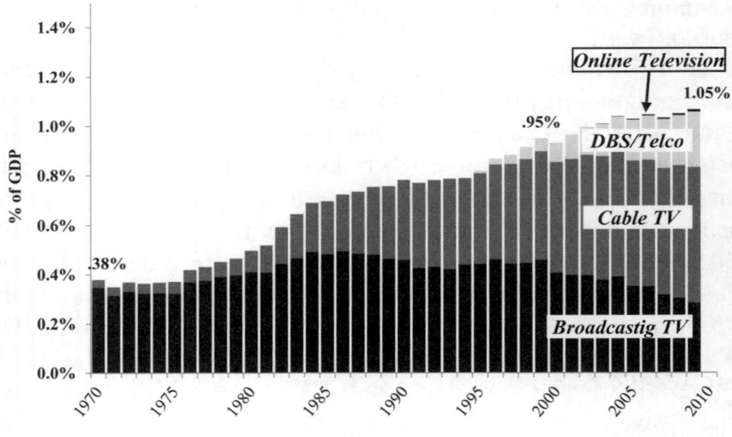

Source: Waterman and Ji (2012).

Figure 2.1 Television industry revenue as a percentage of GDP, 1970–2009

Programming Investments and Original vs. Acquired Programming

To be expected, a comparable increase in programming investments made by television networks accompanied this growth. Figure 2.2 shows available production investment data for the year 2009, broken down for national broadcast, basic cable and premium (monthly subscription) networks. Earlier investment data are fragmentary, but a reasonable estimate indicates a rise in total national television network spending on programming from 0.10 percent to 0.24 percent of GDP over the 1970–2009 period.[7]

As Figure 2.2 suggests, there has been extensive fragmentation of programming investments over this period, especially among basic cable networks. The $18.7 billion in total 2009 basic cable network revenues was shared among about 221 networks tracked by SNL Kagan Research (2010). By any reasonable measure, the overall quality and variety of television programming options has dramatically risen over time.

Figure 2.2 also indicates that a majority of basic cable network investments have been for "acquired" programs. SNL Kagan's definition of acquired includes sports events, which attract relatively large audiences on networks such as ESPN and Fox Sports Networks. It is

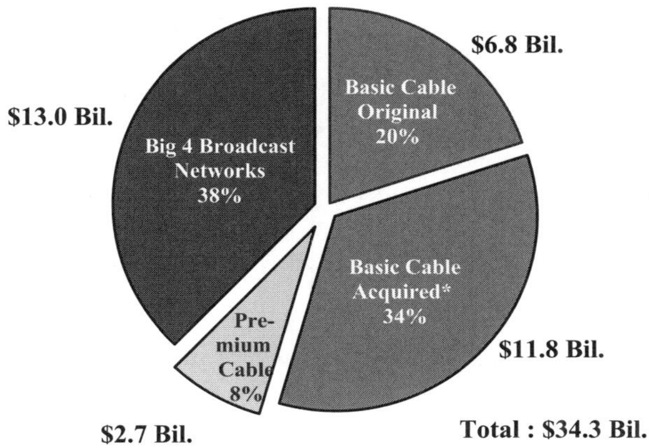

Note: *Definition of "Acquired" includes sports events, which attract relatively large audiences on networks such as ESPN and Fox Sports Networks.

Sources: Authors' estimates from SNL Kagan Research (2010), *Cable Program Investor*, October; SNL Kagan Research (2008); *Media Trends*, 8th edition; Miller and Washington (2011); TVB (n.d.).

Figure 2.2 Program spending by national television networks in 2009

evident, however, that basic cable networks rely substantially on expensively produced "aftermarket" programs, namely theatrical movies and off-broadcast network series programs. A 2011 Screen Digest survey of 79 basic networks indicated that 13.5 percent of basic cable network program hours were theatrical feature films, and that these are generally clustered among the most viewed basic networks, including TBS, AMC, FX and USA (Screen Digest, 2012). Several of the more highly rated basic networks, including USA and TBS, for example, also relied heavily on off-broadcast network programs. By implication, original programming on basic cable networks tends to be inexpensively produced, and in many cases relies upon informational content.

Recent statistical breakdowns of original vs. acquired programs were not available for premium cable or broadcast networks. In the 1970s, broadcast networks were a major outlet for the exhibition of theatrical features, but it is interesting that they have almost entirely abandoned that role to premium and basic cable networks (Screen Digest, 2010). National premium cable networks produce some original series programs and movies, but they rely heavily on theatrical feature films to attract monthly subscribers.

In sum, it is evident that the economic growth and development of multi-channel television in the US has been substantially driven by relatively expensively produced, and thus higher quality "aftermarket" programming appearing on premium and basic cable television networks, especially theatrical movies. To illustrate these economic forces, we now turn to an investigation of movie programming.

The Supply of Aftermarket Theatrical Movies in Historical Perspective

The major role that cable television networks play as an aftermarket for broadcast network programs and especially for theatrical feature films has been modeled by Owen and Wildman (1992) and Wildman (2008). It is reasonable to assume that audience demand for a given program increases, though at a decreasing rate, as investment in that program rises (Crandall, 1974; Park, 1975; Doyle, 2002; Hoskins et al., 2004). Conceptually, the larger is the total market for a given media product, the greater the incentive of the content provider to invest in that program. In effect, addition of the potential revenues from the "original" market (e.g., a prime-time national broadcast network exhibition) and from the aftermarket (e.g., a later exhibition on basic cable) makes the marginal value of a dollar of production investment higher, leading to a more expensively produced, and thus more attractive program.

By far the most complex system of original and aftermarket exhibition is theatrical feature films, which are released to a number of different media over time, typically beginning with theaters, then DVD and VOD (MVPD and online) within the next four months, followed by monthly premium networks after about eight months, then later on basic cable networks. This has been widely recognized as an intertemporal price discrimination system in which high and low value audiences are segmented primarily by waiting time and quality of the medium.

Figure 2.3 displays both the impressive success of the US movie industry in accomplishing this market segmentation, and the role of technology in that success, since the 1970s. The graph shows total payments to movie studios from all US media over time, again as a percent of GDP, from 1970 to 2010. As new media technologies have emerged, there has been an increasingly evident "stacking" phenomenon. Even after a substantial decline since 2005 due to a sharp falloff of DVD/Blu-ray sales and rentals, revenues nearly tripled as a percent of GDP from 1970 to 2010. Of course, Hollywood movies also have a large international market, and in recent years, a similar multi-media release strategy has accounted for more than half of US studio revenues.

The growing role of all television as an aftermarket is also on display in Figure 2.3. In 2002, television contributed 16.2 percent of domestic studio revenues, but that had risen to 27.4 percent by 2010. Reasons for the declining role of broadcast television in movie exhibition are unclear, but both premium networks and the larger basic cable networks (which have relatively lucrative dual income streams of subscriber fees and advertising) are higher value markets for the movie studios and have more than compensated for the broadcasting decline.

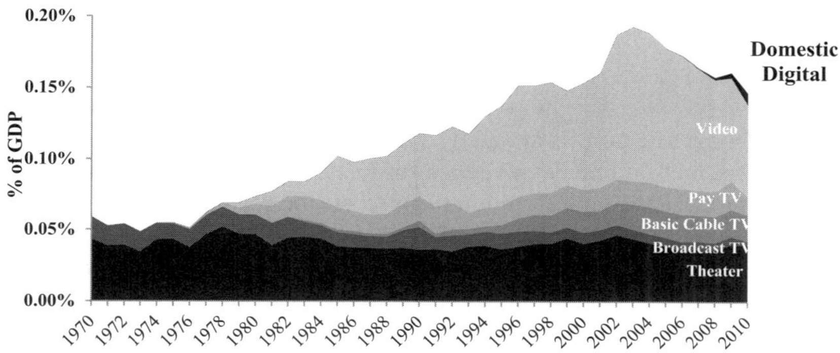

Sources: SNL Kagan Research, *Motion Picture Investor*; *Cable Program Investor*.

Figure 2.3 Movie distributors' domestic revenue as a percentage of GDP, 1970–2010

It is evident as well that production spending on movies, particularly on more expensive movies, has greatly increased over time. Systematic data on total movie production investments over time are not available, but in 1975, MPAA member companies released 138 films at an average cost of $3.1 million, and 179 films in 2007 at an average cost of $74.8 million (Vogel, 1990, p. 86; MPAA, 2008). Television's role as an aftermarket extends far beyond major studio releases. The above referenced Screen Digest survey identified nearly 10,000 different movies that were released in 2011 on the 79 cable channels it surveyed (Screen Digest, 2012).

Thus, the effects of technology on expanding production of one of the main ingredients of multi-channel television programming, theatrical feature films, have been comparable to economic growth of the television industry itself. Similarly, technology has expanded the aftermarket potential of other types of programming.

3. PROSPECTIVE IMPACTS OF THE INTERNET ON PROGRAMMING CONTENT

At this writing, the Internet has yet to develop into a very significant source of revenues for US television, nor has it yet had a very substantial negative effect on "offline" television revenues. Major distributors of television programming online, including Netflix, Hulu, and iTunes are, however, fast growing.

From our perspective, several questions are relevant. First, how will online video affect overall revenues and thus production investments in television and video media entertainment? In effect, we ask, will online video be a positive or a negative sum game for the television industry? Over the longer term, it is apparent that online video offers another stage in the intertemporal release sequence for television programs and movies, and thus potentially, a new complement to offline revenues. As suggested by the decline beginning in the mid-2000s, however, online video also offers a potential substitute for the offline media that exhibit the same or similar programs. On the positive side for television, direct sale of programs via iTunes and other services opens a dual income stream for established networks. The in-program advertising model also translates directly to online video, although it remains unclear if online ad revenues per viewer can match those of standard TV. Finally, there remains the uncertainty of piracy. Copyright control appears to be relatively effective in television, but peer to peer file sharing has likely contributed to the decline in movie studio revenues in the past several years.

A second, related question is how the balance of original vs. aftermarket programs will evolve on the Internet. No systematic research has been conducted on Internet video media content, but it appears to be a dichotomous mix of relatively high quality theatrical movies, broadcast and cable network programs, combined with a few expensively produced, but mostly relatively cheap, original programs. Release windows for aftermarket programs are becoming established: a VOD window at the same time as that of MVPDs, an emerging window for subscription services such as Netflix that compete with the monthly premium network window, and nearly simultaneous, but still short delays of one day or more, for major broadcasting and cable network series programming. In economic terms, it is evident that online video is overwhelmingly dependent on aftermarket programs. In the future, as its user base increases and business models develop, online video seems likely to follow the pattern of cable television in developing an increasingly strong component of original programming.

Finally, we revisit vertical integration. Concerns about favoritism by Internet Service Providers (ISPs) of vertically affiliated content, matched with discrimination against unaffiliated content, have been largely coincident with the network neutrality debate. To date, these concerns have been relatively minor, but they may depend importantly on how the FCC's rules develop.

Probably most of the more recent policy concerns involving vertical integration and online television have involved the potential use by large MVPDs or ISPs of their vertical ties to either inhibit or to dominate the nascent online video industry. As distribution of online video content has become widespread, and various types of online TV aggregators (in the sense of suppliers of large amounts of content through the Internet) such as YouTube and Hulu.com have entered the market, MVPDs such as Comcast, Direct TV and Verizon, have been distributing their licensed TV content to online viewers as offline + online bundles, widely labeled as "TV Everywhere". Since those MVPDs are also broadband ISPs, offline/online service is a form of vertical integration between an online aggregator and an ISP. A concern is that this online/offline bundling strategy could be used by an MVPD to leverage its offline market power into the online TV market.

In some cases, notably Comcast-NBCU, a large ISP and an MVPD owns substantial interests in program supply. The approval of that merger in 2010 was accompanied by a variety of conditions attempting to limit Comcast-NBCU's ability to leverage that content in order to slow the decline of its existing offline market or to advantage its entry into the online market (FCC, 2011b). While it is hard to judge the effectiveness of these constraints, it is evident that established MVPDs have an interest in preserving their offline market position. These constraints on potential leveraging of vertical ownership to protect market positions may affect the progress of new technology diffusion and competition. There seems little doubt that vertically integrated MVPDs or ISPs will also continue to favor their vertically affiliated content, and perhaps disadvantage unaffiliated in cases where they are able to do so.

In evaluating all of these policy concerns with vertical integration, however, we should not lose sight of the dramatic effect that the forward march of technology over the last few decades has had on the quality and variety of television programming available to subscribers. The threats that vertically integrated MVPDs or ISPs will discriminate against unaffiliated programming are important, but are wisely considered within that historical context.

NOTES

1. The Financial Interest and Syndication Rules, known as the fin-syn rules, were a set of regulations promulgated by the Federal Communications Commission (FCC) in 1970, in order to increase programming diversity and limit market power of the three major broadcast TV networks (ABC, NBC and CBS). The FCC tried to prevent those networks from monopolizing the broadcast television industry by forbidding network purchase of a financial interest in any program not produced by them and by restricting ownership of distribution rights in the syndication market. Several authors, however, found that the rules did not achieve the FCC's objectives (Besen et al., 1984; Owen and Wildman, 1992). The rules were partially repealed in 1993, and they completely lapsed in 1995. The Fox network, which was launched in 1987, did not reach full-time network status according to the FCC before 1995, and, therefore, was never subject to the fin-syn rules.
2. This paper was unavailable, but is described in Caves (2005, pp. 201–203).
3. Goolsbee (2007) did find that shows supplied by the production arms of other broadcast networks performed significantly better than either integrated or independent shows, but he did not offer an explanation for this result.
4. The Comcast-NBCU merger in 2011 led to at least a modest reversal of this trend.
5. For further details of this transition and its causes, see Waterman and Han (2010) and Waterman et al. (2013).
6. Online television here includes national TV distribution, such as via hulu.com and CBS Interactive, and local TV station websites. See Waterman and Ji (2012) for further detail.
7. Although we have broadcast network production investment estimates only for sporadic years, that spending has consistently been about two-thirds of their total revenues. Applying that ratio to reported revenues of the (then three) major broadcast networks in 1970 (when cable networks did not exist) indicates total network spending of $1.1 Bil. in 1970, leading to the estimated rise as a percent of GDP.

REFERENCES

Barth, D.K. (2003) 'Essays on the economics of television program supply', Doctoral Dissertation, Northwestern University.

Besen, S.M., Krattenmaker, T.G., Metzger Jr, A.R., and Woodbury, J.R. (1984) *Misregulating Television: Network Dominance and the FCC*, University of Chicago Press.

Bielby, W.T., and Bielby, D.D. (2003) 'Controlling prime-time: Organizational concentration and network television programming strategies', *Journal of Broadcasting & Electronic Media*, 47(4), 573–596.

Caves, R.E. (2005) *Switching Channels: Organization and Change in TV Broadcasting*, Harvard University Press.

Chen, D., and Waterman, D. (2007) 'Vertical ownership, program network carriage, and tier positioning in cable television: An empirical study', *Review of Industrial Organization*, 30(3), 227–251.

Chipty, T. (2001) 'Vertical integration, market foreclosure, and consumer welfare in the cable television industry', *American Economic Review*, 91(3), 428–453.

Crandall, R.W. (1974) 'The economic case for a fourth commercial television network', *Public Policy*, 22(4), 513–536.

Doyle, G. (2002) *Understanding Media Economics*, Sage.

Einstein, M. (2002) 'Program diversity and the program selection process on broadcast network television', *Study# 5: FCC Media Ownership Working Group Paper*.
Einstein, M. (2004) 'The financial interest and syndication rules and changes in program diversity', *Journal of Media Economics*, 17(1), 1–18.
FCC (1993) 'Second report and order' (MM Docket No. 92-264, FCC 93-456), Federal Communications Commission.
FCC (1995) 'In the matter of annual assessment of the status of competition in the market for the delivery of video programming' (Report, CS Dkt. No. 95-61, FCC 95-491), Federal Communications Commission.
FCC (1999) 'In the matter of: Implementation of the Satellite Home Viewer Improvement Act of 1999, Notice of Proposed Rulemaking' (FCC 99-406), Federal Communications Commission.
FCC (2009) 'In the matter of annual assessment of the status of competition in the market for the delivery of video programming' (Report, MB Docket No. 06-189, FCC 07-206) Federal Communications Commission.
FCC (2011a) 'Report on cable industry prices' (MM Docket No. 92-266), Federal Communications Commission.
FCC (2011b) 'In the matter of applications of Comcast Corporation, General Electric Company and NBC Universal, Inc. for consent to assign licenses and transfer control of licensees' (Memorandum Opinion and Order, FCC11-4), Federal Communications Commission.
FCC (2012) 'Fourteenth competition report' (MB Docket No. 07-269), Federal Communications Commission.
Ford, G.S., and Jackson, J.D. (1997) 'Horizontal concentration and vertical integration in the cable television industry', *Review of Industrial Organization*, 12(4), 501–518.
GAO (General Accountability Office) (2004) 'Subscriber rates and competition in the cable television industry' (GAO-04-262T), General Accountability Office.
Goolsbee, A. (2007) 'Vertical integration and the market for broadcast and cable television programming', FCC's 10 Commissioned Economic Research Studies on Media Ownership: Policy Implications, available at https://apps.fcc.gov/edocs_public/attachmatch/DA-07-3470A10.pdf.
Guo, K., and Caves, R. (2001) 'The end of fin-syn and the reorganization of the television broadcast programming market', Working paper, Harvard University.
Hoskins, C., McFadyen, S., and Finn, A. (2004) *Media Economics: Applying Economics To New and Traditional Media*, Sage.
Ji, S.W. (2012) 'Geographical diffusion of video delivery technologies and its policy implications', Doctoral dissertation, Indiana University, Bloomington.
Joskow, P.L. (2005) 'Vertical integration', in C. Menard and M. Shirley (eds), *Handbook of New Institutional Economics*, Springer.
SNL Kagan Research (2008) *Media Trends*, 8th edition.
SNL Kagan Research (2010) *Cable Program Investor*, October 29.
SNL Kagan Research (2013) *Cable Program Investor*, October 25.
SNL Kagan Research *Motion Picture Investor*, various issues.
Kang, J. (2009) 'Entry and growth of basic cable programming networks: an industry and policy analysis', Doctoral dissertation, Indiana University, Bloomington.
Miller, R.K., and Washington, K.D. (2011) *The 2012 Entertainment, Media & Advertising Market Research Handbook*, Richard K. Miller & Associates.
MPAA (2008) 'Theatrical market statistics 2007', Motion Picture Association of America, available at http://brianpuccio.net/files/2007-US-Theatrical-Market-Statistics-Report.pdf.
MPAA (2012) 'Theatrical market statistics', Motion Picture Association of America, available at http://www.mpaa.org/policy/industry.
Owen, B.M., Beebe, J., and Manning, W. (1975) *TV Economics*, London: DC Heath.

Owen, B.M., and Wildman, S.S. (1992) *Video Economics*, Cambridge, Mass.: Harvard University Press.
Papazian, E. (2009) *TV Dimension*, New York, NY: Media Dynamics, Inc.
Papazian, E. (2012) *TV Dimension*, New York, NY: Media Dynamics, Inc.
Park, R.E. (1975) 'New television networks', *The Bell Journal of Economics*, 607–620.
Parsons, P. (2003) 'Horizontal integration in the cable television industry: History and context', *Journal of Media Economics*, 16(1), 23–40.
Parsons, P. and Frieden, R. (1998) *The Cable and Satellite Television Industries*, Boston: Allyn and Bacon.
Perry, M.K. (1989) 'Vertical integration: Determinants and effects', in R. Schmalensee and R.D. Willig (eds), *Handbook of Industrial Organizations*, New York: Elsevier-North Holland, 183–255.
Pew Research Center (2011) 'Internet gains on television as public's main news source', Pew Research Center, available at http://www.peoplepressorg/files/legacy-pdf/689.pdf.
Screen Digest (2010), *Screen Digest*, October, London.
Screen Digest (2012), *Screen Digest*, June, London.
Suzuki, A. (2009) 'Market foreclosure and vertical merger: A case study of the vertical merger between Turner Broadcasting and Time Warner', *International Journal of Industrial Organization*, 27(4).
TVB (n.d.) 'Quarterly and full year ad spending archive', TV Bureau of Advertising, available at http://www.tvb.org/planning_buying/4705/4720.
Vogel, H. (1990) *Entertainment Industry Economics: A Guide for Financial Analysis* (2nd ed.), Cambridge and New York: Cambridge University Press.
Waterman, D. (1985) 'Prerecorded home video and the distribution of theatrical feature films', in E. Noam (eds), *Video Media Competition: Regulation, Economics and Technology*, New York: Columbia University Press, pp. 222–243.
Waterman, D., and Han, S. (2010) 'Broadcasters vs MVPDs: economic effects of digital transition on television program supply', *info*, 12(4), 15–24.
Waterman, D., and Ji, S.W. (2012) 'Online versus offline in the United States: Are the media shrinking?' *The Information Society*, 28(5), 285–303.
Waterman, D., and Weiss, A.A. (1996) 'The effects of vertical integration between cable television systems and pay cable networks', *Journal of Econometrics*, 72(1–2), 357–395.
Waterman, D., and Weiss, A.A. (1997) *Vertical Integration in Cable Television*, Cambridge, MA/Washington, DC: MIT Press/AEI Press.
Waterman, D., Sherman, R., and Ji, S.W. (2013) 'The economics of online television: Industry development, aggregation, and "TV Everywhere"', *Telecommunications Policy*, 37(9), 725–736.
Wildman, S.S. (2008) 'Interactive channels and the challenge of content budgeting', *The International Journal on Media Management*, 10(3), 91–101.

3. Economics of trade in media products

Steven S. Wildman and Sang Yup Lee

Why include a chapter on trade in a book on media economics? The simplest answer is there is a literature to review. While it is not large, economists have been writing about trade in media products for over 25 years. But this begs the question of what makes it a subject worthy of serious investigation. Many thousands of goods and services are traded internationally, but relatively few have generated identifiable bodies of research.

We argue below that our understanding of the economic forces that drive trade in various media products is far from complete and the challenges, both theoretical and empirical, that must be overcome to improve this understanding are of a type that is particularly interesting to economists. There is also the possibility that the conceptual advances required to improve our understanding of trade in media will have broader applications. For example, Rosse's (1970) work on newspapers anticipated by over two decades key insights on pricing with interdependent demands now identified with the still relatively new literature on two-sided markets (or platforms). In their book on trade in computer software, Siwek and Furchtgott-Roth (1993) argue that domestic market size and scale advantages identified in early contributions by economists to the media trade literature (Waterman, 1988; Hoskins and Mirus, 1988; Wildman and Siwek, 1987, 1988) as critical to US producers' success in the motion picture and television programme trades also help explain US firms' success in the global software market. Wildman (1995) suggests that similarities between flows of certain media products among localities within nations and international patterns of trade in media products may reflect the operation of economic forces that are fundamentally the same.

Policy concerns are an additional reason to study trade in media products. Because media play central and often politically sensitive roles in national politics and contribute to the creation and dissemination of national cultures, media firms and industries have long received attention from policy makers that is outsized relative to their shares of national economies. Imported media compete with and reduce the revenues of domestic cultural industries and are sometimes viewed as purveyors of cultural values and political ideas viewed unfavorably by importing countries' political elites. For many decades the United States has dominated trade in TV programmes and in films, and imports from the US have featured prominently in other countries' arguments for cultural exceptions that permit restrictions on imported media in trade agreements that are otherwise intended to liberalize trade.

Table 3.1, which draws on 2007 data collected for studies by Lee and Wildman (2012) and Choi et al. (2013), illustrates the extent of American dominance in films for 30 countries, including the US. Only for Japan and Korea does the US share of the domestic box office dip below 50 percent and only in Korea do domestic films capture more of the home market than American films. For every country in Table 3.1, US films' share of the domestic box office is a sizable multiple of the shares of all other foreign suppliers combined. While the extent of US dominance has varied over time and is greater for films than for television programmes, US domination of the trade in both of these video products has been an established fact for well over 50 years and is a phenomenon worthy of investigation by economists.

The chapter is organized as follows. The next section describes three home market models that have been offered as explanations for observed patterns of trade in films and television programmes and, possibly, for other media. We argue that the range of outcomes allowed by these models precludes their use as self-contained explanations for observed patterns of trade in media. In the end, a definitive assessment of their relevance must be based on an empirical assessment of evidence. The third section summarizes and reviews the empirical studies that constitute the bulk of the media trade literature and concludes that while this research tells us much about various features of the trades in different media products, with one recent exception, the empirical studies have not been designed to generate evidence useful for assessing the validity of the three home market models or making an informed choice among them. We then present for films new evidence and reinterpretation of the results of an earlier study that favors one of the models over the others. The following section proposes a criterion for determining when observed trade patterns are consistent with a large home market advantage and presents results for a preliminary application of that criterion that suggests large home market advantages help explain observed patterns of trade in films. The conclusion offers suggestions for further advancing research on this subject.

Table 3.1 *2007 Domestic box office shares for US, home country and other countries' films*

Country	Own films' share	US films' share	All other countries' share	Ratio of US to own	Ratio of US to other
United States	94.69	94.69	5.32	1.00	17.80
Korea	48.22	42.71	9.07	0.89	4.71
Japan	46.22	48.77	5.01	1.06	9.73
Thailand	43.57	46.76	9.67	1.07	4.84
Turkey	33.97	54.12	11.90	1.59	4.55
Czech Republic	33.36	53.44	13.21	1.60	4.05
France	30.63	57.82	11.55	1.89	5.01
Italy	29.58	58.79	11.63	1.99	5.06
Poland	26.68	60.73	12.59	2.28	4.82
Finland	25.94	57.84	16.22	2.23	3.57
Denmark	23.20	64.45	12.36	2.78	5.21
Germany	21.69	65.07	13.24	3.00	4.91
Hong Kong	21.54	61.24	17.22	2.84	3.56
Sweden	20.46	65.24	14.29	3.19	4.57
United Kingdom	16.83	78.19	4.98	4.65	15.70
Netherlands	15.33	69.91	14.76	4.56	4.74
Norway	14.43	69.77	15.80	4.84	4.42
Greece	12.17	72.09	15.73	5.92	4.58
Spain	11.59	73.72	14.69	6.36	5.02
Chile	8.10	81.47	10.43	10.06	7.81
Mexico	7.60	81.50	10.90	10.72	7.48
Argentina	6.26	79.72	14.02	12.73	5.69
Portugal	3.78	83.45	12.77	22.08	6.53
Romania	3.49	82.81	13.70	23.73	6.04
New Zealand	2.02	76.51	21.46	37.88	3.57
Austria	1.97	73.16	24.87	37.14	2.94
Slovak Republic	1.66	74.82	23.52	45.07	3.18
Switzerland	1.65	75.25	23.10	45.61	3.26
Bulgaria	1.46	82.97	15.57	56.83	5.33
Australia	1.43	83.48	15.09	58.38	5.53

Source: Box Office Mojo (2010).

THEORETICAL PERSPECTIVES

The three trade models discussed below are all home market models: models that identify conditions under which patterns of trade in a particular product or service are shaped by advantages realized by producers located in larger markets by virtue of market size alone. Manifestations of such advantages are often referred to as home market effects. All three models have been offered as explanations for observed patterns of trade in media products. The first two models discussed are adaptions to trade of earlier models of monopolistic competition, with the second modified to include media-specific consumption externalities. The third was developed with media specifically in mind.

Monopolistic Competition Trade Models

Since introduced by Krugman (1979, 1980), monopolistic competition models of international trade have become a touchstone of the economics literature on trade. Krugman's innovation was to incorporate a version of the Dixit and Stiglitz (1977) model of a monopolistically competitive differentiated product industry in a two-country, two-industry model of trade for which the second industry is competitive and sells a homogenous good produced with a constant returns to scale technology. Under these conditions, the country with the larger domestic market for the differentiated good becomes a relative specialist and a net exporter of the differentiated good with shares of global production and number of producers exceeding its share of global consumption (Helpman and Krugman, 1985).

Hanson and Xiang (2004) extended the basic monopolistic competition trade model to allow for a continuum of differentiated product industries that vary in the degree to which consumers view the variants of their products as substitutes for each other. They show that if a sufficiently large fraction of international trade involves differentiated products, the smaller of the two countries in a two-country model must be a net exporter for some subset of the differentiated products drawn from the less differentiated end of the continuum.[1] That both countries can be net exporters of different differentiated products is obvious for the limiting case in which only differentiated goods are traded. Hanson and Xiang report empirical tests that support their differential specialization in differentiated products prediction.

An implication of the Hanson and Xiang (2004) model is that we cannot use monopolistic competition trade models by themselves to predict whether large countries will be net exporters of differentiated media products simply because we can't know a priori where media rank among differentiated product industries in the degree to which consumers view different firms' offerings as substitutes. Monopolistic competition trade models allow for the possibility that media products exhibit home market effects, but they provide insufficient grounds on their own for predicting that this will be the case.

Monopolistic Competition with Consumption Externalities

Pointing to figures illustrating US dominance similar to those in Table 3.1 and positing that, in addition to the direct consumption benefits of media use, consumers also enjoy discussing what they have watched, listened to, or read with other people who have consumed the same media products, Rauch and Trindade (2009) extend the basic two-country two-good monopolistic competition trade model by incorporating in the model's utility function a consumption externality such that the consumption value of any firm's version of the differentiated product increases as its customer base grows. Applying the model to media, they show that if media consumers communicate with their counterparts domestically and in other countries, global demand for the larger country's media products will increase relative to demand for the smaller country's media products if, say, due to differences in language and culture, the cross-country externality is smaller than the within country externality. This would increase the payoff to producers from locating in the larger country. Cross-country consumption externalities would thus increase the likelihood that the home market effects of the basic monopolistic competition trade model would be observed for media industries.

The Budget-based Advantage Model

To our knowledge, the first published research on trade in media products by economists appeared in the late 1980s, when Hoskins and Mirus (1988), Waterman (1988) and Wildman and Siwek (1987, 1988) independently introduced versions of what we will call the budget-based advantage model (BBAM). The BBAM was inspired by the observation that average production budgets for the US films and TV programmes varied from a few times to many multiples of corresponding average budgets for other countries. Further investigation revealed that as a general matter, film and programming production budgets increased with the size of the countries in which their producers were based. This pattern is evident in the film data presented in Table 3.2.

Table 3.2 *2007 GDP and average production budget*

Country	GDP* ($B)	Average production budget** ($M)
United States	13 961.80	31.00
Japan	4 356.33	5.01
Germany	3 323.81	9.05
United Kingdom	2 825.53	12.78
France	2 582.39	7.22
Italy	2 127.18	3.54
Spain	1 441.43	3.46
Korea	1 049.24	4.17
Mexico	1 035.93	1.47
Australia	850.33	7.62
Netherlands	782.57	3.83
Turkey	647.16	1.98
Sweden	462.51	2.54
Poland	425.32	1.66
Norway	393.48	2.42
Austria	375.04	2.55
Denmark	311.42	3.00
Argentina	260.77	0.94
Thailand	246.98	1.01
Finland	246.13	1.50
Portugal	231.74	1.59
Hong Kong	211.60	10.33
Czech Republic	180.51	1.48
Chile	172.87	0.64
Romania	169.28	1.03
New Zealand	134.02	14.73
Bulgaria	42.11	0.95

Notes: * World Bank (2013); ** Screen Digest (2008).

While the three versions of the BBAM differ some in detail, common to all is a core argument with the following elements. First is the assumption that producers of films and programmes can increase their products' appeal and attract larger audiences by committing more resources to their production. Second, producers in financially large countries find it profitable to produce more expensive films and programmes than producers in small countries because the financial return on the extra audience appeal purchased through incremental increases in a production budget increases with the size (or wealth) of the potential audience to which a film or programme might be offered.[2] Third, other things equal, media audiences prefer films and programmes produced in their native languages by producers who understand the domestic culture, which is an advantage in their home markets for domestically produced films and programmes. Fourth, because they benefit from a domestic market advantage in a larger portion of the global market, producers in large markets create more expensive films and programmes than producers in small markets and the added appeal purchased with larger budgets is an advantage in securing distribution in other countries.

The only algebraic representations of the BBAM are Appendix B of Wildman and Siwek (1988) and Frank's (1992) elaboration on Wildman and Siwek's model. The BBAM is considerably simpler than the monopolistic competition models, which incorporate explicit representations of consumer utility functions. BBAM media firms compete for shares of markets with fixed aggregate sales and shares are determined by the relative sizes of production budgets with a cultural or linguistic discount reducing the contribution of budget to audience share for foreign films. While the formula employed to determine films' (or programmes') shares of audience precludes solving for a unique equilibrium as a general matter (Frank, 1992), Wildman and Siwek showed that, starting from an symmetric two-country equilibrium with numerical values assigned to critical parameters, increasing the size of the domestic market for one of the countries increased the equilibrium number of produced films in the country that grew, reduced the number produced in the other country and increased production budgets in both countries, but by more in the country that grew.

The BBAM does not include a second industry, so it does not include the constraint that the aggregate of trade in all commodities must balance. We doubt this is a serious limitation for two reasons. First, for real world countries that trade in thousands of products, many industries record surpluses at the same time many others record deficits. To expect a two-industry, two-country model to predict which countries will realize surpluses (or deficits) in any specific industry when trade across all industries must balance is unreasonable. Second, we see no reason in principle why comparison of a media exporter's shares of audience in different countries should be closely linked to the relative amounts earned from sales to each of them. Hoskins et al. (1989) showed that prices paid for US television programmes by European networks could vary dramatically from country to country, and we should expect per capita prices paid for imported media to vary considerably in a world where a cinema ticket in India may cost less than one thirtieth its price in the US (ZDNet, 2005).

Testable Predictions for the Monopolistic Competition Models and the BBAM

Both monopolistic competition models predict that when there is a home market advantage, the ratio of the number of firms in a large country to the number of firms in a smaller country will be larger than the ratio of their respective market sizes and that the ratio of the amounts of global industry output produced in the two countries will equal the ratio of the numbers of their firms. The BBAM predicts that for the same two countries and a third country that imports media products from both of them, the ratio of the large country's firms' share to the small country's firms' share of the third country's market will be larger than the ratio of the number of large country firms to the number of small country firms. We present preliminary tests of these predictions with data on trade in films at the end of the next section.

THE EMPIRICAL LITERATURE

We start with the studies of trade in films that constitute the bulk of the empirical literature.

Films

Empirical research on trade in films can be separated into a flows branch focused on factors that influence the magnitudes and net directions of flows of films among countries and a much smaller mix branch concerned primarily with the influence of culture on the types of films countries import.

The flows literature

This literature starts with Marvasti (1994), whose regression using United Nations Comtrade data on countries' net exports of films in 1985 generated coefficients for country population, GNP and a dummy variable for English speaking countries that were positive and statistically significant. Marvasti (2000) also used Comtrade data to study US net exports of films from 1961 through 1988, finding that US net exports were positively correlated with the difference between the aggregate population for all OECD countries and that of the US.

While Marvasti was concerned with countries' aggregate film exports, the rest of the literature has focused largely on bilateral trading relationships between individual countries. Accordingly, researchers have looked for ways that trading partners differed to help explain country-pair variation in bilateral trade patterns. With a few exceptions (Fu and Sim, 2010; Marvasti and Canterbery, 2005; Disdier et al., 2010), these studies have used countries' shares of their own and other countries' box office revenues or attendance to assess their relative strengths as suppliers of films for international and domestic consumption. Two findings have held consistently across the highly varied collection of studies that included measures of the size of trading partners' domestic markets as control variables: (1) countries' films capture larger shares of their domestic film markets the larger are those markets, and (2) film exporting countries' shares of other countries' film markets are larger the larger is the exporter's film market. While reporting these studies' contributions to the two consensus findings as we review them, comments on statistical reliability will be reserved for study findings regarding other factors for which study findings conflict or for which the evidence isn't strong enough to support generalized claims.

Waterman and Jayakar (2000), Lee (2002) and Lee and Waterman (2007) all use data sets that span a multi-decade period during which the United States transitioned from being merely the dominant international supplier of films to dominating other countries' box offices as well. Lee and Waterman examine trade among the US, the UK, Japan, Germany, France and Italy, Jayakar and Waterman (2000) study trade between the US and Italy, and Lee (2002) focuses on the US and Japan. All tell the same story. US films' shares of box office in other countries rise and fall as the US film market grows or declines relative to those of its trading partners. Domestically produced films' share of the home box office in these countries moves in the opposite direction.

Jayakar and Waterman (2000) examined the relationship between differences in home market size and shares of box office captured by US films and domestically produced films in 22 other countries in 1994 and found US films' share of other sample countries' film markets varied inversely with the size of the importing country's market, while larger importing countries' films had larger shares of their domestic markets. Coefficients for percent of population fluent in English and, alternatively, a dummy variable for English language countries, were negative for all but one of the domestic films' share regressions and positive for all US share regressions, but the statistical precision of the estimates was generally low.

Oh (2001) focused on importing countries' shares of their domestic markets and reported importer market size results for separate regressions for each year during 1988–94 that agreed with those of Jayakar and Waterman (2000). The coefficient for a dummy for English speaking countries (which did not include the US) varied in sign across regressions. Kogut and Singh (1988) measures of distance from the US along each of Hofstede's (1980) four dimensions of cultural difference were included as controls for cultural distance from the US, with only the power dimension coefficients consistently significant (and positive).

Lee and Bae (2004) used 1997 data for 20 countries and elaborated on Oh's (2001) regression model by adding a screen quota dummy and substituting Kogut and Singh's (1988) four-dimensional measure of cultural distance for Oh's measures along each dimension. Only coefficients for market size measures were statistically significant. They also report that substituting domestic investment in film production for a measure of home market size increased the adjusted R-square to 0.73 from approximately 0.5, which supports the argument that domestic market size affects the success a country's films have in competition with films from other countries through its effect on domestic film investments.

Marvasti and Canterbery (2005) were the first to use a gravity model to study media trade flows. The basic gravity model takes the form of equation (3.1), where λ is a positive constant, $X_{i,j}$ is the flow of good x from country i to country j, M_i and M_j are the sizes of the domestic markets for x in i and j, and a trade barrier reduces the value in j of a unit of x imported from i to $0 \leq \beta_{i,j} < 1$ of its value absent the barrier.

$$X_{i,j} = \lambda M_i M_j \beta_{i,j} \tag{3.1}$$

Gravity models are estimated by taking the natural logs of both sides of an equation like (3.1) and substituting measures of barriers for $\beta_{i,j}$. Using US Commerce Department data for US film exports to 33 countries during 1991–95 and country GDPs for M_i and M_j, Marvasti and Canterbery (2005) estimated equation (3.2), where $\boldsymbol{B}_{i,j}$ is a vector of measures of trade barriers.

$$\ln X_{i,j} = \phi_0 + \phi_1 \ln M_i M_j + \phi_2 \boldsymbol{B}_{i,j}. \tag{3.2}$$

They found that US film exports to another country increased with the product of their GDPs, were reduced by formal trade barriers, and increased with the size of the importing country's English speaking population and with its similarity to the US in general level of education and mix of religious affiliations. Cross-sectional variation in the importing countries' GDPs should account for most of the variation in $M_i M_j$. Therefore, given the consistent finding that US films' shares of other countries' box offices vary inversely with the size of the importing country's domestic market, the positive coefficient for $\ln M_i M_j$ suggests that US films earn more in larger markets, even though their market shares are smaller, a relationship that could have been estimated directly had the authors used the sum of the logs of country sizes rather than the log of their product in equation (3.2).

Building on their two-country trade model (Hanson and Xiang, 2004), Hanson and Xiang (2009) show that for A and B the countries and any good with differentiated variants, the equilibrium ratio of A's share to B's share of B's home market equals the ratio of the number of the industry's firms in A to the number in B multiplied by several terms that capture the effects of trade barriers and differences in production costs. For their empirical model, they substituted the corresponding ratio of GDP sizes for the ratio of numbers of exporting and importing country firms to create equation (3.3), where $S_{a,b}$ and $S_{b,b}$ are A's and B's shares of B's market and Z is a vector with relative production costs and measures for trade barriers. (3.3) was estimated with 1992–2002 panel data for 19 European countries and the US as country A.

$$\ln \frac{S_{a,b}}{S_{b,b}} = \omega_0 + \omega_1 \ln \frac{GDP_a}{GDP_b} + \boldsymbol{\omega}_2 \boldsymbol{Z}. \qquad (3.3)$$

Estimates of ω_1 were positive and statistically significant across model specifications, while coefficients for two alternative measures of the linguistic distance between an importing country's native language and English were negative and significant. The coefficient for an English language dummy in two models was negative, but not consistently significant. The sign of the coefficient for an index of government-created trade barriers borrowed from Marvasti and Canterbery (2005) was not stable across regressions.

The next three studies provide evidence that the earlier findings regarding the effects of relative home market size on US film exports apply to other film exporting countries.

Fu and Sim (2010) used UNESCO data on numbers of films imported by member countries between 1970 and 1999 to estimate an equation with the log of the number of an exporting country's films placed with an importing country in a given year as the dependent variable. Their estimating equation differs from a gravity model by including the logs of two measures of market scale, GDP and domestic cinema attendance. Coefficients for both market scale measures were positive and statistically significant. Estimated importer market scale effects were much smaller than exporter scale effects, which is consistent with Hanson and Xiang's (2008) finding that imports of US films increase with importer

GDP, but very slowly. The number of films imported from an exporting country declined with Kogut and Singh's (1988) four-dimensional measure of cultural distance, but was larger when importer and exporter shared a widely spoken language.

Fu and Lee (2008) used weekly newspaper listings to identify films that played in Singapore's theaters during 2002–04. Lacking attendance data, they used the dominant newspaper's weekly listing of the top 10 films by attendance to assign rank points (descending from 10 to 1) as a proxy for attendance and calculated individual films' shares of total rank points for the sample period. Their regression analysis showed that in general a country's films' combined share of aggregate rank points increased with the average ticket price and total cinema attendance in its domestic market and with its GDP, but fell with Kogut and Singh's (1988) four-dimensional measure of cultural distance from Singapore. For films from major film exporting countries, home market cinema earnings were a good predictor of success in Singapore, which is similar to findings by Elberse and Eliashberg's (2003) for US films in Europe and Lee (2006) for US films in Hong Kong and in seven East Asian countries (Lee, 2008).

Choi et al. (2013) used the data set underlying Tables 3.1 and 3.2 to estimate a three-equation model with separate regressions for number of films produced and for average production budgets by country and an equation for a country's film export's share (penetration) of an importing country's domestic box office, to test the BBAM's assumption that domestic market size affects a country's export success through its effects on production budgets and by affecting the number of films produced domestically. The number of films produced in a country was found to increase with its relative GDP (its GDP divided by the sum of sample countries' GDPs), but statistical significance depended on keeping the US in the sample. Relative GDP explained a substantial portion of the considerable cross-country variation in average production budgets as did the strength of intellectual property rights protection in the home country. Average production budgets were also found to increase with the size of the sum of GDPs for all other countries with the same dominant language.

For the exporter penetration of an importer's market equation, coefficients for exporting country average budget and number of films were positive and highly significant, with exporter average budget explaining much more of the variation in penetration. Exporter penetration was not significantly related to the number of films produced in the importing country, to their average budget size, or to the Kogut and Singh measure of cultural distance between the countries. The coefficient for a common language variable was positive and statistically significant for all model specifications without the US in the sample, but only for a Tobit specification with the US in the sample. The level of intellectual property rights protection, whether in the importing country or the exporting country, did not affect exporters' penetration of importers' markets.

Average production budgets for several small English language countries are much larger than would be predicted by market size. Using the Choi et al. (2013) data, Lee and Wildman (2012) showed that their budget outlier status was largely explained by membership in the globally large English language market for films.

Disdier et al. (2010) used UN Comtrade data covering 1989–2005 to estimate gravity export equations for the Comtrade audio-visual category, which is dominated by films. Because their regression model has exporter-importer fixed effects, it can only be used to examine the effects of trade barriers. Disdier et al. find a country's imports of audio-visual products from a second country decline with the distance between them, are larger if they share a common border, are smaller if they shared a colonial past and are larger if they speak the same language.

The mix literature

Lee (2006) regressed Hong Kong box office revenue against US box office revenue for US films whose Hong Kong revenues ranked among annual top 100 films in Hong Kong during 1988–2004. He found that, relative to films of other genres, science fiction, action and family films did better in Hong Kong than they did in the US, while comedies performed relatively poorly, which he interpreted as evidence of genre preference differences between the US and Hong Kong. A second study (Lee, 2008) comparing genre preferences in the US and seven East Asian countries generated broadly similar results.

Using Box Office Mojo data on US films' box office revenues in the US and other countries during 2002–07, Fu and Govindaraju (2010) showed that the correlation coefficients for American films' 2008 US cinema revenues and their revenues in the other countries were positive and statistically significant but varied substantially in magnitude across countries. They regressed country correlation coefficients on Kogut and Singh's (1988) four-dimensional measure of cultural distance from the US, a year-cultural distance interaction term, and other control variables. Coefficients were negative for cultural distance and positive for the interaction term and both were statistically significant, which they interpreted as evidence that cross-country differences in tastes in films reflect cultural differences and that national tastes in movies are becoming more similar. The latter claim is consistent with Fu's (2006) observation that countries are becoming more similar in the mix of countries from which they import films. For samples of 18 countries in 2003 and 28 countries in 2006, Fu (2012) used a cluster analysis to show that countries with similar distributions of box office across imported US films had similar measures of cultural distance from the US.

Other Media

Television programmes

In a largely descriptive analysis, Waterman and Rogers (1994) examined broadcast schedules for 34 national broadcast networks serving nine East Asian countries with market economies in 1989 and found domestically produced programmes accounted for about 75 percent of total programme hours across the nine countries and more than half for all but the two with the smallest economies, with little difference between public and private networks. In general domestic productions occupied larger fractions of schedules for networks that were better financed and the US was the dominant supplier of imported programmes.

For the television networks serving 17 Western European countries in 1990, a time when the United States accounted for over half of the imported fiction hours for Western European networks as a whole, Dupagne and Waterman (1998) calculated US fiction programmes' shares of each nation's broadcast schedules. Their regression analysis showed that US fiction programmes' share of a country's total television programming hours increased with the fraction of networks that were private rather than public and fell with the importing country's GDP or, in a second regression, with its networks' combined revenues from public and commercial sources. The GDP coefficient was significant only at the 10 percent level, but statistical precision was higher for the total revenues measure. National programming quotas appeared not to influence US fiction programmes' shares of schedules. The coefficient for a measure of domestic populations' English fluency was negative and statistically significant for both regressions.

Recorded music

For a multi-country sample, Ferreira and Waldfogel (2010) use chart ranks for top singles to estimate a Pareto distribution that was used to convert ranks to sales for each country. Estimated sales were then used to calculate shares of sales for domestic and imported recordings. Using 2003–07 data for 22 countries, they show that domestic songs' shares of national sales substantially exceed their country's GDP's share of the 22 country GDP, while countries' shares of sales of all traded music were roughly proportional to their GDPs' shares of the 22 country GDP. This latter finding was interpreted as evidence that, a general preference for domestic recordings notwithstanding, a large domestic market is not an advantage in the international music trade. This contrasts with Schulze's (1999) report, based on a cross-sectional regression with IMF Direction of Trade Statistics data, that large countries tend to be net exporters of sound recordings. However, because trade as a fraction of GDP can be expected to decline with country size (Anderson, 2011), inclusion of a country's sum of exports and imports divided by its GDP as a measure of trade openness may have impacted his estimated GDP coefficient. Another implication of Anderson's observation is that as countries' shares of world GDP grow, their shares of world trade will increase at a slower rate, so large countries' shares of world trade will be smaller than their shares of world GDP. In this light, Ferreira and Waldfogel's finding that the two shares remain approximately equal as country size varies might be interpreted as evidence for a large home market advantage in recorded music.

Ferreira and Waldfogel's estimates for a gravity equation with exporter-importer fixed effects indicated that a shared dominant language increases trade in music between two countries, as does a common border, while increasing the geographic distance between them has the opposite effect. A radio airplay quota was found to increase domestic recordings' share of domestic music sales. Disdier et al. (2010) reported similar findings for distance, a common border and a shared language for recorded media based on a gravity model analysis of UN Comtrade data covering 1989–2005.

Print media

Disdier et al. (2010) also report gravity equation estimates based on Comtrade data for books and for the combination of newspapers and periodicals. For both media categories, coefficients for distance, a common border and a common language were statistically significant and had the same signs as for recorded media. For newspapers and periodicals, bilateral trade was larger if exporter and importer shared a colonial past. Schulze (1999) analyzed IMF Direction of Trade Statistics data for "books and related materials" and reported that larger countries tend to be net exporters, similar to his finding for sound recordings. Because the regression model and data source for this study are the same as for his recorded media study, the same concerns with model specification and data apply to this study as well.

What Have We Learned from the Empirical Literature?

Whatever the media product, it appears that exports to other countries increase with country size. Large countries also capture larger shares of their own and other countries' media markets than small countries. On these findings there is no disagreement.

What else can we say based on the empirical research? The studies that included multiple exporters and multiple importers in their sample all found that a shared language increased the volume of trade in the media product studies. On the other hand, for those studies that looked at US filmmakers' shares of other countries' film markets, there was no consistent evidence that the US films' shares of other English speaking countries' film markets were larger because of shared reliance on English. This may reflect the benefits to small English speaking countries' filmmakers of a low to nonexistent linguistic handicap in the rest of the large and wealthy English language market (Oh, 2001).

The small number of studies that examined the effects of a shared border all found it increased trade, which is consistent with the findings of the same studies that trade volume diminishes with geographic distance between trading partners (Ferreira and Waldfogel, 2010; Disdier et al., 2010). The number of studies that found trade between countries diminished with cultural distance was roughly balanced by those that found no effect. This is true for formal trade barriers as well. On the other hand, at least for films it appears that cultural differences do influence the mix of film genres countries import.

What's Missing?

Setting aside the facts that this is still a pretty thin literature and the preponderance of studies focus on films, we believe the literature has largely ignored two critical questions: (1) Do any of the three trade models typically offered as explanations for observed media trade patterns or support for the design of empirical models accurately describe the economic forces driving trade in media products? (2) How do we design and rigorously apply an empirical test for the existence of a large home market advantage? In the next section, we propose and present a preliminary application of such a test. The remainder of this subsection focuses on tests of certain of the trade models' assumptions and predictions.

The Choi et al. (2013) study of trade in films supports the BBAM argument that home market size affects the competitiveness of a country's media products through its effects on both the number of media products produced and their content production budgets, but we are aware of no other attempts to test assumptions core to the trade models. We observed earlier that both monopolistic competition trade models predict that if there is a large home market advantage and two countries differ in size, the ratio of the larger country's share of the global industry's products (or firms) to the smaller country's share will exceed the ratio of the larger country's GDP to the smaller country's GDP. We use the Choi et al. (2013) data set to directly test this prediction for films. We also offer a test of the BBAM prediction that for the same two countries and a third country that imports media products from both of them, the ratio of the large country's share to the small country's share of the importer's market will be larger than the ratios of their GDPs.

If the monopolistic competition models accurately describe film markets, and if, as seems reasonable, we can treat a film as the equivalent of a firm in these models, then if there is a large home market advantage the elasticity of domestically produced films with respect to market size must be greater than one. To test this proposition, we regressed the log of films produced in a country on the log of its GDP, the log of the summed GDPs for all other countries with the same official language, the number of TV sets per thousand people, the number of movie screens, and a measure of the strength of intellectual property rights protection. With the US included in the sample, the coefficient for the log of GDP, which is the elasticity estimate, is 0.716 and statistically significant at the 0.001 level. Without the US in the sample, the same coefficient is 0.423 and significant at the 0.01 level. Adjusted r-squares were 0.695 and 0.689. If the monopolistic competition models accurately describe the workings of the film trade, there must not be a large home market advantage.

Hanson and Xiang (2009) interpreted the positive estimated value for ω_1 in equation (3.3) as evidence that film producers are concentrating in larger markets as the monopolistic competition models predict when there is a large home market advantage. But this interpretation assumes that the ratio of large country (US) films to smaller (importing) country films is larger than the ratio of their GDPs. For our sample the opposite is true, in which case, consistent with the BBAM, a positive ω_1 means that US films attract larger audiences than Hanson and Xiang's importing countries' films.

To more directly test the BBAM prediction that films from larger countries attract larger audiences, we regressed for all unique country triples in our sample with two exporters and an importer: (1) the ratio of the exporting countries' films' shares of the importer's box office on the corresponding ratio of their GDPs, and (2) the ratio of the numbers of the exporting countries' films acquired by the importing country on the ratio of their GDPs. Figure 3.1 presents regression lines for both equations. The ratio of box office shares regression line is nearly 78 times steeper than the ratio of films imported line, a difference that increases slightly if the US is dropped from the sample. Larger countries' films draw larger audiences.

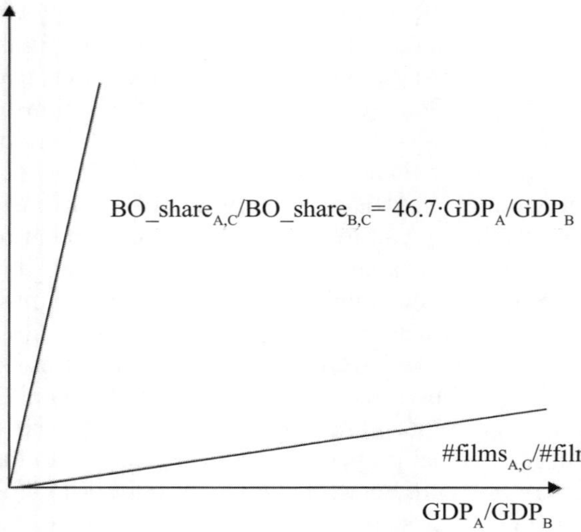

Note: A and B are film exporting countries and C is a film importing country. $BO\_share_{A,C}$ and $BO\_share_{B,C}$ are A's and B's films' shares of C's box office. $\#films_{A,C}$ and $\#films_{B,C}$ are the numbers of films imported by C from A and B. GDP_A and GDP_B are A's and B's GDPs.

Figure 3.1 Relations between box office share ratios, numbers of films ratios and GDP ratios

TESTING FOR LARGE HOME MARKET ADVANTAGE

Here we propose and illustrate the application of a test for a large home market advantage that can be employed with data commonly used for films and that in principle could be employed for other media (and other products).

A Test for Large Market Advantage

If we define a home market advantage to exist for a product when large countries' shares of other countries' markets for that product are larger than can be explained by economic forces other than ones related to market size, then it is possible to construct meaningful tests for home market advantage with data on multiple countries' shares of other countries' markets for the product. Such a test is implicit in the basic gravity model of trade, as we will show using a simple representation of trade with symmetric trade barriers.

To begin, assume a world with n local regions and no national boundaries. Each region produces goods and services with a value of x. For each region, fraction α of x is sold to other regions and $1-\alpha$ is consumed locally. The fraction sold to the other $n-1$ regions is distributed evenly among them, so trade between any two regions is balanced. Thus each region sells $\frac{\alpha x}{n-1}$ to each of the other $n-1$ regions and purchases the same amount from them. If there is no preference for home region goods, $\alpha = \frac{n-1}{n}$. Otherwise α takes some smaller nonnegative value.

Now divide this world into $m < n$ countries indexed by $i = 1, \ldots, m$. Let n_i be the number of local regions contained within country i, so $\sum_{i=1}^{m} n_i = n$. For convenience, we assume $n_j < n_k$ for all $k > j$ and that $n_1 = 1$. Further assume that nations create barriers to trade that reduce trade between regions that are not in the same country to some fraction $\beta < 1$ of what it would be in the absence of national boundaries. Each local region thus sells $\frac{\alpha\beta x}{n-1}$ to every region outside its home country and imports the same amount in return. Assuming goods that would have been sold to other countries in the absence of trade barriers are consumed domestically without loss in value, $GDP_i = n_i x$.[3] To see that the equation (3.1) gravity model is implicit in the relationships described to this point, observe that exports from country i to country j are $\frac{\alpha}{(n-1)x} \cdot \beta n_i x n_j x = \frac{\alpha}{(n-1)x} \beta \mathrm{GDP}_i \cdot \mathrm{GDP}_j$. $\frac{\alpha}{(n-1)x}$ is the positive constant in equation (3.1) and country GDPs are the measures of domestic market size.

We can also show that if country i is larger than country j, the ratio of i's share to j's share of global trade will be less than the ratio of their shares of global GDP. Country i's exports to the rest of the world are $\frac{\alpha\beta x(n-n_i)n_i}{n-1}$ and the expression for j's exports is similar. Because the ratio of i's and j's shares of world trade is the same as the ratio of their exports to the rest of the world, the ratio of their shares of trade is $\frac{(n-n_i)n_i}{(n-n_j)n_j}$ which is smaller than the ratio of their GDPs because $n_i > n_j$.

Define $S_{i,i}$ as country i's purchases of domestically produced products as a fraction of GDP_i and define $S_{i,j}$ as i's purchases of country j's products as a fraction of GDP_i.

$$S_{i,i} = \frac{n_i x - \frac{n_i(n-n_i)\alpha\beta x}{n-1}}{n_i x} = 1 - \frac{(n-n_i)\alpha\beta}{(n-1)}.$$

$$S_{i,j} = \frac{\frac{n_i n_j \alpha\beta x}{n-1}}{n_i x} = \frac{\alpha\beta n_j}{(n-1)}.$$

Now consider a third country, k. Dividing $S_{i,j}$ by $S_{i,k}$, we get

$$\frac{S_{i,j}}{S_{i,k}} = \frac{n_j}{n_k} = \frac{\text{GDP}_j}{\text{GDP}_k}. \tag{3.4}$$

Suppose $GDP_j > GDP_k$ and assume that countries j and k sell product a to country i. If there is a large home market advantage for producing a, then for $s^a_{i,j}$ and $s^a_{i,k}$ the shares of countries j and k in i's market for a, we should observe

$$\frac{s^a_{i,j}}{s^a_{i,k}} > \frac{GDP_j}{GDP_k}. \tag{3.5}$$

As a criterion for identifying home market advantage, (3.5) is simple and straightforward to apply. Other criteria for identifying home market advantage tend to have more complicated formulas than (3.5).

As an example, consider the ratio of country j's share of i's domestic market for a to i's share of its own market for a and call this ratio $R^a_{i,j}$. Absent a home market advantage in a, $R^a_{i,j}$ is determined by equation (3.6). Because the ratio of GDP_i to GDP_j can be substituted for the ratio of n_j *to* n_i, in (3.6), $R^a_{i,j}$ equals the ratio of GDP_j to GDP_i times a second ratio. Call this second ratio the domestic adjustment ratio for country i, or

DAR_i. To see that DAR_i must be positive but less than one, multiply its numerator and the denominator by x. The second two terms of the denominator then becomes $(1 - \alpha\beta)nx - x$, which is the value of global production that is not traded minus the GDP of the world's smallest country. Given the size differences of real world countries, this must be positive. Note that DAR_i would still be less than one if there were no trade barriers ($\beta = 1$) and that DAR_i is larger the larger is n_i (or GDP_i).

$$R^a_{i,j} = \frac{S_{i,j}}{S_{i,i}} = \frac{s^a_{i,j}}{s^a_{i,i}} = \frac{n_j}{n_i} \cdot \frac{\alpha\beta n_i}{\alpha\beta n_i + (1-\alpha\beta)n - 1}. \tag{3.6}$$

A Preliminary Test for a Large Home Market Advantage for Films

We were able to identify 26 countries for which we had shares of domestic box office revenue for at least two countries from which they imported films in the Choi et al. (2013) data set. Across the 26 film importing countries, we were able to calculate box office share ratios and GDP ratios for imported films from 39 countries. Pairs for which both import supplying countries had positive shares of the importer's domestic box office were used to calculate box office share ratios. This produced a sample of 4252 box office share ratios, which we used to estimate equation (3.7).

$$\ln(\mathit{BO\ share\ ratio}) = -\,0.369 + 1.383 \cdot \ln(\mathit{GDP\ ratio}) \tag{3.7}$$

The coefficient of 1.383 for ln(*GDP ratio*) is significant at well beyond the .001 level. While an elasticity of 1.383 may seem rather modest, when the effect is cumulated over a range of GDP ratios that extends from one to nearly 80, the divergence of box office share ratios from the corresponding GDP ratios can be enormous. For GDP ratios of 5, 20, 40 and 60, equation (3.7) predicts box office share ratios of 6.40, 43.51, 113.44 and 198.72. The estimated elasticity drops considerably if the US is dropped from the sample, but the pattern is the same. For the same GDP ratios without the US, predicted box office share ratios are 5.03, 23.59, 51.06 and 80.22. While less dramatic differences, these differences still become quite substantial as the GDP ratio rises. It is fair to say the US bends the curve.

CONCLUDING OBSERVATIONS

Aside from the obvious need for more empirical work and more studies of trade in media products other than films, especially, we have four suggestions for pushing research on this topic forward in a more productive fashion.

First, we need to rigorously test and compare the trade models that currently serve as points of reference for empirical studies of trade in media industries. We put rigorous tests of the models at the top of this list in part because the literature on trade in media products may be starting to separate into two largely self-contained silos. The economics literature on trade in media began in the late 1980s when a small number of economists already working on the economics of media tried to develop a trade model that could explain American productions' overwhelming domination of the international trades in films and television programmes and independently offered three versions of the budget-based advantage model (Hoskins and Mirus, 1988; Waterman, 1988; Wildman and Siwek, 1987, 1988). Their efforts incorporated their common observation that, as a general matter, large countries had larger shares of other countries' film and programme markets than did small countries and that film and programme production budgets were also correlated with the size of their home countries' GDPs. The United States' domination of trade in films and television programmes had been a subject of prominent and lively debate in the communications literature for several decades before economists decided they were phenomena worth investigating, and much of the empirical literature that subsequently developed appeared in communications journals, or journals targeted to an interdisciplinary mix of scholars interested in the economics of media (like the *Journal of Media Economics*), where the audience was already primed for the topic. Economists who have come to the study of trade in media more recently have almost entirely overlooked the earlier research and have instead looked to the mainstream economics literature on trade for theoretical guidance. Because media products are of necessity differentiated, monopolistic competition trade models were a natural choice. At the same time, studies by people steeped in the BBAM tradition rarely give more than a perfunctory nod to the monopolistic competition trade models.

After reviewing the empirical studies described earlier, we have concluded that, with the exception of Choi et al. (2013), none were designed in a way that was influenced by a choice between the two types of models. If empirical research continues on this path, choice of model really doesn't matter, which would be unfortunate because the theories on which we base claims to understanding can only be advanced if they are rigorously tested. We believe the evidence presented and discussed at the end of the section on the empirical literature favors the BBAM, but more work of this nature needs to be done. If in the end both types of models prove inadequate, we can use what was learned in the testing process to construct something better.

Second, we need to develop and apply rigorous empirical tests for large home market advantages. The suspicion that such advantages substantially shaped observed patterns of trade in films and TV programmes has been a key motivator for the empirical and theoretical work surveyed in this chapter. If we find there is no home market effect even for films, this would be further cause for reassessing the models we have been using. We presented our own test and applied it to films in the previous section. If our approach stands up to critical review by other researchers, it should be elaborated further and applied to other media.

Third, we need to do a better job applying what has been learned in the larger economics literature on trade, to trade in media products. We argued above that a reason economists have for so long failed to develop rigorous tests of the trade models used as theoretical touchstones for empirical studies is that they mistakenly thought tests for the effects of home market size on a country's share of its own and/or other countries' media markets were tests for home market effects, when the larger trade literature tells us otherwise. This advice goes beyond tests for large home market advantages. Continued advances in the theoretical underpinnings of empirical trade models has shown that when the relative sizes of countries' domestic markets for individual products differ from the relative sizes of their GDPs, use of GDP as a proxy for home market size, as is common practice, introduces bias that makes the empirical models less than faithful representations of the theoretical models that motivate their use. When the focus is on the effects of trade barriers on trade flows, it is becoming more common to use country fixed effects to control for this source of bias, which is the strategy employed by Disdier et al. (2010) and Ferreira and Waldfogel (2010). Unfortunately, this strategy precludes testing for large home market effects. Therefore, we should be looking for better measures for domestic market size than GDP and developing empirical strategies that allow us to test for market size effects while better controlling for the biases introduced by imperfect proxies. Until we do, we can take some comfort in the fact that some of the earlier studies of trade in films (Jayakar and Waterman, 2000; Oh, 2001; Lee and Bae, 2004; Lee and Waterman, 2007) estimated similar models that used GDP and consumer expenditures on channels through which motion pictures were distributed as alternative measures of domestic film market size and found the signs of the coefficients for market size variables were unaffected by the measure used.

Fourth, the quality of empirical work could be advanced if we were to either find better data for measuring media trade flows or adapt our trade models to the data that is available. The share of domestic audience or sales measures most commonly employed as proxies for exporters' sales in other countries' domestic media markets may be only loosely correlated with the actual payments for distribution rights because the nonrival character and high production costs of media content permit prices paid for distribution rights to vary dramatically across markets. We have cited evidence that such variation is substantial. It is not clear that other measures of the volume of trade in media products are any better. Hanson and Xiang (2008, 2009) show that for the film importing countries in their sample, the figures Comtrade reports for payments for imported films were typically sufficiently small fractions of the revenues American films generated in those countries to suggest that the Comtrade figures substantially understate actual payments for rights to US films. Financial flows are implicitly tied to flows of product in the monopolistic competition models. If financial flows are only loosely coupled with media product flows, the monopolistic competition models should be adjusted to allow for this possibility. This is less of a liability for the BBAM because it predicts shares of audience rather than flows of payments, but the most complete mathematical expression of the BBAM (Appendix B of Wildman and Siwek (1988)) was designed to test the plausibility of the basic intuition and is still fairly rudimentary. If the BBAM is the better model, it could use improvement in this regard.

NOTES

1. The model also predicts that the larger country will become a relative specialist in goods for which barriers to trade are high.
2. See Crandall (1974) and Waterman (1990) for other media market models with endogenous production costs. While not described as a media market model, a model by Economides (1993) is similar in many ways to Waterman's and generates similar results. Krugman's (1984) two-country model of trade with asymmetric trade barriers and R&D expenditures by firms that vary with expected earnings is probably the closest antecedent to the BBAM.
3. If goods that would have been traded are valued in their domestic market at some fraction $\phi < 1$ of the value they would have had in trade, barriers reduce domestic GDP_i by fraction $f_i = \alpha(1-\varphi)(1-\beta)(n-n_i)/n$. This fraction is larger, the smaller is the country.

REFERENCES

Anderson, J.E. (2011) 'The Gravity Model', *Annual Review of Economics,* 3, 133–160.

Box Office Mojo (2010) Retrieved August 1, 2010: http://www.boxofficemojo.com/

Choi, Y.J., Lee, S.Y., and Wildman, S.S. (2013) 'Why Do Large Markets Dominate? A New Look at Sources of the Large Home Market Advantage in the International Film Trade', Michigan State University, Working paper.

Crandall, R.W. (1974) 'The Economic Case for a Fourth Commercial Television Network', *Public Policy*, 22 (4), 513–536.

Disdier, A.-C., Tai, S.H., Fontagné, L., and Mayer, T. (2010) 'Bilateral Trade of Cultural Goods', *Review of World Economics*, 145 (4), 575–595.

Dixit, A. and Stiglitz, J. (1977) 'Monopolistic Competition and Optimum Product Diversity', *American Economic Review*, 67 (3), 297–308.

Dupagne, M. and Waterman, D. (1998) 'Determinants of US Television Fiction Imports in Western Europe', *Journal of Broadcasting and Electronic Media*, 42 (2), 208–220.

Economides, N. (1993) 'Quality Variations in the Circular Model of Variety-Differentiated Products', *Regional Science and Urban Economics*, 23 (2), 235–257.

Elberse, A. and Eliashberg, J. (2003) 'Demand and Supply Dynamics for Sequentially Released Products in International Markets: The Case of Motion Pictures', *Marketing Science*, 22 (3), 329–354.

Ferreira, F. and Waldfogel, J. (2010) 'Pop Internationalism: Has a Half Century of World Music Trade Displaced Local Culture?', *National Bureau of Economic Research*, Working Paper (No. 15964).

Frank, B. (1992) 'A Note on the International Dominance of the US in the Trade in Movies and Television Fiction', *Journal of Media Economics*, 5 (1), 31–38.

Fu, W.W. (2006) 'Concentration and Homogenization of International Movie Sources: Examining Foreign Film Import Profiles', *Journal of Communication*, 56 (4), 813–835.

Fu, W.W. (2012) 'Cross-Country Comparison of Audience Tastes in Hollywood Movies: Cultural Distance and Genre Preferences', in A. Candeub and S. Pager (eds), *Transnational Culture in the Internet Age*, Cheltenham, UK and Northampton, MA, USA: Edward Elgar, pp. 370–388.

Fu, W.W. and Govindaraju, G. (2010) 'Explaining Global Box-Office Tastes in Hollywood Films: Homogenization of National Audiences' Movie Selections', *Communication Research*, 37 (2), 215–238.

Fu, W.W. and Lee, T.K. (2008) 'Economic and Cultural Influences on the Theatrical Consumption of Foreign Films in Singapore', *Journal of Media Economics*, 21 (1), 1–27.

Fu, W.W. and Sim, C. (2010) 'Examining International Country-to-Country Flow of Theatrical Films', *Journal of Communication*, 60 (1), 120–143.

Hanson, G.H. and Xiang, C. (2004) 'The Home-Market Effect and Bilateral Trade Patterns', *American Economic Review*, 94 (4), 1108–1129.

Hanson, G.H. and Xiang, C. (2008) 'Testing the Melitz Model of Trade: An Application to US Motion Picture Exports', *National Bureau of Economic Research*, Working Paper (No. w14461).

Hanson, G.H. and Xiang, C. (2009) 'International Trade in Motion Picture Services', in M. Reinsdorf and M.J. Slaughter (eds), *International Trade in Services and Intangibles in the Era of Globalization*, Chicago: University of Chicago Press, pp. 203–222.

Helpman, E. and Krugman, P. (1985) *Market Structure and Foreign Trade*, Cambridge, MA: MIT Press.

Hofstede, G.H. (1980) *Culture's Consequences: International Differences in Work-Related Values*, Beverly Hills, CA: Sage.

Hoskins, C. and Mirus, R. (1988) 'Reasons for the US Dominance of the International Trade in Television Programmes', *Media, Culture & Society*, 10 (October), 499–504.
Hoskins, C., Mirus, R., and Rozeboom, W. (1989) 'US Television Programs in the International Market: Unfair Pricing?', *Journal of Communication*, 39 (2), 55–75.
Jayakar, K. and Waterman, D. (2000) 'The Economics of American Movie Exports: An Empirical Analysis', *Journal of Media Economics*, 13 (3), 153–169.
Kogut, B. and Singh, H. (1988) 'The Effect of National Culture on the Choice of Entry Mode', *Journal of International Business Studies*, 19 (3), 411–432.
Krugman, P. (1979) 'Increasing Returns, Monopolistic Competition, and International Trade', *Journal of International Economics*, 9 (4), 469–479.
Krugman, P. (1980) 'Scale Economies, Product Differentiation, and the Pattern of Trade', *The American Economic Review*, 70 (5), 950–959.
Krugman, P. (1984) 'Import Protection as Export Promotion: International Competition in the Presence of Oligopolies and Economies of Scale', in H. Kierzkowski (ed.), *Monopolistic Competition and International Trade*, Oxford: Clarendon Press, pp. 180–193.
Lee, B. and Bae, H. (2004) 'The Effect of Screen Quotas on the Self-Sufficiency Ratio in Recent Domestic Film Markets', *Journal of Media Economics*, 17 (3), 163–176.
Lee, F.L. (2006) 'Cultural Discount and Cross-Culture Predictability: Examining US Movies' Box Office in Hong Kong', *Journal of Media Economics*, 19 (4), 259–278.
Lee, F.L. (2008) 'Hollywood Movies in East Asia: Examining Cultural Discount and Performance Predictability at the Box Office', *Asian Journal of Communication*, 18 (2), 117–136.
Lee, S.W. (2002) 'An Economic Analysis of the Movie Industry in Japan', *Journal of Media Economics*, 15 (2), 125–139.
Lee, S.W. and Waterman, D. (2007) 'Theatrical Feature Film Trade in the United States, Europe, and Japan Since the 1950s: An Empirical Study of the Home Market Effect', *Journal of Media Economics*, 20 (3), 167–188.
Lee, S.Y. and Wildman, S.S. (2012) 'Protecting and Promoting National Cultures in a World Where Bits Want to Flow Freely', in S. Pager and A. Candeub (eds), *Transnational Culture in the Internet Age*, Cheltenham, UK and Northampton, MA, USA: Edward Elgar, pp. 389–409.
Marvasti, A. (1994) 'International Trade in Cultural Goods: A Cross-Sectional Analysis', *Journal of Cultural Economics*, 18 (2), 135–148.
Marvasti, A. (2000) 'Motion Pictures Industry: Economies of Scale and Trade', *International Journal of the Economics of Business*, 7 (1), 99–114.
Marvasti, A. and Canterbery, R. (2005) 'Cultural and Other Barriers to Motion Pictures Trade', *Economic Inquiry*, 43 (1), 39–54.
Oh, J. (2001) 'International Trade in Film and the Self-Sufficiency Ratio', *Journal of Media Economics*, 14 (1), 31–44.
Rauch, J. and Trindade, V. (2009) 'Neckties in the Tropics: A Model of International Trade and Cultural Diversity', *Canadian Journal of Economics*, 42 (3), 809–843.
Rosse, J. (1970) 'Estimating Cost Function Parameters Without Cost Data', *Econometrica*, 38 (2), 256–275.
Schulze, G.G. (1999) 'International Trade in Art', *Journal of Cultural Economics*, 23 (1–2), 109–136.
Screen Digest (2008) 'Global Film Production/Distribution: US Makes Fewer Feature Films as World Total Sets New Record', *Screen Digest*, 2008 July.
Siwek, S.E. and Furchtgott-Roth, H.W. (1993) *International Trade in Computer Software*, Westport, Connecticut: Quorum Books.
Waterman, D. (1988) 'World Television Trade: The Economic Effects of Privatization and New Technology', *Telecommunications Policy*, 12 (2), 141–151.

Waterman, D. (1990) 'Diversity and Quality of Information Products in a Monopolistically Competitive Industry', *Information Economics and Policy*, 4 (4), 291–303.

Waterman, D. and Jayakar, K. (2000) 'The Competitive Balance of the Italian and American Film Industries', *European Journal of Communication*, 15 (4), 501–528.

Waterman, D. and Rogers, E.M. (1994) 'The Economics of Television Program Production and Trade in Far East Asia', *Journal of Communication*, 44 (3), 89–111.

Wildman, S.S. (1995) 'Trade Liberalization and Policy for Media Industries: A Theoretical Examination of Media Flows', *Canadian Journal of Communication*, 20 (3), 367–388.

Wildman, S.S. and Siwek, S.E. (1987) 'The Privatization of European Television: Effects on International Markets for Programs', *Columbia Journal of World Business*, 22 (3), 71–76.

Wildman, S.S. and Siwek, S.E. (1988) *International Trade in Films and Television Programs*, Cambridge, MA: Ballinger Pub Co.

World Bank (2013) 'Gross Domestic Product', Retrieved September 1, 2013, from http://data.worldbank.org/indicator/NY.GDP.MKTP.CD

ZDNet (2005) 'Cheapest Movie Tickets Per Capita Price are in India, US, China', Retrieved May 4, 2013, from http://www.zdnet.com/blog/itfacts/cheapest-movie-tickets-per-capita-price-are-in-india-u-s-china/997

4. Media clusters and metropolitan knowledge economy

Charlie Karlsson and Philippe Rouchy

Since the mid-1990s, the interrelationship between ICT, the location of media consortia and their innovation processes have been essential features of agglomeration renewals. In many arenas, academic research as well as policy-orientated projects have focused on understanding the factors operating the re-organization of new media and their development in particular major cities and their agglomerations. Increasing numbers of case studies have investigated particularly remarkable media clusters (Achtenhagen and Picard, 2011; Davis et al., 2009; Picard, 2008 and 2010; Von Streit et al., 2010) which are used as either exemplary models of developments or starting to question traditional industrial and economic growth policies (Backlund and Sandberg, 2002; Bathelt and Boggs, 2003). In this chapter, we will not address the policy implications of media clusters. We rather want to bring some preliminary reflection on media clusters, the dynamic of knowledge and agglomeration. We think it is premature to develop planning policies on clusters when the main issue remains to identify properly the role of knowledge dynamics and its economic implication in both the constitution of media clusters and agglomeration economies (Cheshire and Malecki, 2004; Oinas, 2002). At this moment, it seems unclear to what extent we are able to draw the right lesson of the accumulations of cases on the innovative performance of media clusters. In other words, we think that there are still spaces to investigate conceptually and/or empirically appropriate analytical tools and knowledge bases on media clusters. Studies on media clusters are relatively recently undertaken. One of the lines of study we pursue in this chapter is to what extent the Jacobs' model of city growth dynamics is an appropriate framework to think about media clusters and sector specific knowledge change. In order to explain the issue of knowledge dynamics in media clusters, it is necessary to consider the nature of new knowledge created in new media industry and identify clusters of the cultural industry the best way we can.

Currently McCann's classification of industrial clustering (1995, 2001, 2004, 2008) offers a comprehensive overview of cluster types: the Marshallian type of agglomeration which he calls the model of pure agglomeration, the Weberian type of cluster which is the industrial complex cluster, and the social network model of cluster which specifies types of relations between agents in a network. If those agents are firms, then relation types can vary through joint venture, lobbying, informal alliance and reciprocal arrangements. Scott (1988a) developed a geographical version of social networks by working out the model of "new industrial areas". It aims at describing the characteristics and performance of industrial regions. Researches distinguish between the old industrial areas such as Italy's Emilia-Romagna and new industrial areas such as Silicon Valley (Scott, 1988a; Saxenian, 1994; Castells and Hall, 1994). There are varieties of research that work out the new and old social network theory in the direction of social capital, creativity and space (Glaeser et al., 2002; Caves, 2000; Davis et al., 2012; Florida, 2002, 2004; Scott, 1998a, 2000a).

It seems that the model of pure agglomeration would just fit the new media cluster. Despite its unavoidable importance, notably in the study of the dynamics of productivity, it isn't the best theoretical instrument for media cluster analysis. The Marshallian model assumes that clustering happens by localized external agglomeration economies. In this model, there are positive agglomeration externalities: local information and knowledge spillovers, non-traded local input and skilled labour pool. There are partial elements to consider and some to leave aside (Karlsson, 2008a, b). For that matter, let us review the existing literature developing the Marshallian model in different ways. The first one is called the Marshall-Arrow-Romer (MAR). This line of thought looked at the "increasing return theory of productivity" which assumes that increasing returns play an essential role in the explanation of sustained growth (Krugman, 1991a, b). One of the refinements of the same principle is the "learning by doing" taking place within a single location (Glaeser et al., 1992). We are inclined to think that the endogenous theory of productivity is an imperious necessity in contemporary studies of innovation and wealth creation (Shapiro, 2005). Nevertheless, concerning the study of media cluster, we will logically prefer the second alternative of the pure agglomeration model proposed by the "new economic geography" (Fujita et al., 1999; Fujita and Thisse, 2002) and more traditional approaches of urbanization theory such as Jacobs (1969, 1984). This second branch of the pure agglomeration theory presents the clear advantage to deal with agglomeration diversity-variety in relationship to the dynamics of knowledge. In the new economic geography, the diversity thesis suggests that inter-industry spillover (Ferrando et al., 2008) is generally more important than inter-industry effects (Pandit et al., 2002) to explain growth. As far as the theory goes, the variety version of agglomeration theory is our starting point. We will narrow it down in light of the sectorial characteristics of the new media industry.

The model of new economic geography stipulating diversity as a central component of the clustering phenomenon is still grounded on the idea that knowledge and information stick to particular clustered localities. Although this is partly true for the media cluster, there is an essential part of the story missing. Beside the problem of measuring "knowledge", the media cluster assumes both the stickiness of knowledge and the knowledge flows to the cluster. To be more precise, the geographic location of cultural industries comprises a selective concentration of media industry in large cities and metropolises organized in clusters (Scott, 2000a, b; Braczyk et al., 1999; Krätke, 2002; Krätke and Taylor, 2004). Beside the aspect of clustering, some key players in this industry are also multinationals with a global cultural presence (Morley and Robins, 1995; Robins, 1995; Pratt, 2000; Held et al., 1999; Karlsson et al., 2010; Scott, 1998b). Those globalized consortia work with a worldwide network of subsidiaries and other branch offices. They constitute a network of urban clusters of cultural production. Both their localized clusters and their global metropolitan networks are the core of their cultural production. Both flows of knowledge may be considered contradictory according to the Marshallian pure agglomeration theory.

For that reason, we find it necessary to reconsider essential elements of the new media industry, having in mind a tailor-made dynamics theory based on metropolitan cities (Klaesson et al., 2013). As is well known in economics, the issue of knowledge capture is a recurrent issue forcing us to work with stylized constructs, proxies and other conceptual ideal types. In addition, clearly, we are facing the same problem here when dealing with both knowledge dynamics in the creative industry and agglomeration effects. The existing literatures on creative industry (Andersson and Andersson, 2008; Camagni, 2012; Karlsson et al., 2010; Power and Scott, 2004; Scott, 1997, 1999, 2000a, b; Zukauskaite, 2010) and media clusters (Cook and Pandit, 2008; Karlsson and Picard, 2011; Achtenhagen and Picard, 2011) offer partial but essential parts of the puzzle. Scott (2000a) captures it nicely with the concept "multi-faceted industrial complexes". To start unfolding this puzzle posed by "multi-faceted industry", we will address the media industry by looking at (1) the advent of information technology in the new media sector creating a "weightless economy", (2) the key characteristics of media clusters, (3) a Jacobian metropolitan model of media cluster, and (4) in conclusion, further empirical issues.

NEW MEDIA'S "WEIGHTLESS ECONOMY"

Economic geographers have accepted to a large extent the economic analysis of clustering processes. They have done so stressing that social, cultural and institutional factors also play an important role for clusters to develop, grow, possibly decline, and disappear (Martin and Sunley, 1996). Scott (1998b) claims, for example, that clusters can only create new knowledge and new products and continue to grow if they have linkages with external markets and utilize a mix of local and non-local transactions. Thus, the effects of local interaction and learning are much stronger if they are continuously supported by impulses from other regions and clusters (Bathelt et al., 2004; Bathelt, 2005). In other words, economic geographers have well perceived the tension between local and global economies within some kinds of clusters. To address this tension in their studies, they have taken a classificatory approach (Potts and Cunningham, 2008). For example, Bathelt (2005) has suggested analysing clusters along five dimensions: (i) the vertical dimension, (ii) the horizontal dimension, (iii) the power dimension, (iv) the institutional dimension, and (v) the external dimension. Far from denying the multi-layered structure of transactions taking place within and between clusters, we are not inclined to think that large classification schemes will help solve the issue of catching diversified "knowledge content".

Some more promising ventures in this domain should come from the reflection on technological change affecting media clusters. Today developments within information and communication technologies (ICT) stimulate the birth of new media services including the creation, manipulation and distribution of digital content (Gillespie et al., 2001; Bathelt et al., 2004). An interesting characteristic of these new services, which include software, databases, electronic libraries, new media, videos, broadcasting, etc., is that they do not just embody knowledge – they are knowledge and behave as such (Arrow, 1962; Feldman, 1994). These new services represent what Quah (1999) calls "the weightless economy",[1] that is, an economy whose products are non-excludable, infinitely replicable and electronically transportable costlessly through space. Similar to Arrow's (1962) definition of knowledge, this observation could lead to the conclusion that the location of the production of media products is a non-issue. Since there are no raw materials that should be transported to the producers and no physical goods that should be distributed from the producers to the customers, media firms could locate anywhere. Urban regions would no longer host any clusters of media firms. So why do media firms continue to cluster?

The development of "the weightless economy" is not subtractive of existing economies, but enhancing them through diversification and replacement. To reach this conclusion, we observe tendencies of technology-related industry convergence (Rosenberg, 1963; Sahal, 1985; Dosi, 1988) in the emerging digital economy. There is indeed a breakup of old value chains (Ewans and Wurster, 1997) followed by a new structuring of value chains, where takeovers and strategic alliances play a significant role (Hagel III and Singer, 1999).[2] There are today numerous claims that industries like telecommunications, computing and entertainment are converging. This does not mean that those industries will constitute industrial complexes in the Weberian or Hooverian sense of the term. It certainly might evolve into one huge multi-media industry (Collis et al., 1997; The Economist, 2000) more akin to an endogenous growth of diversified services within metropolises. This industry has received particular attention (Brail and Gertler, 1999; Egan and Saxenian, 1999). In addition, it is noticeable that such services' variety and volume may be best understood in relationship to new media convergence between telecommunications, media and information technology sectors. It is certainly probable that the great growth of services is due to the emergence of the Internet and its subsequent business combinations (Table 4.1, from Krätke and Taylor, 2004).

Those combinations have increased the capability of existing networks to carry both telecommunications and broadcasting services (Kneips, 2003). Developments in digital technologies and software are creating a large innovative technological potential for the production, distribution and consumption of information services. Convergence, characterized as the ability of different network platforms to carry essentially similar kinds of services, may have very different faces: telecommunications operators may offer multi-media systems over their networks; broadcasters may provide data services over their networks; cable operators may provide a range of telecommunication services, and so on.

A cursory look at Table 4.1 suggests that the positive differential between service and media ranking confirms the role of metropolises and urban agglomerations such as London, New York, Paris, Milan, Los Angeles, Toronto, Madrid, Amsterdam, Sydney and Zurich. There is increasing evidence that the digital revolution actually reinforces the position of leading urban regions (Castells, 1989, 1996; Hall, 1998; Wheeler et al., 2000). So why do media firms cluster, when the technological opportunities have seemingly reduced the necessity of proximity in operations between inter-linked firms?[3] Actually, it seems as if the clustering tendencies are even more dominant in media industries than in many traditional industries. Ogawa (2000) shows, for example,

Table 4.1 Top 20 service business cities rank by media connectivity

Service rank	City	Media rank	Difference
1	London	1	0
2	New York	2	0
3	Hong Kong	20	–17
4	Paris	3	+1
5	Tokyo	18	–13
6	Singapore	12	–6
7	Chicago	24	–17
8	Milan	5	+3
9	Los Angeles	4	+5
10	Toronto	8	+2
11	Madrid	6	+5
12	Amsterdam	7	+5
13	Sydney	11	+2
14	Frankfurt	27	– 13
15	Brussels	19	–4
16	Sao Paulo	25	–9
17	San Francisco	33	–16
18	Mexico City	32	–14
19	Zurich	14	+5
20	Taipei	41	–21

Source: Krätke and Taylor, 2004: 464.

that ICT development may not necessarily encourage the dispersal of economic activities due to the network and technology effects of ICT infrastructure supply. Cities are a means of reducing the fixed travel costs involved in face-to-face interactions. Empirical results show that telecommunications complement them rather than exclude them (Gaspar and Glaeser, 1998).

ICT has an effect of enhancing exponential efficiency of transactions both in kind and in cost. ICT rapid diffusion has reduced dramatically transport and communication costs, altering the incentives for clustering of media industries as well as other industries. It is too early to observe the results of the diffusion of ICT but it is possible to identify some possible effects (Venables, 2001). ICT reduces:

- The search and matching costs in product markets, but closeness to customers may still be essential, in particular for products with rich and fluent characteristics.
- The direct shipping costs, since many products can be delivered in digital form.
- The control and management costs for geographically and organizationally fragmented operations.
- The cost of time in transit, that is, the shipping to and communication with distant locations.
- The costs of personal interactions, but knowledge spillovers are stimulated.
- The costs of commuting and of travelling in agglomerations.
- The costs of replicating products.
- The costs of relocation.

These effects are not media-sector specific but apply to it. Furthermore, due to the cultural character of the media sector's products, ICT might have stronger effects on it than on other sectors. It is by no means statistically clear how significant these factors are in affecting the clustering in the media sector. Nevertheless, it seems that ICT plays an essential part as a multiplier in the contemporary diffusion of cultural services. It simply increases the number and variety of producers' services. We do not have a clear solution for appreciating the role of ICT in productivity enhancement of media clusters since media firms add to their existing physical value chain a virtual one having the effect of eliminating stages in the value chain itself (Benjamin and Wigand, 1995; Ghosh, 1998; Bugge, 2010). As a result, we are clearly left with an empirical issue to solve. A question remains: how does the clustering of the media sector function as a multiplier of differentiated services?

KEY CHARACTERISTICS OF MEDIA CLUSTERS

Clusters exist when there is a large enough concentration of media (and related) firms in a city or a metropolitan area. Several firms are normally gathered in a specific, often central location in the city, but the cluster may include other firms in the surrounding area.[4] An important characteristic of clustering is that the firms share resources, such as labour, contract services, information and knowledge, and interact directly or indirectly for mutual advantage and benefit. Those are some of the several obvious reasons why media firms tend to cluster.[5] There is today a growing body of literature dealing with media clusters and in particular with large media clusters (Van den Berg et al., 2001), sometimes characterized as "global media cities" (Krätke, 2003).

Table 4.2 Europe's top 25 regions for CCI: ranking and employment[a]

Region	CCI Rank	CCI Employment	CCI LQ
Île de France (Paris), FR	1	279 361	1.72
Inner London, UK	2	239 983	2.77
Lombardia (Milan), IT	3	175 580	1.31
Madrid, ES	4	164 269	1.65
Cataluña (Barcelona), ES	5	139 278	1.26
Lazio (Rome), IT	6	113 531	1.97
Denmark	7	98 866	1.17
Oberbayern (München), DE	8	94 178	1.57
Attiki (Athens), GR	9	88 195	1.47
Outer London, UK	10	86 884	1.43
Kozep-Magyarorszag (Budapest), HU	11	79 281	1.76
Zuid-Holland, NL	12	78 183	1.44
Berks, Bucks and Oxon (Oxford), UK	13	76 097	1.90
Noord-Holland (Amsterdam), NL	14	74 685	1.80
Andalucia (Sevilla), ES	15	70 914	0.68
Köln, DE	16	68 825	1.37
Stockholm, SE	17	68 212	2.87
Lisboa, PT	18	67 929	1.35
Berlin, DE	19	66 051	1.70
Veneto, IT	20	61 285	0.94
Niedersachsen, DE	21	59 486	0.68
Darmstadt (Hanover), DE	22	58 965	1.15
Piemonte, IT	23	58 068	1.09
Emilia-Romagna, IT	24	58 029	0.95
E Surrey and W Sussex, UK	25	57 837	1.40

Note: a: LQ = 1 is an indicator of Creative and Cultural Industries (CCI) employment relative to the total employment of the region. If LQ > 1 it indicates an over-employment of CCI in the region.

Source: Power, 2011: 9.

As mentioned in the introduction, spatial industrial clustering prevails within the media sector especially in the form of agglomeration economy. However, one interesting question concerns the qualification of distinctive aspects of the media sector. As identified through the weightless economy, media clusters' special traits are guided by fluid value chains grounded in large agglomerations and having global reach. To be more specific, there are clearly metropolitan characteristics of media products, such as their public goods character, the scale economy of media production, important circuits of distribution, high degree of product differentiation, interdependency with advertising content,[6] and the existence of network externalities (Rosse and Dertouzos, 1978; Rosse, 1979; Owen and Wildman, 1992). Following is a review of the main characteristics of media clusters, namely (1) the role of creative activities, (2) the rapid evolution of products, (3) the organization of labour in intra-inter projects structure, (4) the presence of large media oligopolies and (5) the clustering of young firms as service suppliers.

Creative Activities

Because many of the media industries are creative industries, they are within or closely related to the cultural sector. The tendency of creative cultural industries to clusters has been documented in the literature in recent decades (Scott, 1997; Hitters and Richards, 2002; Mommaas, 2004). One important and fundamental characteristic of the media sector's many activities is its relation with creative activities. There is a constant need for creativity and innovation in the design and development of products. Each output is a "one-off" item, which must be experienced by consumers as new or different, even if minimally. Thus, the creation of media output is heavily dependent upon small groups of talented people: authors, actors and crew in film, musical bands, copywriters and designers of advertising, etc. It is well known that creative activities only develop in specific milieus characterized by diverse activities and competencies with synergetic potential, instability and uncertainty, great tolerance, and critical mass (Andersson, 1985). Such milieus are normally found only in large cities.

Rapidly Evolving

Another important characteristic of media products is the short product cycles of cultural content. It implies that important external advantages and stimuli are derived from the incentives of the media firms themselves to generate competing goods and services (Maskell, 2001; Malmberg and

Maskell, 2002). Creative firms in media industries cannot indefinitely reproduce earlier products, limiting the advantage they can take from rent economies. Their ability to generate new products is directly related to their ability to compete in the cultural market. This market is made of customers' choice for visually and functionally novel and/or superior offerings to earlier products. This implies that it is critical for firms in media industries to actively monitor the products of their competitors, and transform and improve their own products accordingly. Presence for a media firm in a cluster with other media firms nearby makes it easier to formally and informally monitor and study the production of others. This kind of monitoring is an important part of the creative process, which stimulates innovation, imitation and competition[7] (Britton, 2007). Innovation in media industries is often incremental and requires new combinations or applications of existing tacit and/or codified knowledge building upon past creative successes and an expanding skill base (Wolfe et al., 2005).

Intra-inter Projects

A third important characteristic of the activities in important parts of the media sector is their organization in intra- and inter-firm projects. Temporary, project-based production networks are set up on a limited time span.[8] This type of governance is a solution to the issue of coordinating of production known in the literature as flexible specialization (Piore and Sabel, 1984; Storper, 1997; Storper and Harrison, 1991; Storper and Venables, 2004) which is very common in the media sector (Starkey et al., 2000; Sydow and Staber, 2002; Mossig, 2004; Ferriani et al., 2005). The flexible specialization model makes it possible for the leading media firms to use freelancers and different small firms in the media cluster as a reserve labour pool and to reduce risks by relying to a high extent on short-term contracts (Christopherson, 2005, 2006). Project-based production is true for film, music and book production, software development, and so on. Authors (Grabher, 2002; Pratt, 2002) have suggested that such project-based enterprises are the archetypical form of the emerging new media industries, as well as of many industries in the cultural sector. Thus, the single talented individual or small group of people are part of a larger production network using a varied supply of specialists. In software development, continuous updating of software demands the employment of large in-house as well as out-sourced teams of designers and managers, preferably with good opportunities for frequent face-to-face communication (Cusumano, 1991; Cusumano and Selby, 1996). Hansen et al. (2005) stress that in the entertainment sector, production systems are often based upon the assembling of new teams of actors, writers and other specialized workers for each new project. Carefully selected staff from different firms,[9] which, for a limited period, dedicate some or all of their time to the tasks specified for the project, constitute such inter-firm projects. These inter-firm projects are based upon a rigorous division of labour within the production chain, i.e. vertical disintegration, and a specialization in small areas of production.

Group of Large Global Media Oligopoly

A fourth important characteristic of the media industry is the existence of a group of large global media oligopolists (McChesney, 1999), strategic alliances between such oligopolists, and mergers and acquisitions. One common picture of industrial clustering is the co-location of many small firms in the same locality. Recognizing the importance of large global actors in the industry makes it necessary to think differently about media clustering. Obviously, large anchor media firms may play a critical role for the clustering of small and medium-sized media firms. To discuss the anchoring role of global media oligopolists in the clustering of media firms, it is necessary to discuss some important characteristics of these firms (Chan-Olmsted and Chang, 2003):

- They offer dual, complementary content and distribution services of media products.
- They rely on dual revenue streams from consumers and advertisers.
- Most media content products are non-excludable and non-depletable public goods. Their consumption by one individual does not exclude another individual from consuming them. Instead, mass consumption adds to scale economies in production.
- Many media content products are marketed under a windowing process. Distribution of a specific content is delivered to consumers via multiple outlets sequentially in different periods.
- Media products are highly subjective to cultural preferences and dependent on the existing communication infrastructure of each geographical market. This includes the regulatory control imposed in different countries.

Today large media firms play a strategic role in the production and delivery of media products. For example, only global firms can afford to deal with the multiple-level legalities involved in trade barriers, distribution exclusivities and other content repackaging to dub or censor. Ultimately, it implies that corporate structure, strategy, management, and behaviour can have a significant influence on industrial clustering of media firms (Fu, 2003; Hendriks, 1995).

Fairly Young Firms in Clusters

A fifth important characteristic is that the firms in media clusters reveal a number of common characteristics (Scott, 1996; Brail and Gertler, 1999; Egan and Saxenian, 1999; Bathelt, 2001). Most of the firms in these clusters are young but many serve older, larger, established media firms. Often existing only for a few years, they supply highly specialized services. They are normally small in terms of employment. The local growth processes of many of the media clusters are driven by innovative regional start-ups. Teams of entrepreneurs rather than individual entrepreneurs play the role of "embryonic city economy" in Jacobs's term. They rely heavily on owner capital. These clusters emerge in inner cities rather than in suburban locations (Storper and Christophersen, 1987; Eberts and Norcliffe, 1998; Brail and Gertler, 1999).

The five characteristics of media clusters are based on the ability of media firms to use local producers of services. At the same time, they use the metropolitan markets to have access to a large pool of services suppliers, which allows them to build a reasonably complete work organization. It allows the clustered media firms to use local suppliers without locked-in dependence toward them. There is clearly a homology between the advantage of cities and the media clusters in the way they can use their rooting in agglomeration to project themselves in global exporting ventures. For that matter, it is necessary to explain further, how a Jacobian model of the metropolitan economies can explain the dynamics of media clusters.

TOWARD A JACOBIAN METROPOLITAN MODEL OF MEDIA CLUSTERS

There are a series of similarities between the way large cities are generating what Jacobs calls an "explosive growth" and the way media clusters are behaving. Both successful media clusters and cities have benefited from each other through the enlargement of their local market and their ability to generate global exports (Fuchs, 2002). In this section, we will review some of the advantage large agglomeration brings to the creative milieu necessary to support a vibrant media clustered industry. The interplay between media cluster and agglomeration economies leads us to consider the Jacobian model of cities' economies. We propose to revisit media clusters in the light of Jacobs' "reciprocating system of city growth" (1969). This system explains the innovation process thanks to two stages. The first stage (Figure 4.1, "Metropolitan System") shows how an agglomeration can reach a critical size thanks to its production and export of goods and services. In turn, growing imports drive renewed production. The second stage (Figure 4.1, "Global System") is the logical extension of the first one through intensified import replacement, which allows the development of global versatile exports. In turn, this global export increases the scale and scope of importation, which affects accordingly the replacement of imports. In Jacobs's research, only large cities are able to generate a diversity of human activities and interests that continually create streams of public goods. In other words, they sustain the workings of what Scott calls "the creative milieu". Socialization dynamics ensure the preservation and development of local knowledge under exposure to global information and knowledge flows. Hence, the clustering of producers in the new media field should occur

> where new communications technologies are insufficient to capture the full range of human expression … clustering of producers will … occur in particular places, namely those that afford a large degree of chance and random encounter with both similar and different producers, and users. (Pratt, 2000: 429)

Large cities also offer "institutional thickness" (Amin and Thrift, 1995) overlapping webs of supporting organizations,[10] such as financing organizations, chambers of commerce, local and regional authorities, marketing, innovation and business support agencies that "create synergy, and a collective sense of identity and purpose within a cluster" (Bassett et al., 2002). These features and the fact that media production requires the overlapping skills of a highly differentiated workforce (Pratt, 1999) imply that full-blown media clusters are normally only present in large cities.

Urban media clusters with both strong intra-regional and strong global networks are essential to explain their innovation dynamics. They have the potential to become worldwide forerunners because the critical mass they have acquired from their growing activities in metropolises allows them to develop versatile exports. Whereas strong intra-regional networks facilitate competitive and creative production, global networks provide inputs of external knowledge and access to distant markets. They have an innovative function, which is to reduce the risk of urban media clusters becoming inflexible. Therefore, a combination of strong intra-regional and strong global networks offers the most favourable conditions for an enduring ability and capacity to secure the long-term competitiveness of urban media clusters (Storper and Harrison, 1991; Freeman, 1995; Marcusen, 1996; Freeman and Soete, 1997; Ernst, 1999). Figure 4.1 is a revised schematic of Jacobs's combination of metropolitan local markets with media clusters' ability to export globally.

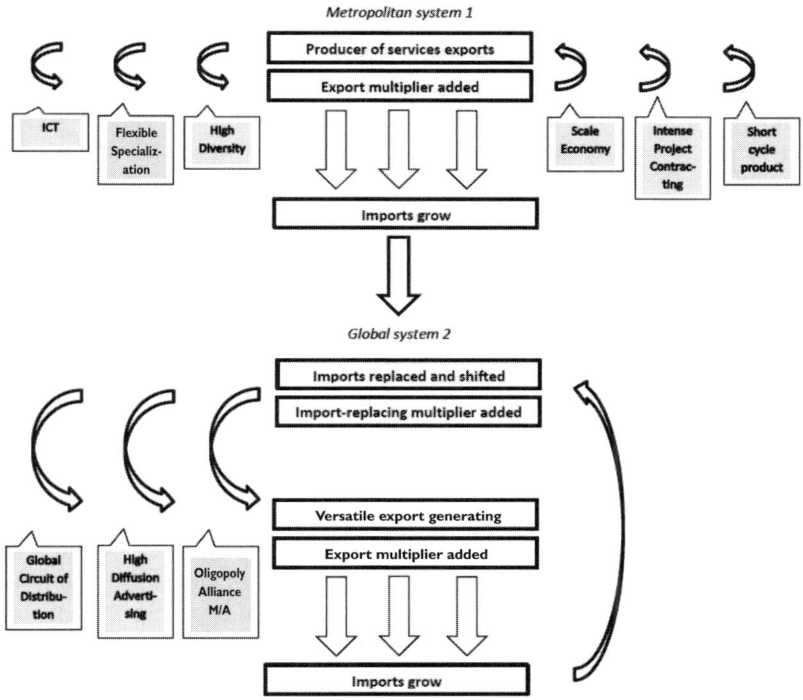

Source: Adapted from Jacobs, 1969: 260.

Figure 4.1 The Jacobian model of agglomeration growth for media clusters

The media value chain is continuously changing, not least due to organizational and technological changes including an increasing digitalization, but also due to changes in transport costs and distribution systems.[11] Seen from a growth perspective, this implies that characteristics of functions within the media sector (ICT, flexible specialization and high diversity, etc.) are not only outsourced but often also relocated from media clusters to other locations nationally and increasingly internationally, that is, off-shored (global distribution and diffusion, advertising, oligopoly, alliances and so on). However, many media functions continue to be clustered irrespective of technological changes and reductions of transport costs, and some media functions might over time even become more clustered. The Jacobian model of media cluster proposed here articulates explicitly the fact that urban clusters can never be studied successfully without considering their inter-regional, national and global connections.[12] The increased importance of global links does not imply that the intra-regional links in clusters lose their importance. What is important for urban media clusters is that they succeed in combining high quantity and high quality intra-regional networking with high quantity and high quality global networking. Certainly, successful urban media clusters need to preserve strategic positions in the organizational structures and networks of global players, but this is impossible if the intra-regional networking is not of a high quantity and quality.

At the bottom, the interrelation between the media clusters based in metropolitan cities and their international reach is explained by the dynamics of economic growth. Jacobs's model explains how media clusters are able to function as import-replacing multipliers. They generate versatile exports, which in turn add up to the global export capabilities of clusters. To specify a little further this virtuous circle, let us look at the linkage between media clusters anchored in metropolises and their global reach. Media clusters are anchored in metropolises because they create a number of projects that engage a large number of different specialists on a temporary basis. Only a relatively large cluster will offer a diverse enough supply of specialists to make such projects economically feasible. Further, they do not always restrict their activities to the local economic milieu. Because of global competition and the need to serve demand elsewhere, media clusters are able to take advantage of economies of scale. Some media firms extend the geographical scale and scope of their external linkages (Nachum and Keeble, 2003). One important aspect of globalization is the continuous scaling-up of markets and the increasing growth of transnational financial and economic networks (Sassen, 1994; Waters, 1995). The critical challenge for urban media clusters is to secure enough synergies between the global and the intra-regional networks to expand import-replacing multipliers in order to add export multipliers. Urban media clusters that successfully secure these synergies might be characterized as global media clusters (Sassen, 1994). Successful global media clusters are those whose networks incorporate an adequate supply of quality knowledge, creativity and design resources. This can only be achieved with the ability, willingness and openness of local firms to cooperate with global firms to make use of external global sources of inspiration, information, knowledge and creativity. Media firms' clear focus on the combination of local and global resources systems is certainly a key to developing new superior media products.

FURTHER EMPIRICAL ISSUES POSED BY THE JACOBIAN INNOVATION PROCESS

As suggested by the research in regional economics (Blien and Maier, 2008), urban regions and large agglomerations in particular are engines of creative activities and innovation, and subsequently sources of economic growth. Media clusters pose two questions for the economics of innovation: 1. What does the Jacobian model of agglomeration growth say about media clusters' innovation? 2. How do urban economists empirically account for the intense knowledge concentration, culture creation and service transactions taking place in media clusters?

Media clusters research faces many challenges, including the need for better comprehension of the social and economic processes underlying their economic development. We think that the Jacobian model of urban media clusters offers several advantages over existing Marshallian, Weberian or social networks models. We nevertheless are well aware that empirical challenges to make this model work are still ahead of us. Let us review its advantages and outline further research needed along the following four topics:

1. Defining the media economy Researchers are continuously working on defining the media economy (Gibson and Kong, 2005; O'Regan, 2011), since many of its components are ad hoc and because ongoing technological and structural changes modify continuously its borders. Media clusters have fluid relations to other sectors in the economy and to consumers. This makes the adoption of traditional Weberian clusters irrelevant and puts the Marshallian in need of a strong specification. Other approaches have emerged, trying to capture an industry based on cultural services for example the sectorial, labour market and organization of production approach (Scott, 1996 and 2001), the occupational approach (for example Florida, 2002 and the creative class), and the convergence of formats approach (Gibson and Kong, 2005). This diversity of perspectives calls for a comprehensive framework reconceptualizing the relation between the creative economy and the city (Pratt and Hutton, 2013).

2. Our solution: a Jacobian definition of urban media clusters based on Jacobs's metropolitan economics The central element of analysis is Jacobs's (1969, 1984: 193) proposition to consider the city as a creative knowledge economy:

> [Cities] vital functions are to serve as primary developers and primary expanders of economic life, functions that work not in the least like perpetual motion. They require continually repeated inputs of energy in two specific forms: innovations, which at bottom are inputs of human insight; and ample replacements of imports, which at bottom are inputs of the human capacity to make adaptive imitations.

One can see how Jacobian urban media clusters can be conceived as creative clusters (Landry and Bianchini, 1995). Jacobs identified well the relevance of tertiary activities at the urban level (Jacobs, 1969, 1984; Simmie, 2002). Without the foresight given to us by the development of new information, multi-media and telecommunications technologies, her approach brings two essential insights on the role of knowledge in innovation: (a) Jacobs's definition of "human insight" echoes Hayek's "relevant knowledge" and (b) Jacobs's definition of "adaptive imitation" echoes Schumpeter's "new combinations". Jacobs's approach of urban centres as "incubating economic life" links more explicitly the urban economics of media clusters with aspects of evolutionary economics accounting for economic development.

3. Jacobs's model offers a mechanism to evaluate value-creation in urban media clusters The superiority of Jacobs's model proposed in this chapter is to offer a mechanism of evaluation of value-creation in media cluster through a genuine economics of socio-cultural knowledge. The strong links between media industries and cultural industries underlines the importance of immaterial assets[13] in innovation processes in these industries. In particular, value-creation in urban media clusters is connected closely to the existence in the city of specific intellectual resources present in unique creative characteristics through individuals and collective creative processes, as well as through a variety of modes of distribution and consumption (Crane, 1992).

4. The Jacobian model explains endogenously the globalization processes in urban media clusters Large cities containing media clusters are today dominated by tertiary activities. The Jacobian model used to describe their development processes leads to an endogenous rather than stochastic characterization of the decline of some factors, a rejuvenation of others and a growth of new ones (Johansson et al., 2001; Scott,

1998b). This is the second aspect of innovation contained in Jacobs's "adaptive imitation".[14] Jacobs's model goes further in the specification of the change of the units of economic analysis themselves. She indicates the mechanics of import and export within urban economics allowing for the articulation of the local and the global level. Further, she specifies the dynamics of urban media clusters, showing a distinctive urban tension allowing local systems to produce global services.

NOTES

1. Quah (1999) indicates that "weightless economy" maybe also be called "knowledge economy", "intangible economy", "immaterial economy" or the "new economy". Kling and Lamb (2000) suggest that the term "information economy" include all informational products such as publishing, R&D, legal and insurance services, entertainment and teaching in all forms. In comparison, "internet economy" addresses only the products whose development, production, sale or distribution is critically depending on digital technologies. Piazolo (2001: 30) defines the digital economy as "an economy where both the modern (digital) information and communication technologies provide worldwide access to almost any available information."
2. One example of the breaking-up of the value chains in the media sector is the increasing role of content intermediaries (Hess and Von Walter, 2006).
3. In the 1980s and early 1990s, some cyber prophets and technological optimists predicted that the emergence of the digital economy would kill distance and make clustering in urban regions superfluous (Cairncross, 1997; Knoke, 1996; Naisbitt, 1995; Negroponte, 1995; Toffler, 1980) and at the same time eliminate the scale disadvantages of smaller and more peripheral regions. The basic idea was that the spread of the use of ICT has the potential to replace face-to-face activities that formerly occurred in central locations. This alone would strongly reduce or even eliminate agglomeration economies and hence make economic activities very "footloose". At the beginning of the 21st century, however, it has become clear that this picture is at least single-sided. New technologies are likely to remain grounded in existing urban regions, which imply that these regions will keep their locational attractiveness and that clusters will remain or even grow. In other words, ICT has not rendered work and organization "space less" (Neff, 2005).
4. At the fundamental level, media differ because they involve a complex interplay among cultural, economic, and political objectives. In media cluster development, issues of national and regional identity, language, and culture play significant roles, as well as desires to promote domestic content production to counter foreign content.
5. The media industry organized itself in clusters in order to be able to manage the high degree of interaction among individual firms in short-project cycles, among a large amount of specialities in order to produce diversified content. Those clusters have significant networks in the agglomeration and with national and international players. Media industries are organized in a specialized form of cluster designed to produce mediated content, such as motion pictures, television programs/videos, broadcasts, audio recordings, books, newspapers, magazines, games, photography and designs, websites, and mobile content for customers often based elsewhere. These clusters may have significant relations with other industries and clusters such as cultural industries (music and theatrical performance; museums and heritage sites;

festivals), sports and entertainment activities (professional sports teams and venues and amusement parks), information and communication technologies (computers, software, telecommunications), and hardware manufactures (television and radio receivers, set-top boxes, game consoles, DVD players, etc.).

6. Media's economic activities have a strong advertisement component. They are directed towards entertaining and informing, seeking to reach and influence a large audience. According to traditional communication theory, it involves a sender signalling a typically large number of receivers (audience), where the relationship between them is one-directional and impersonal (Vogel, 1990). However, the existence of online-commentaries, letters to the press, web-based debates, phone-in-programs, chat-pages, blogs, etc. have radically changed the role of the sender of information. See for example, the issue confronted by the UK newspaper *The Guardian* http://www.economist.com/node/21563334. The output of media activities has to be distributed to the widest possible audience, in order to maximize the returns on investment, making the distribution function a critical determinant of economic success (Vogel, 1990).
7. Competition in media markets is achieved by product differentiation (Rosse and Dertouzos, 1978). To avoid head-to-head competition in homogeneous markets, media firms engage in Hotelling-type competition to distinguish their content products (Hotelling, 1929). The maximum number of differentiated products in monopolistically competitive markets is determined by exogenous variables, such as market size, distribution of taste groups, size of entry barriers, operation costs, etc. Those are difficult for individual media firms to influence (Mankiw and Whinston, 1986; Waterman, 1990).
8. Many of the media sector products, like films, are produced in the form of projects, which run for limited periods.
9. These firms are overwhelmingly made up of small businesses, micro-businesses and self-employed freelancers, which can be described as dependent entrepreneurs (Burton-Jones, 1999).
10. Amongst those institutions, key infrastructures are schools, colleges, universities and training centres. They secure a continuous supply of skilled and specialized labour. Public-private partnerships promote urban renewal and certain technological, creativity and innovation schemes.
11. Driver and Gillespie (1993), in their study of printed magazines in the UK, show that the creative tasks of conception, design and editorial as well as the preliminary production stage of typesetting and reproduction remained firmly tied to London while the printing of magazines was decentralized from London.
12. Many authors have not fully understood the Jacobian model, misrepresenting what globalization implies for firms and regions. They take the globalization process to be morally negative in fading national cultural identities through an increasing of geographical mobility, worldwide migration and resulting ethnic hybridization and apparent cultural homogenization (Zukin, 1995). Some authors have argued that due to the rapid advance of globalization, economic structures and flows are increasingly becoming disembedded from regional contexts. Hence, they conclude that regional embeddedness is losing its importance (Thurow, 1996).
13. Hayek ([1945], 1992: 50–1) gave a definition of "relevant knowledge" proposing to consider the division of knowledge between skills and entrepreneurial ability: "Clearly, there is here a problem of the division of knowledge which is quite analogous to, and at least as important as, the problem of the division of labour. (...) 'Skills' refers only to the knowledge of which a person makes use in his trade, while the further knowledge about which we must know something in order to be able to say anything about the processes in society is the knowledge of alternative possibilities of action of which he makes no direct use."

14. Schumpeter ([1934], 2007) gave a definition of "new combination" as a fundamental phenomenon of economic development: "It is the producer who as a rule initiates economic change, and consumers are educated by him if necessary; they are, as it were, taught, to want new things, or things which differ in some respect or other from those which they have been in the habit of using. Therefore, while it is permissible and even necessary to consider consumers' wants as an independent and indeed the fundamental force in a theory of the circular flow, we must take a different attitude as soon as we analyse change. To produce means to combine materials and forces within our reach. To produce other things or the same things by a different method means to combine these materials and forces differently. As far as the 'new combination' may in time grow out of the old by continuous adjustment in small steps, there is certainly change, possibly growth, but neither a new phenomenon nor development in our sense. In so far as this is not the case, and the new combinations appear discontinuously, then the phenomenon characterizing development emerges. (…) Development in our sense is then defined by the carrying out of new combinations."

REFERENCES

Achtenhagen, L. and R.G. Picard (2011) "Media Clusters: Development Paths and Core Issues", in C. Karlsson and R.G. Picard (eds) *Media Clusters: Spatial Agglomeration and Content Capabilities*, Cheltenham, UK and Northampton, MA, USA: Edward Elgar, pp. 44–71.

Amin, A. and N. Thrift (1995) "Globalization, Institutional Thickness and the Local Economy", in Healey, P. et al. (eds), *Managing Cities: The New Urban Context*, Chichester: Wiley, pp. 92–108.

Andersson, Å.E. (1985) *Kreativitet – Storstadens framtid* (Creativity – The Future of the Metropolis), Stockholm: Prisma.

Andersson, D.E. and Å.E. Andersson (2008) "Infrastructural change and secular economic development", *Technological Forecasting and Social Change*, 75(6), 799–816.

Arrow, K.J. (1962) "Economic Welfare and the Allocation of Resources for Invention", in Nelson, R.R. (ed.) *The Rate and Direction of Inventive Activity*, Princeton: Princeton University Press, pp. 609–625.

Backlund, A.-K. and Å. Sandberg (2002) "New Media Industry Development: Regions, Networks and Hierarchies – Some Policy Implications", *Regional Studies*, 36, 87–91.

Bassett, K., R. Griffiths and I. Smith (2002) "Cultural Industries, Cultural Clusters and the City: The Example of Natural History Film-Making in Bristol", *Geoforum*, 33, 165–177.

Bathelt, H. (2001) "The Rise of a New Cultural Products Industry Cluster in Germany: The Case of the Leipzig Media Industry", *IWSG Working Papers 06-2001*, Johann Wolfgang Goete-Universität Frankfurt.

Bathelt, H. (2005) "Cluster Relations in the Media Industry: Exploring the 'Distanced Neighbour' Paradox in Leipzig", *Regional Studies*, 39(1), 105–127.

Bathelt, H. and J.S. Boggs (2003) "Toward a Reconceptualisation of Regional Development Paths: Is Leipzig's Media Cluster a Continuation or a Rupture with the Past", *Economic Geography*, 79(3), 265–293.

Bathelt, H., A. Malmberg and P. Maskell (2004) "Clusters and Knowledge: Local Buzz, Global Pipelines and the Process of Knowledge Creation", *Progress in Human Geography*, 28(1), 31–56.

Beck, H. (2002) *Medienökonomie. Print, Fernsehen und Multimedia*, Berlin: Springer.

Benjamin, R. and R. Wigand (1995) "Electronic Markets and Virtual Value Chains on the Information Superhighway", *Sloan Management Review*, 36(2), 67–72.
Blien, U. and G. Maier (eds) (2008) *The Economics of Regional Clusters: Networks, Technology and Policy*, Cheltenham, UK and Northampton, MA, USA: Edward Elgar.
Braczyk, H.J., G. Fuchs and H.-G. Wolf (1999) (eds), *Multimedia and Regional Economic Restructuring*, London: Routledge.
Brail, S.G. and M.S. Gertler (1999) "The Digital Regional Economy: Emergence and Evolution of Toronto's Multimedia Cluster", in Braczyk, H.J., G. Fuchs and H.-G. Wolf (eds), *Multimedia and Regional Economic Restructuring*, London: Routledge, pp. 97–130.
Britton, J.N.H. (2007) "Path Dependence and Cluster Adaptation: A Case Study of Toronto's New Media Industry", *International Journal of Entrepreneurship and Innovation Management*, 7(2–5), 272–297.
Bugge, M.M. (2010) "Jacobian Cluster Mutation Across Advertising and Internet-Based Market Communication", *Tijdschrift voor Economische en Sociale Geografie*, 102(5), 515–531.
Burton-Jones, A. (1999) *Knowledge Capitalism – Business, Work and Learning in the New Economy*, Oxford: Oxford University Press.
Cairncross, F. (1997) *The Death of Distance*, Boston, MA: Harvard Business School Press.
Camagni, R. (2012) "Creativity, Culture and Urban Milieux", in L.F. Girard, T. Baycan, P. Nijkamp (eds), *City and Creativity: Promoting Creative Urban City*, London: Ashgate, pp. 183–198.
Castells, M. (1989) *The Informational City. Information Technology, Economic Restructuring and the Urban-Regional Process*, Oxford: Basil Blackwell.
Castells, M. (1996) *The Rise of the Network Society. The Information Age: Economy, Society and Culture*, Vol. 1, Oxford: Blackwell.
Castells, M. and P. Hall (1994) *Technopoles of the world: The Making of 21 Century Industrial Complexes*, London: Routledge.
Caves, R.E. (2000) *Creative Industries: Contracts Between Art and Commerce*, Harvard: Harvard University Press.
Chan-Olmsted, S.M. and B-H. Chang (2003) "Diversification Strategy of Global Media Conglomerates: Examining Its Patterns and Determinants", *Journal of Media Economics*, 16(4), 213–233.
Cheshire, P.C. and E.J. Malecki (2004) "Growth, development and innovation: a look backward and forward", *Papers in Regional Science*, 83(1), 249–267.
Christopherson, S. (2005) "Divide and Conquer: Regional Competition in a Concentrated Media Industry", in Elmer, G. and M. Gasher (eds), *Contracting Out Hollywood: Runaway Productions and Foreign Location Shooting*, Oxford, UK: Rowman and Littlefield, pp. 21–40.
Christopherson, S. (2006) "Behind the Scenes: How Transnational Firms are Constructing a New International Division of Labour in Media Work", *Geoforum*, 37, 739–751.
Collis, D.J., P.W. Bane and S.P. Bradley (1997) "Winners and Losers: Industry Structure in the Converging World of Telecommunications, Computing and Entertainment", in Joffe, D.B. (ed.), *Competing in the Age of Digital Convergence*, Boston: Harvard Business School Press, pp. 159–199.
Cook, G.A.S. and N.R. Pandit (2008) "Clustering in the Broadcasting Industry", in C. Karlsson (ed.), *Handbook of Research on Cluster Theory*, Cheltenham, UK and Northampton, MA, USA: Edward Elgar, pp. 274–291.
Crane, D. (1992) *The Production of Culture: Media and Urban Arts*, Newbury Park, CA: Sage.
Cusumano, M. (1991) "Factory Concepts and Practices in Software Development", *Annals of the History of Computing*, 13(1), 3–32.
Cusumano, M. and R. Selby (1996), *Microsoft Secrets*, London: Macmillan.

Davis, C.H., T. Creutzberg and D. Arthurs (2009) "Applying an Innovation Cluster Framework to a Creative Industry: The Case of Screen-Based Media in Ontario", *Innovation: Management, Policy and Practice*, 11(2), 201–214.

Davis, C.H., J. Shtern, M. Coutanche and E. Godo (2012) "Screenwriters in Toronto: Centre, Periphery and Exclusionary Networks in Canadian Screen Storytelling", draft RTA School of Media, Ryerson University, Toronto.

Dosi, G. (1988) "Sources, Procedures and Microeconomic Effects of Innovation", *Journal of Economic Literature*, 36, 1126–1171.

Driver, S. and A. Gillespie (1993) "Information and Communication Technologies and the Geography of Magazine Print Publishing", *Regional Studies*, 27(1), 53–64.

Eberts, D. and G. Norcliffe (1998) "New Forms of Artisanal Production in Toronto's Computer Animation Industry", *Geographische Zeitschrift*, 86(2), 120–133.

The Economist (2000) "The Great Convergence Gamble", *The Economist*, 357, 67–68.

Egan, E.A. and A. Saxenian (1999) "Becoming Digital: Sources of Localisation in the Bat Area Multimedia Cluster", in Braczyk, H.J., G. Fuchs and H.-G. Wolf (eds), *Multimedia and Regional Economic Restructuring*, London: Routledge, pp. 11–29.

Ernst, D. (1999) "How Globalization Reshapes the Geography of Innovation Systems: Reflections on Global Production Networks in Information Industries", Paper presented at DRUID 1999 Summer Conference on Innovation Systems, Copenhagen.

Ewans, P.B. and T.S. Wurster (1997) "Strategy and the New Economics of Information", *Harvard Business Review*, 78, 71–103.

Feldman, M.P. (1994) *The Geography of Innovation*, Dordrecht: Kluwer.

Ferrando, J., J.J. Gabszewicz, D. Laussel and N. Sonnac (2008) "Intermarket Network Externalities and Competition: An Application to the Media Industry", *International Journal of Economic Theory*, 4(3), 357–379.

Ferriani, S., R. Corrado and C. Boschetti (2005) "Organizational Learning Under Organizational Impermanence: Collective Ties in Film Project Firms", *Journal of Management and Governance*, 9(3–4), 257–285.

Florida, R. (2002) *The Rise of the Creative Class: and How It's Transforming Work, Leisure, Community and EveryDay Life*, New York: Basic Books.

Florida, R. (2004) *Cities and the Creative Class*, London: Routledge.

Freeman, C. (1995) "The 'National System of Innovation' in Historical Perspective", *Cambridge Journal of Economics*, 19(1), 5–24.

Freeman, C. and L. Soete (1997) *The Economics of Industrial Innovation*, 3rd ed., London: Pinter.

Fu, W. (2003) "Applying the Structure-Conduct-Performance Framework in the Media Industry Analysis", *The International Journal of Media Management*, 5 (4), 275–284.

Fuchs, G. (2002) "The Multimedia Industry: Networks and Regional Development in a Globalised Economy", *Economic and Industrial Democracy*, 23(3), 305–333.

Fujita, M., P. Krugman and A.J. Venables (1999) *The Spatial Economy*, Cambridge, MA: MIT Press.

Fujita, M. and J.-F. Thisse (2002) *Economics of Agglomeration: Cities, Industrial Location and Regional Growth*, Cambridge, UK: Cambridge University Press.

Gaspar, J. and E.L. Glaeser (1998) "Information Technology and the Future of Cities", *Journal of Urban Economics*, 43(1), 136–156.

Ghosh, S. (1998) "Making Business Sense on the Internet", *Harvard Business Review*, 76, 126–133.

Gibson, C. and L. Kong (2005) "Cultural Economy: A Critical Review", *Progress in Human Geography*, 29(5), 541–561.

Gillespie, A., R. Richardson and J. Cornford (2001) "Regional Development and the New Economy", *European Investment Bank Papers*, 6(1), 109–131.

Glaeser, E.L., H.D. Kallal, J.A. Scheinkman and A. Shleifer (1992) "Growth in Cities", *Journal of Political Economy*, 100(6), 1126–1152.

Glaeser, E.L., D. Laibson, and B. Sacerdote (2002) "An Economic Approach to Social Capital", *The Economic Journal*, 112(483), 437–458.

Grabher, G. (2002) "Cool Projects, Boring Institutions: Temporary Collaboration in Social Context", *Regional Studies*, 36(special issue), 205–214.

Hagel III, J. and M. Singer (1999) "Unbundling the Corporation", *Harvard Business Review*, 77, 133–141.

Hall, P. (1998) *Cities in Civilization: Culture, Innovation and Urban Order*, London: Weinfield and Nicholson.

Hansen, H.K., J. Vang-Lauridsen and B.T. Asheim (2005) "The Creative Class and Regional Growth: Towards a Knowledge Based Approach", Paper presented at "Regional Growth Agendas" Conference, Regional Studies Association, Aalborg, Denmark, March 28–31.

Hayek, F. ([1945], 1992) "Economics and Knowledge" in *Individualism and Economic Order*, Chicago: University of Chicago Press, pp. 33–56.

Held, D. et al. (1999) *Global Transformations: Politics, Economics and Culture*, Stanford, CA: Stanford University Press.

Hendriks, P. (1995) "Communications Policy and Industrial Dynamics in Media Markets: Toward a Theoretical Framework for Analysing Media Industry Organisation", *Journal of Media Economics*, 8(6), 61–76.

Hess, T. and B. Von Walter (2006) "Toward Content Intermediation: Shedding New Light on the Media Sector", *International Journal of Media Management*, 8(1), 2–8.

Hitters, E. and G. Richards (2002) "The Creation and Management of Cultural Clusters", *Creativity and Innovation Management*, 11(4), 234–247.

Hotelling, H. (1929) "Stability in Competition", *Economic Journal*, 39(153), 41–57.

Jacobs, J. (1969) *The Economy of Cities*, New York: Vintage Books.

Jacobs, J. (1984) *Cities and the Wealth of Nations: Principles of Economic Life*, New York: Random House.

Johansson, B., C. Karlsson and R.R. Stough (2001) (eds) *Theories of Endogenous Regional Growth – Lessons for Regional Policies*, Cheltenham, UK and Northampton, MA, USA: Edward Elgar.

Karlsson, C. (2008a) (ed.), *Handbook of Research on Cluster Theory*, Cheltenham, UK and Northampton, MA, USA: Edward Elgar.

Karlsson, C. (2008b) (ed.), *Handbook of Research on Innovation and Clusters*, Cheltenham, UK and Northampton, MA, USA: Edward Elgar.

Karlsson, C. and R.G. Picard (2011) (eds) *Media Clusters: Spatial Agglomeration and Content Capabilities*, Cheltenham, UK and Northampton, MA, USA: Edward Elgar.

Karlsson, C., B. Johansson and R.R. Stough (2010) "Introduction", in Karlsson, C., B. Johansson and R.R. Stough (eds), *Entrepreneurship and Regional Development. Local Processes and Global Patterns*, Cheltenham, UK and Northampton, MA, USA: Edward Elgar, pp. 1–27.

Klaesson, J., Johansson, B. and Karlsson, C. (eds) (2013) *Metropolitan Regions: Knowledge Infrastructures of the Global Economy*, Collection Advances in Spatial Science, Berlin: Springer.

Kling, R. and R. Lamb (2000) "IT and Organizational Change in Digital Economies: A Socio-technical Approach", in Brynjolfsson, E. and B. Kahin (eds), *Understanding the Digital Economy – Data, Tools, and Research*, Cambridge, MA: MIT Press, pp. 295–324.

Kneips, G. (2003) "Competition in Telecommunications and Internet Services: A Dynamic Perspective", in Barfield, C.E., G. Heiduk and P.J.J. Welfens (eds), *Internet, Economic Growth and Globalisation. Perspectives on the New Economy in Europe, Japan and the US*, Berlin: Springer, pp. 217–227.

Knoke, K. (1996) *Bold New World: The Essential Road Map to the Twenty-First Century*, New York: Kodansha.

Krätke, S. (2002) "Network Analysis of Production Clusters: The Potsdam, Babelsberg Film Industry as an Example", *European Planning Studies*, 10(1), 27–54.

Krätke, S. (2003) "Global Media Cities in a World-Wide Urban Network", *European Planning Studies*, 11(6), 605–628.

Krätke, S. and P.J. Taylor (2004) "A World Geography of Global Media Cities", *European Planning Studies*, 12(4), 459–477.

Krugman, P.E. (1991a) *Geography and Trade*, Cambridge, MA: MIT Press.

Krugman, P.E. (1991b) "Increasing Returns and Economic Geography", *Journal of Political Economy*, 99(3), 483–499.

Landry, C. and F. Bianchini (1995) *The Creative City*, London: Demas.

Malmberg, A. and P. Maskell (2002) "The Elusive Concept of Localisation Economies – Towards a Knowledge-Based Theory of Spatial Clustering", *Environment and Planning*, A34(3), 429–449.

Mankiw, N.G. and M.D. Whinston (1986) "Free Entry and Social Efficiency", *Rand Journal of Economics*, 17 (Spring), 48–58.

Marcusen, A. (1996) "Sticky Places in Slippery Space – A Typology of Industrial Districts", *Economic Geography*, 72, 293–313.

Martin, R. and P. Sunley (1996) "Paul Krugman's Geographical Economics and Its Implications for Regional Theory: A Critical Assessment", *Regional Studies*, 77(3), 259–292.

Maskell, P. (2001) "Towards a Knowledge-Based Theory of a Geographical Cluster", *Industrial and Corporate Change*, 10(4), 921–943.

McCann, P. (1995) "Rethinking the Economics of Location and Agglomeration", *Urban Studies*, 32(3), 563–577.

McCann, P. (2001) *Urban and Regional Economics*, Oxford: Oxford University Press.

McCann, P. (2004) "Urban scale economies: statics and dynamics", in R. Capello and P. Nijkamp (eds) *Urban Dynamics and Growth: Advances in Urban Economics*, Amsterdam: Elsevier, pp. 31–56.

McCann, P. (2008) "Agglomeration economics", in Charlie Karlsson (ed.) *Handbook of Research On Cluster Theory*, Cheltenham, UK and Northampton, MA, USA: Edward Elgar, pp. 23–38.

McChesney, R.W. (1999) "The New Global Media", *The Nation*, November 29, 11–15.

Mommaas, H. (2004) "Cultural Clusters and the Post-Industrial City: Towards a Remapping of Urban Cultural Policy", *Urban Studies*, 41(3), 507–532.

Morley, D. and K. Robins (1995) *Spaces of Identity: Global Media, Electronic Landscapes, Cultural Boundaries*, London: Routledge.

Mossig, I. (2004) "The Networks Producing Television Programmes in the Cologne Media Cluster: New Firm Formation, Flexible Specialization and Efficient Decision-Making Structures", *European Planning Studies*, 12(2), 155–171.

Nachum, L. and D. Keeble (2003) "Neo-Marshallian Clusters and Global Networks. The Linkages of Media Firms in Central London", *Long Range Planning*, 36(5), 459–480.

Naisbitt, R. (1995) *The Global Paradox*, New York: Avon Books.

Neff, G. (2005) "The Changing Place of Cultural Production: The Location of Social Networks in a Digital Media Industry", *Annals, AAPSS*, 597(1), 134–152.

Negroponte, N. (1995) *Being Digital*, New York: Vintage Books.

O'Regan, T. (2011) "Styles of National and Global Integration: Charting Media Transformation in Australian Cities", *Studies in Australasian Cinema*, 5(3), 223–238.

Ogawa, H. (2000) "Spatial Impact of Information Technology Development", *The Annals of Regional Science*, 34(3), 537–551.

Oinas, P. (2002) "Competition and Collaboration in Interconnected Places: Towards a Research Agenda", *Geografiska Annaler: Series B, Human Geography*, 84(2), 65–76.

Owen, B.M. and S.S. Wildman (1992) *Video Economics*, Cambridge, MA: Harvard University Press.

Pandit, N.R., G.A.S. Cook and G.M.P. Swann (2002) "A Comparison of Clustering Dynamics in the British Broadcasting and Financial Services Industries", *International Journal of Economics and Business*, 9(2), 195–224.

Piazolo, D. (2001) "The Digital Divide", *CESifo Forum 2*, No. 3, 29–34.

Picard, R.G. (2008) "Media Clusters: Local Agglomeration in an Industry Developing Networked Virtual Clusters", Working Paper 2008-3, Jönköping International Business School.

Picard, R.G. (2010) *The Economics and Financing of Media Companies*, 2nd ed., New York: Fordham University Press.

Piore, M.J. and C.F. Sabel (1984) *The Second Industrial Divide: Possibilities for Prosperity*, New York: Basic Books.

Potts, J. and S. Cunningham (2008) "Four Models of Creative Industries", *International Journal of Cultural Policy*, 14(3), 233–247.

Power, D. and A.J. Scott (2004) "A Prelude to Cultural Industries and the Production of Culture", in Power, D. and A.J. Scott (eds), *The Cultural Industries and the Production of Culture*, London: Routledge, pp. 3–15.

Power, D. (2011) *The Creative and Cultural Industries*, The European Cluster Observatory: Priority Sector Report, European Commission, Enterprise and Industry, Europa Innova, Paper no. 16, Uppsala University.

Pratt, A.C. (1999) *Digital Places*, London: London School of Economics.

Pratt, A.C. (2000) "New Media, the New Economy and New Spaces", *Geoforum*, 31(4), 425–436.

Pratt, A.C. (2002) "Hot Jobs in Cool Places: The Material Cultures of New Media Product Spaces: The Case of the South of Market, San Francisco", *Information Communication and Society*, 5(1), 27–50.

Pratt, A.C. and T.A. Hutton (2013) "Reconceptualising the Relationship Between the Creative Economy and the City: Learning from the Financial Crisis", *Cities: Special Issue on the Creative Economy and the Financial Crisis*, 33, 86–95.

Quah, D. (1999) "A Weightless Economy", *The Unesco Courier*, Summer, 4(2), 30–32.

Robins, K. (1995) "The New Spaces of Global Media", in Johnston, R.J., P.J. Taylor and M.J. Watts (eds), *Geographies of Global Change. Remapping the World in the Late Twentieth Century*, Oxford: Basil Blackwell, pp. 232–247.

Rosenberg, N. (1963) "Technological Change in the Machine Tool Industry, 1840–1910", *The Journal of Economic History*, 23(4), 414–446.

Rosse, J.N. and J.N. Dertouzos (1978) "Economic Issues in Mass Communication Industries", in *Proceedings of the Symposium on Media Concentration*, Volume 1, Washington, D.C.: Federal Trade Commission, pp. 40–192.

Rosse, J.N. (1979) "The Evolution of One-Newspaper Cities", in Federal Trade Commission, *Proceedings of the Symposium on Media Concentration*, Volume 3, Washington, D.C. : Federal Trade Commission, pp. 429–471.

Sahal, D. (1985) "Technological Guideposts and Innovation Avenues", *Research Policy*, 14(2), 61–82.

Sassen, S. (1994) *Cities in a World Economy*, Thousand Oaks, CA: Pine Forge Press.

Saxenian, A.-L. (1994) *Regional Advantage: Culture and Competition in Silicon Valley and Route 128*, Cambridge, MA: Harvard University Press.

Schumpeter, J. ([1934], 2007) *The Theory of Economic Development: An Inquiry into Profits, Capital, Credit, Interest and the Business Cycle*, New Brunswick, USA: Transaction.

Scott, A.J. (1988a) *New Industrial Spaces*, London: Pion.

Scott, A.J. (1988b) *Metropolis: From the Division of Labor to Urban Form*, Berkeley: University of California Press.

Scott, A.J. (1996) "The Craft, Fashion, and Cultural-Products Industries of Los Angeles: Competitive Dynamics and Policy Dilemmas in a Multisectoral Image-Producing Complex", *Annals of the Association of American Geographers*, 86(2), 306–323.
Scott, A.J. (1997) "The Cultural Economy of Cities", *International Journal of Urban and Regional Research*, 21(2), 323–339.
Scott, A.J. (1998a) "From Silicon Valley to Hollywood: Growth and Development of the Multimedia Industry in California", in Braczyk, H.-J., Cooke P. and Heidenreich M. (eds), *Regional Innovation Systems*, London: UCL Press, pp. 136–162.
Scott, A.J. (1998b) *Regions and the World Economy: The Coming Shape of Global Production, Competition and Political Order*, Oxford: Oxford University Press.
Scott, A. (1999) "The Cultural Economy: Geography and the Creative Field", *Media, Culture and Society*, 21(6), 807–817.
Scott, A.J. (2000a) *The Cultural Economy of Cities*, London: Sage.
Scott, A.J. (2000b) "The Cultural Economy of Paris", *International Journal of Urban and Regional Research*, 24(3), 567–582.
Scott, A.J. (2001) "Capitalism, Cities, and the Production of Symbolic Forms", *Transactions of the Institute of British Geographers NS 26*, pp. 11–23.
Shapiro, J.M. (2005) "Smart Cities: Quality of Life, Productivity and the Growth Effects of Human Capital", NBER Working paper 11615, National Bureau of Economic Research, September.
Simmie, J. (2002) "Trading Places: Competitive Cities in the Global Economy", *European Planning Studies*, 10(2), 201–214.
Starkey, K., C. Barnatt and S. Tempest (2000) "Beyond Networks and Hierarchies: Latent Organizations in the U.K. Television Industry", *Organization Science*, 11(3), 299–305.
Storper, M. and S. Christopherson (1987) "Flexible Specialisation and Regional Industrial Agglomerations: The Case of the US Motion-Picture Industry", *Annals of the Association of American Geographers*, 77(1), 260–282.
Storper, M. and B. Harrison (1991) "Flexibility, Hierarchy and Regional Development: The Changing Structure of Industrial Production Systems and their Forms of Governance in the 1990s", *Research Policy*, 20(5), 407–422.
Storper, M. (1997) "Regional Economies as Relational Assets", in Lee, R. and J. Willis (eds), *Geographies of Economies*, London: Arnold, pp. 248–258.
Storper, M. and A.J. Venables (2004) "Buzz: Face-to-Face Contact and the Urban Economy", *Journal of Economic Geography*, 4(4), 351–370.
Sydow, J. and U. Staber (2002) "The Institutional Embeddedness of Project Networks: The Case of Content Production in German Television", *Regional Studies*, 36(3), 215–227.
Thurow, L. (1996) *The Future of Capitalism: How Today's Economic Forces Shape Tomorrow's World*, New York: William Morrow and Company.
Toffler, A. (1980) *The Third Wave*, New York: Bantam Books.
Van den Berg, L., E. Braun and W. van Winden (2001) "Growth Clusters in European Cities: An Integral Approach", *Urban Studies*, 38(1), 185–205.
Venables, A.J. (2001) "Geography and International Inequalities: The Impact of New Technologies", paper presented for World Bank Annual Conference of Development Economics, Washington, D.C., May 2001.
Vogel, H. (1990) *Entertainment Industry Economics*, 3rd ed., Cambridge, UK: Cambridge University Press.
Von Streit, A., G. Montanari, M. Popp, S. Hafner, G. Heinritz, and M. Miosga (2010) *Policies and Strategies for the Creative Knowledge Economy in the Region of Munich: How To Enhance the City's Competitiveness*, ACRE report 10.7, Accommodating Creative Knowledge – Competitiveness of European Metropolitan Regions within the Enlarged Union, University of Amsterdam, Amsterdam.
Waterman, D. (1990) "Diversity and Quality of Information Products in Monopolistically Competitive Markets", *Information Economics and Policy*, 4(4), 291–303.

Waters, M. (1995) *Globalization*, London: Routledge.
Wheeler, J.O., Y. Aoyama and B. Warf (2000) *Cities in the Telecommunications Age. The Fracturing of Geography*, New York: Routledge.
Wolfe, D.A., C. Davis and M. Lucas (2005) "Global Networks and Local Linkages: An Introduction", in Wolfe, D.A. and M. Lucas (eds), *Global Networks and Local Linkages: The Paradox of Cluster Development in an Open Economy*, Kingston: McGill-Queen's University Press, pp. 1–22.
Zukauskaite, E. (2010) "Innovation in Cultural Industries: The Role of University Links", Centre for Innovation, Research and Competence in the Learning Economy (CIRCLE), Paper no. 2010/15, Lund University, 24 pages.
Zukin, S. (1995) *The Cultures of Cities*, Cambridge, MA: Blackwell.

5. Economics of advertising: the role of commercial media

Anthony Dukes

Firms and organizations have the need to communicate with the public. For instance, a consumer package goods manufacturer informs its customers about a new product, or a retail merchant announces its upcoming price reductions. We define this form of communication as *advertising*. As with any form of communication, a medium is necessary to deliver the message. Commercial media is the typical medium for advertising. In this chapter we study the economics of advertising with particular attention to the role that commercial media play in facilitating businesses' and non-profits' desire to communicate with consumers.

We examine advertising from an economic perspective. That is, we assume that advertising is a market activity in which participants respond to their private incentives. The market for advertising is a significant aspect of economic activity – typically over 2 percent of the US gross domestic product in recent years.[1] But where does this money go? Until recently, economists had not addressed this question. Rather, they focused on the demand side of advertising, trying to understand the effects of advertising on consumers and on the markets for the advertised products. Such a focus, however, overlooks the supply side of advertising: the role of commercial media to supply consumer attention to advertisers. The primary source of revenue for commercial media is, in fact, through the sale of advertising. There has been a surge of academic activity that examines the supply side aspects of advertising into which this chapter taps. Doing so provides us a broader perspective on the economics of advertising than simply examining the relationship between advertisers and consumers. The objective is to provide a framework for the media economist to think about the commercial media industry and an important market it serves: the market for advertising. This perspective provides an understanding of how the media shape advertising and its impact on consumers.

The first part of this chapter is devoted to the demand side of the advertising market. We present the classic and modern approaches to advertising. Specifically, we address the following questions: (1) why do advertisers advertise? (2) what are their motives? (3) how do these motives differ depending on the product being advertised? There is a long and rich literature addressing these questions for which we provide an overview.

More recently, economists have turned their attention to the advertising medium. We define the advertising medium as a commercial entity, which earns profits in the sale of commercial advertising. In the second part of this chapter we describe the supply side of the advertising market. We examine how media facilitate the communication process between advertisers and their audiences. Specifically, we answer the question: What is the source of value that media provide to advertisers?

MOTIVES FOR ADVERTISING: THE DEMAND SIDE

This section explores the various roles of advertising as identified in the economics literature. This literature takes advertising as a costly activity undertaken by the seller of a product, a good or service, which presumes to have an impact on the demand for that product. The nature of this effect, however, is a varied issue to which we turn below.[2]

Advertised Products

A common view of advertising that economists adopt is that it informs buyers about products or persuades them that a product is suitable to their needs. The value of advertising and the type of advertising that sellers employ is likely to be determined, at least in part, by characteristics of the products that they are selling. In particular, we can distinguish four types of products: search goods, experience goods, credence goods, and conspicuous goods.

Search goods are products that consumers can fully evaluate before a purchase. For example, a consumer can inspect a shirt (for quality, fit, and so on) and accurately anticipate its net benefit before buying. Such products are referred to as search goods because a consumer search is sufficient by itself to make an informed purchase decision. For search goods, advertising is used to lower the consumer's search cost by informing the consumer about the product's existence, helping the consumer locate where it is available, identifying the price that must be paid, and describing product characteristics.

For some products, however, the consumption benefits cannot be known until after purchase. We refer to these products as *experience goods* to reflect that they must be experienced before fully knowing the level of quality. We distinguish between two types of experience goods:

convenience goods and shopping goods. Convenience goods are products for which consumers cannot be sure of the quality until they consume it, but because the product is low priced and purchased on a frequent basis, consumers are able to use information from past purchases to make informed choices. Beverages are a good example of this type of product. As repeat business is important to suppliers of convenience goods, suppliers have an incentive to provide stable quality levels so that consumers experience the same level of quality across their purchases. Given these product characteristics, product sampling is a cost-effective learning strategy for convenience goods. Because suppliers want to encourage customers to include their product in their sampling, they have an incentive to advertise to encourage trial of their product. The accuracy of claims made in these advertisements are subject to repeated checks by consumers that may lead them to become confident in the accuracy of claims made by particular brands and thus more willing to try new products introduced by those same brands. Moreover, with respect to an individual convenience good, the stability of the product and the information provided by historical trial may move the particular brand from having the characteristics of an "experience good" towards having the characteristics of a "search good" and may force retailers who resell these products to be careful about how they price them, as comparison shopping can be done relatively easily.

In contrast, shopping goods are high-priced goods that are purchased on an infrequent basis. Automobiles are a good example of a shopping good. Because sampling is costly, consumers will make greater use of the information and signals contained in advertising when buying shopping goods than when buying convenience goods (Laband, 1986). However, because the detailed information that consumers often demand before buying shopping goods can sometimes be provided in other, less costly ways, such as through point-of-sale instruction by a salesperson, advertising levels are not always as high for these goods as one might expect. For instance, Porter (1974) found that the average advertising outlay as a percentage of sales was 4.7 percent across 19 convenience goods industries and only 2.1 percent across 23 shopping goods industries.

Another category of goods are *credence goods*. The quality of these goods cannot be fully assessed even through trial. A typical example is the maintenance service of an auto mechanic because the driver can never know for sure whether the car would continue to perform without that service. As another example, suppose a bar patron buys a certain brand of beer to impress friends of his refined taste in malt beverages. Beyond the enjoyment of the beer itself, added benefit accrues to the purchaser because of what he believes others think of him. But because he may never know how much his fellow bar goers are impressed, he cannot be sure of the benefit of the product even after consumption. For these goods, advertising may be used to reinforce the notion that a product will provide high levels of utility. In the beer example, for instance, brand advertising conveys positive associations of those who drink the beer. These associations are communicated not only to the consumer but also to his friends.

The utility of consuming *conspicuous goods* depends in part on third-party's reactions because these goods not only satisfy material needs but also social needs such as prestige. Conspicuous goods include things such as jewellery, perfumes, and watches that obtain some of their value from the prestige that individuals get when others recognize that the individual is consuming exclusive goods (Amaldoss and Jain, 2005). In fact, unlike typical products, the demand for conspicuous goods may rise with price. As discussed below, conspicuous goods are often associated with mass advertisements.

Roles of Advertising

Not only are there different types of products, there are different types of advertising. Classical treatments of advertising sometimes distinguish three types of advertising: informative, persuasive, and complementary (Tirole, 1988).

Informative advertising is advertising that firms undertake to communicate product information to the consumer. This information enables the consumer to evaluate the utility she will obtain from buying the product, thus making informative advertising more suitable for search goods. A magazine advertisement might, for example, show pictures of the product, describe its features, and inform upon how or where to purchase it. To be fully informative, the advertisement must also indicate the price of the product. Grocery or department store "mailers" that announce sales and special product offers are prototypical examples of informative advertising.

The lack of hard information on a typical television commercial, however, suggests that the advertising often does not involve the direct provision of detailed information about a product. Classical treatments of advertising explain this observation by suggesting that advertising also has a *persuasive* role. Specifically, advertisers use advertising to communicate messages designed to raise the consumers' willingness to pay for their product. It is in this sense that advertising "persuades" a potential buyer that there is greater benefit from the product than she had previously believed.

A key difference between these two roles is that, with informative advertising, a consumer's knowledge of the product (existence, price, where to buy, and so on) is updated upon seeing the advertisement, while her fundamental preferences remain unchanged. In contrast, a persuasive advertisement affects a consumer's preference for the product.

The persuasive role of advertising assumes that consumer preferences are subject to change and that affected consumers are unable to overcome the persuasive intention of the advertising firm. Such an assumption might be difficult to maintain if consumers are rational. Any seller of an experience good, for instance, may claim that its product is high quality, regardless of the true quality level. A rational consumer should then consider all persuasive messages meaningless.

We offer an explanation of how persuasive advertising can credibly communicate a product's quality to a rational consumer. Nelson (1974) was the first to suggest the signalling role of advertising.[3] To illustrate his argument, consider the case when sellers of an experience good cannot make credible claims about high quality – a low-quality seller loses little by claiming its quality is high. A seller of high-quality experience goods can, however, signal its quality by spending a sufficient amount on advertising. Suppose consumers become repeat customers only if they enjoy high quality upon the first trial. Due to repeat sales, the high-quality seller has more potential profit than a low-quality imitator. In order to credibly convince the consumer it is high quality, the seller can publicly spend off or "burn" some of these future profits by advertising to such an extent that a low-quality producer would find it unprofitable to imitate. The rational consumer observes this seller spending lots of money on advertising and concludes that it is offering a high-quality product. It is worthwhile to note that the advertising message itself is irrelevant beyond the cost to provide it so long as consumers know how much money was burned. Hence, a widely publicized charitable donation can be a credible signal in the same way as a costly advertising campaign.

The signalling theory offers an alternative to the persuasive advertising theory when trying to explain why certain types of persuasive advertising contain little direct information. To the extent that high levels of advertising signal higher quality, the mere act of advertising conveys reliable quality information to consumers and is thus consistent with the observation that famous brands of cars, dish detergent, and other goods with experience attributes are heavily advertised on television and contain little hard information other than "look how much money I'm spending on advertising".

One still has difficulty using the signalling argument to explain all forms of persuasive advertising. Products such as popular brands of cola and beer have long been in existence, and it is likely that most people have experienced them at some point or another. The signalling story, therefore, is an unlikely role for the ubiquitous advertising for these popular brands given that most people have tasted them and evaluated their true quality. As a result, the signalling role of advertising has been more commonly attributed to new product launches (Milgrom and Roberts, 1986).

The quality-signalling role of advertising has received some, but limited, empirical support. The strongest support comes from experimental marketing studies (Kirmani, 1990). Caves and Greene (1996), on the other hand, find few correlations between advertising outlays and consumer reports' ratings of quality.

Complementary advertising, typically used for credence and conspicuous products, involves the notion that advertising provides an image that complements the physical characteristics of the product (Becker and Murphy, 1993). For instance, consider a television commercial that shows a famous basketball player wearing a particular brand of footwear. Such an advertisement might give a teenager a chance to enjoy an association with the famous player when wearing the shoes. The teenager then accrues an added benefit from this association beyond any inherent quality characteristics of the shoe itself. The seller may accordingly charge a premium for the product in order to capture this added value.

Closely related to complementary advertising is its ability to facilitate social interactions within consumer segments. To illustrate, suppose a man smokes and wants to smoke what other men smoke. Perhaps more specifically, he would rather not smoke something that women smoke. If there are several brands of cigarettes and men do not know what their peers are smoking, then they will guess among existing brands. If, on the other hand, a cigarette brand Y designs and airs advertising that appeals only to men, then men conclude that brand Y is for them. Furthermore, men also know that women saw this advertisement and do not buy brand Y. Hence all men coordinate on the "right" brand. This *coordination role* of advertising was introduced by Chwe (1998) and is a compelling explanation for the prominence of advertising for conspicuously consumed products, such as status goods (Kuksov and Xie, 2012).

Given the different types of advertising and types of products, it is not surprising that different products are associated with different levels and types of advertising. For example, products that are pure search goods, such as homogeneous products that are easily graded (such as commodities), are observed to have much lower levels of advertising than experience goods (Greer, 1992). While the hypothesis remains to be fully tested, it seems that when a consumer's utility depends directly on who else consumes the good, advertising may serve more of the coordinating role than other roles. However, these types of generalities may not hold in particular circumstances because firms can convey information and brand image to consumers using other forms of promotion, such as sales support, product packaging, and trial sampling. Moreover, because consumers have diverse preferences, different advertising and promotional strategies may be used to target distinct types of consumers.

ROLE OF THE MEDIUM: THE SUPPLY SIDE

The motives of advertising described above concern only one side of the market for advertising. Economic research over the past decade has explored the supply side of the advertising market (Dukes, 2004). Specifically, the market for advertising requires that there is a supply of consumer attention to commercial advertisements. While many consumers seek advertising messages (for example, in fashion magazines, tourist brochures, and internet search advertising), a lot of advertising is bundled with non-advertising content, which is the primary focus of the consumer (for example, viewer, listener, or reader). The media provide such non-advertising content to lure the viewer, subject her to commercial messages, and sell this attention to advertisers. In fact, advertising sales are typically the primary source of revenue for commercial media. This is the supply role of commercial media.

The idea that media serve as the supply side of advertising arises from the notion of a two-sided market (Rochet and Tirole, 2003; Armstrong, 2006). Commercial media tend to the market needs of viewers on one side and to the advertisers' needs on the other. The economics literature utilizes this perspective to understand the role of the advertising market on the structure of media industry (Goettler and Shachar, 2001; Gal-Or and Dukes, 2006; Wilbur, 2008b) and the corresponding impact on media pricing (Kaiser and Wright, 2006; Godes et al., 2009).

The benefit of this two-sided market perspective is in recognizing that the media have a stake in the success of its advertisers. The attention that consumers pay to advertising messages ultimately determines advertisings' financial returns. These returns take the form of purchases (or some desired action) by the viewer, which correspondingly benefits the advertiser. The extent to which media affect advertising's financial return helps us understand many of the strategies observed in the media industry. In this section, we explore this notion in detail. We focus on three functions of the media that serve advertisers. First, media attract the attention of viewers in order to serve them advertising. Second, media provide a means to segment viewers for the purpose of targeting. Finally, media, in an increasing number of cases, provide cover, or stealth, for advertisers to deliver their messages with more credibility.

Attracting Attention

The success of commercial media relies on the fact that its viewers will be exposed to advertisers' messages (Anderson and Coate, 2005; Dukes, 2006; Wilbur, 2008b). In many settings consumers may actively seek out these messages (as discussed later) but often they view such commercial advertising as a nuisance (Kaiser and Song, 2009) and too much of it may reduce a medium's audience. In fact, Wilbur (2008b) estimates that a 10 percent reduction in advertising time leads to a 25 percent increase in television viewing. So, while attractive content encourages viewers to subscribe to a medium, there is no guarantee that viewers will be exposed to or react to an advertisement. Media have various techniques to control the viewer's or listener's engagement in the advertisement and the degree of this control depends on the form of the media. We explore this issue below.

Classical print media typically have the least control over how much attention the reader pays. For instance, readers can simply turn the page or overlook ads on a page in lieu of focusing on the content of interest. Print media have strategies to intervene in the readers' experience and direct their attention to the advertisement. Newspapers utilize colour print, attractive pictures, or other means to draw the readers' attention to the advert. Alternatively, magazines devote thicker pages to print ads or use drop-out cards, which must be picked up off the floor, to direct consumers' attention away from the content and toward the advert. Internet media, with purely readable content (that is, non-video), have more control over viewers' attention than print media. Banner ads can be customized for relevance and updated instantly, and pop-up ads are more likely to be acknowledged because an action must be taken to avoid or close the ad window.

Informative and persuasive roles for advertising occur in print form. Detailed information or persuasive arguments are well suited for print since interested consumers can engage in the advertisement at length. The signalling role of advertising may also be at play in print. Recall that for the signalling role, the reader need only notice that a significant amount of money was spent by the advertiser. An expensive full-page, colour ad in a prominent location, such as the back cover of a publication, can serve this purpose.

Audio media such as radio and online streaming rely on listeners to stay through the commercials to hear more of the content of interest. Unlike readers of print media, listeners of audio media cannot skip commercial messages without disengaging with that medium altogether. Listeners may often be simultaneously engaged in another activity (for example work) and disengaging with the medium simply to avoid commercials is not worth it. In addition, music or talk radio programs typically bait listeners just before commercial breaks by suggesting that there is something worth sitting through the commercial for.

Visual media, such as television and online video, typically have more control over the engagement of their viewers to advertising. Relative to audio media, viewers must be visually engaged with the medium to enjoy the content. Because of this engagement, visual media hook the viewer to "stay tuned" through the commercials to continue with or conclude the content. Because viewers dislike sitting through adverts, they may tend to drift from the channel to another one or to a different activity if the commercial breaks are too long (Siddarth and Chattopadhyay, 1998). Zhou (2003) investigates the scheduling and length of commercial breaks that optimize the number of viewers that see adverts. He finds that, due to the increasing level of the viewer's engagement as the program progresses, the best scheduling strategy places longer commercials toward the end of the program.

Online video platforms, user-generated content (UGC) sites (such as Youtube.com) and online television ventures (such as Hulu.com) typically force the viewer to sit through an advertisement before being shown the desired content. Interestingly, these online video media are more interactive and tend to be shorter. This may be due to the greater levels of distractions online. One potential implication of this is that commercial breaks tend to be shorter than those on television. Nevertheless, the mechanism of retaining viewer attention is the same.

The visual media discussed above pose another advantage over print and audio media with respect to control over viewers' engagement in advertising. Unlike audio, a visual medium can intrude with advertising messages, albeit modestly, into the content without fully interrupting it. Product placement and "ad bugs" are techniques seen in television broadcasting. Ad bugs appear on the screen during regular programming and convey little more than brand logos (Kaplan, 2001). Such logos serve as reminders of the brand but convey little additional information. Product placement, however, is considerably more intertwined with the content. Finally, with UGC platforms like Youtube.com, ads appear at the bottom of the viewing screen and offer a link to learn more about the advertised product.

The above discussion focused on media for which viewers eschew advertising messages. But, in some cases, a commercial medium may serve as a destination for consumers who seek out advertising to learn about products. This may be why home decorating and fashion magazines contain more advertising pages than editorial content.[4] Media's role in these cases is to identify relevant advertisers for their audiences and provide advertising in accessible ways. Search advertising, which was traditionally facilitated by Yellow Pages, is now largely done with internet search engines. Here the consumer indicates his or her interests by entering the search query. This enables the medium to determine context-specific ads for the consumer. Search engines such as Yahoo! and Google auction off keywords that are matched with the consumers' search queries. Search engines are media in which the consumer's level of interest in the advertising is a direct result of the search for information. In that sense, her participation is direct, rather than passive as in more conventional media forms such as television or radio.

The emergence of ad avoidance technology (AAT), such as digital video recorders (DVRs), has posed a recent challenge to the role of media to bring advertising to television viewers (Wilbur, 2008a). In response, television has increased the use of product placement in its content. One might also reason that AAT has had a negative impact on the amount of advertising aired by television channels. Wilbur (2008b), however, finds the opposite. He reasons that those viewers who remain without AAT tend to be less averse to commercials, creating the incentives for television broadcasters to provide more of them.

Targeting

Another role of the media for advertisers is to improve the ability of advertisers to target their communication to potential customers. By targeting, advertisers avoid ad spending on those who are unlikely to buy their product regardless of the advertising message (Iyer et al., 2005). Furthermore, by sending the most relevant advertisements, consumers tend to be more engaged in the advertising they do see. The advertising industry consistently expresses concerns over "ad clutter" – a tendency for advertisers to bombard consumers with ad messages creating the tendency of consumers to tune out of all ads (Kent and Allen, 1993). Better ad targeting is, therefore, believed to generate an industry-wide benefit by making each individual ad more effective (Kim and Sundar, 2010).

The ability for media to provide targeting opportunities for advertisers requires knowledge about consumers' preference over products they might be interested in buying. There are two ways this knowledge is obtained. Knowledge about preferences can be collected directly by the medium or it may be inferred by the viewer's behaviour. The latter is referred to as behaviour-based targeting because it utilizes a consumer's behaviour to facilitate ad targeting. Otherwise, targeting simply uses direct information provided to the medium for the purposes of better targeting. We first discuss behaviour-based targeting.

Conventional media, like television, radio, and print, largely utilize behaviour-based targeting strategies. Such strategies rely on a correlation between a viewers' taste for content and for product interest (Belk, 1988). For instance, a consumer's choice of what radio station to listen to and when can provide an indication of the type of person she is. A country music listener in Kansas, for example, is more likely interested in American-made automobiles than a jazz radio listener in Los Angeles. Media research firms such as Arbitron study the psychographic patterns present in listening audiences for the purposes of targeting (Lane et al., 2005). Recognizing this, media provide a variety of content in order to provide targeting opportunities for their advertisers. In fact, over the previous 20 years, there has been a proliferation of specialized cable channels. According to Nielsen research, in 2007, the average home received 118.6 channels (The Nielsen Company, 2008). By allowing viewers to more precisely indicate their preferences or lifestyles, advertisers can better know who is likely to be interested in their messages.

An association of a viewer's content interest and product preference has provided radio and television advertisers ample targeting opportunities. However, the internet permits additional opportunities for media to facilitate targeting. In contrast to television viewing or radio listening, internet use is more interactive. This distinction gives online media additional opportunities to facilitate targeting that is more precise than with conventional media. Online news media and other online providers of content often ask readers to register so that they can collect useful information for their advertisers (Loviglio, 2004). Online media also facilitate the use of browsing behaviour to identify what advertisements are most relevant. Cookies allow online media to track an internet user's browsing behaviour, which may indicate the user's interests and product preferences. The use of such data allows online media to customize ads based on what websites the user has visited before.

Not all behaviour-based targeting methods on commercial media involve an association between content interest and product preferences. Traditional forms of print media, such as magazines and newspapers, offer a platform for advertisers to elaborate on informative or persuasive claims that an interested reader can pursue. Similarly, in written online content, hyperlinks provide an avenue for interested consumers to pursue more information. In contrast, such advertising messages may be overlooked by readers who are not interested in the product in the first place. This process of self-selection conveniently separates readers based on their level of interest and allows marketers to focus their messages accordingly. This process is particularly salient for internet media. For instance, a consumer who arrives at an advertiser's website via a link from a YouTube video knows she has at least an initial interest in that advertiser's product.

It is not only browsing behaviour that online media collect. Social media such as Facebook have recognized that users willingly provide information about their interests and preferences to share with social contacts. The growth of Facebook has relied on advertisers' demand for such information to use for targeting. This form of targeting, which is based on information freely provided by users, permits the use of non-behaviour-based ad targeting because consumers explicitly express what their interests are rather than let their behaviour speak for them. Some on-demand internet video sites and UGC platforms (such as YouTube) also utilize non-behaviour-based targeting when they prompt viewers for their ad preferences. In this case, the website asks the viewer whether or not the advertisement they just saw was relevant for them.[5]

Until now, we have discussed media's role in targeting to an audience for which advertisements are most relevant. However, media may also use targeting to help alleviate competition for advertised products. For instance, some media strategies are aimed at limiting competing product information. Exclusive advertising contracts assure the advertiser that the media will not sell advertising space to any of its competitors. Such contracts are common for major sporting events. Media can charge a premium for exclusive advertising rights because they are likely able to give market power to the advertiser in the sale of its product (Dukes and Gal-Or, 2003).

Providing Stealth

Another means by which commercial media enhance the value of an advertiser's message is to hide the source of advertising or disguise the fact that it is a paid endorsement. Commercial media sometimes try to disguise an advertiser's message so as to make it appear as if it comes from a more credible authority. This is the notion of stealth advertising and it is a fairly recent practice that has emerged as a result of suspicion of marketers and advertising avoidance (Kaikati and Kaikati, 2004). Stealth advertising is utilized in cinema, television, and by online media.

Product placement in movies and television programs is perhaps the most common form of stealth advertising. The advantage of product placement over conventional advertising is that viewers may not easily notice that they are being pitched a product and are therefore less resistant to the association. Furthermore, this gives exposure to an advertiser's product when the consumer is paying the most attention. But product placement offers more than exposure. Under the complementary view of advertising, marketers want to create desirable associations with their product. This can be achieved with product placement since the brand interacts with actors or characters in movies and television programs (Manly, 2005).

Online, many bloggers promote or endorse products without acknowledging that they are being compensated for it. Bloggers can be trusted sources of new information or content and readers value their critiques of products they may have used. Under the persuasive role of advertising, the credibility of the message is often discounted by the recipient. To overcome this, some bloggers can exploit the trust of the readers by not admitting to being compensated for their endorsements (Mayzlin, 2006).

Many consumers object to stealth advertising. They argue that a consumer has the right to know the source of the message. Some advertisers also object to the use of stealth on the grounds that it makes consumers suspicious of all advertisers and sceptical of their messages. Another controversy surrounding stealth advertising, particularly with regard to product placement, is the possibility that artistic or creative content will be dominated by advertisers' interests (Manly, 2005). The controversy surrounding stealth advertising, however, seems to depend on its form. For example, viewers have grown accustomed to product placement, and advertisers' identities are revealed in the credits of the program or movie. On the other hand, bloggers' organizations in the US have lobbied regulators to enforce disclosure rules for paid endorsements (Schatz and Bustillo, 2010).

CONCLUSION

This chapter has introduced the economics of advertising for the reader interested in media economics. As such, we discussed in detail the role of commercial media for the advertising market. Specifically, we view media as the supply side for this market because without it, advertising demand would be considerably harder to fulfil. This approach provides a new perspective on the role of commercial media as a business enterprise. Much of media economics has focused on content choices, journalistic issues, and audiences. However, given that most media survive because of their funding by commercial advertising, media must be cognizant of advertisers' motives to also make a profit. Understanding advertisers' incentives is essential to explain the patterns in commercial media markets.

NOTES

1. Based on author's data from 100 Leading National Advertisers, *Advertising Age*, and Bureau of Economic Analysis, United States Department of Commerce.
2. This section borrows from Dukes (2009).
3. See Klein and Leffer (1981), Kihlstrom and Riordan (1984), and Milgrom and Roberts (1986) for formal extensions of Nelson's idea.
4. While this may typically be informative advertising, it may also be advertising of the coordinating type. For instance, the status conscious who may turn to a fashion magazine to learn the latest are also believed to inform status conscious audiences about which products are "it" (Kuksov and Wang, 2012).
5. See hulu.com/support/article/166625.

REFERENCES

Amaldoss, W. and Jain, S. (2005) 'Pricing of Conspicuous Goods: A Competitive Analysis of Social Effects', *Journal of Marketing Research*, 32, 30–42.

Anderson, S. and Coate, S. (2005) 'Market Provision of Broadcasting. A Welfare Analysis', *Review of Economic Studies*, 72(4), 947–72.

Armstrong, M. (2006) 'Competition in Two-Sided Markets', *RAND Journal of Economics*, 37(3), 688–711.

Becker, G. and Murphy, K. (1993) 'A Simple Theory of Advertising as a Good or Bad', *Quarterly Journal of Economics*, 108(4), 941–64.

Belk, R. (1988) 'Possessions and the Extended Self', *Journal of Consumer Research*, 15(4), 139–68.

Caves, R. and Greene, D. (1996) 'Brands' quality levels, prices and advertising outlays: Empirical evidence on signals and information costs', *International Journal of Industrial Organization*, 14, 29.

Chwe, M. (1998) 'Believe the Hype: Solving Coordination Problems with Television Advertising', University of Chicago, Department of Economics, Working Paper.

Dukes, A. (2004) 'The Advertising Market in a Product Oligopoly', *Journal of Industrial Economics*, 52(3), 327–48.

Dukes, A. (2006) 'Media Concentration and Consumer Product Prices', *Economic Inquiry*, 44, 128.

Dukes, A. (2009) 'Advertising and Competition'. In Wayne Dale Collins (ed.) *Economics of Antitrust*, American Bar Association.

Dukes, A. and Gal-Or, E. (2003) 'Negotiations and Exclusivity Contracts for Advertising', *Marketing Science*, 22(2), 222–45.

Gal-Or, E. and Dukes, A. (2006) 'On the Incentives for Media Mergers', *Journal of Business*, 79(2), 489–525.
Godes, D., Ofek, E., and Sarvary, M. (2009) 'Content vs. Advertising: The Impact of Competition on Media Firm Strategy', *Marketing Science*, 28(1), 20–35.
Goettler, R. and Shachar, R. (2001) 'Spatial Competition in the Network Television Industry', *RAND Journal of Economics*, 32, 624–56.
Greer, D. (1992) *Industrial Organization and Public Policy*, New York: MacMillan.
Iyer, G., Soberman, D., and Villas-Boas, M. (2005) 'The Targeting of Advertising', *Marketing Science*, 24(3), 461–76.
Kaikati, A. and Kaikati, J. (2004) 'Stealth Marketing: How to Reach Consumers Surreptitiously', *California Management Review*, 46(4), 6–24.
Kaiser, U. and Wright, J. (2006) 'Price Structure in Two-Sided Markets: Evidence from the Magazine Industry', *International Journal of Industrial Organization*, 24(1), 1–28.
Kaiser, U. and Song, M. (2009) 'Do Media Consumers Really Dislike Advertising? An Empirical Assessment of the Role of Advertising in Print Media Markets', *International Journal of Industrial Organization*, 27(2), 292–301.
Kaplan, D. (2001) 'UPN May Welcome Infestation of Ad Bugs', *The New York Post*, August 20.
Kent, R. and Allen, C. (1993) 'Does Competitive Clutter in Television Advertising "Interfere" with Recall and Recognition of Brand Names and Ad Claims', *Marketing Letters*, 4(2), 175–84.
Kihlstrom, R. and Riordan, M. (1984) 'Advertising as a Signal', *Journal of Political Economy*, 92, 427.
Kim, N.Y. and Sundar, S.S. (2010) 'Relevance to the Rescue: Can "Smart Ads" Reduce Negative Response to Online Ad Clutter?' *Journalism and Mass Communication Quarterly*, 87(2), 346–62.
Kirmani, A. (1990) 'The Effect of Perceived Advertising Costs on Brand Perceptions', *Journal of Consumer Research*, 17, 160.
Klein, B. and Leffer, K.B. (1981) 'The Role of Market Forces in Assuring Contractual Performance', *Journal of Political Economy*, 89, 615.
Kuksov, D. and Wang, K. (2013) 'A Model of the "It" Products in Fashion', *Marketing Science*, 32(1), 51–69.
Kuksov, D. and Xie, Y. (2012) 'Competition for Status Goods', *Journal of Marketing Research*, 49(5), 609–23.
Laband, D. (1986) 'Advertising as Information: An Empirical Note', *Review of Economics and Statistics*, 68(3), 517–21.
Lane, W.R., King, K.W., and Russell, J.T. (2005) *Kleppner's Advertising Procedure*, 16th edn, Prentice Hall: New Jersey.
Loviglio, J. (2004) 'Newspapers Riding Out Complaints Over Online Registration', *The Associated Press*, June 13.
Manly, L. (2005) 'When the Ad Turns into the Story: On Television, Brands Go from Props to Stars', *New York Times*, October 2.
Mayzlin, D. (2006) 'Promotional Chat on the Internet', *Marketing Science*, 25(2), 155–63.
McClellan, S. (2005) 'Nielsen: Ad clutter spikes', *Mediaweek*, 15(39), 6–8.
Milgrom, P. and Roberts, J. (1986) 'Price and Advertising Signals of Quality', *Journal of Political Economy*, 94(4), 796–821.
Nelson, P. (1974) 'Advertising as Information', *Journal of Political Economy*, 82(4), 729–54.
Nielsen Company, The (2008), 'Average US Home Now Receives a Record 118.6 TV Channels, According to Nielsen', Press Release, June 6.
Porter, M. (1974) 'Consumer Behavior, Retailer Power, and Market Performance in Consumer Goods Industries', *Review of Economics and Statistics*, 56(4), 419–36.

Rochet, J.-C. and J. Tirole (2003) 'Platform Competition in Two-Sided Markets', *Journal of the European Economic Association*, 1(4), 990–1029.

Schatz, A. and Bustillo, M. (2010) 'U.S. Tells Bloggers to Reveal Financial Ties', *Wall Street Journal*, October 7.

Siddarth, S. and Chattopadhyay, A. (1998) 'To Zap or Not to Zap: A Study of the Determinants of Channel Switching During Commercials', *Marketing Science*, 17(2), 124–38.

Tirole, J. (1988) *The Theory of Industrial Organization*, MIT Press.

Wilbur, K. (2008a) 'How the Digital Video Recorder (DVR) Changes Traditional Television Advertising', *Journal of Advertising*, 37(1), 143–9.

Wilbur, K. (2008b) 'A Two-Sided, Empirical Model of Television Advertising and Viewing Markets', *Marketing Science*, 27(3), 356–78.

Zhou, W. (2003) 'The Choice of Commercial Breaks in Television Programs: The Number, Length, and Timing', *Journal of Industrial Economics*, 52(3), 315–26.

6. The pricing of advertising

Agostino Manduchi

1. INTRODUCTION

This chapter is devoted to a survey of the literature on the pricing of advertising. The term 'advertising' is understood in the sense that is most common among practitioners, namely as the various forms of communication initiated by the sellers and finalised with the cooperation of third parties whose goal is 'to inform and/or persuade one or more people' (Fletcher, 2010). Thus, the chapter does not cover activities that are often classified as advertising, in common language, but that are not covered by this definition, such as promotional initiatives related to the design and the packaging of products, sales and communications through the seller's own channels. Consistently with the scope of the Handbook, the chapter focuses on the pricing of the transactions related to advertising in which one of the parties is a media outlet – in particular, the sale of advertising slots in newspapers and magazines, published either on-line or on paper, search engines, websites, TV and radio programmes. In 2012, the sellers of products and services spent an estimated US$483 on advertising (*The Economist*, 2011).

Some forms of advertising were already observed in ancient societies. In classical Athens, for example, the public announcements of the town criers were interspersed with sponsored messages (Fletcher, 2010). The introduction of the printing press with movable type and the appearance of newspapers made advertisements cheaper to produce, and multiplied the opportunities for the sellers to advertise their products. In 1759, the lexicographer Dr Samuel Johnson apparently had already reasons to complain that 'advertisements are now so numerous that they are very negligently perused' (Fletcher, 2008). The industrial revolution brought about further far-reaching developments, as the division of labour and the economies of scale made possible by the intensive use of machinery increased the need for communication among possible exchange partners. Additionally, the advertisement of brand names allowed the manufacturers to increase their bargaining power *vis-à-vis* the intermediaries (Norris, 1980). Recent innovations in information and communication technology have spurred new, dramatic developments in advertising, both directly, by making new tools available to the advertisers, and also indirectly, by introducing new products and services and by re-shaping the production and distribution processes of the existing ones.

The interest in the economic analysis of advertising is however a relatively recent phenomenon. Following Bagwell (2003), we can identify three broad threads in the literature. The 'persuasive' thread, pioneered by Chamberlin (1933), views advertising as a tool used to create product-specific attributes, which can artificially lower the substitutability between products, and thereby allow their producers to charge higher prices. The 'informative' thread, pioneered by Ozga (1960) and by Stigler (1961), focuses on the provision of information in markets in which the buyers are imperfectly informed about the features, the quality and the price of the products offered, and face significant search and learning costs. The 'complementary' thread, started by Stigler and Becker (1977), postulates the existence of synergies between advertising and the products advertised, already built into the buyers' preferences.

The systematic analysis of the pricing of advertising is an even more recent phenomenon, whose development started around the turn of the millennium. Interestingly, the historical paucity of academic literature on the topic does have a counterpart in the literature aimed at practitioners. For example, the analysis of the day-to-day management of an advertising agency presented in two classical references such as Ogilvy (1985) and Ogilvy (2004) essentially disregards pricing. The only exception is a brief comment on the transition witnessed in the 1980s from the traditional system – in which the advertising agencies received a fixed rate-commission on the price charged by the media outlets, typically set at the rate of 15 per cent (Fletcher, 2010) – to the current system of negotiated fees (Ogilvy, 1985, p. 55). This state of affairs was probably due both to the smaller set of analytical tools available, and to a generally profitable environment in which a small number of media outlets and advertising agencies, crafting the advertising campaigns and acting as intermediaries, were faced with a relatively large number of advertisers, and the audiences' brand loyalty was relatively strong. This close-knit supply chain, with relatively stable interactions, may have made experimentation and fast adaptation less important than they are in today's environment, and may therefore have made the market players relatively unwilling to engage in the search for formal accounts of the market mechanics.

The traditional fixed commission payment created a strong incentive for the agencies to sell large numbers of advertising slots. In general, the media outlets would only accept as counterparts agencies that were formally 'recognised' by their industry associations, and the agencies could not offer rebates on their commissions. The limited opportunities for price competition induced many agencies to offer subsidiary services as loss-leaders (Fletcher, 2010). The argument in Choi and Stefanadis (2006) suggests that this bundling of different services may have contributed to deterring entry. In the US, a standard contract provision requiring the advertisers to pay a commission to the old agency for two additional years, after a switch to a new agency, was in place for some time until the mid-1950s, when the government intervened to eliminate it (Tungate, 2007, p. 156). The anti-competitive effects of an artificial switching cost of this type can again be especially penalising for the potential new entrants (Farrell and Klemperer, 2003). The abandonment of the fixed-rate commission was motivated both by explicit restrictions, introduced as law-makers and industry regulators became aware of its anti-competitive effects, and by the growing competition for clients, in a scenario in which many specialists decided to create independent firms targeting specific segments of a larger and more complex market (Fletcher, 2010).

The analysis of the pricing of advertising received a key impulse from the developments of the analysis of 'two sided platforms' and from the emergence of internet advertising. Two-sided platforms are economic subjects mediating the interactions between two (or more) groups of agents (Anderson and Gabszewicz, 2006; Armstrong, 2006; Levin, 2013; Rochet and Tirole, 2006). From this point of view, media outlets represent a link between the audiences, to which they provide information and entertainment, and the advertisers. As we shall see, this analytical framework allows us to take explicit account of the fact that the appeal of any given channel, for the advertisers, depends on the size and the demographic structure of the audience. The same framework makes it possible to consider the attitude of the audience members towards advertising. Some audiences – in particular among the audiences of TV and radio broadcasts – may not appreciate unsolicited advertisements; by contrast, newspaper readers may even be willing to pay a premium for outlets publishing classified advertisements.

Internet advertising emerged in the first half of the 1990s. By 2011, the advertisers' expenditure on this activity reached a level estimated at \$70 billion (Fletcher, 2010). The interactive nature of the medium has created both new opportunities and new challenges. Initially, internet advertisements took the form of 'banners' shown to all visitors of a given website. Advertisements of this type are superficially similar to those published by traditional newspapers. However, their electronic format makes it possible to base the calculation of the price on especially accurate estimates of the number of viewers, if a viewership-based price is charged. Additionally, the possibility to track the viewers' responses to the advertisements allows the media outlets and the advertisers to make the price contingent on measures such as the number of individuals who either visit any websites indicated in the advertisement, or purchase the products advertised.

The opportunities to adapt the set of advertisements displayed to the users' features provided by the internet introduced a further element of novelty. The 'engines' through which the internet users search for information on specific topics typically respond to the users' queries by listing a few sponsored links, along with the 'organic' links – the links that the algorithms used to scan the web identify as especially relevant. The slots allotted to the sponsored links are offered to advertisers registered with the search engine, together with some keywords related to the specific search on which the (automated) purchase strategies can be made conditional. The website managers who wish to 'monetise' the popularity of their sites can offer their advertising slots on similar terms, by participating in programmes offered by specialised intermediaries such as Google's AdSense. In all these cases, fast and efficient matching and pricing routines are critical factors for the success of the advertisements.

The remainder of this chapter is organised as follows. Section 2 discusses the main formats used to set the price of advertising slots. Section 3 presents the approach to media economics based on two-sided platforms, with a special focus on pricing. Section 4 presents the standard auction format used to price internet advertising, and discusses its main features. Section 5 contains some concluding remarks, and indicates possible research directions. Due to space limitations, the chapter does not cover models building on the theory of revenue management. Talluri and van Ryzin (2005) give an excellent coverage of the analytical apparatus and of its applications; an example of an application to the pricing of online banners can be found in Roels and Fridgeirsdottir (2009).

2. THE MAIN PRICING FORMATS

The classic quote 'Half the money I spend on advertising is wasted, and the trouble is I do not know which half' suggests that the effectiveness of advertising has historically been both very uncertain and difficult to identify.[1] Thus, assessing the success of different campaigns – and possibly also the contributions of the single activities within each campaign – has always been regarded as a top priority by the advertisers.

In general, the media outlets and the advertisers can share the effectiveness risk by making the price contingent on some performance measure. Even if the parties featured a similar risk attitude, hedging the advertisers' risk could generally improve the precision of the information about the managerial skills and the project quality conveyed by the accounting data (DeMarzo and Duffie, 1995). Prices conditional on effectiveness also create incentives for the media outlets to provide appealing information and entertainment to their audiences. In the absence of these incentives, a standard 'lemon' problem (Akerlof, 1970) could in principle set in: The advertisers could only accept relatively low prices, providing weak incentives for the media outlets to achieve high levels of exposure, and/or drive the high-exposure outlets out of the market. These effects could ultimately lead to a situation in which either only 'low quality' advertising slots are offered, or the market collapses altogether. Additional strategic factors that may affect the choice of the pricing format are presented in Section 3.

Even traditional advertising channels can provide some reliable measures of effectiveness, for example in the form of coupons handed out by the referrals. The modern information and communication technologies provide an enriched array of measures, which have in turn led to the development of new pricing arrangements. The price – or cost, to use the expression more commonly used by practitioners – of the advertising slots can be specified as:

- A flat fee
- A cost per impression
- A cost per click
- A cost per action

Flat Fee

A flat fee is a price set in terms of the potential exposure received by the advertisements, measured for example by the number of slots in a newspaper or a magazine – either electronic or on paper – or by the broadcasting time. Nominal flat-fee contracts sometimes feature a 'minimal exposure' clause, entitling the advertiser to a price reduction if the audience falls short of a set target; this pricing scheme is a hybrid form between the flat fee, properly understood, and the cost per impression.

If the audience of the media outlet is relatively stable over time – possibly with predictable peaks or troughs, as was and to some extent still is the case for traditional newspapers and magazines – the exposure of the advertisements can be based on historical data, usually collected and made available by certifying agencies. The reliability of the data can be enhanced by the administrative records of the transactions related to the media products imposed by the tax, labour and business laws in general, by the prevailing accounting principles, and by the requirements of the payment system. Predictability can be further enhanced by a relatively large fraction of subscribers over the total readership. From this point of view, the smaller amount of records available may put the free newspapers offered in modern cities at a disadvantage, in comparison with the newspapers and the magazines that are actually sold to the public.

The relation between the circulation of major US newspapers and the prices for the publication of advertisements, even in a system of flat fees, is documented by Cover et al. (1931). In the period covered by this study, the newspapers with a larger circulation typically charged higher prices for the publication of advertisements, but also lower prices per reader reached, possibly due to the lower incidence of the fixed production costs. On a related note, Corden (1952–53, p. 182) identifies the circulation of the newspapers as the primary determinant of the advertisers' willingness to pay for ads.

Cost Per Impression

With a cost per impression, the price paid by the advertiser is explicitly referred to some measure of the actual exposure of the advertisements. The price is most often a linear function of exposure – namely, it is calculated as the product of the estimated size of the audience and the unit price of exposure. Typically, the audience is measured in thousands of individuals; this pricing scheme is thus indicated by the acronym 'CPM', where 'M' stands for *Mil*, from the Latin for 'thousand'. If refined estimates of the audience are available, the parties may choose to focus on some subset(s) of the audience of particular interest for the advertiser.

The difference between a price measured in terms of impressions and a flat fee is most significant if the historical data do not allow the advertisers to form reliable estimates of future exposure. In the case of radio and television, the price is typically referred to the rating points measuring the success of the programme during which the advertisements are broadcast; one rating point corresponds to 1 per cent of the potential audience members tuned in on the given programme, in the relevant geographic area(s). Thus, the rating of a programme effectively expresses the fraction of the households in the sample who chose to follow the programme, as opposed to following a competing programme, or just engaging in other activities. The audience can in principle be tracked at very short time-intervals; the standard contractual reference is the average rating over the time covered by any given programme.

Already in the early stages of the commercial development of radio broadcasting, in the 1920s, announcers often invited the audience members to send cards and letters about the programmes to specialised agencies (Lotz, 2007, Chapter 6). Similarly, the measurement of the TV audiences initially relied on the information collected from randomly selected samples of viewers. More systematic procedures were subsequently adopted. Daily ratings for the US were produced by Nielsen by 1973. In the UK, a similar service has been provided by *Television Audience Measurement Limited* (Fletcher, 2008). Constant progress was also made both in the identification of the demographic attributes of the audiences, and in the provision of data for local and regional markets. The measurement services were subsequently extended to the audiences of cable TV, TV networks, and VCRs.

The more refined measures of the audiences available eventually led to the development of conditional pricing arrangements. From the point of view of the TV advertisers, the effects of uncertainty are exacerbated by the traditional partition of time into 'seasons' and by the long planning horizons resulting from this practice (Lotz, 2007, p. 159). Since the late 1960s, most TV networks have provided audience guarantees for the advertisement slots purchased in the 'upfront' market – generally held throughout the planning stage, a few months ahead of the start of the season – with compensatory slots. The adoption of this hybrid pricing arrangement (see sub-section on flat fees) effectively marked the onset of a transition towards a more widespread use of prices contingent on estimated exposure.

Measures of the audience of internet sites, providing the basis for the use of the CPM, are also provided by specialised certifying agencies. The price of exposure of internet advertising banners was initially expressed as a flat fee or as a CPM (Hoffman and Novak, 2000). Nowadays, banners are typically priced by using the CPM (Edelman et al., 2007).

In general, exposure to an advertisement does not automatically guarantee that each single audience member will actually pay attention to the advertising message. The gap between the number of impressions and the number of audience members paying attention to the advertisements can be boosted by the use of different 'advertising avoidance' strategies – such as switching to a different channel when an advertisement is broadcast, or actively skipping advertisements while watching time-shifted shows, possibly even by using special recorders. Nevertheless, the CPM is still a very common pricing format. The estimates in PwC

(2010), based on 2009 data for the USA, indicate that the CPM was used to price the exposure of advertisements in approximately 39 per cent of the cases considered, whereas a performance-related price, of the type described in the two following sub-sections, was used in approximately 57 per cent of the cases, and hybrid pricing formats were used in the residual 4 per cent of the cases. Performance-related prices are generally based on relatively 'immediate' measures of the performance of the advertisements. Hence, the CPM may be a more suitable pricing scheme in the case of advertisements aimed at general brand-building, rather than at the immediate conclusion of transactions.

Cost Per Click

In the case of internet advertisements, information on browsing behaviour, which can be collected with relative ease, can be used as an indicator of the attention received. In particular, if the advertisements contain links, the price of the media exposure can be set as a cost per click ('CPC'), calculated by multiplying the number of 'clicks' received by the links displayed by a given unit price. The price of the advertisements displayed by search engines in response to the users' queries is generally set as a cost per click, with a unit price determined in an auction – see Section 4.

The rate between the number of clicks received by an advertisement and the number of viewers is known as the click-through rate ('CTR'). The CTRs for specific advertisements may take on values ranging from 0 to a few percentage points, depending on the slots in which the advertisements are displayed and on the relevance of the product advertised, given the viewer's interests. A low CTR may be due either to the intrinsic lack of appeal of the offer, as presented in the advertisement, or to a weak connection between the user's query and the product advertised, for advertisements displayed by search engines. To limit the risk of a penalty effectively imposed by a low number of clicks, in the former case, the media outlets may consider the advertisers' historical performance when they decide the assignment of the slots available.

In general, the CPC exposes the advertisers to the risk of clicks from users whose goal is to manipulate the counting. These 'fraudulent clicks' may be the expression of the competitors' attempt to drain an advertiser's budget, or perhaps to make the information on the effectiveness of the campaigns more noisy. Jansen (2011) estimates that fraudulent clicks representing a fraction slightly higher than 1 per cent of the total may not be detected. Considering this possibility, the advertisers often compare the reports on the number of clicks on which the billing of the advertising slots is based with the activity records of their own servers.

Cost Per Action

The actions taken by the internet users may in principle be tracked beyond the act of clicking on the links displayed in the advertisements, possibly down to the actual purchase of the products. The price of the advertisement slots can correspondingly be made conditional on whether the actions tracked are taken, or not. This pricing scheme is generally known as cost per action ('CPA') – or also as 'cost per sale' or 'cost per transaction'. The payment can be based either on the number of individuals taking the actions, or on the revenues generated. An important example of a CPA scheme is Amazon.com's Associates Program. This scheme applies to each sale of Amazon.com for which a website participating in the programme acts as referral, and entitles the latter website to a fraction of the revenue from the transaction (Edelman et al., 2007). As the actions on which the payments are conditional entail a significant cost for the users, unlike in the case of the CPC, the CPA is generally not exposed to manipulation via fraudulent clicks.

3. MEDIA OUTLETS AS TWO-SIDED PLATFORMS

The present section illustrates a number of models in which the pricing problems of the media outlet are seen as a part of the broader strategic problem faced by the manager of a two-sided platform. The qualifying element of the literature on two-sided platforms is the focus on the externalities across the groups whose interactions are mediated by the platform, which are an important feature of many practical situations – see Anderson and Gabszewicz (2006), Armstrong (2006), Levin (2013) and Rochet and Tirole (2006). For example, credit card companies facilitate payments between buyers and sellers, and a card that is more widely used or accepted by one group is also more valuable for the members of the other group. Computer operating systems and video game consoles link the developers and the users of software and games. Also in these cases, a larger size of one group generally makes the platform more appealing for the members of the other group – save for effects such as the greater diffusion of internet viruses and spyware, and the greater ease with which copies of software can be made and exchanged, against the will of the patent holders, if the transactions are mediated by more popular platforms.

Media outlets provide news, general information and entertainment to their audiences, and channel the attention of the audience members towards the advertisers' messages. The advertisers derive greater benefits from messages presented to larger audiences of potential interest, as defined by the members' demographic features, while the single audience members may have different views about the desirability of the advertisements of different types. The audience members may not appreciate advertisements that interrupt TV or radio programmes, or intrusive internet banners, if they are not interested in the advertising messages. By contrast, they may be willing to pay a premium for outlets providing classified advertisements, particularly if they are free to disregard advertisements of little interest, as is more often the case for newspapers. The literature distinguishes between 'ad-averse' and 'ad-loving' audience members (Anderson and Gabszewicz, 2006); clearly, any given individual may match both profiles, in different situations. The broad focus of the literature surveyed in the present section is on the interactions between the pricing decision and the decisions that affect the size and the structure of the audience, through the service provided and the price charged for it.

One issue that has received a substantial amount of attention is the analysis of the incentives for media channels who do have information about their users' preferences – as is often the case for social media and internet platforms in general – to suggest the best matches between the users and the products advertised. Eliaz and Spiegler (2011) investigate a model with a continuum of buyers, an intermediary and a continuum of sellers, characterised by different probabilities that their products will be a suitable match for each buyer. The intermediary posts a single CPC charged to all sellers included in a 'search pool' which is presented to the buyers at no charge, in the main version of the model. Visiting each seller allows the buyers to learn their respective match-values, and entails a positive cost. In equilibrium, the intermediary may set a relatively low CPC, and thereby induce sellers whose products are relatively unlikely to be a good match for the buyers to join the search pool. Essentially, a very heterogeneous pool of sellers softens competition, and leads to higher prices and a larger expected number of sellers visited by the buyers. The search pool that maximises the intermediary's profit is actually independent of whether a CPC or a CPM is charged to the sellers; the effect identified may emerge even if the intermediary charges a fee to the buyers, but is sensitive to the introduction of competition between intermediaries. Hagiu and Jullien (2011) investigate a related model featuring two sellers of horizontally differentiated products, and a set of buyers who can learn their idiosyncratic valuations for each seller's product by visiting the seller, at a cost that differs across buyers. The intermediary can give 'informed' recommendations to the buyers; its revenues derive from a CPC charged to the sellers. In equilibrium, the intermediary may 'divert' search – namely, she may purposely refer some of the buyers to the 'wrong' seller. Essentially, the intermediary maximises the revenues induced by the CPC by trading off the incentive for the buyers to follow her recommendations and the number of diverted buyers, who may effectively be forced to visit both sellers. Additionally, diversion may allow the intermediary to profitably manipulate the prices charged by the sellers. The paper identifies rather stringent conditions under which diversion is ruled out. Armstrong and Zhou (2011) investigate a number of settings in which a seller can become 'prominent' for the buyers, compared to the competitors, by paying a fee to an intermediary. As in Eliaz and Spiegler (2011) and in Hagiu and Jullien (2011), the intermediary does not always give the best possible advice to the buyers. Nevertheless, the intermediary's advisory activity may improve the market performance, particularly if substantial differences exist between the sellers, and/or if the sellers' payments take the form of a CPM. Taylor (2013) studies the effects of the tension between the search engines' incentives to present sponsored and 'organic' links, given the competition for the users' attention between the links presented and the fact that only sponsored links yield positive revenues. This tension may induce the search engines to deliberately include sub-optimal organic links in the lists of results presented to the users.

Baye et al. (2011) investigate two related settings where an intermediary who can recommend differentiated products to their potential buyers can charge either a CPM, or a CPC, or a combination of the two to the sellers. The intermediary maximises her profit by charging a pure CPC. In a nutshell, the key advantage of the CPC lies in the higher expected revenue that it generates, subject to the condition that the sellers must be willing to pay the price charged by the intermediary.

To illustrate competition for audiences, I consider a model building on, among others, Anderson and Coate (2005) and Armstrong (2006). The model features two horizontally differentiated media outlets, (Outlet) A and (Outlet) B, typically interpreted as TV or radio broadcasters, or newspapers. The preference space is a [0,1] interval, *à la* Hotelling (1929), and outlets A and B are located at 0 and at 1. There are a continuum of potential users of the media outlets/buyers of the products advertised, whose finite total measure is set equal to 1, without loss of generality, and whose preferences are uniformly distributed over the interval [0,1] (Figure 6.1).

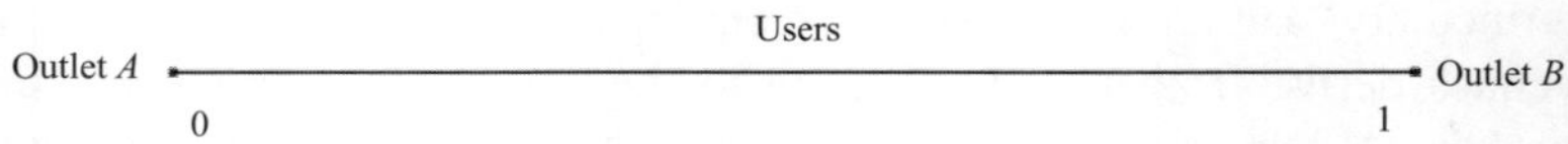

Figure 6.1 Media outlets and users

The manager of each media outlet $m \in \{A, B\}$ chooses the prices $p_m \in \mathbb{R}$ and $q_m \in \mathbb{R}$ that the users and the advertisers must respectively pay to access her outlet. I conveniently express the price of advertising per unit of audience, so that the price of publishing an advertisement is the product of the unit price q_m and the measure of the outlet's audience, denoted by $h_m \in \mathbb{R}_+$. Generality compels us to allow for prices that can be either positive, or negative. A key insight of the literature on two-sided platforms is indeed that if a greater size of one group makes the platform more appealing for the members of the other group, the effect on the revenues from the latter group may induce the platform's manager to reward the members of the former group for their participation. Media outlets do not usually offer cash to their users, possibly also because it is costly to monitor the attention devoted to the advertisements. However, newspapers may offer free supplements and coupons to their readers, and search engines may offer free news sections and free email to their users; in both cases, the costs may be more than offset by the increased revenues from the sale of advertising spaces deriving from a larger audience. The effects of restrictions on the prices charged by the media outlets on the content provided and the advertising levels are considered for example by Anderson and Coate (2005) and by Peitz and Valletti (2008).

Each user's address identifies the 'ideal' outlet, as defined by the type of information and entertainment provided. The utility that a user with address $x \in [0,1]$ derives from the use of media outlet m, with address $\gamma_m \in \{0,1\}$ net of the price p_m, is

$$u_x(m) = v - rh_m - t|x - \gamma_m| - p_m.$$

The exogenous parameters $v \in \mathbb{R}_{++}$ and $t \in \mathbb{R}_{++}$ respectively measure the highest utility from the outlet's content, achieved by a user whose address coincides with that of the outlet, and the pace at which utility decreases as the distance between the two addresses $|x - \gamma_m|$ increases. $r \in \mathbb{R}_+$ measures the effect of the advertisements published on the reader's utility. The restriction to non-negative values entails a focus on the cases of ad-averse or ad-neutral users; some comments on the case of negative values of r, identifying ad-loving readers, are made below. Each audience member can use at most one outlet; v is assumed to be sufficiently large that, in equilibrium, each audience member does indeed use one outlet. A buyer who receives the same utility from both outlets can choose either one of them with probability 1/2. Models in which each audience member can 'multi-home' – namely use multiple outlets – are investigated by Bergemann and Bonatti (2011) and by Kind et al. (2007).

The advertising slots are offered to the monopolist producers-sellers of a set of new products. Each potential advertiser produces a single product; the population of the advertisers is a continuum with exogenous measure $\mu \in \mathbb{R}_{++}$. The willingness to pay for each product is equal to some $w \in [0,W]$, where $W > r$, for all buyers, and the range of the products is such that w is uniformly distributed over the given interval. Each buyer only purchases the products advertised in the media outlet of choice. The model could be adjusted to account for the possibility that only a fraction of the media users actually purchase each product advertised, and/or a fraction of the users are already aware of each product, so that some media exposure is necessarily 'wasted', for each advertisement. Production takes place under constant returns to scale, and the unit production cost is set equal to 0 with no further loss of generality – the willingness to pay could be re-interpreted as a margin over the unit cost. Each seller decides whether to advertise in one or both media outlets, or to refrain from advertising, and exploits her monopoly power by setting the price of the respective product equal to the buyers' willingness to pay for it.

The costs of providing media content and advertisements are set equal to 0 – again, a proportional cost could be readily incorporated in the model. We consider subgame-perfect equilibria, at which the media managers effectively act as Von Stackelberg leaders: They simultaneously set their respective prices, taking into account the agents' optimal responses to any prices chosen both on and off the equilibrium path. The profit of each seller who advertises through a media outlet charging an access price q, for each buyer reached by the outlet, is equal to $w - q$. As only the sellers for whom the profit is positive actually advertise, both the set of the advertisers and the set of the advertisements published by the outlet have measure

$$H(q) = \begin{cases} \mu, \text{ if } q \le 0, \\ \mu\left(1 - \dfrac{q}{W}\right), \text{ if } q \in (0, W), \\ 0, \text{ if } q \ge W. \end{cases}$$

If both media outlets have a positive audience, the address of the critical user is defined by the equality $u_X(A) = u_X(B)$, and the sizes of the audiences of the two outlets can be expressed as

$$X_A(p_A, p_B, q_A, q_B) = \frac{1}{2} - \frac{p_A - p_B + r(H(q_A) - H(q_B))}{2t},$$

$$X_B(p_A, p_B, q_A, q_B) = \frac{1}{2} + \frac{p_A - p_B + r(H(q_A) - H(q_B))}{2t}.$$

We can then express the profit of outlet $m \in \{A,B\}$ as

$$\pi_m(p_A, p_B, q_A, q_B) = (p_m + q_m H(p_m))\, X_m(p_A, p_B, q_A, q_B),$$

and write the problem faced by the outlet's manager as

$$\max_{(p_m, q_m) \in \mathbb{R}^2} \pi_m(p_A, p_B, q_A, q_B)$$

where the prices set by the other media outlet are taken as given.

Focusing directly on symmetric cases, we can say that the system formed by the first order conditions for the outlets' problems identifies a symmetric equilibrium with $p_A = p_B = p^e$ and $q_A = q_B = q^e$, where

$$p^e = t - \frac{\mu}{4}\left(W - \frac{r^2}{W}\right), \tag{6.1}$$

$$q^e = \frac{W + r}{2}; \tag{6.2}$$

each outlet's audience is the half-interval closest to it. The outlets' optimised profits are both equal to $\frac{t}{2}$, and thus independent of advertising. This result does not hold in more general versions of the model; for example, Manduchi and Picard (2009) show that if the outlets are asymmetrically positioned, the outlets' profits may be a decreasing function of the number of the potential advertisers.

In a benchmark setting with no advertising ($\mu = 0$), the outlets' managers would set their prices equal to t. Comparison with p^e in (6.1) reveals that the possibility to publish advertisements makes a larger audience more valuable, and therefore induces the outlets to charge lower and possibly negative prices to their users. The gap between the prices charged to the users with and without advertising increases together with the size of the advertisers' population μ and with the upper bound to the value of the advertisers' products W; by contrast, it decreases as the advertising nuisance parameter r increases.

A further benchmark is the solution to the problem of a monopolist facing a set of buyers with valuations uniformly distributed over $[0,W]$; this is effectively the position of each media outlet *vis-á-vis* the advertisers, as the outlet is an exclusive gatekeeper for the respective users. With a unit production cost $c \in \mathbb{R}_+$, the monopolist would set her price equal to $\frac{W+c}{2}$, for any size of the buyers' population. If we regard the nuisance parameter r as the unit production cost of advertising exposure, this price coincides with q^e in (6.2). Both the price per unit of audience charged to each advertiser and therefore the advertising revenues, given that each outlet's audience has always size 1/2, in equilibrium, are increasing in W and in r.

A hypothetical central planner maximising the total surplus generated by the media content and the exchanges made possible by advertising would choose identical prices and levels of advertising for the media outlets. These necessary conditions are both verified at the equilibrium of our model, in which the media outlets are symmetrically positioned. The conditions may not hold, however, if the media outlets are asymmetrically positioned, due to the strategic effects identified in Fudenberg and Tirole (1984). The planner would also set the price of advertising equal to the nuisance parameter r. Thus, the price charged to the advertisers is higher than the level that maximises aggregate surplus, and equilibrium features an excessively small number of advertisements published. In general, the welfare losses due to the media outlets' monopoly power could be tempered by price discrimination of the advertisers. The possibility of multi-homing for the audience members can also lead to lower prices faced by the advertisers; see Anderson et al. (2012) and Kind et al. (2007).

Equilibria in which both outlets are active may not exist in settings with ad-loving audiences; intuitively, this happens because the incentives for the media outlets to pursue larger audiences are very strong, in settings of this type. Gabszewicz et al. (2007) investigate a model in which the media outlets may also choose the quality of the content provided to their audiences, and identify conditions under which this 'circulation spiral' is possible. Manduchi and Picard (2009) show that any intrinsic competitive advantages of one of the outlets can be amplified by advertising, if publishing the advertisements entails a fixed cost.

Crampes et al. (2009) investigate free entry in a market of competing media outlets. Their main result is that with non-decreasing returns to scale in the audience size, the equilibrium may feature both an excessively large number of media outlets, and an excessively small number of advertisements displayed. This result is in line with the result obtained by Kind et al. (2007) in a setting with no entry, if the media are close substitutes; in both cases, the nuisance that the advertisements impose on the audience plays an important role in the derivation of the results. On this note, Chandra (2009) shows empirically that US newspapers facing stronger competition charge lower circulation prices and higher advertising prices. The author argues that this result follows from the increased opportunities for the newspapers to segment their readers, in a more competitive environment, leading to higher returns from the advertisements. This result suggests that the theoretical investigations of the effects of competition on advertising could usefully be complemented by studies allowing for the possibility of targeted advertising, along the lines of Bergemann and Bonatti (2011).

4. AUCTIONS FOR ADVERTISING SLOTS

Internet advertising slots allocated in response to the users' queries, whose sale generates yearly revenues of the order of many billions of US dollars, are typically assigned to the advertisers and priced by using auctions. To illustrate these auctions, I consider a version of the models in Edelman et al. (2007) and Varian (2007). The setting features $A > 1$ (potential) advertisers and $S > 0$ slots offered by a media outlet. Advertisers and slots are formally described by two sets $(\varphi_1, \ldots \varphi_A) \in \mathbb{R}^A_{++}$ and $(\rho_1, \ldots \rho_s) \in (0,1]^s$, whose generic elements φ_A and ρ_s are respectively interpreted as the profit per click for advertiser a and as the CTR for slot s. Thus, the profit realised by advertiser a if her advertisement is posted in slot s, gross of the fee paid for the slot, is equal to $\varphi_a \rho_s$. All decision-makers are risk-neutral, and maximise their expected payoffs.

The profits per click and the CTRs could in principle measure the expectations of non degenerate random variables whose realisations become known after the matches are formed, provided the variables φ_a and ρ_s are uncorrelated for each pair (φ_a, ρ_s). I assign lower indices to advertisers and slots featuring respectively a higher profit per click and a higher CTR, so that we have $\varphi_1 \geq \varphi_2 \geq \ldots \geq \varphi_{A-1} \geq \varphi_A$ *and* $\rho_1 \geq \rho_2 \geq \ldots \geq \rho_{S-1} \geq \rho_S$. The indices of the slots could for example express the order in which the links are listed by a search engine; the evidence suggests in fact that the viewers are typically more likely to follow links closer to the top of the list (Jansen, 2011, Chapter 4). As in Edelman et al. (2007) and Varian (2007), the CTRs of the slots and the advertisers' profits per click are common knowledge.

The matching between advertisers and slots is expressed by a set of binary variables denoted by

$$T = \{\theta_{a,s}\}_{a=1,\ldots,A;\, s=1,\ldots,S},$$

where the generic variable $\theta_{a,s}$ is equal to 1 if advertiser a is assigned to slot s, and to 0 otherwise. The total expected surplus for the market participants is then

$$\sigma(T) = \sum_{s=1}^{S}\left(\sum_{a=1}^{A}\theta_{a,s}\varphi_a\rho_s\right). \tag{6.3}$$

The constraints are that each advertiser can use at most one slot, and each slot can be assigned to at most one advertiser:

$$\sum_{s=1}^{S}\theta_{a,s} \in \{0,1\}, a \in \{1,\ldots,A\},$$

$$\sum_{a=1}^{A}\theta_{a,s} \in \{0,1\}, s \in \{1,\ldots S\}.$$

A hypothetical planner maximising $\sigma(T)$ in (6.3), subject to these constraints, should assign the slots to the advertisers with the S highest valuations. Hence, a standard result in the theory of inequalities (Ross, 2000, Proposition 1.3.2) allows us to conclude that maximisation of the surplus in (6.3) requires the planner to set either $\theta_{a,s} = 1$ or $\theta_{a,s} = 0$, depending on whether $a = s$ or $a \neq s$, respectively, for every slot $s \in \{1,\ldots,S\}$; the planner should thus assign the slot with the s-th highest CTR to the advertiser with the s-th highest profit per click.[2]

Internet slots are typically offered to advertisers who state a set of keywords of interest, along with a bid for each keyword and the advertisement to be published, containing a link to the advertiser's website. Each advertiser may also state a maximum budget or other restrictions, involving for example the users' locations. When an internet user submits a search query or a request to view a page on a site that accepts advertisements, an electronic routine identifies the keywords more closely related to the topic of the query or the page content, and retrieves the bids of the advertisers interested in them. If the slots are auctioned, unit demands and 'separability' of the CTRs and the profit per click of each advertiser guarantee that the relevant information can be conveyed by using one-dimensional bids, regardless of the number of slots offered. In principle, a Vickrey-Clarke-Groves ('VCG') auction could be used. In this auction format, each advertiser presents a sealed bid; the advertiser submitting the s-th highest bid, for $s \leq S$, receives the slot with the s-th highest CTR, and pays a price equal to the payoff loss induced by the exclusion from the slot of the advertisers who presented lower bids, evaluated by using the very CPCs in their bids. Ties between bids can be broken by randomisation. The VCG auction has a dominant strategy equilibrium in which each advertiser 'truthfully' bids her profit per click, the advertisers and the slots are efficiently matched, and the price charged for each slot coincides with the actual cost of the exclusion of other advertisers from the slot, in surplus terms (Ausubel and Milgrom, 2006).

VCG auctions are not very common in practice, possibly due to a number of potential weaknesses featured by them: The revenues may be relatively low and non-monotonic in the number of bidders and in the bidders' valuations, and the auction format is vulnerable both to collusion by a coalition of bidders and to the use of aliases by the participants (Ausubel and Milgrom, 2006). Historically, a CPM set by the website's manager was the first format used to sell advertising slots, followed by the generalised first price-auction ('GFP-auction'), in which the s-th slot is assigned to the s-th highest bidder, upon payment of the amount of the respective bid – and the seller may state a minimum acceptable bid, or 'reserve price'. GFP-auctions may admit no pure-strategy equilibria, and may effectively create an incentive for the bidders to 'game the system', thus leading to inefficient assignments and to inefficient investments in bidding robots – see for example Edelman et al. (2007, p. 246, 'Example').

The main mechanism currently in use is the generalised second price auction ('GSP auction'), in which the assignment rule is the same as in the GFP-auction, but the advertiser receiving the s-th slot pays the amount of the $(s+1)$-th highest bid, rather than the own bid. If a single slot is offered, the GSP auction is a VCG auction. Equivalence does however break down if multiple slots are offered; hence, the GSP auction may not have an equilibrium in dominant strategies with truthful bidding.

To illustrate some aspects of the GSP auction, I consider an example with three advertisers and two slots, similar to the examples in Aggarwal et al. (2006) and Edelman et al. (2007). The profits per click, in dollars, are $\varphi_1 = 200$, $\varphi_2 = 120$ and $\varphi_3 = 50$. The CTRs in the first and the second slot are $\rho_1 = 0.5$ and $\rho_2 = 0.25$. If the advertisers bid their respective profits per click, the GSP auction would assign the first and the second slot to advertisers 1 and 2, respectively, at the prices of 120 and 50; the advertisers' net profits would be equal to $(200-120)\times 0.5 = 40$ and $(120-50)\times 0.25 = 17.5$ – both preferable to the no-bidding profit of 0. Advertisers 2 and 3 would face a negative profit if they increased their bids to obtain a slot with a higher CTR, and the only potentially profitable deviation is thus a lowering of advertiser 1's bid to some value in the interval $(50, 120)$. *Ceteris paribus*, a bid of this type would allow the advertiser to obtain the second slot at the price of 50. The corresponding profit would however be $(200-50)\times 0.25 = 37.5 < 40$. Hence, truthful bids would indeed be an equilibrium of the auction.

To pinpoint the possibility of a failure of truthfulness in a GSP auction, we can modify the example by making the second slot relatively more appealing. For example, if we increase its CTR to $\rho_2 = 0.4$, while leaving the remaining features of the example unchanged, then under truthful bidding advertisers 1 and 2 would still receive the first and the second slot at the prices of 120 and 50. The higher CTR would increase advertiser 2's profit, while advertiser 1's profit would still be equal to 40. Any bid in the interval $(50, 120)$ would then allow advertiser 1 to obtain the second slot at the price of 50, and to thereby realise a profit per impression equal to $(200-50)\times 0.4 = 60 > 40$. Hence, the assumed equilibrium with truthful bidding would unravel.[3]

In a VCG auction, if only the first slot were available, assigning that slot to advertiser 1 would necessarily leave advertiser 2 unmatched. With truthful bids, the CPC would therefore be equal to 120, as in the GSP auction – recall that a GSP auction for a single item is in fact a VCG auction. By contrast, in our two-slot example, advertiser 2 is moved to a less profitable slot, to replace an advertiser who would in turn have made a less profitable use of it. The difference between the expected surplus corresponding to the hypothetical case in which advertiser 1 is left unmatched and the case in which advertiser 1 receives the first slot, for the remaining advertisers – namely the actual price charged to advertiser 1, in a VCG auction – is equal to $120\times(0.5-0.4) + 50\times 0.4 = 32$.

Advertiser 1 would then face an expected profit per impression of $200 \times 0.5 - 32 = 68$. As the expected profit from a deviation to a bid in the interval $(50, 120)$ is still equal to 60, the equilibrium in dominant strategies of the VCG auction does feature truthful bidding also in this scenario. (See Varian, 2009, Section 3, for additional details.)

Gomes and Sweeney (2014) characterise the efficient Bayes-Nash equilibrium of the GSP, and provide a necessary and sufficient condition for its existence. Bounds for the equilibrium revenues of the standard GSP auction can be provided by considering the *locally envy-free equilibria*, in which each advertiser prefers the slot assigned to her to the slot assigned to the advertiser ranked one position above or below her (Edelman et al., 2007). Let us suppose that $L \leq S$ slots are actually assigned in the auction, and let q_s denote the price paid for slot $s \in \{1,\ldots,L\}$; either the $(s+1)$-th highest bid or the greatest between the first omitted bid and the reserve price set by the seller, in the case of last slot assigned L. The analysis of the set of the locally envy-free equilibria allows us to establish the following lower and upper bound for the revenue from the GSP auction:

$$\sum_{s=1}^{L} q_s \rho_s \geq \varphi_2 (\rho_1 - \rho_2) + 2\varphi_3 (\rho_2 - \rho_3) + \ldots + (L-1) q_L \rho_L,$$

$$\sum_{s=1}^{L} q_s \rho_s \leq \varphi_1 (\rho_1 - \rho_2) + 2\varphi_2 (\rho_2 - \rho_3) + \ldots + (L-1) q_L \rho_L.$$

The given lower bound coincides with the revenue from the VCG auction – see Edelman et al. (2007) and Varian (2009).

Systematic differences between the CTRs of any given slot, if used by different advertisers, may in principle be observed due to the relevance of the keywords and the quality of each advertiser's offer, advertisement and on-line support. The relative CTRs of different slots may also differ across advertisers. For example, the users who are more likely to click on the advertisements in slots with a lower position in the list may be either intrinsically more interested in niche products or more sophisticated and 'tech-savvy', or they may have a low opportunity cost of time; in each case, we could expect systematic differences in the probabilities of a visit to the websites of different advertisers. The routines used by some platforms are adjusted to better handle differences of this type. For example, Google multiplies the bids by a 'quality score' based on each advertiser's estimated CTRs to determine the ranking of the advertisers and the prices of the slots – see Varian (2009) for additional details.

Lahaie and McAfee (2011) consider a model in which the platform's manager is uncertain about the advertisers' CTRs. They identify a sufficient condition under which an adjusted quality score, obtained by raising the estimated quality score to a power between 0 and 1, can improve the efficiency of the auction. Borgers et al. (2006) investigate a setting in which the advertisers' profits per click may depend on the position of the advertisements and the CTRs for different advertisers may change by different proportions as their position changes. Goel et al. (2009) consider a class of generalisation of the standard second price auction that they label 'contract auctions', and illustrate their use in a setting whereby the parties have conflicting information about the CTRs, and the price paid by each advertiser is the sum of a CPM and a CPC.

Athey and Ellison (2011) and Chen and He (2011) investigate models of auctions for advertising slots in which the buyers' search routines are explicitly modelled, and a visit to each advertiser's website, allowing each buyer to discover the own match-profit, entails a 'search cost'. These models make it possible to explore the links between the advertising market, the total surplus generated by the intermediated exchanges and the division of the surplus among the market participants. In both papers, the advertisers are vertically differentiated and have private information about their idiosyncratic probabilities of meeting each buyer's need, which are generally keyword-dependent. In Athey and Ellison (2011), the advertisers' match-profits conditional on the presence of a match are exogenous, and the focus is on auction design. In Chen and He (2011), the advertisers' profits are endogenous, and the focus is on the equilibrium of the market for products, taking into account the 'hold-up' problem identified in Diamond (1971). In both cases, the sellers' bids and therefore the CTRs of the slots assigned to them are (possibly weakly) monotonic in the probability of a match, and the matching of advertisers and slots therefore provides valuable information to the searching buyers.

5. CONCLUDING REMARKS

This chapter has surveyed the economic literature on the pricing of advertising. In particular, the chapter has focused on the different criteria used to price the media exposure of advertisements, on the main models accounting for the pricing decisions, and on the links between the pricing decisions and the competition for audience and the selection of the advertisements published.

Advertising markets are subject to very fast changes, and their analytical investigation is a relatively young subject. Hence, the area presents many opportunities for future research. Some topics related to issues covered in the survey are:

1. The relative performances of the alternative pricing formats presented, in different scenarios, as well as the development of new formats, possibly building on the existing ones.
2. Competition among media platforms, and its consequences from the point of view of the platforms' pricing strategies.
3. The efficient use of information about the intrinsic appeal of the advertisements and the advertisers' previous performance in the allocation and the pricing of the advertising slots.

In all likelihood, the literature will continue to develop at a fast pace in the coming years, and the results of the extant literature will prove to be valuable building blocks in this process.

NOTES

1. Ogilvy (2004, p. 86) attributes the quote to William Hesketh Lever, first Viscount Leverhulme, 1851–1925.
2. The requirement must hold up to permutations of the CTRs and/or the profits per click that happened to have identical values.
3. It is readily verified that a reserve price in the interval [100,120] would guarantee both truthful bidding and an efficient assignment of the slots, in this example. In more general cases, however, a reserve price may create a trade-off between truthful bidding and the full utilisation of the slots.

REFERENCES

Aggarwal, G., Goel, A. and Motwani, R. (2006) 'Truthful Auctions for Pricing Search Keywords', in Joan Feigenbaum, John Chuang and David Pennock (eds), *Proceedings of the 7th ACM Conference on Electronic Commerce*, pp. 1–7.

Akerlof, G. (1970) 'The Market for "Lemons": Quality Information and the Market Mechanism', *Quarterly Journal of Economics*, 84 (3), 488–500.

Anderson, S.P. and Coate, S. (2005) 'Market Provision of Broadcasting: A Welfare Analysis', *Review of Economic Studies*, 72 (4), 947–972.

Anderson, S.P. and Gabszewicz, J.J. (2006) 'The Media and Advertising: A Tale of Two-sided Markets', in Victor A. Ginsburgh and David Throsby (eds), *Handbook of the Economics of Art and Culture*, Volume 1, London: Elsevier Science, pp. 567–614.

Anderson, S.P., Foros, Ø., Kind, H.J., and Peitz, M. (2012) 'Media Market Concentration, Advertising Levels, and Ad Prices', *International Journal of Industrial Organization*, 30 (3), 321–325.

Armstrong, M. (2006) 'Competition in Two-sided Markets', *RAND Journal of Economics*, 37 (3), 668–691.

Armstrong, M. and Zhou, J. (2011) 'Paying for Prominence', *Economic Journal*, 121 (556), F368–F395.

Athey, S. and Ellison, G. (2011) 'Position Auctions with Consumer Search', *Quarterly Journal of Economics*, 126 (3), 1213–1270.

Ausubel, L.M. and Milgrom, P. (2006) 'The Lovely but Lonely Vickrey Auction', in Peter Cramton, Yoav Shoham and Richard Steinberg (eds), *Combinatorial Auctions*, Cambridge, MA: MIT Press, pp. 17–40.

Bagwell, K. (2003) 'The Economic Analysis of Advertising', in Mark Armstrong and Robert H. Porter (eds), *Handbook of Industrial Organization*, Amsterdam: North-Holland, pp. 1701–1844.

Baye, M.R., Gao, X. and Morgan, J. (2011) 'On the Optimality of Clickthrough Fees in Online Markets', *Economic Journal*, 121 (556), F340–F367.

Bergemann, D. and Bonatti, A. (2011) 'Targeting in Advertising Markets: Implications for Offline versus Online Media', *RAND Journal of Economics*, 42 (3), 417–443.

Borgers, T., Cox, I., Pesendorfer, M. and Petricek, V. (2006) 'Equilibrium Bids in Sponsored Search Auctions: Theory and Evidence', Mimeo.

Chamberlin, E. (1933) *The Theory of Monopolistic Competition*, Cambridge, MA: Harvard University Press.

Chandra, A. (2009) 'Targeted Advertising: The Role of Subscriber Characteristics in Media Markets', *Journal of Industrial Economics*, 57 (1), 58–84.

Chen, Y. and He, C. (2011) 'Paid Placement: Advertising and Search on the Internet', *Economic Journal*, 121 (556), F309–F328.

Choi, J.P. and Stefanadis, C. (2006) 'Bundling, Entry Deterrence, and Specialist Innovators', *Journal of Business*, 79 (5), 2575–2594.

Corden, W.M. (1952–1953) 'The Maximisation of Profit by a Newspaper', *Review of Economic Studies*, 20 (3), 181–190.

Cover, J.H., Thompson, P.J. and Cohenour, V.J. (1931) 'Newspaper Advertising Rates and Circulation', *Journal of Business of the University of Chicago*, 4 (2), 115–126.

Crampes, C., Haritchabalet, C. and Jullien, B. (2009) 'Advertising, Competition and Entry in Media Industries', *Journal of Industrial Economics*, 57 (1), 7–31.

DeMarzo, P.M. and Duffie, D. (1995) 'Corporate Incentives for Hedging and Hedge Accounting Reviewed', *Review of Financial Studies*, 8 (3), 743–771.

Diamond, P.A. (1971) 'A Model of Price Adjustment', *Journal of Economic Theory*, 3 (2), 156–168.

The Economist (2011) 'The World in Figures', November 12.

Edelman, B., Ostrovsky, M. and Schwarz, M. (2007) 'Internet Advertising and the Generalized Second-Price Auction: Selling Billions of Dollars Worth of Keywords', *American Economic Review*, 97 (1), 242–259.

Eliaz, K. and Spiegler, R. (2011) 'A Simple Model of Search Engine Pricing', *Economic Journal*, 121 (556), F329–F339.

Farrell, J. and Klemperer, P. (2003) 'Coordination and Lock-in: Competition with Switching Costs and Network Effects', in Mark Armstrong and Robert H. Porter (eds), *Handbook of Industrial Organization*, Amsterdam: North-Holland, pp. 1967–2072.

Fletcher, W. (2008) *Powers of Persuasion – The Inside Story of British Advertising: 1951–2000*, Oxford, UK: Oxford University Press.

Fletcher, W. (2010) *Advertising: A Very Short Introduction*, Oxford, UK: Oxford University Press.

Fudenberg, D. and Tirole, J. (1984) 'The Fat-Cat Effect, the Puppy-Dog Ploy, and the Lean and Hungry Look', *American Economic Review*, 74 (2), 361–366.

Gabszewicz, J.J., Garella, P. and Sonnac, N. (2007) 'Newspapers' Market Shares and the Theory of the Circulation Spiral', *Information Economics and Policy*, 19 (3–4), 405–413.

Goel, S., Lahaie, S. and Vassilvitskii, S. (2009) 'Contract Auctions for Sponsored Search', in Stefano Leonardi (ed.), *Internet and Network Economics, Proceedings of the 5th International Workshop (WINE)*, Berlin Heidelberg: Springer, pp. 196–207.

Gomes, R. and Sweeney, K. (2014) 'Bayes-Nash Equilibria of the Generalized Second-Price Auction', *Games and Economic Behavior*, 86 (2014), 421–437.

Hagiu, A. and Jullien, B. (2011) 'Why do Intermediaries Divert Search?', *RAND Journal of Economics*, 42 (2), 337–362.

Hoffman, D.L. and Novak, T.P. (2000) 'Advertising and Pricing Models for the Web', in Brian Kahin and Hal R. Varian (eds), *Internet Publishing and Beyond: The Economics of Digital Information and Intellectual Property*, Cambridge, MA: MIT Press, pp. 45–61.

Hotelling, H. (1929) 'Stability in Competition', *Economic Journal*, 39 (153), 41–57.

Jansen, J. (2011) *Understanding Sponsored Search*, Cambridge, UK: Cambridge University Press.

Kind, H.J., Nilssen, T. and Sørgard, L. (2007) 'Competition for Viewers and Advertisers in a TV Oligopoly', *Journal of Media Economics*, 20 (3), 211–233.

Lahaie, S. and McAfee, R.P. (2011) 'Efficient Ranking in Sponsored Search', in Ning Chen, Edith Elkind and Elias Koutsoupias (eds), *Internet and Network Economics, Proceedings of the 7th International Workshop (WINE)*, Berlin Heidelberg: Springer, pp. 254–265.

Levin, J. (2013) 'The Economics of Internet Markets', in Daron Acemoglu, Manuel Arellano and Eddie Dekel (eds), *Advances in Economics and Econometrics*, Volume I, Cambridge, UK: Cambridge University Press, pp. 48–74.

Lotz, A.D. (2007) *The Television Will Be Revolutionized*, New York: New York University Press.

Manduchi, A. and Picard, R. (2009) 'Circulations, Revenues, and Profits in a Newspaper Market with Fixed Advertising Costs', *Journal of Media Economics*, 22 (4), 211–238.

Norris, V.P. (1980) 'Advertising History: According to the Textbooks', *Journal of Advertising*, 9 (3), 3–11.

Ogilvy, D. (1985) *Ogilvy on Advertising*, New York: Vintage Books, Random House.

Ogilvy, D. (2004) *Confessions of an Advertising Man*, London: Southbank Publishing (first published in 1963).

Ozga, S.A. (1960) 'Imperfect Markets through Lack of Knowledge', *Quarterly Journal of Economics*, 74 (1), 29–52.

Peitz, M. and Valletti, T.M. (2008) 'Content and Advertising in the Media: Pay-tv versus free-to-air', *International Journal of Industrial Organization*, 26 (4), 949–965.

PwC (2010) *Measuring the Effectiveness of Online Advertising*, study conducted by PwC for IAB France and the SRI.

Rochet, J.-C. and Tirole, J. (2006) 'Two-Sided Markets: A Progress Report', *RAND Journal of Economics*, 37 (3), 645–667.

Roels, G. and Fridgeirsdottir, K. (2009) 'Dynamic revenue management for online display advertising', *Journal of Revenue & Pricing Management*, 8 (5), 452–466.

Ross, S.M. (2000) *Topics in Finite and Discrete Mathematics*, Cambridge, UK: Cambridge University Press.

Stigler, G.J. (1961) 'The Economics of Information', *Journal of Political Economy*, 69 (3), 213–225.

Stigler, G.J. and Becker, G.S. (1977) 'De Gustibus non Est Disputandum', *American Economic Review*, 67 (2), 76–90.

Talluri, K.T. and van Ryzin, G.J. (2005) *The Theory and Practice of Revenue Management*, Berlin Heidelberg: Springer.

Taylor, G. (2013) 'Search Quality and Revenue Cannibalization by Competing Search Engines', *Journal of Economics & Management Strategy*, 22 (3), 445–467.

Tungate, M. (2007) *Adland: A Global History of Advertising*, London and Philadelphia: Kogan Page.
Varian, H. (2007) 'Position Auctions', *International Journal of Industrial Organization*, 25 (7), 1163–1178.
Varian, H. (2009) 'Online Ad Auctions', *American Economic Review, Papers & Proceedings*, 99 (2), 430–434.

PART II

PLATFORM APPLICATIONS

7. Economics of print media

Robert G. Picard

Print media such as newspapers, magazines, and books share some common economic features because of physical production and distribution, but each also has unique issues because of different demand characteristics and because they integrate or outsource elements in their value chains in various ways. They also operate with different business models that create economic incentives and constraints that differ among the print industries. Fundamental to understanding these factors and differences are comprehension of the differing cost structures, the role of economies of scale, and constraints on prices created by multi-sided markets in the print media industries.

The most significant and common economic factor is that print media share a similar underlying technology – the printing press. Although the characteristics of presses used to produce the three main print media can differ, the manufacturing of copies on presses creates conditions in which all three operate in unit cost economies. In this type of economic setting, the costs of producing and distributing single units are important and efficiency is influenced by the number of copies printed. This creates economies of scale in production and distribution and transaction costs involved in individual unit sales and distribution.

Daily newspapers encounter strong barriers to entry because of capital costs for printing presses and facilities (Busterna, 1988; Lacy and Simon, 1993; Picard and Brody, 1997), something not faced by most book and magazine publishers that typically outsource production (Dealy et al., 1997; Mogul, 1998; Greco, 2004).

Such factors create pressures and incentives for publishers to produce, sell, and distribute the largest viable amount of the printed product and make it more difficult for publishers who produce smaller amounts to operate as efficiently and profitably given the same production equipment. These factors consequently promote consolidation and concentration in the industries.

The basic threshold costs for creating and manufacturing the content of a newspaper, magazine, or book are the same regardless of the amount manufactured and distributed. Consequently, the first copy printed is said to bear all the fixed costs of production. These fixed costs include all costs required to produce the content and for any amount of the product to be published, such as essential facility, equipment, supplies, and personnel for editorial, production, marketing, distribution, and administration (Udell, 1978; Picard, 2011). Among the print media, these fixed costs are highest for daily newspapers, which have traditionally owned and operated all elements in their value chains, and are lowest for book publishing, which typically outsources not only content creation, but production and distribution as well. A few large publishers own and operate production and distribution facilities and equipment and the capacity of those assets is often marketed to other publishers, thus turning these cost centers into profit centers. Some independent specialized firms also provide these services for publishers.

The costs that change when the amount of print production and distribution is altered – variable costs – include printing supplies, ink, paper, binding, packaging, warehousing, and shipping costs. In the short run these tend to be rapidly declining costs, so the marginal cost of producing each additional unit is low. However, if the scale of production and distribution is dramatically increased it will push these variable costs significantly upwards and may require additional investments in fixed assets to acquire necessary production and distribution capacity.

The combined fixed and variable costs are significantly affected by economies of scale, with rapidly declining total average costs, which create advantages for larger producers and tendencies toward concentration (Rosse and Dertouzos, 1979; Norton and Norton, 1986; Doyle, 2013).

Print media thus have significant technological dependencies and are technology intensive industries with reliance on skilled production labor. Before production, however, they vary widely in terms of labor intensity. Newspapers tend to be the most labor intensive, requiring significant staffs of reporters and editors, advertising and circulation sales personnel. After production, because they tend to operate their own distribution systems, they also require large numbers of delivery personnel. Most magazines have relatively smaller staffs, because they tend to heavily rely on freelance writers and usually outsource production and distribution. Book publishers are the least labor intensive of the three because writers are not employed by the firms and their staffs are primarily editors, designers, marketing personnel, and administrative staffs.

One of the unique business issues faced by print media is that the majority of their costs are not related to their core activities – text and illustrative content. Instead, the bulk of the costs are associated with production and distribution. This has made some particularly vulnerable to digital only producers and distributors that have emerged and are challenging traditional publishers in all three print media products, and it has led companies in the print industries to begin significant digital activities of their own in hopes of reducing overall costs and maintaining a larger portion of revenue.

The processes and cost incurred in creating print media vary depending upon whether they involve single creation or continuously created product (Picard, 2011) and the frequency of continuous creation. Books are examples of single creation products and newspapers exemplars of continuous creation products. The requirements of single and continuous creation differ significantly, and fundamentally affect the investments and fixed costs of their producers and the organizational structures of the enterprises.

The characteristics of books and magazines have led many publishers to establish portfolios of titles serving various genres and niches, so they may benefit from providing a breadth of service that produces economies of scale and scope and reduces the risks of single titles. Publishers tend to manage these titles like investment portfolios with performance expectations for individual titles as well as the portfolio as a whole.

In the process portfolio publishers tend to rely on high performing 'hit' titles to cross-subsidize average- or lower-performing titles, especially in the book publishing industry where there is a low success rate among titles. This leads publishers to pay very high compensation to writers of bestsellers and to seek multiple ways to exploit the hit content through other media and activities.

Book titles involve different contracted authors and are typically produced individually, as part of a portfolio of book titles being produced by the publisher. Books are sold in separate submarkets including trade books intended for the general public, books for use in professions, and books used in education. It has long been recognized that demand for each varies, as does the economic risk (Blackwell, 1954). Trade books are particularly risky because they exhibit the highest characteristics of goods of uncertain quality and most are not successful commercial products. Demand for textbooks is created by official adoption of specific texts by faculty or schools and thus is less risky to publishers because consumption is forced on readers, particularly in higher education (Horovitz, 1965), and publishing and distribution factors appear to have more effect on price than even local monopoly retailers (Siegfried and Latta, 1998).

There are few time constraints on the appearance of books, so highly cost effective production and distribution services can be sought out and contracted as a means of lower costs. The production of time sensitive newspapers and magazines, however, generally requires keeping more creation and production, sales, and distribution services inside the company or close at hand and thus tends to reduce the number of distribution options that can be considered.

Because print media involve physical distribution to points of sale or home delivery, distribution structures and costs are important aspects of their economics. Three important factors come into play in distribution economies: distances covered in delivery, time required for delivery, and the density of distribution points. These factors influence how far print product can be delivered without having to establish satellite printing facilities and the actual costs of delivering a print product to customers in different locations (Picard, 2011).

These distribution factors create incentives to serve customers in closer geographic proximity to the publisher, to refuse to serve customers elsewhere, or to institute differential pricing based on geographic considerations – a price choice that influences demand. It also provides advantages to publishers that distribute multiple products simultaneously – thus promoting concentration – or to those using joint distribution services with other publishers (a very common practice in magazine and book publishing).

THE TRADITION OF TWO-SIDED PLATFORMS IN MAGAZINES AND NEWSPAPERS

Books are sold to consumers, and publishers rarely have other significant income streams from each title. They are thus fairly traditional products in market terms, subject to normal demand functions, with consumers' sovereignty based on consumer choice and price preferences.

Nearly all magazines and newspapers traditionally operate in a different environment from books. They normally have two significant revenue streams, from sales to reading consumers and sales to advertisers. They are thus two-sided platforms that require different economic understanding. In such platforms, the simple demand functions and consumer price signals do not play as prominent a part in determining content, quality, and consumption. Instead, the needs of both sets of consumers are addressed and there is an interaction between strategies and choices for each (Chaudhri, 1998). Prices for content affect consumer consumption quantity and this, in turn, affects the prices for and consumption by advertisers. Optimal revenues can only be achieved by dealing with both groups of consumers simultaneously (Corden, 1953; Reddaway, 1963; Picard, 1988; Picard, 1998).

Getting prices right in this model is crucial, but most media have traditionally been relatively unsophisticated in setting prices. Few have used demand-oriented pricing, based on what the market will bear, or target return pricing based on achieving a specific rate of return. Instead most have set prices based on what the closest competitors are doing or on industry average price. They were historically able to get away with it because elasticity and price resistance were relatively low because of the near monopolies in many markets.

The two-sided platform model in print media is dependent upon attracting sufficient numbers of readers so advertisers will want to use the publication to convey marketing messages to the readers (Kaiser and Wright, 2006). Consequently, there is an incentive for publishers to keep prices to consumers low to increase consumption and to raise prices on advertisers who have few choices for reaching the audience produced. In this model, success in selling the content product affects ability to sell advertising access because more readers make a paper more attractive to advertisers; conversely, success in selling advertising affects ability to sell the printed product to readers because it provides resources that improve content and make the paper more attractive (Picard, 2011). Although there is a direct relationship between circulation and advertising demand (Picard, 1998), getting prices correct in this relationship is difficult because it involves multiple choice factors that go beyond mere circulation and price (Kalita and Ducoffe, 1995; Depken II, 2004; Kaiser and Wright, 2006).

The challenges this poses are particularly evident in newspapers, which have for much of the past century obtained the majority of their income from advertisers. This reliance on advertisers has ranged from 60 percent to 80 percent of revenue in most developed nations. Many of the content choices of the twentieth century newspaper were made to serve advertiser interests – the additions of real estate, automotive, and real estate sections, for example. Choices to increase entertainment, lifestyle, and sports sections and feature stories were made to attract portions of audiences less interested in news – thus increasing circulation that made it possible to sell more advertising. The incentives to do so were thus provided by the two-sided platform and the most important demand function and price signals were those of the advertiser, with the price signals and quality demands of the reader playing secondary roles.

Two-sided platforms become more complex with the arrival of digital distribution because publishers sell print products separately and in conjunction with online products and products for tablets and smartphones. This shifts print media from two-sided to multi-sided platforms in which the relationships among consumers are compounded (Venkatesh and Chatterjee, 2006). This complexity is evident in the difficulties newspapers and magazines are having determining how to provide and sell content and advertising online and what kinds of bundling with print media are most effective.

The problem occurs because there are paying audiences and advertisers for the print edition, free or paying audiences and paying advertisers for online editions, and some joint audience and advertisers who use both the print and online offerings. If one alters a free price online to create a paying audience, it not only affects the willingness of online advertisers to pay, but affects the willingness of joint audiences and advertisers to pay and thus affects performance of the print sales as well.

These relationships are illustrated in Figure 7.1, showing that eight relations are affected and eight price decisions have to be made. The relationships and price choices grow exponentially with the addition of tablets, e-reader, and mobile services, making decisions even more difficult for publishers.

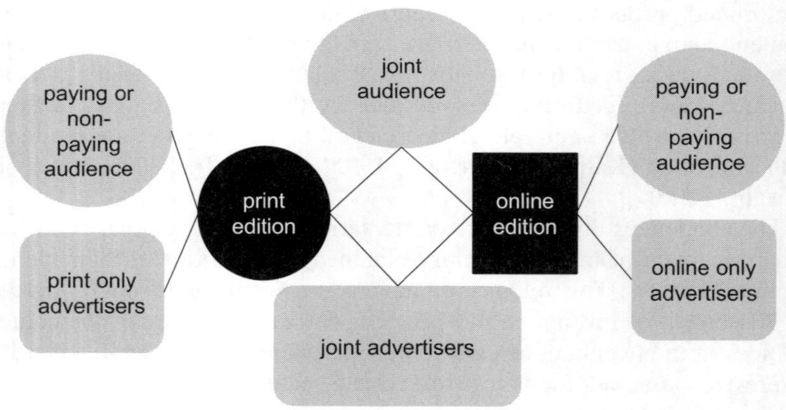

Figure 7.1 Complexity of price decisions increases as platforms are added

Creating the correct combination of content available in print and digital distribution, getting the content prices right, generating audiences in all places that are right for advertisers, and properly pricing advertising is no mean feat. Those who think newspapers and magazines can easily be monetized on digital platforms ignore the significant challenges posed by multi-sided platforms on product and price choices.

Even when effective pricing strategies are in place, print media are particularly susceptible to changes in the economy. Because of cyclical effects on advertising, magazines and newspapers are significantly affected by downturns in the economy, with declines in advertising of 4–5 percent for every 1 percent decline in GDP (Picard and Rimmer, 1999; Picard, 2001; Bakker et al., 2008).

Book publishers do not rely on advertising, but are also affected by downturns in the economy because consumer spending on discretionary purchases falls. Consequently book sales – particularly books intended for the general public – tend to fall and rise with business cycles and other economic fluctuations.

The interactions of cost and competition factors have led many countries to provide a range of tax incentives and subsidies to print media. Newspapers are often supported to overcome monopolistic tendencies and support or preserve their political and other social effects. Many smaller nations also provide support for book publishing for cultural reasons with a variety of interventions (Picard, 2007; Picard, 2008; Nielsen, 2011). These alter some of the negative economic factors that would otherwise influence the structure and output of print media.

DISTRIBUTION AND PRICE CHALLENGES

Physical distribution is highly influenced by unit cost economics, and digital distribution is significantly affected by transaction costs, thus requiring attention to be paid to distribution arrangements. When physical copies of books, magazines, and newspapers are involved, the cost of getting each copy to consumers is critical and will affect pricing throughout the distribution chain.

Three factors are particularly significant in physical distribution: distribution distance, density of delivery, and time available for delivery (Picard, 2011). This is because costs increase as distribution distance rises, decrease as delivery density mounts, and increase when distribution time is short. When digital copies are involved the distribution cost itself is near zero, but costs for intermediaries such as online retailers and payment transactions can be significant.

The complexity of distribution created by large geographic markets and distribution density produce challenges that make many publishers heavily reliant on independent wholesalers and retailers. In addition, few publishers own and operate their entire distribution chains, in order to save investment and operating costs, and most publishers outsource activities to specialized firms that provide expert services. An important driver for this is that distribution is a particularly labor intensive aspect of the print media value chain, and involves high wage and benefit costs, and structures that are often inefficiently utilized in the distribution of single titles.

In these retail distribution processes, publishers sell copies of newspapers, magazines, and books to wholesalers. The wholesalers operate warehouses and distribution centers, manage and account for sales to retailers and returns of unsold copies, and carry out other functions serving the retail establishments (Buchan and Siegfried, 1978). Newspapers often use independent distributors and carriers to deliver to homes.

When physical copies are distributed through retail establishments, publishers have incentives to keep shelves well stocked because they receive money from advertisers based on the total amount sold. They would rather have too many copies left on shelves and at newsstands than risk lost sales, a choice that does not apply normal demand principles. The choice creates significant sales inefficiencies with 15–20 percent of single copy sales newspapers typically remaining unsold at points of sale, 30–40 percent of books delivered to shops unsold, and about 60 percent of single copy sales magazines at newsstands unsold. The unsold copies create uncompensated costs for production, distribution, and product return that are ultimately passed on to consumers. Although the uncompensated production costs are borne by publishers, the distribution and product return costs are borne by wholesalers and retailers and this creates tensions over pricing and terms of service (Koschat et al., 2003; Picard, 2011).

Prices for print media products are influenced by the two- and multi-sided platforms through which they operate, but they are also affected by price challenges arising from distribution mechanisms employed. When a producer sells its product directly, it can respond clearly to price signals in its market. This is the norm for publishers who set their price and sell directly to consumers through subscriptions or single copy sales. Subscribed sales are particularly desirable because they lock consumers into purchases for a period of time, reducing uncertainty over the number of copies that need to be printed and lowering the amount of marketing costs required for operation. Newspapers and magazines have traditionally used subscriptions, and some books publishers have created a similar sales channel through the establishment of book clubs. Today, many publishers – especially book publishers – are engaging in direct and indirect single copy sales to consumers through the internet and other digital platforms.

The ability to perceive and respond to price signals is reduced when a producer is separated from a buyer. This, of course, is the norm when a producer uses a retail distribution mechanism. In these settings publishers sell copies to wholesalers, wholesalers sell copies to retailers, and retailers sell copies to end consumers, with each essentially retaining a portion of the final retail price. The publisher will normally suggest a retail price, but rarely has the complete authority or power to enforce it. The publisher, however, is able to set the price to wholesalers based on price signals from the wholesaler and, subsequently, the wholesaler can set prices for the retailer based on their price signals. Nevertheless, the price signals are somewhat weak and most prices are set using industry standards, which tend to favor large publishers over smaller publishers with fewer or slower moving titles.

Subscription and single-copy prices tend to be stable in the short term because of marketing costs and demand issues in raising nominal prices, but nevertheless publishers regularly adjust prices for inflation. It has been shown that consumer magazine prices tend to rise in the fiscal quarter after real prices have fallen and that higher levels of inflation lead to more frequent adjustments (Cecchetti, 1986).

Print media producers are typically more directly influenced when setting prices for advertisers, but the rise of media buying agencies that make the decisions on behalf of larger buyers has introduced an intermediary that can also muffle price signals because their decisions are based on many non-price criteria.

The importance of large retailers to print media – particularly books and magazines – is increasingly reducing their bargaining power against these sellers. When price rivalry between large publishers and small bookstores and magazine stands exists, there is little market power in the retailers. Large brick-and-mortar retailers such as Wal-Mart, Target, and major grocery chains are particularly important in sales of bestselling book and magazine titles, but carry a limited number of titles, making it difficult for publishers to negotiate price. This tends to push down the prices publishers obtain from such retailers. Digital retailers such as Amazon, Apple, and Google have become increasingly important distributors and provide a large number of both physical and digital titles – even for smaller publishers. They tend to use their abilities to move large numbers of books and magazines to turn publishers into price takers with little effective ability to negotiate or influence the wholesale or retail prices.

Although publishers have incentives to ensure the entire distribution system functions, they tend to pressure wholesalers and retailers to maintain cover prices, and have incentives to pay these parts of the distribution chain as little as possible. They also attempt to control the behavior of wholesalers through contractual obligations and arrangements that benefit publishers and push costs toward wholesalers and retailers with less market power (Ferrari and Verboven, 2012).

COMPETITION AMONG PRINT MEDIA

Competition amongst the three types of print media is limited by the significant differences in content, format, and timeliness. Even when they deal with a similar topic – international development, for example – newspapers convey it as breaking news, news/public affairs magazines analyze developments and their impact, and books deal with it in broader historical terms. Although not directly substitutable for readers, there is some broader competition for consumer sales because neither money nor time is boundless for consumers. With regards to advertisers, there is some broad level competition for advertising expenditures at the industry level, but the differences in the frequencies of publication of newspapers and magazines, the purposes of advertising typically placed in newspapers and magazines, and different presentational styles keep them from being highly substitutable.

Greater competition is evident within each type of print media, however. All books compete for consumers' attention and money, for example, but not all books are alike and equally desirable to individual consumers. Some are designed for education and professions and some for the general public. Children's books do not compete with adult fiction and university textbooks do not compete with coffee table books (Greco, 2004). Similar types of differences and further refined genres exist in the magazine industry, reducing direct competition to usually a few titles in genres such as home magazines, sports magazines, men's magazines, and so on (Mogul, 1998). Titles are usually heavily segmented and highly branded, and seek long term relationships with consumers to reduce competition for attention and money. The number of directly competing titles in a country is related to the size of audience; in countries with smaller populations there may be only two or three women's magazines, whereas there may be a dozen in larger countries.

TRADE IN PRINT MEDIA

Unlike many other kinds of products, print media are primarily domestic products because their content is interest- and culture-specific, and linguistic factors affect demand more than for audio-visual media. These factors limit international trade in print media, but not altogether. When direct exports are involved, the primary economic issues are costs for marketing and distribution, demand for copies, and revenue produced. It has been shown that there is a greater tendency toward international diversification of European publishers than US publishers (Van Kranenburg et al., 2004), perhaps because of smaller domestic market sizes and greater incentives to internationalize operations.

Newspapers provide news from within a specific geographic area and interpret news from elsewhere with a domestic – usually national – framework. This, combined with linguistic differences, highly limits trade in newspapers and such trade tends to involve national newspapers of record or cross-border distribution to nearby towns. When copies are exported, the primary economic issues are primarily distribution cost and price. Because advertisers are typically uninterested in international readers, the economic context changes from a two-sided to a one-sided platform, and normal consumer demand functions emerge. In international trade, newspapers tend not to be substitutes for papers in the countries to which they are imported, but act as supplements or complements to newspapers produced in that nation.

Magazines also face linguistic challenges in exportation, but their trade is further limited by differences in lifestyles and culture. This makes exportation of copies of consumer magazines particularly difficult, so the industry tends to export popular titles through licensing, co-production arrangements, or foreign direct investment that allows creation of multiple editions in different languages and countries, reflecting the original brand but with local content (Hall, 1983; Hafstrand, 1995). In these cases, the economics of trade are rather straightforward market transactions over rights or analysis of investment choices.

Books have historically been the most traded print media, especially those in major world languages. This is particularly true for literature, professional, and higher education materials (Altbach and Hoshino, 1995). Linguistic difference affects demand for such books, as well as their comprehension and enjoyment, so trade in translation rights is vigorous with publishers buying rights to translate and print popular titles from other countries (Hall, 1983).

DISCUSSION

The economics of print media are fundamentally affected by different economic factors than audio, audio-visual, and digital media because of physical production and distribution. Print media companies are increasingly moving into digital distribution as well, altering their traditional distribution economic environment and forcing them to address economic issues more akin to those in broadband and peer-to-peer activity.

In both print and digital operations, however, issues of advertising and advertising pricing are central, as are those of intellectual property rights, taxes, and subsidies. Because they are operating on multiple distribution platforms, economic issues involving multi-sided platforms are becoming increasingly complex and they are not well understood.

Although the structures and operations of print media are being altered, there is still significant demand for their products and services by both content consumers and advertisers. However, as that demand progressively shifts to digital platforms, the importance of the print operations will diminish and issues related to portfolio operations, costs, and pricing will become increasingly significant and offer significant new avenues for investigation.

REFERENCES

Altbach, P.G. and Hoshino, E.S. (eds) (1995). *International Book Publishing: An Encyclopedia*. Routledge.

Bakker, P., van der Wurff, R. and Picard, R.G. (2008). Economic growth and advertising expenditures in different media in different countries, *Journal of Media Economics*, 21(1):28–52.

Blackwell, R. (1954). The pricing of books, *The Journal of Industrial Economics*, 2(3):174–183.

Buchan, R.P. and Siegfried, J.J. (1978). An economic evaluation of the magazine distribution industry, *The Antitrust Bulletin*, 23:19–50.

Busterna, J.G. (1988). Concentration and the industrial organization model, in R.G. Picard, Maxwell McCombs, James P. Winter, and Stephen Lacy, *Press Concentration and Monopoly: New Perspectives on Newspaper Ownership and Operations*. Norwood, N.J.: Ablex Publishing.

Cecchetti, S.G. (1986). The frequency of price adjustment: A study of the newsstand prices of magazines, *Journal of Econometrics*, 31(3):255–274.

Chaudhri, V. (1998). Pricing and efficiency in the circulation industry: The case of newspapers, *Information Economics and Policy*, 10(1):59–76.

Corden, W.M. (1953). The maximisation of profit by a newspaper, *Review of Economic Studies*, 20:181–190.

Dealy, C.P., Henry, P. and Ryder, E. (1997). *The Book Publishing Industry*. Boston: Allyn and Bacon.

Depken II, C.A. (2004). Audience characteristics and the price of advertising in a circulation industry: Evidence from U.S. magazines, *Information Economics and Policy*, 16(2):179–196.

Doyle, G. (2013). *Understanding Media Economics*, 2nd ed. London: Sage.

Ferrari, S. and Verboven, F. (2012). Vertical control of a distribution network – an empirical analysis of magazines, *RAND Journal of Economics*, 43(1):26–50.

Greco, A. (2004). *The Book Publishing Industry*. Boston: Allyn and Bacon.

Hafstrand, H. (1995). Consumer magazines in transition: A study of approaches to Internationalization, *Journal of Media Economics*, 8(1):1–12.

Hall, L.B. (1983). *International Book and Magazine Licensing*. Greenwood, CT: Praeger.

Horovitz, P.M. (1965). A note on textbook pricing, *The American Economic Review*, 55(4):844–848.

Kaiser, U. and Wright, J. (2006). Price structure in two-sided markets: Evidence from the magazine industry, *International Journal of Industrial Organization*, 24:1–28.

Kalita, J.K. and Ducoffe, R.H. (1995). A simultaneous-equation analysis of pricing, circulation, and advertising revenue for leading consumer magazines, *Journal of Media Economics*, 8(4):1–16.

Koschat, M.A., Berk, G.L., Blatt, J.A., Kunz, N.M., LePore, M.H., and Blyakher, S. (2003). Newsvendors tackle the newsvendor problem, *Interfaces*, 33(1):72–84.

Lacy, S. and Simon, T.F. (1993). *The Economics and Regulation of U.S. Newspapers*. Norwood, NJ: Ablex.

Mogul, L. (1998). *The Magazine: Everything You Need to Know to Make It in the Magazine Business*, 4th ed. Routledge.

Nielsen, R.K. (2011). *Public Support for the Media: A Six-Country Overview of Direct and Indirect Subsidies*, RISJ Report, Reuters Institute for the Study of Journalism, University of Oxford.

Norton, S.W., and Norton Jr., W. (1986). Economies of scale and new technology of daily newspapers: A survivor analysis, *Quarterly Review of Economics and Business*, 26:66–83.

Picard, R.G. (1988). Pricing behavior of newspapers, in R.G. Picard et al. (eds), *Press Concentration and Monopoly: New Perspectives on Newspaper Ownership and Operation* (pp. 55–69). Norwood, NJ: Ablex.

Picard, R.G. (1998). A note on the relationships between circulation size and newspaper advertising rates, *Journal of Media Economics*, 11(2):47–55.

Picard, R.G. (2001). Effects of recessions on advertising expenditures: An exploratory study of economic downturns in nine developed nations, *Journal of Media Economics*, 14(1):1–14.

Picard, R.G. (2003). Temporal aspects of media distribution, in Alan B. Albarran and Angel Arrese (eds), *Time and Media Markets* (pp. 49–60). Mahwah, NJ: Lawrence Erlbaum.

Picard, R.G. (2007). Issues and challenges in the provision of press subsidies, in Isabel Fernández Alonso, Miquel de Moragas, José Joaquín Blasco Gil and Núria Almiron (eds), *Press Subsidies in Europe* (pp. 211–220). Barcelona: Generalitat de Catalunya.

Picard, R.G. (2008). Subsidies for the media, in Wolfgang Donsbach (ed.), *The International Encyclopedia of Communication*, Volume 11 (pp. 4891–4895). Oxford: Wiley-Blackwell.

Picard, R.G. (2011). *The Economics and Financing of Media Companies*, 2nd ed. New York: Fordham University Press.

Picard, R.G. and Brody, J.H. (1997). *The Newspaper Publishing Industry*. Boston: Allyn and Bacon.

Picard, R.G. and Rimmer, T. (1999). Weathering a recession: Effects of size and diversification on newspaper companies, *Journal of Media Economics*, 12(1):1–18.

Reddaway, W.B. (1963). The economics of newspapers, *The Economic Journal*, 73: 201–218.

Rosse, J.N. and Dertouzos, J.N. (1979). The evolution of one newspaper cities, in Federal Trade Commission, *Proceedings of the Symposium on Media Concentration*, Volume 2 (pp. 429–471). Washington, DC: Government Printing Office.

Siegfried, J.J. and Latta, C. (1998). Competition in the retail college textbook market, *Economics of Education Review*, 17(1):105–115.

Udell, J.G. (1978). *The Economics of the American Newspaper*. New York: Hastings House.

Van Kranenburg, H., Hagedoorn, J. and Pennings, J. (2004). Measurement of international and product diversification in the publishing industry, *Journal of Media Economics*, 17(2):87–104.

Venkatesh, R. and Chatterjee, R. (2006). Bundling, unbundling, and pricing of multiform products: The case of magazine content, *Journal of Interactive Marketing*, 20(2):21–40.

8. The economics of television: excludability, rivalry, and imperfect competition

Patrick Barwise and Robert G. Picard

Television is a part of everyday life and it is easy to overlook the complex economic factors and choices underpinning it. This chapter is designed to clarify those factors and choices by reviewing the fundamental elements of broadcasting economics, the economics behind different structural and financing choices, the economics of multichannel and pay television, how and why different forms of television are able to compete and coexist, and how digital switchover and convergence change, and might change, television economics.

The fundamental questions of broadcasting economics involve how spectrum is allocated, who owns broadcasting, and how it is funded. The answers to these questions in different countries emerged from both economic rationales and technical, social, and political factors. The very nature of broadcasting requires governmental involvement: because it uses electromagnetic spectrum and spectrum is constrained, not all who might like to broadcast have been able to do so, thus fundamental policy decisions created the structure of television markets and also influenced their economic characteristics.

Governments worldwide took different paths in creating television systems, usually following policy choices and trajectories they earlier created for radio. Some initially established television as a branch of government, some as public service television, and some as commercial television. In most countries the systems have evolved over time to create a mixture of state/public service and commercial television (or vice versa if they started with commercial broadcasting), with the size and wealth of countries greatly influencing the scale and scope of television services provided. All, however, have had to accommodate the fundamental economic characteristics of broadcasting.

Television, like radio before it, relies on scarce spectrum, a valuable public asset that is managed by governments. Because spectrum is a public resource with multiple uses, governments have to decide how it is allocated and who gets to use it. This process is undertaken at the global, regional, and national levels. In the initial development of radio and television, the spectrum available for broadcasting was highly constrained due to the limitations of early analogue transmission systems, making fully competitive broadcast markets impossible. Although technological advances throughout the twentieth century expanded the spectrum available and allowed it to be used more efficiently, demand for spectrum has always exceeded supply and constrained the development of a fully competitive broadcast market. Even today, the availability of spectrum for broadcasting is limited by the voracious appetite for the same spectrum by the larger and better-resourced mobile telecommunications industry. Auctioning spectrum – most economists' preferred allocation method – will almost always lead to mobile operators outbidding broadcasters. Whether this leads to increased welfare is debatable but beyond the scope of this chapter.[1]

Another factor inhibiting the creation of markets in broadcasting has been excludability problems. The ability to exclude those who have not paid from consuming a product or service is fundamental to the existence of any economically efficient market. Because of the open nature of broadcast signals, those who are unwilling to pay cannot be excluded from receiving them. Further, anyone can receive broadcasts without reducing their availability to others. Broadcasting is thus a public good, that is, a good which is both 'non-excludable' and 'non-rivalrous' (Owen et al., 1974; Wolpert and Wolpert, 1986; Owen and Wildman, 1992). These economic factors meant that the development and effective operation of the broadcast marketplace would be constrained by 'free-riding', with those who did not pay enjoying the benefits of others' expenditure, like someone riding a bus or train without paying. Unlike most products and services, including media such as print and traditional recorded music (vinyl, CDs, and so on), broadcasting requires investment in additional ('conditional access') technology in order to become excludable. Even with such technology, it remains non-rivalrous, with the partial exception of online distribution, where too many households viewing at the same time can lead to local and/or system-wide performance degradation.

Related to its non-rivalrous nature, television enjoys even greater economies of scale than other traditional media because of its very high fixed costs and low – or zero – variable costs. As we discuss more fully later, television content with sufficiently high production values to attract viewers in a competitive market combines high production costs (typically, a factor of at least ten times the hourly production cost for radio), low unit consumption costs, significant but effortless audience engagement, and imperfect competition. This has made television the dominant, highly cost-effective mass medium in nearly every country around the globe.

The cost per viewer hour depends on the production cost and the number of viewers over whom this is spread. The latter is partly determined by regulators and governments who control where broadcast stations are located and the power of transmitters (which determine the distances that signals will travel) but the main factors are the size and affluence of the overall population: countries with large, affluent populations can support many more channels, greater production, and much higher production values.

Because of these structural and economic factors, government policy has always been needed to create workable television broadcasting systems and markets.

The fundamental economic challenges led some governments to select compulsory collective financing designed to provide a universal broadcasting service. Many countries in Europe and beyond chose this public ownership route, creating some form of public or state broadcasting funded by licence fees or general taxation – with varying degrees of independence from government control. The US and other countries took a commercial route because of financial constraints on governments or ideological and other cultural factors, with financing initially provided by advertising. Both the public ownership and commercial policy choices produced free-to-air (FTA) television available to anyone within signal range who has a TV set. This remains the fundamental form of television broadcasting worldwide today.

From an economic standpoint, the public ownership choice spreads costs efficiently across the population, but does not create a market in which economic efficiency emerges from the interplay of producer and consumer self interest. Public ownership typically established a monopoly provider for television, with its attendant economic inefficiencies, although those monopolies were progressively reduced in most democracies during the later twentieth century.

Advertising funded FTA broadcasting spreads costs somewhat less efficiently than public ownership because it does not spread costs evenly across the population (some viewers are worth more to advertisers than others) and does not provide universal service (viewers in remote areas may not generate enough revenue to warrant incurring the high unit cost of distribution). In practice, these problems are limited because (a) terrestrial transmissions supplemented by local cable systems fed by community antennas (CATV) enable near-universal service in many developed nations and (b) relative to other media, audience preferences for different types of TV content are rather weakly segmented (Barwise and Ehrenberg, 1988; Sharp et al., 2009) so FTA commercial broadcasters do not underprovide programmes for less affluent viewers. The problem is almost the opposite: some types of programmes (for example challenging drama, heavyweight current affairs, demanding culture) for which enough viewers would be willing to pay to cover the cost of supply, attract audiences that are too small to generate enough advertising revenue to pay for them. In other words, because the funding comes from advertisers rather than directly from consumers, FTA commercial TV tends to suffer a restricted range of easy-viewing programmes. Nevertheless, consumers do influence the available content and, if there is competition, the self interest of broadcasters does promote efficiency. Commercial television is still not a free market, however, because spectrum and policy barriers limit the ability of new broadcasters to enter the market and advertisers have significant influence over programmes offered – thus keeping audiences from balancing producers' market power with the power normally provided consumers in efficient markets.

The removal of monopolies in television – as was the case when competition to the British Broadcasting Corporation (BBC) was introduced in 1955 or when second commercial broadcasters began appearing in various markets in the US in the late 1940s – created competition for audiences, that is, rivalry between broadcasters for viewers. This competition exists whether there is competition between publicly owned broadcasters, commercial broadcasters, or a combination of the two. Such competition also creates a labour market in which broadcasters vie to employ the most talented people, increasing demand for their services. Finally, competition among broadcasters creates a programme acquisition market in which they contend to acquire rights to carry sporting events, films, and syndicated programmes. As in all markets, competition in television-related markets increases pressures for efficiency and lowers many costs, but it also leads to higher costs as competing broadcasters bid up the price of top talent and premium acquired content (big sporting events, first-run Hollywood movies, and high-rating TV series).

When free-to-air broadcasting was the only form of television, regulators and broadcasters jointly created workable and well-funded television broadcast systems. These were based on monopoly and oligopolistic structures that funnelled large amounts of revenue to major players and allowed them to grow and create large, well-funded organisations. However, both publicly owned and commercial broadcasters had imperfect incentives to pursue economic efficiency in these systems or to offer consumers significant choice of programmes. That situation began to change significantly when technological developments produced opportunities for new types of television service to compete with free-to-air television. The next section turns to how developments outside of terrestrial broadcasting and the development of pay television services altered the environment and created new economic influences on television.

MULTICHANNEL CABLE, SATELLITE, AND SUBSCRIPTION TV

Multichannel television emerged from simple CATV cable technology that extended television distribution to areas where broadcast reception was limited – usually by geographic impediments. These systems initially only re-transmitted broadcasts from nearby cities. Consumers paid the cable operators the costs of the community antenna and cabling needed to bring the signals to their homes in a relatively straightforward service market. Cable companies soon realised, however, that they could provide additional channels that were not available locally, adding value that allowed them to charge higher prices and increase revenue and profit. Over time, community antennas picking up local terrestrial broadcasts were replaced by a system of geostationary satellites with nationwide 'footprints', whose signals were received by large satellite dishes for local cable distribution. Some non-broadcast channels such as HBO (Home Box Office), that were available only on cable systems, emerged as pay TV networks, while others, such as CNN and MTV, began seeking funding through advertising as well as payments from cable operators. The number of available channels on cable increased from a handful of local stations to several dozen national networks, with the number limited only by the capacity of the satellites and cables.

By the 1980s, more powerful satellites made it possible to broadcast direct to any home that mounted a small dish with a direct line of sight to the satellite, avoiding the huge infrastructure costs of laying cable lines to homes. Cable and DTH satellite TV services initially used analogue technologies with limited channel capacity. Conversion to digital began in the late 1990s, gradually increasing the number of channels from dozens to hundreds and enabling new features, such as electronic programme guides and digital video recorders.

These new systems circumvented the broadcast spectrum limitations that constrained terrestrial television but increased demand for other spectrum needed to operate their microwave, satellite, and other wireless telecommunication links. Despite the growing demand for that new spectrum, multichannel television providers were able to increase dramatically the number of channels available to viewers.

Multichannel systems began operating in nations and regions around the globe, providing viewers new options for obtaining television services. In most cases these were provided as market-based, commercial systems in which operating companies acquired rights to channels and sold subscriptions for consumers to access the channels.

Cable and satellite operators provided set-top boxes to convert the signals so subscribers could view them on their television sets. To avoid the free-rider problem of free-to-air television and inhibit use by those who might intercept signals, companies added conditional access technologies that scrambled the signals – providing excludability – so that only those who had paid could watch the programmes.

Unlike FTA terrestrial TV services funded by the licence fee, taxation or advertising, cable services were not available in all homes within the limits of the broadcast signal for two reasons: (1) decisions about where to offer services were based on analysis of demand, infrastructure costs and the potential for return on investment – typically creating incentives to invest in urban and suburban areas, and (2) ability and willingness to pay varied significantly across households.

Satellite services largely removed the first of these constraints because the cost per home was relatively low and largely independent of both population density and location. The number of available channels available no longer depended on the number of terrestrial stations or cable capacity where one lived, but on one's willingness and ability to pay.

Subscription, pay television is a 'purer' television market than free-to-air television because it is based on market prices, consumer payments, and more consumer channel and programme choices. These services also increase the overall competition for audiences, advertising revenue (because many of the new channels carry advertising), content rights, and on- and off-screen talent, driving up costs for all broadcasters.

Most pay television operators benefit from both subscription and advertising revenue. Advertising accounts for only a small proportion of pay TV operators' revenue but a higher proportion of their gross profit margin since it has relatively low incremental fixed costs and minimal variable cost. Many consumers are willing to pay much more for premium channels than either the level of the licence fee or the revenue per home that can be generated by advertising alone. Despite their lower availability (due to price elasticity and, in the case of cable, lower geographical availability), pay TV operators have been able to pay higher prices for rights than FTA broadcasters, so many sporting events, most first-run movies, and some other premium content is increasingly no longer universally available on free-to-air channels.

The developments in non-terrestrial broadcasting have created television environments that now blend the different types of television services. It is important to comprehend how their economics and business dynamics differ, and how they coexist. We address those issues in the next section.

THE MIXED ECONOMY OF CONTEMPORARY TELEVISION

Three main funding models are now evident in television: (1) FTA television wholly or partly funded by licence fees or general taxation; (2) FTA television funded by advertising; and (3) Pay TV funded by consumer subscriptions and sometimes with advertising.

Although each is part of the wider television market, each operates with a different economic logic in a separate submarket because the economic characteristics and incentives differ. Each model has relied on a different primary funding source, although that is changing somewhat. In many other countries, public broadcasters are funded by a combination of licence fees or taxation and advertising, with the proportion of advertising growing over time as governments seek to hold down the level of the licence fee. Satellite and cable platforms and channels have always been funded by a combination of subscriptions (and some pay-per-view for major sporting events, concerts, and other events) and advertising. Although subscription revenue is starting to mature in the most developed markets, it is still expected by most analysts to increase further, and advertising to decrease further, as a percentage of total industry revenue. Many are now gaining additional revenue by syndicating programmes they own to FTA channels after their use on the pay TV window.

Funding, ownership, and regulation models determine to whom broadcasters are accountable and who their main customers are. These models significantly influence programming policies, cost structures, competition, and many other aspects of how broadcasters serve the public and deliver value for money and social welfare. Economic incentives differ between the three submarkets, but there are two generic, interrelated factors that apply to all television services, regardless of how they are funded: the cost structure of production and distribution, and the nature of the audience's programme preferences.

As already mentioned, the underlying cost structure of television is simple: high fixed production cost, zero variable production cost (that is, the production cost of a programme is unaffected by the number of people who then watch it unless producers choose to increase investment for other purposes), and – usually – relatively low physical distribution cost. This is therefore a market with extreme economies of scale, in which the unit cost of production for a given programme falls inversely with the number of viewers. Although consumer video cameras and editing equipment now mean that nearly anyone can create TV programmes, the cost of long-form video content that audiences will choose to watch on a mainstream channel, far from falling, is generally rising faster than general inflation and makes such competition rare. Viewers are accustomed to high production values and quality in performance (in the studio, sport arena, and theatre), direction, editing, and technical standards (sound recording, camera work, and so on). The market for talent is increasingly winner-take-all, with the top few performers earning – and costing – much more than others who are either not quite as accomplished or are simply less well known. Digital technology is increasingly used to enhance programme quality through, for example, more live feeds from around the world, better graphics, and computer-generated images, at least as much as to reduce costs. Increased competition for the best acquired content further drives up costs.

The high fixed cost of programmes able to attract large audiences is one of the fundamentals of TV economics.[2] It applies globally and regardless of the funding method. Internationally, the economics favour countries with large populations and high GDP per capita and allows them to produce more high quality programming and rely less on imported and syndicated programming (Lowe and Nissen, 2011).

The audience's general preference for high production values (reinforcing the extreme economies of scale of TV) is, however, mitigated by a preference for local content, where 'local' mainly means 'national'. Other things being equal, American viewers prefer American content, Malaysian viewers prefer Malaysian content, and Germans prefer German content because national content is generally more culturally and individually relevant. This relevance is reinforced because audiences generally prefer content created in their own language rather than that which is dubbed or subtitled.

These factors are present in all three funding models of television, but each of the three has specific economic characteristics and incentives, creating significant differences in their operations and performance.

Licence Fee Funded Television

Licence fee funding is used to provide FTA television services through public service broadcasters. The system was introduced for radio in the UK when the only way to hear radio programmes was by buying a radio set, listening to BBC broadcasts, and paying a licence fee to fund the content. The TV licence, introduced in 1946, simply extended the same approach to television when the BBC was the only UK television broadcaster. This funding mechanism is still used in the UK and many other countries.

With licence fee funding and public ownership, there is no direct financial incentive to make particular investment and programming decisions. Licence funding frees the broadcaster from paying attention to the needs of investors (as in the case of commercial firms) and advertisers (as in the FTA advertising funded model), or of dealing directly with viewers as consumers (as in the pay TV model).

Licence funded broadcasters do, however, need to take account of viewers' interests in order to maintain public and political support, including by attracting enough viewing hours and 'audience reach' (the proportion of homes or individuals watching at least some of the time in a given time period, such as a week) to ensure that the licence fee is seen as good value for money – for example as measured by the cost per viewer hour – as well as to meet audience appreciation and overall satisfaction standards set by regulators. Compared with purely commercial broadcasters, they can, and must, also pay attention to broader social interests to justify their continued existence (Picard, 2006a, b). There is an inherent tension between these two broad aims – maximising viewing, to ensure high reach and good value for money, and increasing the number and quality of less popular programmes that commercial broadcasters will not show.

In principle, it would be possible to combine licence fee funding with private ownership. A government could auction a time-limited licence for monopoly access to the money raised, with some regulation of the level of the licence fee and/or how the money is spent. Alternatively, the funding might be distributed programme by programme or channel by channel through a public body that allocated resources in response to competitive bids. This approach appeals to free-market economists because it forces applicants to focus on public service criteria and avoids 'distorting' the market, by making funds available to all who wish to contest for them (Peacock, 2004; Broadcasting Policy Group, 2004).

The universal licence fee can be a cost-effective way of funding television because it generates a large programme budget at a low cost per home compared with the price of subscription TV. There are several reasons for this:

- All television homes contribute to the programme fund and operational overheads through licence fees, whereas with pay TV subscriptions, costs have to be covered by a smaller customer base – those willing to pay for the service.
- As a consequence of the 'non-rival' aspect of broadcasting as a 'public good', once a transmission network is in place and a programme has been made, it costs nothing to make it available to everyone reached by the network and there is even a small cost saving compared to pay TV because investment in conditional access technology is not needed.
- Licence fee revenue generation costs are lower than for advertising or subscriptions because large expenditure on sales or marketing is not required, allowing a higher proportion of revenue to be invested in content.

Because of these factors, a well-managed and well-regulated licence fee funded broadcaster can provide remarkable value for money in pure consumer terms, as measured by universal access, high reach, and a lower cost per viewer hour than for pay TV.

Public ownership, regulation, and licence fee funding also force and enable public broadcasters to address public service rather than private objectives. This makes it possible for them to provide a wider and more diverse range of programmes and news and current affairs coverage independent of commercial interests, and potentially, because of the stability of funding, to take a longer-term perspective and more creative risks.

The downside of the public's ownership is that there will always be disagreements about its scale, scope, content, and priorities. Popularity with audiences invariably creates resentment among commercial competitors, as can commercial activities such as programme sales, DVDs, and on-demand services that supplement the licence fee. Such criticisms are leading to increasing economic debates about licence fee supported television.

Free-market economists object on ideological grounds to the existence and market impact of large publicly owned, licence fee funded players. Underlying their objections is an implicit assumption that a publicly owned broadcaster funded by the licence fee is inevitably less efficient – and therefore provides less value for money in pure consumer terms – than a commercial broadcaster funded by advertising or subscriptions. Although many economists make this assumption, some do not. Up to this point, there has been only one systematic attempt, to our knowledge, to evaluate the evidence in this contested area (Barwise and Picard,

2014). In addition, most economists agree that some public service objectives have societal value beyond the cost of achieving them, that the market will under-provide at least some such content, and that there is a case for some public intervention to address this 'market failure'.

Economists embracing free-market ideology see the implication of these points as being that a publicly owned broadcaster should provide only those types of programme that the market will not and whose value against some criterion (other than the ability to generate commercial revenue) exceeds their cost, for example 'Public service broadcasting should consist of supplying consumer wants where such wants, for some reason, cannot be provided through the market' (Booth, 2004: 18). Economists taking a welfare economics approach argue that limiting a publicly owned broadcaster to providing only programming the market is uninterested in does not allow it to make other contributions to social, cultural, and economic well-being (Graham and Davies, 1997; Graham et al., 1999).

Advertising-supported Television

Advertising-supported television is usually operated as a commercial enterprise, but many publicly owned public service broadcasters globally are at least partially funded by advertising.

In economic terms, free-to-air advertising funded commercial TV is accountable to its owners and, like other private enterprises, governed in ways that ensure that their interests are prioritised, subject to regulation. Programme quality is judged only on the ability to generate income from selling advertising airtime. Programming investments are made only to the point that they are expected to generate a return equal to or exceeding the risk-adjusted opportunity cost of capital, thereby maximising shareholder value. Commercial broadcasters also need to divert a portion of profits to compensate investors for their capital, thus reducing the proportion of revenue available to invest in programmes.

Commercial TV is not a pure economic market, however, because those who consume the programming – the viewers – do not pay for it and they have no direct ability to influence managerial actions through price evaluation and purchase choices. It is a 'two-sided' market in which viewers are attracted by free-to-air programming and access to them is sold to the advertisers who are the revenue source for the enterprise (Coase, 1950, 1966; Picard, 2011).

There is a rivalry between advertisers and broadcasters over the price of commercial airtime. Advertisers have an incentive to pay only to the extent that they believe that their investment will produce returns by adequately increasing brand awareness and the sales and prices of the advertised products and services. Broadcasters have an incentive to raise the price of airtime to the point that maximises revenue, that is, beyond which the reduction in the volume of airtime sold would more than offset the higher revenue per unit.

As already noted, FTA commercial broadcasters' reliance on advertising income influences their programming. There is no incentive to serve broader social interests and little incentive to show programmes that increase viewers' satisfaction but attract insufficient ratings and advertising revenue to cover their costs. FTA commercial TV broadcasters also have little incentive to invest in innovative and risky original programming, since a programme that attracts fewer viewers than expected will lead to the broadcaster having to compensate advertisers, but programmes that attract more viewers than expected do not lead to increased payments from advertisers, at least in the short term.

The result of these factors is that certain culturally and socially useful programme types, such as serious drama and demanding factual programmes, cost more to produce and distribute than the advertising revenue they generate so they are dropped in favour of more profitable types. Advertisers also generally avoid advertising on programmes involving controversial topics or that otherwise provide an unhelpful environment for their products and services.

Because of the incentive to control programme costs while generating large audiences, the major free-to-air commercial networks tend to produce heavy offerings of relatively low-cost entertainment such as game shows, talent shows, and reality shows, and all channels usually offer a rather similar mix of undemanding 'middle-of-the-road' programmes (Owen and Wildman, 1992) in a way reminiscent of Hotelling's (1929) economic theory.

Because the programming is provided free-to-air, advertising funded television maintains the 'public good' economic characteristics of licence fee funded television: no one is excluded and the marginal cost of homes tuning in is zero. A significant difference from licence fee funded broadcasters, however, is that revenue for advertising-supported television fluctuates from quarter to quarter and year to year, depending upon the ability of its programmes to attract audiences (a challenge because programming is a good of uncertain ex ante quality even to the producer) and also because advertising expenditure is strongly affected by economic conditions. This further reduces mid- and long-term planning of programme expenditures and makes it hard to take a longer-term investment perspective.

The main focus of commercial TV broadcasters funded by advertising is maximising their channels' share of commercial viewing (relative to the cost of programmes), thereby maximising their advertising revenue. Although some might assume the share of total television advertising revenue is equal to its share of commercial viewing, this is not the case because channels sell different amounts of air time and the prices for air time are not the same on all channels at a particular time of day. These differences exist for strategic reasons and because some programme audiences are less valuable than others because of size or characteristics. In some countries, regulations limit the total amount of advertising per hour or in certain categories of programming also constrain advertising revenues.

Revenue generation costs for advertising-supported television tend to be higher than for licence fee funding because they include substantial selling costs and media agency fees.

Advertiser funded television is a major source of original and syndicated programming in most countries but, because of its economic characteristics and advertisers' priorities, it cannot serve the full range of programme wants and needs of audiences and society. With the growth of pay TV, regulators are increasingly allowing FTA commercial broadcasters to narrow their programme offerings in order to remain viable.

Subscription Television

Subscription TV operates in a purer economic market than either licence fee or advertising funded television because platform operators generate their subscription revenue directly from consumers rather than by selling audiences to advertisers, and they are purely commercial activities without public service obligations.[3] Most of the economic features of this market are therefore those of standard microeconomic theory.

As with all commercial markets, the operators aim to maximise profits by charging what the market will bear. Many homes are unable or unwilling to pay the market price, so subscription television does not provide universal service (Bloch and Wirth, 1984; Wirth and Bloch, 1989).

Although it is more firmly market-based, even subscription/pay TV is not a pure market, because of multiple bundling practices. First, content is bundled with the platform, usually a satellite or cable service (and increasingly also bundled with broadband and fixed/mobile telephony). Consequently, subscribers do not pay content suppliers directly. Second, individual programmes are bundled into channels and paid for almost entirely through monthly subscriptions. In a pure-market textbook world, programmes would be unbundled and bought on a pay-per-view basis. This does happen for occasional high-value sport events and, with internet-based video-on-demand (VoD) services, some other content, especially movies, but the dominant pay TV model continues to be subscription-based because it avoids the transaction and choice costs of pay-per-view. Finally, operators bundle channels together into packages with different price points. This again simplifies the choice process for consumers but also means that subscribers may be paying for more channels than they wish to buy.

Despite these limitations, subscription TV is highly responsive to viewers' preferences because platform and channel operators have a direct incentive to offer consumers attractive – and if possible exclusive – programming (Baldwin et al., 1991).

The markets for subscription TV platforms and channels, like many information markets, tend to be highly concentrated because of economies of scale in content acquisition, marketing, and distribution (Wu, 2010; Savage and Wirth, 2005). This leads to a small number of dominant platforms offering a few high-priced movie, sport, and other premium channels, with a larger second tier of lower-priced and FTA channels.

Pay television services differ fundamentally from free services in that they use conditional access technologies (such as encryption, set-top boxes, and smart cards) to exclude those who do not pay for the services. They are thus normal paid-for services, not public goods. Although they aim to serve large audiences, their main commercial objective is to maximise subscription revenue, not audience size, and their audiences tend to be significantly smaller than if the same programmes were shown on one of the main FTA channels. For instance, in the UK, test match cricket and the US show *Mad Men* both suffered a collapse in ratings when they moved from Channel 5 and BBC4, respectively, to the dominant pay-TV platform BSkyB.

Nevertheless, pay TV introduces significantly greater competition and choice (for those willing and able to pay for it) by greatly increasing the number of channels and competitors compared with a market with only FTA television supported by licence fee and/or advertising.

Pay TV services have higher marketing, distribution, and customer service costs than free-to-air broadcasters because they must (i) attract new subscribers to replace those lost, (ii) meet the capital and operating costs of distribution using satellite or cable technology, including the costs of conditional access equipment and installation, and (iii) provide more extensive invoicing and customer service functions. Subscription TV services' relatively high overhead costs reduce the proportion of revenue they can afford to spend on programmes compared to FTA commercial and licence fee funded broadcasters.

The dual product, or two-sided market, nature of free-to-air commercial broadcasting becomes even more complex in the pay television market, where broadcasters must typically maximise a combination of subscription and advertising income (Bel et al., 2007). Most of these broadcasters' revenue comes from subscriptions, but their advertising revenue generates high gross margins and is also important for profitability of many channels.

The consequences of the economic characteristics, consumer demand, and business strategies of subscription television are that it does not provide universal service and is governed by the economic interests of both suppliers and consumers. It is given scope by regulators to operate more independently than free television supported by licence fees and advertising because the power exercised by consumers over programme choice and price acts as a countervailing power to that of the suppliers, albeit moderated by pay TV operators' tendency towards high market concentration.

HOW LICENCE FEE, ADVERTISING, AND SUBSCRIPTION FUNDED TELEVISION COMPETE AND COEXIST

Like other media businesses, all broadcasters compete for talent and acquired content on the supply side. On the demand side, however, they compete in three conceptually distinct submarkets, for audiences, consumer payments, and advertising (Figure 8.1).

In the audience market, TV also competes for viewers' time and attention against other media and leisure activities. In the advertising market, it competes against other ways of spending marketing money, including other advertising media. In the consumer payment market, it ultimately competes against all other consumer products and services, but especially against other leisure activities, including other consumer media that charge for content. In all three submarkets, the big new player is the internet, but TV is competing remarkably successfully, especially in comparison with print media.

Where a television provider locates within these markets depends on its funding model (Figure 8.2). TV broadcasters are in head-to-head competition for revenue only if they have the same business models or mix of business models. Licence fee, advertising, and subscription funded TV broadcasters all compete for audience time and attention

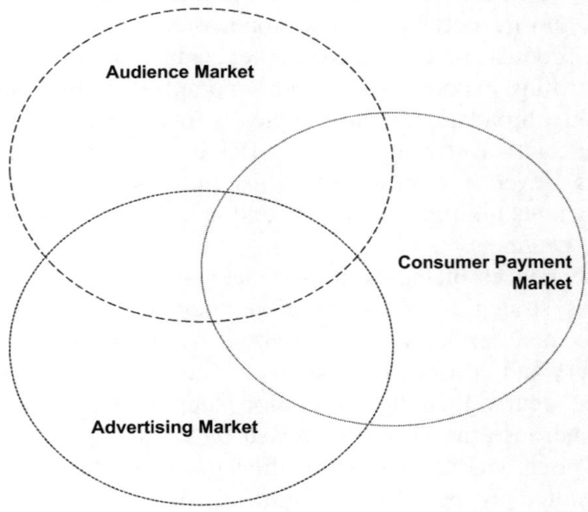

Figure 8.1 Television's three demand-side markets

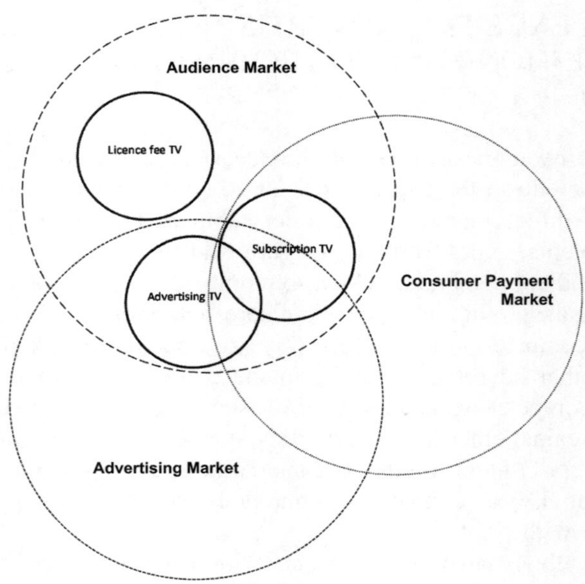

Figure 8.2 Competition among television providers based on funding

within the audience market, but that is where their demand-side similarities largely end.

Advertising funded free-to-air television competes within the advertising market, whereas licence fee funded TV does not. This difference has helped commercial broadcasters coexist with licence fee funded broadcasters. Similarly, subscription TV competes in the consumer payment market, whereas FTA commercial television does not. This difference has allowed pay TV and FTA commercial TV businesses to coexist.

Because some channels on pay TV platforms rely at least partly on advertising revenue as well as on subscriptions, pay TV operates in the advertising as well as in the consumer payment market, competing against FTA players. The decision to operate as a paid broadcaster with advertising is strategic in that the broadcaster is giving up the large mass audience of FTA broadcasting – thus gaining much lower income from advertising but gaining potentially much more revenue through consumer subscriptions.

Because television is still such good value for money (the cost per viewer hour is less than for almost every other leisure activity apart from radio listening), subscriptions – already the biggest revenue source in the USA and UK – are still growing in most countries. Although all three types of broadcaster compete for the audience's time and attention, the only type that fully aims to maximise audience size (subject to programming costs and, to a lesser extent, viewer demographics) is advertiser funded TV (Barwise and Ehrenberg, 1988, pp. 111–113).

Licence fee funded broadcasters also look for large audiences in order to demonstrate value for money but they also measure their performance against a wide range of other public service criteria including audience appreciation (Barwise and Ehrenberg, 1988, Chapter 5; Barwise et al., 1979; Barwise and Ehrenberg, 1987). For pay TV broadcasters, the aim is to maximise the number of consumers willing to pay a high monthly subscription, which in turn comes down to consumer satisfaction – especially for the content not available on FTA channels – rather than audience size *per se*.

Because subscription TV competes primarily in the consumer payments market, is premium-priced, and attracts smaller audiences than free-to-air television, it has relatively little competitive impact on FTA television on the demand side (its impact on the supply side is much bigger) except insofar as it competes for advertising. In contrast, FTA television – especially high-quality, commercial-free, licence fee funded TV – almost certainly does reduce consumers' willingness to pay for subscription TV.

All three forms of television are being affected by digitalisation, and the change to digital free-to-air broadcasting has significant implications for television environments and the economics of television.

HOW MIGHT DIGITAL SWITCHOVER AND CONVERGENCE FURTHER CHANGE TELEVISION ECONOMICS?

The switchover to digital television – where analogue broadcasts are switched off and all TV is delivered using digital channels – is occurring at varying paces in different countries. Some have already completed switchover, some are in the process of doing so, and some have yet to begin. Digital switchover continues the tradition of broadcasting using spectrum, but does so more efficiently, creating opportunities for more broadcast channels. It replaces analogue television receivers with sets or set-top-boxes that are digitally adapted, allowing easy connections to digital terrestrial, cable and satellite services and some other digital technologies such as digital video recorders (DVRs) and camcorders. However, digital switchover should not be confused with digital convergence, which in the context of television refers to the adoption and usage of new online technologies for the delivery of TV content over the internet.[4] Digital convergence has the potential to shift the fundamental economics of broadcasting towards being inextricably linked to the economics of broadband telecommunications (covered in Chapter 10).

Even digital switchover, however, could have radical implications for the financing and business models of television because the combination of conditional access technology and the reduction in the reliance on scarce spectrum means that one could in principle move to a free-market system funded entirely by subscriptions and/or advertising. It could also produce media systems with no or much smaller publicly owned broadcasters because the main historical economic rationale for their existence – spectrum scarcity – would no longer be as significant a constraint. The debate over whether that would be desirable would not be only about market economics but would also focus on welfare economics questions related to cultural and social objectives. Because digital switchover is already complete in some countries and in process in many others, this debate may happen imminently in democratic countries that still have significant public service broadcasters funded by licence fees or taxation.

Looking further ahead, in a fully converged environment, television programmes would be converted to Internet Protocol data packets and distributed online, sharing networks and devices with other internet traffic – social media, online shopping, news, user-generated content, and so on. In this purely technological sense, all online media and content would be converged. On the internet there is no clear-cut technical distinction between TV content and other video content such as YouTube clips and videos embedded in newspaper sites and company websites. In this environment content can be sliced and diced, combined with other content, supplemented with additional content at the click of a button, shared between consumers in different places, and bought and sold in any convenient way, including pay-per-view (PPV). Viewers can watch whenever and increasingly – with mobile internet – wherever they want on the platform of their choice.

These long-predicted radical technological changes[5] have the potential for powerful impact on the economics of television. Among the possibilities is the movement from so-called 'linear' to 'non-linear' television (Barwise, 2011) in which the primary way people watch television moves from a linear stream to online video-on-demand. This change would mean that people switch from 'passive [viewing] through the linear schedule' to 'active [consumption] using search and on-demand' (Department of Culture, Media and Sport and Department for Business, 2009). In this situation, one can distinguish between six categorically different viewing behaviours:

1. Live viewing of traditional linear TV.
2. Time-shifted viewing using a DVR or similar offline device.
3. Online catch-up viewing, which is also time-shifted viewing but does not require viewers to pre-set the recording.
4. Online preview viewing, for example watching a future episode immediately after the linear broadcast of an episode.
5. True online video-on-demand (VoD) viewing of original content not previously (or recently) broadcast.
6. Viewing of retail or rental video content distributed via offline, removable storage media such as DVDs.

The speed and scale of changes that will occur in the converged world are uncertain because they are not merely questions of technology availability but also of consumer adoption and usage and various supply-side developments. It is still early days, especially for superfast broadband and connected TVs, and there is a lot of individual variation within and between homes. Early results, however, indicate that most people in households with converged TV technology remain predominantly viewers of traditional linear TV (1 in the above list) and that a high proportion of their non-live viewing comprises offline or online time-shifted viewing, but of much the same content from the same favourite channels, that is, 2 and 3 in the list (Barwise, 2011). However, true on-demand viewing (5 in the list) is growing – especially as a substitute for removable storage media such as DVDs (6 in the list) and many analysts expect the long-predicted change to predominantly online, on-demand viewing to happen over the next few years, facilitated by fast broadband networks (see Chapter 10).

One reason for our scepticism about the speed and scale of digital convergence is that research on *why* people watch online television (Deloitte, 2010) finds that the main reasons are to watch recent TV programmes which they missed, to watch a TV programme or movie a second time, and to view something for free rather than paying. All of these are still about traditional 'linear' content on traditional channels. Less important reasons are to see content that is not available on television, to keep informed during a breaking news story, and to see additional content about a programme. Even these are often driven by or derived from traditional television.

There is also a technological quality issue, at least for now. Compared with broadcasting, the internet still offers a relatively unreliable, poor-quality and expensive physical distribution channel for video. To replace quality video broadcasting the technology will need to mature and either viewers or advertisers will have to pay the internet service providers for significant extra bandwidth costs. Capacity and price hurdles are being reduced, of course, but we are still a long way from a point where it makes economic sense to replace the digital terrestrial TV networks with online distribution.

Finally, there are well-established habitual and social factors to overcome. For over half a century, viewers have watched a mixture of drama, comedy, news, sport, documentaries, and general entertainment, mostly to relax, in the evening, in the living room, with other family members. Despite all the changes in video technologies, viewing patterns have proved remarkable stable. How much, what, when, where, with whom, and even how people watch TV has changed surprisingly little since the 1960s (Sharp et al., 2009). The biggest change is that viewing is now spread over hundreds of channels, but with a few still capturing the majority of the viewing in most countries.

To whatever extent the connected non-linear television world develops, it will further alter the economics of what we call television by disaggregating the stream into individual programmes that can be sold directly to consumers or traded with them in exchange for exposure to marketing messages. If and when this happens, it will create something much closer to a textbook market because the constraint on the number of stations is no longer a factor. This will alter supply of programmes, but will also affect their costs because each will be a separate product to be marketed and distributed individually. Suppliers will seek economies of scale and scope through bundling multiple programmes on common platforms, probably still using channels and mainly subscription payments to reduce uncertainty and transaction and choice costs. However, the business models, consumer responses and revenue sources for those operations are only now emerging and their effects on choice are far from clear.

CONCLUSIONS

There are unique elements in the economics of the various forms of television (licence fee, advertising, and subscription funded) and their market dynamics differ because of their varying relations to revenue sources, number of direct competitors, costs of marketing and distribution, and the degrees of rivalry and excludability afforded. The different forms of television do not thus directly compete in the same demand-side market (although, on the supply side, they do compete for talent and acquired content). As has been shown, however, the forms of television compete to varying degrees in overlapping markets and the competition is far more nuanced than often suggested.

Although television shares the high first-copy cost factor for the creation of content with other media, it differs from them in significant ways. Television differs from print media (newspapers, magazines, and books) because it does not have to cope with the unit cost factors created by production and distribution of a physical product, because the number of competitors is still somewhat limited by spectrum, and because of the difficulties of excludability that it faces. It differs from radio in that it has much higher production costs and also requires much more spectrum, and thus has fewer competitors. It also generates much more revenue per hour, whether from consumers (subscriptions or licence fees) or advertisers. It differs from the internet because it remains a one-to-many medium for distributing compelling long-form audio-visual content and advertisements, whereas the internet is a protean many-to-many communication and transaction channel with multiple uses for both individuals and organisations. TV is currently able to generate more revenue than the internet from both subscriptions and display advertising but much less from individual transactions and from search and classified advertising.

It is clear, however, that new technologies and the attendant new forms and operations of television are significantly altering the economic characteristics and dynamics of television provision and consumption and will continue to do so in the coming decades. The overall trend is toward the creation of more effective markets for television by overcoming or avoiding factors that inhibited the operation of the market in the past. This change has implications for those who view television as more than a mere product and service and are thus concerned with welfare aspects of television markets.

NOTES

1. Barwise and Picard, 2012, pp. 8–9.
2. The production cost varies greatly between genres and individual programmes and is typically much lower for daytime programmes, children's programmes, etc. These differences do not affect the overall cost structure discussed here.
3. There is no inherent reason why a subscription funded broadcaster could not be publicly owned and/or have public service obligations, although we are not aware of any country that has introduced this system.
4. Barwise and Picard, 2012, pp. 33 and 38.
5. See Barwise, 2011. The digerati have been predicting an imminent radical switch to online on-demand viewing for over 20 years, e.g. Gilder, 1990; Negroponte, 1995; Gates, 1995.

REFERENCES

Baldwin, T.F., Connie L. Ono, and Seema Shirkhande (1991), 'Program Exclusivity and Competition in the Cable Television Industry', *Journal of Media Economics*, 4/3, 29–45.

Barwise, Patrick (2004), *Independent Review of the BBC's Digital Television Services* (October), DCMS.

Barwise, Patrick (2011), 'Waiting for Vodot', *Market Leader* (March), 30–3.

Barwise, Patrick and A.S.C. Ehrenberg (1987), 'The Liking and Viewing of Regular TV Series', *Journal of Consumer Research*, 14 (June), 63–70.

Barwise, Patrick and Andrew Ehrenberg (1988), *Television and its Audience*, Sage.

Barwise, Patrick and Robert G. Picard (2012), *The Economics of Television in a Digital World: What Economics Tells Us for Future Policy Debates*, RISJ Report, Reuters Institute for the Study of Journalism, Oxford University, September.

Barwise, Patrick and Robert G. Picard (2014), *What If There Were No BBC Television? The Net Impact on UK Viewers*, RISJ Report, Reuters Institute for the Study of Journalism, University of Oxford, February.

Barwise, T.P., A.S.C. Ehrenberg and G.J. Goodhardt (1979), 'Audience Appreciation and Audience Size', *Journal of the Market Research Society*, 21, 269–89.

Bel, G., Joan Calzada, and Raquel Insa (2007), 'Access Pricing to a Digital Television Platform', *Journal of Media Economics*, 20/1, 29–53.

Bloch, H. and M. Wirth (1984), 'The Demand for Pay Services on Cable Television', *Information Economics and Policy*, 1(4), 311–32.

Booth, P. (2004), 'Introduction', in Peacock, A., *Public Service Broadcasting Without the BBC?*, Institute of Economic Affairs.

Broadcasting Policy Group (2004), *Beyond the Charter: The BBC after 2006*, Premium Publishing.
Cave, M. and Kiyoshi Nakamura (eds) (2006), *Digital Broadcasting: Policy and Practice in the Americas, Europe, and Japan*, Cheltenham, UK and Northampton, MA, USA: Edward Elgar.
Coase, R.H. (1950), *British Broadcasting: A Study in Monopoly*, Longmans Green for LSE.
Coase, R.H. (1966), 'The Economics of Broadcasting and Government Policy', *American Economic Review*, 56 (1 March), 440–7.
Committee on Financing the BBC (1986), *Report of the Committee on Financing the BBC*, chairman Alan Peacock, CMND 9824 (July), London: HMSO.
Deloitte (2010), presentation at Edinburgh Television Festival.
Gates, W. (1995), *The Road Ahead*, Viking Penguin.
Gerbarg, D. (1999), *The Economics, Technology, and Content of Digital Television*, Kluwer Academic.
Gilder, G. (1990), *Life After Television*, Norton.
Graham, A. and Gavyn Davies (1997), *Broadcasting, Society and Policy in the Multimedia Age*, University of Luton Press.
Graham, A. et al. (eds) (1999), *Public Purposes in Broadcasting: Funding the BBC*, University of Luton Press.
Hotelling, H. (1929) 'Stability in Competition', *Economic Journal*, 39, 41–57.
Lowe, Greg F. and Christian S. Nissen (2011), *Small Among Giants: Television Broadcasting in Smaller Countries*, Nordicom / Gothenburg University.
Negroponte, N. (1995), *Being Digital*, Knopf.
Nissen, C.S. (ed.) (2006), *Making a Difference: Public Service Broadcasting in European Media Landscape*, John Libbey.
Owen, B.M. and Steven S. Wildman (1992), *Video Economics*, Harvard University Press.
Owen, B.M., Jack H. Beebe, and Willard G. Manning Jr. (1974), *Television Economics*, D.C. Heath.
Peacock, A. (2004), *Public Service Broadcasting Without the BBC?*, Institute of Economic Affairs.
Picard, R.G. (2006a), 'Financing Public Media: The Future of Collective Funding', in Christian S. Nissen (ed.), *Making a Difference: Public Service Broadcasting in European Media Landscape*, John Libbey, pp. 183–96.
Picard, R.G. (2006b), 'Audience Relations in the Changing Culture of Media Use: Why Should I Pay the Licence Fee?', in Gregory F. Lowe and Per Jauert (eds), *Cultural Dilemmas in Public Service Broadcasting*, Nordicom, pp. 277–92.
Picard, R.G. (2011), *The Economics and Financing of Media Companies*, 2nd edn, Fordham University Press.
Savage, S. and M. Wirth (2005), 'Price, Programming and Potential Competition in US Cable Television Markets', *Journal of Regulatory Economics*, 27/1, 25–46.
Seabright, P. and Jürgen von Hagen (eds) (2007), *The Economic Regulation of Broadcasting Markets: Evolving Technology and Challenges for Policy*, Cambridge University Press.
Sharp, B., Virginia Beal, and Martin Collins (2009), 'Television: Back to the Future', *Journal of Advertising Research*, 49/2, 211–19.
Wirth, M. and H. Bloch (1989), 'Household-Level Demand for Cable Television: A Probit Analysis', *Journal of Media Economics*, 2/2, 21–34, 57.
Wolpert, S.A. and Joyce Friedman Wolpert (1986), *Economics of Information*, Van Nostrand Reinhold.
Wu, T. (2010), *The Master Switch: The Rise and Fall of Information Empires*, Knopf and Atlantic.

9. The economics of broadband

Benjamin J. Bates, Nick Geidner and Yi-Xi Zhu

"Broadband" generally refers to high-speed (or high-bandwidth) digital data networks connected to the Internet and its available content and services. What speed/capacity qualifies as "broadband" is an evolving standard. And while broadband networks have previously referred primarily to wired networks, wireless data networks have become an increasingly important in-house wireless extension of broadband, and are starting to develop as viable regional wireless broadband networks (through 4G mobile systems, as well as dedicated wireless broadband data services).

Still, the fundamental economics of telecommunication/data networks and the economics of the Internet apply regardless of speed – fixed costs for infrastructure are fairly high (although falling over time), particularly compared to operating (variable) costs, leading to generally falling average costs (at least to the point of network saturation), and generally high economies of scale in terms of infrastructure; the presence of network economies on the demand side; the quasi-public good nature of both networks and content services and accompanying pricing issues; and so on. Of course, the desired bandwidth will impact the specific costs of any particular broadband system, as will a number of other factors.

On the demand side, the wealth of content and services available online have created a substantial demand for access. Expanding access speeds open up markets for high bandwidth content and services such as higher quality video streams and interactive online gaming. The world has seen an explosion in the amount of content available online over the last few years, particularly in terms of high-quality entertainment content and streams. Online video, once dominated by YouTube and short low-res clips of kittens and home video excerpts, now includes a wealth of movies and old TV programs in standard definition and HDTV (where licensing has been worked out), for sale and for viewing, from Internet giants such as Apple, Amazon, Hulu, and Netflix (among others). Video-based data traffic can account for half of the data traffic for some times and areas, and is primarily additional traffic loads overlaid on more traditional traffic levels rather than substitutes or replacement for alternative uses.

Broadband access has replaced basic Internet access and basic telephony as the primary goal for telecommunications networks. In some nations, broadband has become the base level for Universal Service goals.

In this chapter, we address the evolving nature of broadband, general digital data network economics, the specific economics of key broadband infrastructures and technologies, and some of the key issues facing broadband implementation and utilization.

DEFINING AND MEASURING BROADBAND

Early digital telecommunication authorities often described broadband systems as having bandwidth of at least 256 Kbps – roughly four times the bandwidth available via modems through standard analogue telephone lines. After telecommunication networks started integrating digital services, the broadband standard for Internet connections was first formally established by an international standards committee (CCITT) in 1988 as anything higher than the established telecommunications "primary rate" then widely available in North American and Japanese (as T1) and European (as E1) telephone/telecomm networks. That amounted to bandwidths in the neighbourhood of 1.5–2 Mbps.

The standard was a bit too high for many countries eager to brag about having broadband access, and so "basic" broadband was widely defined in the 1990s as Internet connections with 200–256 Kbps download speeds. These were data rates easily achieved by cable-based digital Internet access services and DSL services – the dominant local Internet access services available. Data speeds and consumer expectations soon exceeded those levels, pushing for new definitions for broadband service.

The US FCC definitions of the term "broadband" offer an example of the evolving standard. Initially, the FCC defined broadband as anything faster than 200 Kbps (to include basic ISDN offerings), and then quickly upgraded the "broadband" standard to include anything faster than 768 Kbps downstream and 200 Kbps upstream as high-speed cable modem services proliferated and offered Internet access at higher data speeds. The FCC formally changed its definition in 2010, requiring minimal data speeds of 4 Mbps downstream and 1 Mbps upstream. These levels reflected the continuing upgrading of cable and telecommunications networks and the widespread availability of higher bandwidth Internet services.

Currently, the FCC is under pressure to move the broadband bar even higher – its Household Broadband Guide suggested that speeds of 6–15

Mbps could be needed to satisfy multiple device uses in the home; recent broadband adoption progress reports suggest schools should have access to 25 Mbps or higher broadband Internet connections; and the 2010 National Broadband Plan calls for a goal of roughly half of US homes having "affordable access" to 100 Mbps broadband connections, a goal now near achievement.[1]

The EU has also provided several different baseline definitions for broadband service as part of the EU Digital Agenda initiative. They defined basic broadband as download speeds in excess of 144 Kbps, Next Generation Access (NGA) broadband was set at 30 Mbps, and Fast Broadband defined as achieving download speeds of 45 Mbps or greater. The stated goal of the Digital Agenda was to provide universal NGA broadband access by 2020. A 2012 report for the European Commission found that 95.7 percent of homes already had Basic Broadband access, and more than half had NGA broadband access.

The OECD (2012) uses 256 Kbps download rate to define basic broadband access, keeping the lower rate to reflect bandwidth and data traffic levels in less economically developed countries. As access at that low rate became ubiquitous in the more digitally developed regions, baseline data rates for broadband status became faster, moving from 2–9 Mbps almost a decade ago, to 30–45 Mbps in recent years (OECD, 2008).

The ever-evolving broadband standards have several consequences for the economics of broadband. Although the costs of telecommunications systems and services continue to decline over time, networks and services are generally designed to a certain set of capabilities and standards. A network designed and built to provide a 15 Mbps "broadband" service today is likely in a few years to require an upgrade to a 50 Mbps or 100 Mbps service capacity to remain classified as "broadband." The changes in user demands and regulatory requirements can force broadband service providers to either significantly overbuild initially (as with Google's Giganet 1-Gbps (1000 Mbps) service) or can require network upgrades to occur more frequently than normal depreciation standards would suggest.

Another factor driving increased standards for "broadband access," as well as requiring continued expansion of networks (through upgrading existing networks and building new nets), has been the rise of new Internet uses (video, mobile) that are adding new levels of demand and resulting in rapidly increasing data traffic. Cisco (2012) reported that video-based data traffic accounted for more than half of all consumer Internet data traffic in 2011, and predicted that it will grow six-fold by 2016 – at which point video will account for 12 percent of all global

Internet traffic. As for mobile, the ITU (2011) puts the number of global mobile broadband subscriptions at 1.1 billion in 2011, roughly twice the number of fixed (wired) broadband subscriptions. Ericsson (2012) predicts a twelve-fold increase in mobile data traffic from 2010 to 2018, at which point mobile data traffic will account for 9 percent of global Internet data traffic. Most of this traffic is new, rather than replacing other uses, and is growing more rapidly than other types of services and uses.

As broadband speeds increase, and content and services expand to take advantage of those higher speeds, data traffic and data loads approach capacity levels more quickly, providing another force for rapid network upgrades and expansion. Data traffic increases and demand for faster connection speeds mean that broadband access providers require higher infrastructure investment costs than prototypical telecommunication networks.

BROADBAND NETWORK STRUCTURE

Since "broadband" essentially refers to a high-speed digital network connection to the Internet, we start this examination of the economics of broadband with a quick review of digital networks, the Internet, and their economics.

Digital telecommunication networks are characterized by high fixed costs (the physical network infrastructure), and generally very low variable costs (operations) and marginal costs. Digital telecomm networks generally demonstrate significant economies of scale, economies of scope, and network economies. The actual cost of the physical infrastructure required can be quite high, and in general is positively correlated with network capacity and distances or areas that networks transit to deliver signals. The number and density of users served can also be a factor. Costs can also vary significantly, based on the specific technologies used and/or geographic factors. Still, history demonstrates that telecommunication network costs have consistently declined over time – for a given type and level of service. For example, costs for a Gigabit Ethernet port in New York and Sao Paulo declined 22 percent per year from 2007 and 2012. Over the same period, Hong Kong experienced a 26 percent annual decline in cost, and London saw a 31 percent annual decline (TeleGeography, 2012).

Internet economics is very similar, but takes into consideration the nature of the Internet as a network of networks and the distinctive nature of its operating system. That is, what we call the Internet is a conglomeration of myriad networks that can be based on various technologies and infrastructure designs that are connected with one another. These networks may have different primary uses, employ different networking technologies, and have different capacities. Still, one can differentiate some basic Internet network sectors that play different roles, and within the roles have some common economic features.

First, there is the Internet backbone – a collection of very high capacity digital network infrastructures that interconnect countries and major ISPs (Internet Service Providers). Then there is the internal network infrastructure of the major ISPs, which connect different local nodes, and interconnect those with backbone network nodes. A third major sector is the user connections to the ISP, which often can occur over a range of possible telecommunications networks.

A fourth sector is emerging in many countries, utilizing what the telephone industry used to call CPE, Customer Premises Equipment. This fourth sector refers to any additional network infrastructure provided by the user to expand the number or type of broadband connections within their home or business. At this point the fourth sector primarily consists of homeowner Ethernet networks providing multiple access points within the home, and/or WiFi wireless networking providing locally mobile connectivity.

The underlying Internet operating system (TCP/IP packet-switched) was designed to accommodate a variety of uses while being usable on a wide range of computing hardware and telecommunications networks with little added cost. This flexibility has several significant economic implications. First, operating costs, other than the price of connection, are minimal. Second, the digital packet-switching foundation has allowed the network to accommodate any content or service that can be converted to a digital format – the network is not constrained by form, format, or data bandwidth requirements of a piece of content or a service. The Internet OS has added features over time, but remains inexpensive and flexible, at least compared to the infrastructures used for data transmission. Those can and do impose constraints, and can require upgrades and replacement as the amount of data traffic grows, and user demand for greater bandwidth and faster data speeds increases.

As anticipated in the original design of the Internet operating system, today's Internet incorporates a wide variety of networking technologies and infrastructure, and a corresponding wide range of infrastructure and operating costs. One can, however, divide these into two basic types – wired networks, where the telecommunication infrastructure is based on a physical conduit that connects nodes and users; and wireless networks, which use radio spectrum as the conduit.

Wired Networks

At this point, the network infrastructure of the Internet backbone is primarily terrestrial wired-based using fibre optic technologies. (There are a few links that use satellites or microwave broadcasting as lower-cost alternatives to connect distant or remote backbone nodes.) Fibre optics tend to offer the greatest potential bandwidth (especially when installed in bundles) and lowest operating costs of digital telecommunication network structures. Fibre infrastructure is significantly less costly to install and operate than any copper-based physical telecommunication network of similar capacity, and is rapidly becoming less costly than basic coax, DSL, and even twisted pair copper networks. As a result, fibre has been replacing copper infrastructure in telecommunication networks. The cost advantage was highest in high traffic areas, so that was where the upgrade to fibre occurred first. As the costs of digital fibre networks have fallen, they have become the dominant technology used to build new network infrastructure, bringing the fibre installation all the way to the user.

Just as Internet backbone operators quickly shifted to fibre for network infrastructure, so have digital network operators in the second sector of Internet and digital telecommunication service providers, starting with the high traffic parts of their internal networks (interconnecting their nodes and service centres). Initially, the lower bandwidth demand and huge installed base of copper wired networks favoured copper-based technologies for the local user loop. As demand for bandwidth (for voice, video, and data) grew and fibre network technologies developed (and their costs fell), the relative cost advantage of digital fibre over analogue copper in wired networks encouraged operators to replace copper coax with digital fibre as they upgraded networks to try to keep pace with increased user demand. As fibre costs continued to decline while the cost of copper rose, and demand for and use of telecommunications networks increased, networks invested more and more in fibre upgrades to existing copper/coax installations. Over time, the proportion of fibre in these hybrid fibre/coax systems worked its way closer and closer to the home/business user, enabling higher data speeds.

In many of the industrialized countries, the continuing drop in fibre installation costs has made fibre to the node (FTTN) or fibre to the user premises (FTTx) infrastructures cost effective.[2] In many areas, new telecommunications infrastructure builds are all-fibre. This has been a factor in the push for broadband; the faster broadband speeds in wired networks require the speeds and bandwidth that fibre provides. FTTx (or really close, say to the curb) seems to be the only wired technology that can currently bring 100 Mbps to 1 Gbps (or higher) data speeds to individual users. For many, the future of wired broadband access requires the transition to, and expansion of, FTTx networks as the primary user/network access link (Samanta et al., 2012a, b).

Infrastructure construction costs can vary wildly, and an example from the US illustrates some of the differences. SNL Kagan has estimated that FTTN new construction from 2004 to 2009 averaged $404 per home passed, while FTTx new infrastructure construction averaged $994 per home passed. By 2014, SNL Kagan estimates that FTTx per home costs will drop by more than a third, to $651 per home passed. That would still make it twice as expensive as FTTN, which they predict will come in at $330 per home passed in 2014. At this point, the mix of network construction runs about 60 percent FTTN and 40 percent FTTx, and the choice seems to be driven more by corporate strategy than local conditions. It should be noted that much of the difference in cost results from whether the cost of the optical digital converter equipment is shared or not, and by how many potential users. In addition, the FTTx network will be inherently faster than the FTTN network, and thus less likely to require upgrades as users demand more and more bandwidth and data traffic increases.

How rapidly are broadband demand and increased data traffic flows in the Internet growing? There are two interrelated drivers of growth. First, Internet access continues to expand into new service areas, adding new Internet users and their early stage data needs. That basic user growth fosters content and service creation, and new and valued services increase demand and traffic flows. Internet content and services explode as a result of the cost advantages and expanding global markets that the Internet provides. The expansion of broadband access provides another major driver of demand. Faster speeds and access have made high-bandwidth types of content and services economically viable.

From the early days of text, increasing network speeds made images viable, then audio/music, and then low-resolution video. For many people, having broadband access equates with the ability to handle live, full-resolution, video streaming. The opening of the online video market has led to explosive growth in use, and in the heavy data flows video requires. In addition, we are also experiencing similar explosive growth in mobile-generated data traffic coming from widespread diffusion and use of smartphones[3] and tablets.[4]

Global data traffic has been more than doubling every year historically, with recent growth in no small part due to the explosion of video and mobile data traffic. In the US, backbone data traffic has grown from around 20 TB/month at the start of 2000 to over 3,000 TB/month at the start of 2011. Similar growth can be seen throughout the developed economies. As the expansion of broadband continues, the increased amount of data traffic will hasten the potential for reaching existing capacity limits – and nearing capacity requires network infrastructure expansion (increasing capacity) or trying to reduce demand through increased pricing or limiting customer data use (or customer data speeds). Either can prove costly to network suppliers, in effect pushing them to speedier upgrades to maintain a certain level of over-capacity. In these sectors of the network, the push for broadband primarily shows up in the need for increasingly frequent network capacity upgrades.

Luckily, two aspects of fibre optic network infrastructure have allowed backbone service providers to cope with this rapidly expanding data traffic and demand. First, fibre network capacity is multiplied by the normal practice of installing fibre networks as bundles of fibres, most of which are initially unneeded and unused. This allows the backbone operators to tap the unused ("dark") fibres as data traffic increases over time. While fibre bundles are slightly more expensive to install initially, the unused capacity can delay the need for significant infrastructure upgrades for some time. While good estimates are hard to come by (and will differ across networks), it was generally believed that 50–90 percent of installed fibre was unused (dark) a decade ago. While network operators initially held dark fibre in reserve, markets for leasing that dark fibre have emerged in recent years. New uses and increased traffic have taken advantage of some of the excess capacity, even as newly installed fibre networks create more dark fibre. Data currently suggests that even at peak uses, there is plenty of excess capacity; in the Americas and Europe, current data traffic peaks at around 45 percent of total capacity, peak traffic uses 60 percent of Asian Internet capacity, and 80 percent of African capacity (TeleGeography, 2012).

The second advantage of fibre networks is that they employ optical transmission systems. As a result, network capacity in fibre networks can often be improved by expanding the optical bandwidth used, by increased multiplexing, and/or improved data compression algorithms. This means that bandwidth and data flows can be improved by merely switching out the electronics in the network, rather than having to lay additional fibre. As technology continues to develop, and its costs decrease, this provides networks with additional ability to greatly expand per-fibre strand capacity at fairly low costs (compared to installing additional networks).

The combination of extensive dark fibre and significant improvements in data traffic capacity for each fibre reduces the need for extensive and expensive overbuilds and upgrades, particularly among the backhaul networks (Internet backbone and ISP intranetworks and backbone interconnections).

For many of the same economic and market reasons, larger ISPs have adopted fibre optics based networks for their internal infrastructure, at least within the high-traffic portions of the network (their backbone and extending into local fixed networks). Some are also beginning to take the fibre network all the way to the end user, installing that last bit in anticipation of eventual economic viability driven by increased demand and declining equipment costs. The conversion to full FTTH (fibre to the home) was, until recently, considered to not be economically feasible, primarily due to the relatively high cost of the equipment needed to convert the optical digital signal emerging from the fibre to the various analogue and digital pathways needed by home equipment (computers, TVs, phones). One early test of FTTH estimated that at that time, conversion systems would cost around $10,000 per unit (or home). With the inherent bandwidth of a single fibre optic strand falling well above any current definition or conception of broadband capacity, the lack of demand (at least for bandwidth in excess of that a fibre channel can provide) and the high signal conversion costs pushed the conversion point upstream (where costs could be spread across multiple users). Today, however, the optical conversion box is approaching the costs of other set-top boxes used by cable, DBS, and other multichannel video and data suppliers. This allows farsighted providers to go fully fibre in their fixed wired infrastructure, which will facilitate their ability to expand bandwidth offerings in the future.

In the meantime, the data flows and bandwidth users' desire and demand continue to grow in a positive feedback loop. As users experience broadband, they discover new services and content that drive their data usage higher, and as user demand increases, that should drive the supply of content and services higher, which should also drive demand higher, ad infinitum. This suggests that users will periodically increase their perceived need for greater bandwidth, with data traffic expanding to fill available bandwidth (even as vehicle traffic expands to fill expansion of concrete highways). As both the number of users and their demand for bandwidth grow, the consequent rapid growth in aggregated data traffic puts pressure on the ISPs' internal network to expand capacity to keep pace. In addition, individual and aggregated data traffic loads and increasing demand will also put pressure to extend the fibre infrastructure further and further into the local connection loop to keep pace with growing bandwidth demand. Eventually, this means taking the network all the way to the user.

Wireless Networks

The same basic factors are also at play in the development and construction of wireless networks, as wireless signal bases still need to be connected to the operator's network, as well as the Internet. As the radio spectrum available for wireless/cellular networks is generally limited, the higher bandwidth offered by fibre optic networks makes it the technology of choice for intra- and inter-operator networks.

The recent explosion of mobile data traffic, driven by the diffusion and adoption of smartphones, and then tablets, is creating pressure for more spectrum for wireless data, enabling higher data rates. Even so, growing data traffic loads threaten to overload the wireless component of the network's ability to handle the growing mobile data traffic demands. With that last consumer loop being in the broadcast spectrum, however, there is the problem of standards. Wireless systems need standards, for both state licensing and the development of consumer markets. However, part of the standards-setting process is a determination of what bandwidth will be available for which services, including data services. As data traffic flow increases, it can eventually overwhelm the limited capacity inherent in the initial standards. While wireless services can tweak data traffic flows somewhat, through improved compression/multiplexing, expanding coverage, and shifting data flows through strategic pricing, eventually more bandwidth is needed than the existing system can provide.

In that case, a new set of technologies and standards need to be developed, accommodating the increased demand for data speeds and bandwidth. It takes time and money, however, for new standards to be set, licenses granted, systems built, and for consumers to buy new devices that utilize the new standards. That has been the case in WiFi, with a series of improved standards (802.11b, g, n) each allowing greater bandwidth to be used, and mobile cellular's transition from 2G to various versions of 3G and now 4G, with each generational upgrade significantly improving available data bandwidth.

THE BROADBAND MARKET

When activists, politicians, and Internet users talk about "broadband," they are usually referring to the third Internet sector – the connection between the user and the ISP. Their concern is centred on the apparent speed/bandwidth at the end-user's device. One of the most basic aspects of the Internet is that the apparent end-user data bandwidth is set by the slowest network connection employed in the transmission. As noted above, the data traffic capacity of the Internet backbone nodes, the connections between ISPs and backbone nodes, and the internal ISP networks, are for the most part far greater than what generally constitutes "broadband." The limiting factor in almost all cases is the data speed/capacity of the connection between the ISP and the user.

That connection is also the one with the greatest range of network technologies and infrastructures available – ranging from analogue phone lines to all-fibre networks (physical, land-based, networks) to a range of wireless network alternatives. For now, pure fibre-to-the-user is marginally cost-effective, and there are a number of alternative existing network infrastructures that can be used for digital data, although their data speeds and capacities are limited by their existing infrastructure design and technologies used. In this section we will discuss a number of systems, their costs, and their viability as broadband connections.

Basic Data Network Economics

While there are many types of networks generally employed by media outlets, with a concomitant wide range of infrastructure costs and limitations, for the most part "broadband" networks are limited to digital data, Internet-connected (IP-based) telecommunication networks, allowing us to focus on a more specific set product and market circumstances.

The Internet refers to an interconnected global network of data networks based on a common meta-operating system known as TCP/IP.

WiFi

For most of the world, wireless Internet access is equated with WiFi. WiFi is fundamentally a wireless LAN (local area network) operating under the IEEE 802.11 family of technical standards and protocols. It requires no licensing, is relatively cheap, and is easy to install and operate. The primary limiting factor of WiFi is coverage area. Signal range for early versions was about 20 meters within structures, and up to 100 meters outdoors, and accommodated data streams of 1–2 Mbps.

Upgraded protocols (802.11b, 802.11g, 802.11n) allowed multiplexing of multiple signals, with 802.11n allowing data speeds of 70–150 Mbps and two to three times the coverage area of previous versions.

As such, 802.11n WiFi easily provides broadband speeds to the ISP access point. Work on further upgraded systems continues, with the draft 802.11ac standard providing multi-station throughputs of 1 Gbps, and with the 802.11ad standard offering data throughput speeds up to 7 Gbps. WiFi mobile connections are primarily used in homes and smaller fixed locations, although WiFi stations can be networked to provide coverage over larger areas. Most academic campus wireless networks, for instance, use networked WiFi.

WiMax

WiMax systems operate similarly, but were designed to provide coverage over larger areas, with single base station signal range of 5–7 miles, and allowing for networked multiple coverage extending out to 30 miles (radius). The initial WiMax protocol called for downstream data flows of 30–40 Mbps, although that would be shared among synchronous users across that expanded coverage area. Depending on the number of simultaneous users, the actual data speeds can be less than WiFi (with enough users splitting available bandwidth). The newer WiMax2 standard calls for data throughput speeds in the range of 110–365 Mbps. WiMax is currently used around the world to provide wireless coverage across cities and communities (although the system can become overloaded and slow if used by too many people); many early efforts at municipal efforts had issues with costs and pricing, while others found that as users increased, speeds slowed as aggregated data traffic overloaded local nodes. In some countries, WiMax systems have been used to provide mobile Internet access in the early stages of Internet diffusion, or for smaller communities and rural areas; the lower user-density in such cases suggests this seems to be the most efficient use of WiMax as a primary Internet access provider.[5]

National Wireless Broadband

In some nations, access providers are building regional and/or national networks of WiFi and/or WiMax stations that are linked to a separate data backbone. Many of these get around capacity issues by targeting their use as a supplementary access point for users roaming outside their normal service areas or for dedicated commercial connections, rather than as a primary means of Internet access.

The US has proposed using a newly recovered bit of wireless bandwidth as the foundation for building a new type of wireless broadband service using a yet-to-be-determined technology. The added spectrum would be helpful, and the plan calls for subsidies to help expansion of the new system into rural areas as well as the continued subsidy of rural operations (through Universal Service fees). However it is not clear, at this point, that the system is needed, or would achieve the desired goal of universal access. Furthermore, many of the newer technologies being proposed have proved to be problematic. One early plan proposed to use spectrum set aside for satellite use to establish ground stations for a national wireless broadband system, but had to be discarded due to technical problems (including interference with civilian and military GPS systems) and potential conflicts of interest in the licensing process.

Satellite Wireless

Satellites have been publicly used for digital telecommunications since the mid-1960s. The last few years have seen the widespread implementation of satellite-based digital data services. Two-way data channels through satellites have been commercially available since the mid-1980s in the form of VSAT services, and have been primarily used by businesses to connect outlets for real-time inventory and tracking, and maritime services. Early systems were fairly expensive (in large part due to the cost of equipment for the uplink portion of the two-way signal), and offered limited bandwidth (256 Kbps–1 Mbps). Some providers tried to reduce costs by splitting the service – using satellites for downloads, and terrestrial links (telephone, cellular, and so on) for uploads. Improvements in technology lowered costs and gave greater available bandwidth, first with the deployment of Ka band satellites after 2000, and in the last few years the deployment of satellites designed explicitly for high-throughput data services. These allow for increases in download speeds to broadband levels, up to 15 Mbps with the latest generation of satellites. Pricing remains high (in the US, satellite data plans typically run two to three times higher than similar speed fixed wireline costs – plus equipment costs and a monthly cap). Geosynchronous satellites, while minimizing customer equipment needs compared to lower orbit satellite systems, create one problem for typical Internet use. The distance to the satellite creates a delay of around a quarter of a second for each satellite leg, which can be a problem for highly interactive uses. Signal lag is less of an issue with normal browsing or with content streaming services.

Still, these services provide near 100 percent coverage within their operating footprint, and thus can greatly extend Internet and broadband access, particularly to remote and rural areas. Since satellite broadband services are generally slower and more costly than terrestrial-based broadband options, they generally are not competitive with wired or terrestrial wireless options (if any are available). Thus, satellite wireless tends to be primarily used in rural areas, or when users want a dedicated data connection. As noted above, the newer satellites allow Internet access providers to offer plans (1.5 Mbps–15 Mbps) that fall in the definition of basic broadband. Europe currently offers public satellite broadband at 2 Mbps, and Eutelsat recently announced plans to offer a 20 Mbps service to rural areas, starting in the UK (Judge, 2013) – enough to qualify as basic broadband, but too slow to contribute to the goal of offering universal 30 Mbps coverage by 2020 (EU, 2012). Multiple satellite-based public Internet services in the US offer broadband plans with download speeds of 1.5 Mbps to 15 Mbps. Globally, advanced consumer satellite broadband services are coming online or are planned, at least for more developed countries and regions around the world. In the meantime, commercially focused VSAT data services are globally available. While the VSAT satellite services tend to be much more costly and are primarily marketed for commercial uses, they may also be made available to individual users.

Mobile Wireless (Cellular)

Mobile wireless is defined as data services offered by digital cellular technologies. Data standards for mobile began with the various 2G technical standards (GSM, CDMA, TDMA). While 2G systems were initially designed primarily for voice, their digital basis allowed for data transmission. The success of text and messaging services encouraged updated systems to include specific data traffic components. The 2.5G systems and later upgrades provided for data rates up to 156 Kbps (average user speeds fell in the 60–80 Kbps range) – enough to encourage non-voice uses, but not broadband speeds.

The use of mobile for data services and Internet access began in earnest with the advent of 3G systems. The minimal technical standard to qualify as 3G cellular service called for data speeds of at least 200 Kbps, just qualifying under the earliest broadband definitions, but certainly not meeting current expectations for broadband capability. This was enough to provide fast Internet access for text and graphic based uses. The mobile data boom, though, started with Blackberry cell phones and service, which included access to email, calendar, and directory services. This led other handset manufacturers to expand data-based features, eventually integrating full Internet access from handsets. The development of these smartphones enabled users to significantly extend their opportunities for Internet access, including audio and low-res video streaming. As a result, mobile data traffic greatly expanded.

Handset operating systems became more flexible, permitting users to download apps for virtually any purpose. Continuing improvements within the basic 3G standards brought data speeds up (GSM-EDGE to 1.6 Mbps, CDMA2000 to 2.45 Mbps, GSM-HSPDA to 14.4 Mbps (max)). As handset functionality and data speeds improved, users found more and more reasons to use smartphones for more than voice, resulting in a positive feedback loop, with improved devices and services (including apps) driving increases in data traffic, which drives system upgrades, which promotes greater demand. Some form of 3G mobile access is available globally in almost all urban regions, and 2G mobile services reach an estimated 90 percent of the world's population. Mobile is quickly becoming a primary Internet access point, particularly in rural and less-developed areas.

The increased data traffic, however, is threatening to overload local capacity in some areas.[6] The anticipated massive growth in mobile data traffic placed an emphasis in 4G technical standards development on incorporating a significant increase in data handling capacity. Another emphasis was to make 4G a system capable of offering broadband access. As a result, the minimal global standards for true 4G mobile/cellular services require IP-based data transmission capabilities at fast broadband data speeds. The 4G Advanced standard has a hypothetical 1 Gbps data download speed (for stationary use), and 100 Mbps downloads when rapidly moving (as in cars or trains), although mobile service providers are likely to market services at lower speeds initially. Currently, only two mobile technologies reach that standard – 4G-LTE and WiMax2. A number of upgraded 3G services with significantly improved data speeds are marketed as 4G, although they do not meet the formal 4G technical standards.

The diffusion of true 4G mobile services is just beginning, and is expected to remain fairly slow for the next few years. The ITU (2013) reports that 45 percent of the world's population currently has access to 3G services. Various estimates indicate that true 4G networks will reach 50 percent of the world's population by 2017.

BROADBAND ISSUES: AN ECONOMIC PERSPECTIVE

Social and Economic Impact of Broadband

Jaffer and Lee (2012) reviewed a number of studies looking at the economic and social impact of broadband investment. The World Bank found that a 10 percent increase in broadband household penetration increased GDP by up to 1.5 percent in low- and middle-income countries. This was supported by market research reports that suggested that improved penetration had a lasting impact (over five years), and was even higher for countries with high broadband penetration levels. Broadband's impact on economies was about twice as strong as that of fixed telephony, and higher than the impact of mobile telephony and basic internet penetration. The report also found significant social impacts from broadband penetration – improving access to information markets, public services and education, as well as expanding social networks and social capital.

Pricing Issues

Pricing policies can have a significant impact on the adoption and use of telecomm networks. With high fixed costs and comparatively minimal operating (variable) costs, pricing often becomes strategic. For system operators, the primary concern is finding the price point that reflects average costs (after any subsidies) over the long term, rather than the equation of price with marginal costs that is typical with fully competitive markets. With price at average cost, the system covers both infrastructure and operating costs and is economically viable.

Of course, pricing policy can be used for other purposes as well. Price discrimination can be used to shift demand patterns, to slow down or speed up adoption by new users. For digital data networks, flat-rate pricing can also encourage exploration of new services and help better establish demand, while caps and usage-based pricing will discourage exploration and the use of lower-value services. In recent years, a lot of attention has been given to pricing strategies and the impacts they have on markets and demand – for example, one cable MSO instituted fairly low data caps on their broadband service, while exempting their own video streaming and VOD services. Other video streamers (Netflix, Hulu+, YouTube, for example) have challenged the move as anti-competitive, in effect making their content more expensive.

Another example is the wireless (cellular) services shifting data plans from flat-rate pricing packaged with voice and messaging, to instituting data plans with flat-rate caps with significant overage charges.[7] In this case, the move is less anti-competitive (as virtually all mobile operators are doing so), and more a result of the boom in mobile devices and the expanding use of high-bandwidth services. The growth of mobile devices, particularly tablets, has significantly increased data traffic over older cellular networks – which were not designed to handle broadband-level data loads. The move can be seen as an effort to shift data-heavy traffic from 2G and 3G networks to WiFi/landline systems that can more easily handle the traffic.

While one might expect a return to flat-rate pricing with the expansion of true 4G services, there are two mitigating circumstances that could require maintaining pricing plans incorporating usage caps for some time to come:

1. The new 4G services are being implemented incrementally, and it is likely that mobile operators will continue to use a combination of 2G, 3G, and 4G networks for some time to come. Cisco's Visual Networking Index (VNI) reports predict that 4G will account for only 6 percent of global connections by 2016 (2012), so concerns about overloading 2G/3G networks will remain for the near future and provide mobile service operators with an incentive to maintain caps to control and shift data traffic patterns (at least for use on the older networks).
2. The growth of broadband access and broadband services (high data traffic services needing broadband for optimal operation) has contributed to the continuing explosion of data traffic loads – Cisco's VNI (2012) indicates that half of all current mobile data flows are generated by video services; and that growth in such high-bandwidth services, combined with the further diffusion of connected mobile devices (smartphones, tablets) will contribute to a predicted 18-fold increase in mobile data traffic by 2016. The report indicates that there are already more than 100 million smartphone users globally who generate at least 1 GB of data traffic a month, and that in 2016, the average mobile device will generate 2.6 GB of data traffic monthly. The speed at which data traffic, particularly mobile data traffic, is expanding and will continue to provide mobile system operators with incentives to shift traffic where possible.

There are many ways that flat-rate and usage-based pricing can be combined, alone or in combination with price discrimination. Such strategies are likely to have the following kinds of impact:

- Price discrimination – setting different prices for different groups, or for different varieties of services. The general impact is to reduce demand for the higher-priced options, and increase it for the lower-priced (shifting demand patterns).
- Price discrimination via versioning – different "versions" of a product or service are offered, with different sets of features or

attributes. Variation in features means that the different versions may have different values to users, and create different demand curves. The typical versioning is to offer a low quality version and a high-quality or specific featured version at a significantly higher price. Producers can thus capture the higher value from those with high demand, which may then justify differential pricing.

- Price subsidies – setting prices below market level (usually with the subsidies recovered from a different funding source). This increases demand by reducing the real costs.
- Price taxes/surcharges – setting real prices higher than market level, which decreases demand by increasing real costs to users.
- Flat-rate (access) pricing – a purchase is tied to the ability to access and use a service or good, rather than the amount of use. User demand is determined by the value a user gains from anticipated (normal) usage levels. As a result, the marginal cost of additional usage is zero, which encourages users to experiment and use services with low separate value or unknown value. Flat-rate pricing can create significant social and public value by encouraging use of lower-value, and non-commercial services. Flat-rate pricing increases demand in terms of the range and amount of services used. The incentive to experiment and discover additional valued uses will shift (increase) demand, and increase user tolerance of price increases over time. (Users may increase anticipated usage levels, and aggregated total value of the access package as the incentives to explore new valued uses.) The strategy can also be very useful in early stages of diffusion, by allowing users to find the value in new services and content, and thus increase the perceived value of the service.
- Pure usage pricing – when price is based on some combination of service and its use. This strategy works best with low demand users and when value is fixed and certain. However, it has the impact of setting the marginal cost of additional use at the usage price. As such, users are less willing to explore uses with less certain value, or with low perceived value, reducing or limiting demand. In addition, users are likely to shift to lower-priced or flat-rate close substitutes if available.
- Plans with caps plus overages – with this pricing strategy, the user faces a mix of flat-rate pricing up to a certain level of total usage, and then encounters usage-based pricing after that point. The general economic effects of such pricing strategies depend on both the cap level and the overage pricing. If the cap is high enough to

accommodate the expected normal usage of all but a few high-demand users, then the flat-rate portion still encourages exploration, growing demand, and swings in demand. It also shifts more of the cost burden to those very high traffic users while helping to control data traffic loads. However, when caps fall below normal or likely usage levels, or overage costs are disproportionately high, the negative impact on demand will be spread more widely, discouraging exploration (and the serendipity effects of discovering new valued uses), and lower-value content and services (including much cultural and narrow interest usage) in favour of very high-value content and services (primarily commercial). The higher the cost of overages, the more likely consumers will shift usage patterns (and possibly shift completely to alternative providers). The basic effect is to shift (or reduce) demand, particularly from low value or uncertain value use to high-value (that is, commercial) content and services. The impact will thus depend significantly on what levels of use the cap is set at, and whether overage prices (or penalties) are significantly higher than average price under the cap.

State Broadband Policy and Divides

Telecommunications networks generally have high fixed costs, which is based at least partially on the areas served and population density in those areas. The relationship with area/distance is clearest for physical wired networks, which have to provide physical connections to each user. It is also somewhat true for wireless networks – although they can use the airwaves for the final connecting leg, terrestrial broadcast ranges are distance-limited by the combination of power, antenna height, and frequencies used. A cellular system, for example, needs more sites/towers the greater the area it seeks to cover. Still, user density also matters – both in terms of impacting average costs (more users, lower average fixed costs), and more specifically for telecommunications networks, by impacting total usage loads and the possibility of system overloads and service performance, particularly in wireless segments (overloads are more likely in very high density networks).

Broadband services are increasingly widespread in urban and suburban markets (where distances tend to be shorter and density higher, keeping average costs down), and in regions where significant demand already exists for media content (particularly streaming high-quality video), online gaming, and other high data-traffic generating Internet content and services. In these areas, the lower average infrastructure cost curves intersect the growing service demand curves at points where broadband services are economically viable. The prospect of growing demand for service and uses that require or benefit from broadband data flows, and the profits that will generate, push infrastructure diffusion and the provision of broadband access at prices that large user segments find reasonable. State action in these markets can perhaps speed up diffusion and use, but may not be strictly necessary.

The problem is that those trends and conditions don't apply uniformly. Infrastructure costs in rural areas tend to be more expensive, particularly on a per capita or per user basis. In addition, while interest in services requiring broadband connections may be high, perceived value and demand for the high-traffic uses driving much broadband adoption is less well established. The lower available Internet connection speeds and typically higher prices that users experience in rural and less economically developed areas, combined with licensing issues for much high-value entertainment content, hinder the ability of users to experience and discover the value of high-speed broadband access, and ability to afford it (in low-income areas). Limited demand also slows the creation and provision of services and content requiring broadband access, and slows development of markets.

These differences in demand are one factor driving the rise of various "divides" – Urban/Rural, Rich/Poor, Developed/Undeveloped. There is a long and colourful history of "divides" across myriad telecommunication systems, and of state efforts to minimize them through state action and policy (for example, "Universal Service" policies). Telecommunication services have become a critical component of economic development, and Internet access and content is almost as widely seen as having educational, socio-cultural, economic, and even political impacts. As more and more countries see broadband Internet access and services as an important, if not critical, component of their economic and telecommunications/Internet policy, states are developing and publishing plans to promote broadband access and use.[8]

Exemplar: China's broadband policy[9]

For most of the recent past, China's national telecommunications policies have focused on upgrading and expanding telecommunications infrastructure, with an occasional emphasis on specific markets or media. Policies going back to 2001 promoted expansion of telecommunications networks and Internet backbones capable of providing "broadband" speeds, although not specifically focusing on or defining "broadband." That came in 2009, when China's Ministry of Industry and Information Technology (MIIT) put forth a plan to "accelerate the next generation of the Internet and broadband fibre access network construction."[10] In the meantime, achieving broadband capability was part of formal and informal local and regional policies aimed at improving local infrastructure development.

Another 2009 program focused on national/local collaboration in promoting more universal diffusion of broadband networks. The Information Infrastructure Enhancement Program recognized that outside of the largest urban markets, the best option for rapid development of broadband access was the local cable systems, mostly owned and operated by local government authorities or firms, who might not have the capital or resources to fund infrastructure upgrades or expansion of the systems into nearby rural areas. The Program provided some national funding, and started to restructure cable rules to permit more consolidation of cable systems, giving cable a better foundation for getting funds for infrastructure upgrades (as well as programming development).

In the larger urban areas, the scale of network operations and user demand facilitated more localized arrangements, such as the partnership between China Telecom and the Shanghai government – an arrangement that expanded broadband service to 750,000 new users in the first year.

In 2010, MIIT and other national state agencies collaborated on setting fibre broadband standards and access goals.[11] Through these, the state set a goal of 80 million broadband users by the end of 2011, with average access speeds above 8 Mbps in urban areas, and 2 Mbps in rural areas, and provided subsidies for basic network construction (150 billion Yuan over three years) as well as 50 billion Yuan in user (ISP/local access) subsidies. MIIT also noted the role that newer mobile cellular systems could play, noting the state plan for complete nationwide 3G coverage and existing subsidies for mobile wireless network infrastructure. With China's upgraded and proprietary 3G system capable of providing low-end broadband data rates, and rapid diffusion (212 million 3G users in two years), wireless broadband access will play a significant role in providing basic broadband access. Recent stats suggest that there is more wireless Internet access (388 million) than desktop Internet access (380 million) in China.

In May 2012, a new national plan (Broadband Strategy Project) set more expansive goals, setting a goal of reaching 250 million broadband users by 2015, and increasing "broadband" target speeds to 20 Mbps (urban) and 4 Mbps (rural). The long-term goal is for broadband services to become ubiquitous across both urban and rural areas, and for those networks to provide integrated and secure connections at an "advanced" level.

The development of China's "broadband" policy has evolved from an initial focus on extending basic infrastructure, to focused improvements on the speed and quality of Internet connections and telecommunications networks. In line with the US, the EU, and other developed countries, the policy has since placed an emphasis on universal coverage, and providing funding and subsidies to push access into rural and undeveloped areas. With the most recent policies, China has also recognized the importance of broadband access in the development of information and content industries, both as increasingly important industries and markets, and as drivers for broadband adoption.

The growth of broadband, particularly wired access built up from cable, also plays a significant role in China's overall telecommunication strategy and policy. Currently, the broader telecom sector is highly concentrated, with China Mobile and China Unicom dominating mobile telecomm, China Telecom and China Netcom dominating fixed-line telecommunications, and state operators dominating broadcasting. Local cable, while historically dominated by local authorities, is the least concentrated. The focus of most of the broadband policy actions is directed to building up the cable sector to be a competitive player in the cross-media broadband market, eventually to the point where it can be a competitive challenge to the other big telecomm operators. The cable sector is on track to become the third largest player in China's broadband market, particularly when the "Next Generation Broadcast Networks" currently under construction come on line.

Urban/Rural Divides

The same forces that provided the foundation for Universal Service concerns and the first digital divide (any Internet access) apply to broadband today, setting the stage for a broadband digital divide, with rural areas not getting the access needed. At the foundation is the question of basic access, and the building of critical infrastructure.

In Europe, a report (European Union, 2012) found that while half of EU homes had NGA broadband access, only 12 percent of rural homes did so. While DSL service[12] was the dominant fixed access throughout Europe, offering near universal coverage (92 percent), coverage was significantly lower in rural areas (78 percent). A similar gap existed in wireless (cellular-based) services. HSPA, the data standard employed in most 3G cellular services, had an overall 95 percent coverage, but only 79 percent reach in rural areas. Still in the early stages of diffusion, 4G broadband access had reached only 9 percent of all European homes, and had minimal coverage in rural areas – except for two countries that had mandated rural coverage when awarding 4G licenses. As a result, 40 percent of rural homes in Germany have access to 4G wireless broadband, as do 14 percent of rural homes in Sweden. Several reports suggest a similar urban/rural gap in the US. A National Broadband Map report (NTIA, 2014) suggests a minimal gap (2–3 percent) for broadband speeds below 1.5 Mbps, largely due to the widespread diffusion of 3G wireless networks and the availability of satellite-based data services. However, the gap widens considerably for higher access speeds provided by fixed wireline technologies, reaching a coverage gap of around 40 percent for broadband download speeds of 25–100 Mbps.

Further expansion of wired networks into rural areas is hampered by the higher infrastructure costs that longer distances and lower population density bring; and the diffusion of 4G wireless services, which will provide higher broadband speeds, remains in the early stages of adoption.

Those nations with commercial telecomm systems have experienced difficulty in attracting commercial telecomm operators to provide broadband access in rural areas, thus delaying their goals of universal broadband access. The fundamental issue is the significant cost differentials. Ims et al. (1998) provide a dated, but still illustrative, analysis of the costs of upgrading wired networks to broadband speeds across urban, suburban, and rural areas.[13] Average costs of upgrading to 2 Mbps in densely populated downtowns and urban areas were estimated at 400 Euros per connected home. In low density suburban and rural areas, costs rose to 800 to 900 Euros. Upgrading to 8 Mbps would increase average costs to 700 Euros in urban areas, and 1400 Euros in suburban and rural areas. Upgrading to 26 Mbps service would run from 400 Euros in downtown areas, to 1600 Euros per connection in urban areas, while average costs in rural areas could exceed 5000 Euros per connected home (depending on the local loop length). They reached two interesting conclusions: first, that the costs of installing new networks would be about the same as upgrading existing infrastructure; and second, that extending high-speed (26 Mbps and higher) broadband into rural areas "significantly increases financial risk."

If rural areas are going to get high-speed broadband access, states are going to have to step in, and develop policies to incentivize broadband network operators. Some states have gone the route of subsidies – requiring state operators to provide access, subsidizing operators through tax breaks or subsidized loans for infrastructure, subsidizing local users in high-cost areas, or encouraging local demand in the hope of increasing data traffic enough to make broadband more commercially viable. Others are trying cross-subsidies, tying access to high value markets to providing access in low-value areas. Some states are looking at various wireless technologies and networks; while costs tend to run higher than urban wired broadband networks, the urban/rural cost differentials are much less. And some are hoping that the two broad economic trends in broadband – declining infrastructure and operating costs and rapidly expanding market demand in terms of users and usage – will someday intersect at a point where broadband services become economically viable in rural areas.

While rural areas are unlikely to have the same wide range of broadband access options[14] as downtown urban areas for the foreseeable future, they do have near-universal basic broadband access via wireless satellite data services and/or mobile/cellular services. In the US and EU, gaps in term of having any access to broadband are (or should soon be) fairly small.

Network Neutrality and Open Access

The problem with catchphrases like "network neutrality" and "open access" is that people use them to refer to a wide range of different, even contradictory, issues. For some, network neutrality means the freedom to choose what ISP you want, and not be locked into the one selected by the network connection provider. As discussed in the last section, the Internet is not neutral in this manner. Individuals in some populations have greater freedom to choose an ISP than individuals in other populations. The federal government, through various broadband outreach programs, has worked to increase access and choice in underserved populations. With that said, the FCC has unambiguously stated that broadband providers are allowed to charge more for faster access. From a freedom of choice standpoint, this ruling creates a less neutral Internet, which favours wealthy subsets of the population.

For others, net neutrality means maintaining the end-to-end principle that defined the early Internet. The end-to-end principle refers to the design of the network of computers that makes up the Internet. In this design, most of the intelligence of the network is located at the ends of the network (for example, the end user's computer or the server hosting a website). The computers inside the network act as blind information processors – moving information through the network and completing other simple tasks. The end-to-end principle allows for quick user-side innovation. For example, when an application like Skype is created, nothing in the middle of the network has to change. The user installs the program on their computer at the end of the network and can immediately communicate with other individuals, who have installed the program on their ends of the network. The end-to-end principle results in a neutral network. Neither the computers in the middle of the network nor the network owners discriminate between types of information. Skype traffic does not get processed in a systematically faster or slower manner than traffic from its competitors (such as AOL Instant Messenger or Yahoo Messenger).

Although the principle of network neutrality is argued to be a basic right by groups like the Electronic Freedom Foundation, network owners argue that they should be allowed to manipulate information flow in certain cases, particularly when there are economic and social impacts. First, network owners argue they should be allowed to "throttle" (cap usage) for users with extreme levels of data usage. Relying on a variation of the "tragedy of the commons" hypothesis, they argue that in order to give fair and equal access to all users, they should have the right to prevent such individuals from overusing the network. Throttling high-bandwidth users also reduces infrastructure costs by lessening strain to the network and delaying upgrades to allow for the increased use. Second, network owners argue for the ability to favour certain types of content that is socially desirable, or that subsidizes users. In contrast, proponents point to examples where ISPs have limited individuals' access to certain VOD services (such as Hulu), while allowing unfettered access to the VOD owned by the ISP. In 2010, the FCC approved a new set of rules banning this practice, but members of the US Congress and numerous ISPs have threatened to challenge this rule through legislation and lawsuits, respectively.

Broadband Costs and Prices

Worldwide broadband costs vary greatly, but are rapidly trending downward. This tends to be true both in terms of actual prices, price controlling for bandwidth and/or data usage, and price/cost as a percentage of income. The combination of infrastructure costs and average income leads to some significant differentials. According to a 2012 report by the International Telecommunication Union (ITU), broadband costs, as a share of GNI per capita, ranged from 0.3 percent (Macao) to 747.4 percent (Gambia).[15] In 84 countries, the cost of entry-level broadband was equivalent to 5 percent or less of GNI per capita. Broadband costs stand at over 25 percent of GNI per capita in 39 countries and over 100 percent of GNI per capita in 17 countries. The ITU reported that in developed nations, the average cost of basic broadband access was 1.7 percent of per capita GNI; the average in developing nations was 40.3 percent of per capita GNI. Using a different approach, TeleGeography (2013) found that broadband prices in the US and Europe can be as low as 50 cents per Mbps per month, although prices more typically ran in the $1–$6 per Mbps per month range for major ISPs and carriers. Median prices in Hong Kong were two to five times the median price in London, for example. They found that prices can increase even more rapidly in other areas, running over \$100 per Mbps per month in a number of markets in sub-Saharan Africa and small island nations, although the study notes that the number of markets with prices that extreme is falling.

Although costs can vary significantly between counties, they are all moving in the direction of greater affordability. The cost of entry-level broadband access has dropped about 75 percent between 2008 and 2011. The plummeting costs are most evident in developing nations. For example, broadband costs have dropped more than 90 percent in both Zimbabwe and Ethiopia. In developed countries, broadband costs have dropped about 30 percent during the same period. While the differences in cost and affordability between developing and developed countries are tightening, there are still great disparities. TeleGeography (2013) tracked service rates for Gigabit Ethernet ports in several major cities around the globe from 2007 to 2012. They found that costs/prices were falling 20–30 percent annually, with drops up to 50 percent in the last year. They also found regional differentials. Prices fell at a compounded annual rate of 22 percent in New York and Sao Paulo, 26 percent in Hong Kong, and 31 percent in London.

Table 9.1 Worldwide broadband costs

Economy	Cost as percent of GNI per capita
1. Macao	0.3
2. Israel	0.4
3. United States	0.5
4. Switzerland	0.5
5. Luxembourg	0.6
World Average	28.5
157. Swaziland	399.1
158. Togo	405.5
159. Tajikistan	543.7
160. Eritrea	720.0
161. Gambia	747.4

CONCLUSIONS

The economics of broadband, in terms of network operations and various infrastructure costs, are similar in many ways to Internet economics. An important difference is that broadband access is a rapidly growing and rapidly shifting target, with significant implications for a range of related markets. Another difference is that most of the concern is narrowly targeted on the final local loop, the ISP access point, supplemented by the user's own networking. For the most part, the rest of the components of Internet networks already operate well in excess of broadband norms. This allows the focus on user demand and the range of ISP access technologies and networks. Here, economics is driving the transition to fully fibre networks, even in the local loop, while technological innovation is enabling wireless systems to be competitive alternatives, at least for basic and midrange broadband speeds. It is also clear that substantial variations in costs and prices remain, mostly as a result of differences in geography, density, and competition.

Demand for broadband is growing rapidly, fed to a large degree by the explosion in demand for, and use of, various forms of IP-video. Interest and demand is also being driven by the introduction of a whole new access market: mobile. More than 100 million Americans report watching online video daily (more than half of all Internet users), and they are watching more, and longer, videos. Smartphones, which provide base broadband access, already account for more than a quarter (27.4 percent) of all cellular/mobile devices; and tablets another 2.3 percent (Cisco, 2012). These are large and growing segments of demand, and, more importantly, data traffic. Both are also driving an explosion in the markets producing and supplying content, applications, and services appropriate for video and mobile use. And both online video and mobile markets are seen as transformative, impacting how, when, and where users access information and entertainment.

Several issues related to broadband diffusion are in play. Pricing strategies can have significant impacts on broadband adoption. State policy can facilitate or retard diffusion. Regional differences in income and access can contribute to growing divides – urban/rural, rich/poor, among others. Governance issues, including open access and network neutrality concerns, can play a significant role in shaping network development, broadband diffusion, access, and eventually the social impact of broadband access.

Despite the uncertainties at work, there is good news for broadband access. Fundamental and long-term cost trends in network infrastructure, user devices, and production technologies provide strong evidence that costs and prices will decline over time, and that connection choices (including access speeds) will increase, if authorities permit. Access to broadband will increase as networks upgrade and expand, and prices should fall as competition among access providers increases, and technological efficiencies continue to emerge. Content markets will expand, and new applications and services will emerge, if not hamstrung by intellectual property issues and the rise of localized content regulation. The trends should positively reinforce each other, as well. As broadband diffuses, the issues and differences should reduce, if the markets are left to their natural course.

Overall, the economics of broadband suggest that broadband access is good, and likely to get better – at least if authorities do not meddle too much, and/or until some new transformative innovation comes along.

NOTES

1. The National Broadband Map reports suggest that almost half of US homes (46 percent) currently have access to broadband networks offering 100 Mbps or higher download speeds.
2. FTTx is a generic reference to what is variously called fibre to the home (FTTH), fibre to the building (FTTB) and fibre to the premises (FTTP), and describes networks that bring the fibre cable all the way to the individual user. Fibre to the node (FTTN), also referred to as fibre to the curb (FTTC), describes networks where the fibre gets close to the user, but stops at a point where several (25–100) users are connected by coax or copper to the local node. Another way of looking at the difference is that FTTx networks place the optical digital signal converter at each user's premises, while the node users in FTTN share the cost of the converter.
3. Smartphones offer Internet access, and allow users to expand their Internet usage away from home and office computers. More than half of all mobile customers in the EU and the US own and use smartphones as their primary mobile device.
4. Tablets are mobile devices with larger screens that facilitate their use as content displays. Tablet diffusion is nearing 20–25 percent in the US and UK (the vast majority of content available is English language; also licensing deals for much content are country-specific). Recent studies suggest heavy tablet use for data-heavy video and multimedia content, increasing data traffic even more quickly.
5. WiMax also makes sense as a secondary or supplemental access server, if the number of users and data traffic levels can be controlled.
6. Internet traffic, particularly from mobile devices, caused several slowdowns during the 2012 London Olympics, and crashed one local mobile site outside of London during the cycling road course events.
7. A pure flat-rate pricing plan is one that charges a flat rate for some fixed time period, regardless of how much or how little the covered services are used. Flat rate plus cap pricing refers to a fixed basic charge per period, but puts a limit (cap) on the use of some particular service, with further use during that period charged at a higher rate (usually significantly higher).
8. Wikipedia (n.d.) offers an outline of broadband plans that reflects some of the efforts.
9. Information for this section contributed by Yi-Xi Zhu.
10. MIIT, The Industrial Restructuring and Revitalization Planning of Electronic Information Industry, 2009.
11. The Opinions on Promoting Fiber Broadband Construction, 2010.

12. DSL refers to a family of digital data services primarily offered by local telephone operators, and can offer download speeds of 256 Kbps to 40 Mbps, depending on how it is implemented.
13. The calculated cost figures are average per connected home, based on upgrades occurring over a 10-year period and a 25 percent adoption rate.
14. In the US, the NTIA's report on Broadband Availability in Urban Areas (2014) indicates gaps in access to high-speed broadband; in the number of broadband service providers; and in the range of network technologies available.
15. GNI per capita can be interpreted roughly as the average income for the given population. Therefore, the cost of broadband access in Macao is approximately 0.3 percent of the average individual's income.

REFERENCES

Cisco (2012). *Cisco Visual Networking Index: Global Mobile Data Traffic Forecast Update, 2011–2016.* Cisco.

Cisco (2013). *Cisco Visual Networking Index: Global Mobile Data Traffic Forecast Update, 2012–2017.* Cisco. Accessed at http://www.cisco.com/en/US/solutions/collateral/ns341/ns525/ns537/ns705/ns827/white_paper_c11-520862.html

Ericsson (2012). *Ericsson Mobility Report: On the Pulse of the Networked Society.* Ericsson. Accessed at: http://www.ericsson.com/res/docs/2012/ericsson-mobility-report-november-2012.pdf

European Union (EU) (2012). *Broadband Coverage in Europe in 2011: Mapping Progress Towards the Coverage Objectives of the Digital Agenda.* Accessed at: http://ec.europa.eu/information_society/newsroom/cf/dae/document.cfm?action=display&doc_id=1102

Federal Communication Commission (FCC) (2012). *A Report on Consumer Wireline Broadband Performance in the U.S.* Accessed at: http://www.fcc.gov/measuring-broadband-america/2012/july

Ims, L.A., Myhre, D., and Olsen, B.T. (1998). 'Costs of upgrading the residential telecommunications infrastructure to broadband', *IEEE Global Telecommunications Conference, 1998: The Bridge to Global Integration,* 6, 3153–3158.

International Telecommunication Union (ITU) (2011). *The World in 2011: ICT Facts and Figures.* Accessed at: http://www.itu.int/ITU-D/ict/facts/2011/material/ICTFactsFigures2011.pdf

International Telecommunication Union (2012). *Key ICD indicators for developed and developing countries and the world.* Accessed at: http://www.itu.int/ITU-D/ict/statistics/at_glance/KeyTelecom.html

International Telecommunication Union (ITU) (2013). *Measuring the Information Society, 2013.* Accessed at: http://www.itu.int/en/ITU-D/Statistics/Documents/publications/mis2013/MIS2013_without_Annex_4.pdf

Jaffer, F. and Lee, B.H.L. (2012). 'National Broadband Networks: Enlightening the Future of Nations', *2012 14th International Conference on Transparent Optical Networks (ICTON),* 1–4.

Judge, P. (2013). 'New Eutelsat Tooway Packages Bring 20Mbps Broadband To Rural UK', *Techweek Europe*, February 1. Accessed at: http://www.techweekeurope.co.uk/news/tooway-eutelsat-broadband-20mbps-rural-106129

National Telecommunications and Information Administration (NTIA) (2014, July). Broadband Statistics Report: Broadband Availability in Urban vs. Rural Areas. Accessed at: http://www.broadbandmap.gov/download/Broadband%20Availability%20in%20Rural%20vs%20Urban%20Areas.pdf

Organisation for Economic Co-operation and Development (2008). *Broadband Growth and Policies in OECD Countries.* Accessed at: http://www.oecd.org/internet/broadbandandtelecom/40629067.pdf

Organisation for Economic Co-operation and Development (2012). *OECD Broadband Portal.* Accessed at: http://www.oecd.org/internet/broadbandandtelecom/oecdbroadbandportal.htm

Samanta, S.K., Martin, R. and Pan, H. (2012a). 'Drivers and Barriers to Investment in High Speed Broadband Infrastructure', *Social Science Research Network.* Accessed at: http://ssrn.com/abstract=1997107

Samanta, S.K., Martin, R., Guild, K. and Pan, H. (2012b). 'The Diffusion of High Speed Broadband: A Cross Country Analysis', *Social Science Research Network.* Accessed at: http://ssrn.com/abstract=1997113

TeleGeography (2012). 'International Market Trends', Presentation by TeleGeography to Pacific Telecommunications Council conference, January 15. Slides accessed at http://www.ptc.org/ptc12/images/papers/upload/PTC12_TeleGeograph%20Wkshop.pdf

TeleGeography (2013). 'International Market Trends', Presentation to Pacific Telecommunications Council conference, January 20. Slides accessed at http://www.ptc.org/ptc13/images/papers/upload/PTC13_TeleGeo_PPS.pdf

Wikipedia (n.d.). 'National broadband plans from around the world', Wikipedia. Accessed at http://en.wikipedia.org/wiki/National_broadband_plans_from_around_the_world

10. Economics of peer-to-peer file exchange

Nodir Adilov, Peter J. Alexander and Brendan Cunningham

Peer-to-peer file sharing reflects a technological change and subsequent "cultural revolution" that began in the late 1980s, and fully blossomed in the late 1990s and early 2000s. The technological element of this change was the transition from analog production and physical distribution to digital production and distribution; the cultural aspect refers to the changing mindset of consumers of digital products. When products were produced physically, a substantial and explicit infrastructure reflected perceived value-added that may have helped rationalize the existing pricing structure. After the transition from physical to digital production and distribution however, the analog pricing structure, constructed to reflect physical costs (including distribution networks and retail stores), may not have made as much sense in the minds of consumers, and may have induced a certain amount of "piracy" or "sharing" of content in response.[1] That is, among the many reasons individuals might have for exchanging digital products, the price for peering substantially undercut the retail price. In this sense, consumers responded rationally to the "market" price signal. Arguably, a digital duplicate of a creative work is almost costless to produce, on the margin. And perfectly competitive prices would, therefore, be arbitrarily close to zero, an outcome which is almost perfectly replicated through free exchange. The response to consumer file exchanges from content providers has been fierce, and some changes in the regulation of the internet reflect, to some degree, the struggle between content providers and a substantial fraction of their consumers.

In what follows, we explore peer-to-peer (P2P) technology and digital file sharing, beginning with some elementary technical background information. While the concept of peering and sharing files may seem mysterious, implementation of peer-to-peer protocols are straightforward, and there are multiple software platforms readily available for any computer user with internet access.

We examine the transition from analog to digital products in so-called creative or culture-based industries, and the implications of this transition for consumers, firms, and policy-makers.[2] As we suggest, the transition from analog to digital production and distribution has had, in certain respects, significant influence over communications policy-making. Put another way, the conflict that emerged between consumers and producers in creative industries after the transition to digital technology has, in a sense, "punched above its weight" relative to its economic importance, in cultivating actual and potential changes in the legal and economic terrain of the internet. The current debate over so-called "network neutrality" illustrates this point, at least to the extent that content providers have battled to compel cable operators (the companies that provide internet services to households and institutions) to stop consumers from exchanging certain copyright-protected content. This action was a beachhead in a broader, much more general debate over whether cable operators might favor some internet traffic (and perhaps implement tiered-pricing schemes).

We conclude the chapter by examining effects of the transition from analog to digital and subsequent peer-to-peer file exchanges on the evolution of production and distribution in creative industries, such as music recording. The music recording industry was on the early front lines of the analog-to-digital transition and peer-to-peer exchanges, and while the trajectory of the industry does not map perfectly to other creative industries, the evolution of the music industry provides a useful case study.

BASIC TECHNICAL BACKGROUND

When an internet user visits a website, such as www.nytimes.com or www.bbc.com, the user's computer (or more generally, a user's internet capable device) establishes a connection with a central server that holds the content for the website. The server receives the request for content, and, if possible, delivers the content the user requests. At any given time, the user may be one of many thousands of "clients" requesting and receiving content from the website's central server(s).

This situation is depicted in Figure 10.1, where six individual clients are requesting and receiving content from one central server.[3] Notice there are no direct interconnections between the six individual clients.

In Figure 10.2, note the absence of a central server. Instead, the individual computers are connected via a series of so-called "peered" connections; that is, the individual "clients" have multiple independent connections with each other.[4] If the individual clients are using compatible peering software, they can communicate with each other, and can exchange files. In this configuration, each individual computer can be

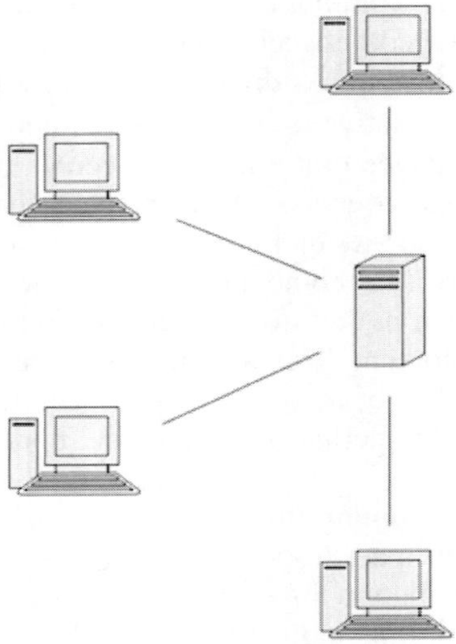

Figure 10.1 Client-server model

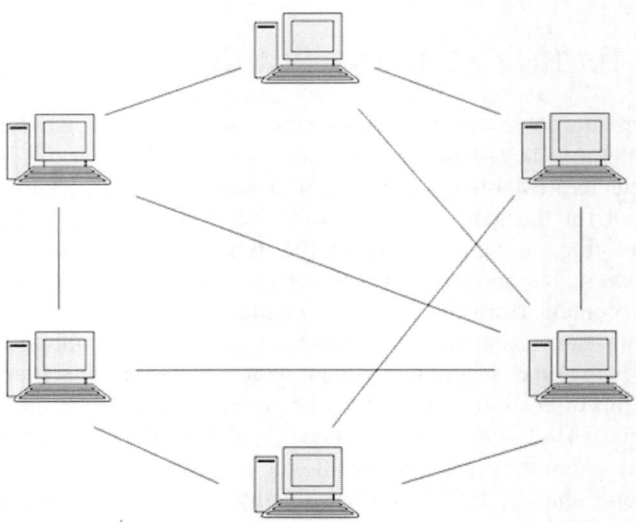

Figure 10.2 Peer-to-peer network

both a client and a server, in that they can receive files and exchange them with others. Moreover, a single file can be obtained piecemeal from multiple peers. This is what is meant by "peer-to-peer".

Specialized peering software facilitates the peering interconnection. At a basic level, peering software, like that previously used by Napster, provides an index of files available for exchanges on an individual machine. If another user is interested in obtaining a file, the user, in essence, sends a request to the computer hosting the file, and begins downloading.

Unlike the client-server framework, all computers in the peer relationship that have an existing copy of the requested file can provide or "serve" parts of the file to the machine that sent the request. The various parts of the file are then re-assembled on the recipient's computer. Once the recipient has obtained the file, the recipient's computer can now also act as a server if other peers request the file. One benefit of this arrangement is that file transfer speeds can be improved, since the request is being distributed over multiple "servers". Another benefit is that if some computers are unable to respond to the request, peering provides redundancies, unlike a single central server. These redundancies are beneficial to internet users, since bottlenecks or various other sorts of disruptions can often be routed around.

Evolution of Peering (Software) Technology

The technology of peering has evolved substantially since Napster, a pioneering peer-to-peer software technology, was released in 1999. The earliest systems, like that deployed by Napster, were actually quasi-peer-to-peer since they relied on central servers that indexed the exchangeable files of users, and then directed users to peers who could provide the file. The exchange of files, however, took place between two individual computers, and not the Napster servers. Peer-to-peer communications have also extended in new directions. For example, Skype provides voice and video communications over a P2P protocol.

Current peer-to-peer software technology, such as uTorrent (among many others), has advanced well beyond this early structure, and individual computers currently do not require the explicit intermediation of a central server. Instead, using uTorrent (or similar software) individual computers communicate directly with one another, using self-created indexes of files available for exchange. Moreover, if multiple computers contain the file to be exchanged, multiple computers can provide parts of the file simultaneously, a redundancy which improves download speeds and makes peer-to-peer exchanges more resilient to network slowdowns. Peer-to-peer also plays an important role in balancing traffic on the internet. File distribution through P2P eliminates the need for a single server with a high bandwidth capacity in order to accommodate multiple simultaneous downloads.

P2P in the Context of Network Neutrality

Network neutrality is difficult to define, but an informal definition might be that all network packets, irrespective of their content, are treated equally. This impressionistic treatment is improved by Felton (2006). Felton notes that digital information flows across the infrastructure of the internet in discrete packets, each of which contains data of some kind or another. Sometimes the packets are subject to simple, unavoidable congestion, and cable operators (again, the companies that provide physical access to the internet for households and institutions) have to decide which packets to discard or delay. Felton refers to this type of intervention as "minimal discrimination", since it only occurs at congestion, and is done out of necessity. On the other hand, "non-minimal discrimination" occurs when cable operators willfully choose to discard or delay packets in the absence of congestion.

In 2008, the Federal Communications Commission (hereafter, FCC), concluded that Comcast, a cable operator, engaged in widespread non-minimal discrimination against BitTorrent (a general peer-to-peer software protocol upon which specific applications are built) users, among others. According to the FCC, Comcast undertook this widespread non-minimal discrimination without informing its customers of such activity, and, when asked about the practice, initially denied that it was "throttling" traffic in a non-minimally discriminatory fashion.

TRANSITION FROM ANALOG TO DIGITAL

In this section, we explore the emergence and introduction of digitization and digital technologies. The relationship, and importance, of this section relative to what we explored above is this: exchanging goods and information via physical copies, such as a photocopy of a book, a tape recording of a musical performance or motion picture, and other analogous products, has been superseded by exchanging these goods and information in a digital format, and peering technologies provide a substantial platform for these exchanges. Moreover, digitization has significantly reduced many of the costs that were formerly associated with analog production and distribution, including many large-scale physical plants related to pre-digital processes. In most industries, for example the computer industry itself, lower production costs would ultimately lead to lower consumer prices and greater consumer (and potentially producer) surplus. However, creative industries were initially resistant to digitization of their products, in part due to the ability to easily redistribute digital versions and, also in part, due to a disruption in their pricing structure and strategy.

Computers

At the center of the transition from analog to digital is the computer. Computers are ubiquitous in most advanced economies. Computers are used to write papers and email, read newspapers, watch movies or listen to music, and a myriad other tasks or activities; computers are also used to fly airplanes, operate automobile engines, and control fully automated production technologies, among many other things. By implication, computers have supplanted or replaced various pre-computer technologies that were used to perform these tasks. For example, instead of writing this chapter on a typewriter and sending photocopies by land mail, computers and associated software implement the production of originals and distribution of copies. Similarly, digital cameras, a small computer of sorts, have replaced, in a popular sense, their analog counterparts, which rely on reflected light to induce a chemical change.

Creative or Culture-based Markets

Computers and computing technology have also had a revolutionary influence in creative or culture-based industries (such as music recording, motion pictures, and book publishing) in terms of production, distribution, and consumption. For example, the production of music, motion pictures, and books all substantially involve digital technologies. Moreover, product distribution, which used to have a significant physical component in these industries, is largely conducted digitally. Finally, the ways in which consumers consume the output of these industries has been radically altered.

For example, theaters and network television continue to be supplanted by video-on-demand, which allows consumers to choose not only the product to be consumed, but also the time and place. Books can be instantly downloaded to (portable) computing devices and entire libraries can be carried on a single portable tablet device. Entire libraries of music can be carried on a portable device no larger than a package of chewing gum. All of these products can be stored in the "cloud" which allows access at a time and place determined by the consumer.

A HELPFUL EXAMPLE: THE MUSIC RECORDING INDUSTRY

It is useful to provide a specific industry framework to illustrate the substance and magnitude of the changes brought by the transition from analog to digital, from both a technological and legal perspective. While each creative or culture-based industry has its own particular contours, there are some core aspects of the transition from analog to digital that might be usefully explicated by a single industry focus.

A Very Brief History of Technological Change in the Industry[5]

The recorded audio music recording industry is over a century old. In the industry's infancy, playback devices and audio products initially utilized wax cylinders and crude vinyl records. From a scale perspective, production (recording) and reproduction (manufacture) of the wax cylinders used for music playbacks was relatively costly, as each cylinder had to be individually produced.[6] Less costly methods for mass-producing cylinders emerged by 1901. One new manufacturing method employed a pantographic technique in which a master recording was used to make copies by replaying the master as a cutting device for reproducing the same sound vibrations on new cylinders. Each original master could be copied approximately 25 times before it wore out. A session using ten machines to record a single song could ultimately yield 250 cylinders, a 2,500 percent increase over the original technique.[7] Perhaps more important for the music recording industry, however, was another innovation in the technology of supply: magnetic tape recorders. The pre-tape recording technology used for recording music was limiting in two ways: first, it was expensive to purchase, and second, it was unforgiving in production. By unforgiving we mean that if a mistake was made in the production process, the entire process was stopped, the master disk discarded and replaced by a new master, and the process begun again. In addition to reducing fixed costs (that is, a lower purchase price of production technology), tape machines also provided an easy way to edit musical performances and thus reduced the marginal costs of recording music. Tape technology made it possible to correct mistakes by rerecording a flawed musical passage and then cutting the tape and replacing the flawed passage with the correction.

The development and refinement of digital production and reproduction in the 1980s is the most recent technological change in the industry's history. Prior to the 1980s, the production and playback technologies of the music recording industry were analog-based, and music was produced and distributed using vinyl disks and magnetically encoded tape.[8]

Compact disks, introduced to consumers in the 1980s, were the first important element in the music industry's shift to digital technology. The transition from analog to digital production and reproduction has had a significant effect on supply-side costs within the industry: with digital products the marginal cost of producing, reproducing, and distributing perfect copies is functionally zero. Thus, unlike the case where the tape player made production cheaper but did not alter the costs of distribution, digital technology has significantly reduced costs throughout the entire process – production, reproduction, and distribution. However, it has also made illicit redistribution far easier and introduced a demand for additional technologies, often referred to as "digital rights management," which maintain the scarcity of copies and limit the ability to illicitly redistribute.

Given that a compact disk player uses a sequence of 0s and 1s to reproduce sound waves, consumers can use computers to play compact disks, as well as transfer songs (rip) from compact disks for storage and replay them on their computers and other devices (iPod, Rune, mobile phones, and so on). These types of files, until relatively recently, were generally not shared with large numbers of other users, since, as late as 1997, the transfer of three minutes of music required 50 megabytes of hard-drive storage space and an enormous amount of time and bandwidth to move them across the internet.

However, the development of the MP3 file format changed substantially these storage and bandwidth requirements. MP3 is an audio compression format that generates near compact disk-quality sound at approximately one-tenth to one-twentieth the size of the original file. For example, while each minute of music on a compact disk requires the equivalent of 10 megabytes of computer storage space, an MP3 format of the same piece can be stored on 1 megabyte or less.[9]

File compression technology made digital file distribution more efficient. This increased efficiency is amplified given more computers are connecting to the internet via cable and fiber rather than modem, which significantly improves the speed at which files can be transferred.

The Legal and Technological Evolution of Digital File Exchanges in the Music Industry

The music recording industry is currently at (or very near) the center of a highly-contentious debate about digital file exchanges, a debate that in some ways has already shaped, and is shaping, the regulation of the internet. The music industry's trade association, the RIAA, asserts that digital file exchange is substantially diminishing industry profits and harming the industry. The evidence for this claim, as we shall see, is less clear. We begin by reviewing file exchanges that rely on central servers. We then explore pure peer-to-peer systems, and finally so-called private trackers.

The music industry initially responded to nascent large-scale organized digital file exchange by taking legal action against the most prominent and sizable digital file distributors, MP3.com and Napster.com. These firms claimed protection citing "fair use" and "safe harbor," respectively. However, in UMG Recording, Inc. et al. v. MP3.com, Judge Jed S. Rakoff concluded that "defendant's infringement of plaintiffs' copyrights is clear" (92 F. Supp. 2d 349 [2000]). During the trial, MP3.com argued that its repository of legally purchased copyrighted material, which it distributed to registered users, was protected by "fair use." Judge Rakoff concluded that the "defendant's 'fair use' defense is indefensible and must be denied as a matter of law" (92 F. Supp. 2d 349 [2000]). Moreover, in the Napster.com case, US District Judge Marilyn Hall Patel refused a motion by Napster.com to dismiss the lawsuit against them, ruling that Napster.com was not entitled to "safe harbor" status as provided in the Digital Millennium Copyright Act (DMCA) of 1998.[10] Judge Patel subsequently issued a preliminary injunction against Napster.com, ordering them to stop distributing copyrighted materials.

Note that MP3.com and Napster.com share common features, the most important of which may be that as distribution systems they rely on a series of central servers to guide the distribution of digital products. So, for example, if a user of either system sends out a request for a file, the request is routed through one of the firms' servers. Because requests for information relating to the location of MP3 files are routed through their servers, and because a federal judge has held such activity to violate existing copyright law, companies like MP3.com and Napster.com were obvious targets for legal remedy.[11]

In contrast, as we noted above, pure peer-to-peer file exchange systems are decentralized and do not require a central server. Rather, each individual computer that has peer-to-peer software installed on it can become a server via (a series of) peer connections. Thus, if a computer has the required software and internet connection, it can connect with another similar computer, which itself is connected to another similar computer, and so on.

The music industry's initial response to peer-to-peer file exchange, at the individual consumer level, was to physically copy protect its products through various Digital Rights Management schemes. Despite many attempts, however, these efforts failed. The industry's current response is multi-pronged. First, the industry is tracking individuals who exchange copyrighted files online, and issuing pre-litigation letters and subpoenas to these users for alleged damages. Second, the music recording industry coordinated with Apple Computers to introduce the first platform for selling an almost-comprehensive catalogue of music digitally: iTunes. This reasonably priced legal source for music provided a competitor to peer-to-peer exchanges and, in conjunction with lawsuits, reduced the level of activity on exchanges. Subsequently, the formal distribution channels for music have expanded to include Amazon, Google Play, and a number of subscription-based streaming services such as Spotify and Rhapsody. It is worth noting that these platforms (like peer-to-peer file exchanges) also provide an easy means to unbundle albums, and allow consumers to purchase singles. It is highly probable that unbundling is welfare-enhancing for consumers.

More generally, the RIAA tracks file sharing by hiring computer consulting firms who monitor peer-to-peer networks for copy-protected works being made available for exchange. These firms report the IP (Internet Protocol) address of the alleged infringing user to the RIAA. The RIAA then issues a subpoena to the user's ISP (Internet Service Provider), requesting that the ISP reveal the name and address of the alleged infringing user. The RIAA then uses this information to issue pre-litigation letters or subpoenas.

Besides tracking users, it is alleged that the RIAA and their consulting firms use a variety of other means to thwart peer networks, such as introducing malformed files (packets) into the network. One counter-technique common in peer networks is the use of "blocklists", which filter out IP addresses known to be used by the RIAA or their consultants to track users. In addition, peer software that employs encryption and proxy service (or simply using VPNs) is becoming more common and user friendly. While not providing complete privacy (and generally operating at slower speeds), the architecture of this software is such that tracking online file sharing is much more difficult, while peer users obtain greater levels of privacy.

File exchanges have also migrated to private trackers. Private trackers are, roughly, smaller groups of individuals that make files available to other "club" members. Since membership is based on contributions and referrals, private trackers have a relatively high level of security.

Tragedy of the Commons?

Early versions of peer-to-peer software built-in "share" as the default setting for users, but once users became increasingly sophisticated, many users began to stop making files available for others to download.[12] Using an analogy to the classic "Tragedy of the Commons", Adar and Huberman (2000) conjecture that peer-to-peer file exchange might be extinguished by free-riding, noting that "in order for distributed systems with no central monitoring to succeed, a large amount of voluntary cooperation is required, a requirement that is very hard to fulfill in systems with large user populations that remain anonymous."[13] In fact, Adar and Huberman track peer-to-peer traffic on the Gnutella (peer-to-peer) network and conclude exchanges were not symmetric; about 70 percent of users did not provide any files (songs, in this study) for exchange. Adar and Huberman suggest privatizing the public good might overcome these effects, and propose setting up a market that allowed users to buy and sell computer processing resources.[14] Golle et al. (2003), among others, offer a detailed model of how such systems might be structured. To the best of our knowledge, these markets have not yet emerged.

The probability of being detected sharing, and the substantial penalties associated, may further dissuade users from providing files. The penalties for file exchange can be substantial, such as the recent case of Joel Tenenbaum, who was fined $675,000 for making 31 songs available for downloading by other users.[15] Hughes et al. (2005) notes that as free riding become prevalent, the probability of detection among those who continue to make files available increases, which may create a positive feedback loop among users, further reducing exchanges.

ECONOMIC DAMAGE TO THE MUSIC INDUSTRY FROM FILE EXCHANGE?

How economically damaging, if at all, is digital file exchanging activity to the music recording industry? In the following section we review literature relating to this question. Most of the research we review has a focus on the music industry, since the music industry was and is at the epicenter of digital file exchanges.

Before we begin our review however, it is useful to observe that the implications of file exchanges might impact different digital industries in different fashions. That is to say, the economic welfare and social effects of file exchanges might be more or less severe in certain industries. In short, we suggest the cost structure of the industries might be an important, and largely overlooked, aspect of actual (social) costs.[16]

For example, the music recording industry's production and distribution cost structure has evolved over the past 100 years from high fixed-cost/high marginal-cost to low fixed-cost/low marginal-cost.[17] This low fixed and low marginal cost structure, to some degree, differentiates the music recording business from other creative and culture-based industries that currently have high fixed or first copy costs (such as motion pictures and software) and low marginal costs.

It is worth noting that this distinction in fixed cost structure might also suggest very different legal remedies and approaches to property rights and infringement because high upfront costs and uncertain profitability (possibly due to infringement) might actually diminish the flow of certain media and cultural products. If protecting the flow of new products, rather than the stock of existing product, is the focus of public policy, the underlying cost structure of the industries may be an important feature to consider. The argument, for example, that the flow of new products from the music industry has been harmed by file exchanges is simply contradicted by the evidence. The same may not be true for other creative or culture-based industries.

A Review of Some Economic Literature

The economic theory literature relating to peer-to-peer file exchange is relatively modest, but not insubstantial.[18] Much of this literature has been produced, unsurprisingly, in the past decade, although the broader issue of copying and piracy can be traced back still further. For example, photocopy machines, analog tape devices (known as cassette tape recorders), and video cassette recorders, provided a means to provide copies of printed materials, music, and motion pictures, respectively, prior to the digitization of these products.

The earliest models exploring the implications of these pre-digital technologies, such as Novos and Waldman (1984) and Johnson (1985), typically posit a monopolist providing a single product, copies of which are lower quality, and consumers who are heterogeneous with respect to demand for quality. In these frameworks, copies compete with originals for some consumers, and producers may be incentivized to lower price (see also Takayama, 1994). The welfare implications in these models are ambiguous, since static economic efficiency increases with copying because it expands the market; however, dynamic efficiency, the flow of new products, may be negatively affected.

From a welfare perspective, there are three additional elements explored in the literature which provide bridges to the newer literature. Extensions to the early models noted above introduced the idea that consumers benefit from increased product information (or sampling) derived from copies or samples. Liebowitz (1985), for example, identified the potential information-revelation benefit of photocopies for books and journals. Alexander (1994) observed that music is an experience good and conjectured that on-line digital distribution in the music industry would benefit consumers by reducing uncertainty about product quality and characteristics, and would expand the market by increasing competition from new entrants. Zhang (2002) and Gopal et al. (2006) provide formal models of this conjecture, and find that peer-to-peer exchanges (1) enhance welfare by reducing uncertainty, and (2) benefit new entrants more than established superstars. In addition, Peitz and Waelbroeck (2006) suggest that information revelation benefits music producers since consumers are willing to pay more for products that better meet their preferred specification.

Network effects and indirect appropriation are additional extensions that bridge some of the earlier copying literature to some of the recent peer-to-peer. Network effects suggest interdependencies among consumers in that progressively larger networks of users provide additional benefits. Thus, Conner and Rumelt (1991) suggest software piracy may be beneficial in the presence of network effects. Dewenter et al. (2012) analyze the interdependency between the market for music recordings and concert tickets, assuming that there are positive indirect network effects both from the record market to ticket sales for live performances and vice versa. File sharing can increase profits through increased concert ticket demand and thereby also lead to additional market entry and additional variety.

Indirect appropriability, proposed by Liebowitz (1985), suggests that the capacity to make (photo) copies increases a consumer's willingness to pay a higher price for originals, thereby compensating producers for copies the consumer might make. Watt (2005), however, suggests the scale of digital copying and exchanging vitiates the notion that producers are meaningfully compensated, indirectly or otherwise, for the number of potential copies.

For the music industry, the empirical economics literature relating to the economic damage (lost sales) from file exchanges is mixed, in terms of data sources, modeling choices, and hence results. Of the studies explored here, which we believe reflect more or less the "state of the art", the sales or displacement losses to producers range from approximately 0 percent to 30 percent.

Oberholzer-Gee and Strumpf (2007) find that file sharing has no statistically significant negative effect on the sale of compact disks, and that most individuals who share files would not have purchased the music they downloaded. The authors find that peer-to-peer file sharing increases the sales of the most popular compact disks, and that every 150 peer-to-peer exchanges of the most popular music increases compact disk sales by one unit.

Bhattacharjee et al. (2007) employ a survival analysis and find significantly reduced hit chart duration for all albums, except those that debut high on the hit charts. In particular, music "superstars" and female performers display enhanced survival. They also find that file exchange does not negatively affect the survival of top-ranked albums, but does have a negative impact on lower-ranked albums.

Zenter (2006) estimates the effect of music downloads on music sales and shows that individuals who download music online are more likely to buy music. However, when controlling for simultaneity, this preliminary result suggests that peer-to-peer exchange reduces the probability of buying music by an average of 30 percent. Based on these findings, Zenter suggests that music sales would be approximately 8 percent higher absent peer-to-peer networks.

Rob and Waldfogel (2006) collect data on albums obtained via purchase and downloading, as well as consumers' valuations of these albums, among a sample of US college students in 2003, and find that album download reduces purchases by about 10 percent in their sample, although possibly by more. The authors measure the effect of exchanges on welfare and find that exchanges reduce per capita expenditure on hit albums released in the years between 1999–2003 from $126 to $101, but increases per capita consumers' surplus by $70.

Gopal et al. (2006) suggest that peer-to-peer exchanges decrease sampling costs, leading more potential consumers to sample unknown music, and also more consumers to purchase the music they have sampled. Lower sampling costs have a positive effect on consumer surplus, and purchases. For high value songs, online search and sampling capabilities have a beneficial impact on sales while the sale of lower value songs suffers.

Peitz and Waelbroeck (2004) find that music downloading could have caused a 10 percent reduction in compact disk sales worldwide in 2001, but does not explain the 9 percent observed reduction in sales observed in

2002. Thus, Peitz and Waelbroeck suggest that legal actions and protection schemes for compact disks may be poorly motivated.

Mortimer et al. (2012) find that concert ticket sales significantly increased after the introduction of Napster, particularly for newer and less well-known artists. This result suggests that the overall financial impact of file exchanges on artists is complicated due to the potential promotional value associated with wider distribution of music. Concert revenues are relatively more remunerative for artists, in comparison to album sales.

It is clear, even from these brief empirical sketches, that a good deal of heterogeneity exists in approach and results, and it is difficult to draw meaningful conclusions about actual damage to the industry. Part of the lack of convergence in these econometric music industry studies results from the choice of data, and part from the choice of technique. For example, some studies rely exclusively on student surveys, which may not be representative, and thus produce biased results. However, data relating to actual file exchanges are expensive and difficult to obtain, while survey data are relatively cheap and easy to generate. Unobserved heterogeneity presents another difficulty for empirics. Researchers have responded using difference-in-difference and instrumental variable techniques. Difference-in-difference approaches require time invariance for the estimates to be unbiased, a requirement that is unlikely to be met. Instrumental variable techniques, a promising approach, require good judgment and more than a bit of luck, since weak instruments generate poor predictions.

CONCLUSION

Peer-to-peer computer connections are one means of facilitating the exchange of digitized products, and more generally information and data. Some of these exchanges, however, are non-sanctioned, and violate existing copyright laws. To put a fine point on this, we specifically refer to unauthorized exchanging of music, movies, books, software, and other products of this type. Many of the established firms in industries affected by unauthorized file exchanges claim that they are materially damaged by such actions.

When digital copyrights management (copy protection) failed to staunch unauthorized exchanges, some firms, in particular and especially the trade association of the music industry, the RIAA, began to track down those engaging in exchange, and taking at least some of them to court. In many of these cases, like that of Joel Tenenbaum, large monetary awards were granted to the industry.[19] Despite these legal efforts, it appears that file exchanges continue, and end user technology has become more sophisticated, that is, encrypted files, use of proxy servers, private tracker, and so on. In one sense, this resembles a technological sophistication arms race. Whether society benefits from this is uncertain.

It does appear, however, that public policy in a broader sense is implicated in the creative or culture-based industries' efforts to squelch non-sanctioned exchanges. Specifically, we refer to network neutrality. It appears that at least some internet providers, including Comcast, have engaged in what Felton (2006) describes as non-minimal discrimination, specifically the throttling of bandwidth of users downloading "torrents," an effort no doubt applauded by the music industry. Other efforts have included the proposed SOPA legislation, which would dictate (and perhaps censure), returned domain search results on internet search engines. Given the uncertainty over actual damages to any of the creative or culture-based industries, and in particular the music recording industry, it may be unwise to drive public policy on such a thin evidential reed, especially when the potential broader consequences of such actions are unknown. We are left to conclude, as we noted in our introduction, that the music recording industry is "punching well above its economic weight" in the public policy arena. As Romer (2002) notes, "even in the worst case in which the government takes no action and all the traditional music firms go out of business, the net harm to the economy in the United States or the rest of the world would be trivial."

We do not, however, conclude that all damage to all creative or culture-based industries, in particular in the aggregate, is trivial. We observe that these products do have value and that appropriate incentives must be utilized to call forth new products from these industries. It is also the case that protecting the stock of products from these industries is distinct from protecting the flow, which we believe to be the appropriate focus of copyright policy. In this respect, we suggest, as we have noted previously, that the cost structures of the industries might provide a piece of a useful foundation for public policy. In particular, industries with low fixed and low marginal costs are less likely than those with high fixed and low marginal costs to see a reduction in the flow of new products. Evaluating the flow of new products might help policy makers better evaluate the damage (or benefit) to society.

NOTES

1. We will, henceforth, use the term "exchange" as a substitute for sharing or piracy. Both of the latter terms appear to carry value judgments that we seek to avoid. We suggest that exchange, on the other hand, conveys a more neutral description.
2. We use these imprecise terms, creative and culture-based, for lack of anything better.
3. http://upload.wikimedia.org/wikipedia/commons/thumb/f/fb/Server-based-network.svg/200px-Server-based-network.svg.png
4. http://upload.wikimedia.org/wikipedia/commons/thumb/3/3f/P2P-network.svg/200px-P2P-network.svg.png
5. Alexander (1994) provides additional detail on the evolution of technology in the industry.
6. To make 10 copies of a recording, the performer either had to perform the song 10 times, or 10 recorders had to be recording simultaneously (or some combination of the two). After recording the performance, the recorded cylinders were replaced with new cylinders and the song was performed again. If a mistake was made during the performance, all 10 of the recording devices were stopped, the cylinders discarded and replaced, and the process began anew.
7. Another more efficient technique for mass producing cylinders used a reverse metal master stamper; several thousand copies could be made from the original before the stamper wore down and had to be discarded. These techniques greatly reduced the cost of reproducing recorded products.
8. The primary difference between analog and digital signals is that analog is a continuous form of encoding information, while digital is a discrete form. Thus, for analog technologies, information is encoded in a continuous stream while in digital technologies sound is encoded in discrete bits.
9. To give a practical example of the compression savings, consider that Elvis Presley's *Hound Dog* on compact disk requires 24 megabytes of hard disk space, but when converted to MP3 the storage requirement is 2 megabytes. On a 28.8-kilobit-per-second modem, the compact disk version of *Hound Dog* would take at least 1.5 hours to download from another computer; if the file were first converted to MP3, it would take approximately 8.5 minutes.
10. The safe harbor provisions of the DMCA were established to protect internet service providers from liability and court-issued injunctions regardless of their knowledge, in the event that users of the service committed illegal actions.
11. In general, copyright law is designed to protect copyright holders from substantial unauthorized use of copy-protected objects. This legal protection, and the resulting capacity on the part of the copyright holder to exploit the benefits of innovation, is thought to provide appropriate incentives to create.
12. This default setting is an interesting example of the type of "nudge" described in Thaler and Sunstein (2008). Since users tend to accept the default the networks tend to function despite the noticeable costs associated with sharing.
13. According to Cunningham et al. (2004), individual self-interest is a sufficient explanatory element of the success of file sharing communities, as users share files to reduce own search and congestion costs; thus, the virtual common is continuously and endogenously restored. They suggest a dynamic of group cooperation can emerge from the interplay of a modest amount of altruism, in conjunction with a large aggregate percentage of self-interested types, which itself could emerge when the technology of sharing imposes (non-binding) sharing restrictions as the default behavior of users. This last finding is consistent with the recent work of Thaler and Sunstein (2008).
14. They also suggest that Usenet is a better venue for file exchanges.

15. http://news.cnet.com/8301-13578_3-57499519-38/court-affirms-$675000-penalty-in-music-downloading-case/
16. Alexander (2008).
17. Alexander (1994) details the evolution of production and distribution costs in the music industry.
18. A helpful overview of some past and recent literature is given in Belleflamme and Peitz (2010).
19. Tenenbaum was fined $675,000 for making 31 songs available for downloading by other users. http://news.cnet.com/8301-13578_3-57499519-38/court-affirms-$675000-penalty-in-music-downloading-case/

REFERENCES

Adar, E. and Huberman, B.A. (2000) 'Free Riding on Gnutella', *First Monday*, 5(10), October (peer-reviewed journal on the internet) http://firstmonday.org/htbin/cgiwrap/bin/ojs/index.php/fm/article/viewArticle/792.HUMPHREY/701

Alexander, P.J. (1994) 'New Technology and Market Structure: Evidence from the Music Recording Industry', *Journal of Cultural Economics*, 18, 113–123.

Alexander, P.J. (2002) 'Peer-to-Peer File Sharing: The Case of the Music Recording Industry', *Review of Industrial Organization*, 20, 151–161.

Alexander, P.J. (2008) 'The Music Recording Industry', *The Structure of American Industry*, James Brock, Editor, 11th edition.

Belleflamme, P. and Peitz, M. (2010) 'Digital Piracy: Theory', *The Oxford Handbook of the Digital Economy*.

Bhattacharjee, Sudip, Ram D. Gopal, Kaveepan Lertwachara, James R. Marsden, and Rahul Telang (2007) 'The Effect of Digital Sharing Technologies on Music Markets: A Survival Analysis of Albums on Ranking Charts', *Management Science*, 53(9), 1359–1374.

Conner, K.R., and Rumelt, R.P. (1991) 'Software Piracy – An Analysis of Protection Strategies', *Management Science*, 37, 125–139.

Cunningham, B.M., Adilov, N. and Alexander, P.J. (2004) 'Peer-to-Peer File Sharing Communities', *Information Economics and Policy*, 16, 197–213.

Dewenter, Ralf, Haucap, Justus and Tobias Wenzel (2012) 'On File Sharing With Indirect Network Effects Between Concert Ticket Sales and Music Recordings', *Journal of Media Economics*, 25(3), 168–178.

Felton, E.W. (2006) 'Nuts and Bolts of Network Neutrality', Center for Information Technology Policy, Department of Computer Science, and Woodrow Wilson School of Public and International Affairs, Princeton University.

Golle, P., Leyton-Brown, K., Mironov, I. and Lillibridge, M. (2003) 'Incentives for Sharing in Peer-to-Peer Networks', Working Paper, Stanford University, Palo Alto, CA.

Gopal, Ram D., Sudip Bhattacharjee and G. Lawrence Sanders (2006) 'Do Artists Benefit from Online Music Sharing?', *Journal of Business*, 79(3), May, 1503–1533.

Hughes, D., Coulson, G. and Walkerdine, J. (2005) 'Free Riding on Gnutella Revisited: The Bell Tolls?', IEEE Distributed Systems Online 1541-4922, 6(6), http://comp.eprints.lancs.ac.uk/1136/1/BellTolls.pdf

Johnson, W.R. (1985) 'The Economics of Copying', *Journal of Political Economy*, 93, 158–174.

Liebowitz, S. (1985) 'Copying and Indirect Appropriability: Photocopying of Journals', *Journal of Political Economy*, 93, 945–957.

Mortimer, Julie, Nosko, Chris and Alan Sorensen (2012) 'Supply Responses to Digital Distribution: Recorded Music and Live Performances', *Information Economics and Policy*, 24(1), 3–14.
Novos, I.E. and Waldman, M. (1984) 'The Effects of Increased Copyright Protection: An Analytic Approach', *Journal of Political Economy*, 92, 236–246.
Oberholzer-Gee, Felix and Koleman Strumpf (2007) 'The Effect of File Sharing on Record Sales: An Empirical Analysis', *Journal of Political Economy*, 115(1), 1–42.
Peitz, Martin and Patrick Waelbroeck (2004) 'The Effect of Internet Piracy on Music Sales: Cross-section Evidence', *Review of Economic Research on Copyright Issues*, 1(2), 71–79.
Peitz, M. and Waelbroeck, P. (2006) 'Why the Music Industry May Gain from Free Downloading: The Role of Sampling', *International Journal of Industrial Organization*, 24(5), 907–913.
Rob, Rafael and Joel Waldfogel (2006) 'Piracy on the High C's: Music Downloading, Sales Displacement and Social Welfare in a Sample of College Students', *Journal of Law and Economics*, 49(1), 29–62.
Romer, Paul (2002) 'When Should We Use Intellectual Property Rights?', *American Economic Review*, 92(2), 213–216.
Takayama, L.N. (1994) 'The Welfare Implications of Unauthorized Reproduction of Intellectual Property in the Presence of Network Externalities', *Journal of Industrial Economics*, 42, 155–166.
Thaler, Richard and Sunstein, Cass (2008) *Nudge: Improving Decisions about Health, Wealth, and Happiness*, Yale University Press.
Watt, R. (2005) 'Indirect Appropriability 20 Years On', *Review of Economic Research on Copyright Issues*, 2, 1–4.
Zenter, Alejandro (2006) 'Measuring the Effect of Music Downloads on Music Purchases', *Journal of Law & Economics*, 49(1), 63–90.
Zhang, M.X. (2002) 'Stardom, Peer-to-Peer and the Socially Optimal Distribution of Music', mimeo, Sloan School of Management, MIT.

11. Video games, virtual worlds and economics

Isaac Knowles, Edward Castronova and Travis Ross

Video games have undergone a number of facelifts, transformations, and reinventions since the humble days of Pong and Pac-Man. The most advanced modern games are based in huge, immersive virtual worlds that are fully-rendered in 3D. Players interact with computer-controlled characters, many of them voice-acted by well-known celebrities and capable of the most minute facial expressions. The quality of music and sound production in today's games rivals that of any contemporary big-budget film. Storylines can be as expansive as any novel, and may include tie-ins with real world events and references to political or social issues.

The incredible graphics and sharply written stories of virtual worlds are impressive, but we believe that the most important development in games over the last ten years has been the dual moves toward persistence and massively multiplayer interaction, which have resulted in the emergence of complex virtual economies. What makes this achievement even more striking is that these dynamics were not designed into the game. They simply emerged as a product of persistence and massively multiplayer interaction. Games that were once single player experiences now feature complex, persistent social dynamics.

Player to player trade is now a common feature in an ever-growing number of multiplayer videogames. This means that there are literally thousands of different virtual economies, of varying size and complexity, found in games across the world. These economies make for fascinating objects of study, both in their own right and for the insights they give us into how real-world economies function (Castronova, 2009b; Ross et al., 2012). Moreover, trends indicate that a large and growing number of economically significant transactions are taking place within these economies; that is, goods and services with significant economic value are to be found inside of virtual economies. The value of virtual economies is already being stated in the billions.[1] Thus, their stability may soon begin to matter for the stability of the real economy.

In this chapter, we review the history of virtual economies and virtual economic research. In doing so we discuss the value of virtual economies to players and game developers alike. We also discuss the unique challenges faced by game developers managing such large-scale social interaction. Finally, we discuss an intriguing possibility: that games, and the economies within them, can be a laboratory for large-scale economic policy experiments.

The rest of this chapter proceeds as follows. In section 1, we will review the history of virtual worlds, virtual economies, and virtual assets. In section 2, we will examine in detail how a virtual economy interacts with the real world through virtual asset markets. In section 3, we review some of the available academic literature in the economics of videogames and virtual worlds, consider the prospects of using games as laboratories to test economic theories and policies, and suggest some ideas for further research. Section 4 concludes.

1. BACKGROUND

This section provides some background for those new to the economies in virtual worlds and video games. We begin by reviewing what virtual worlds are and how they are currently manifested. We'll then delve into virtual economies and discuss how they are constructed and managed. In the course of playing a game or using a virtual world, a person will produce virtual assets that have real-world value, and which are frequently traded on real-world markets. We'll analyse these markets in preparation for section 2, where we discuss the intersection of real and virtual economies.

Virtual Worlds

Virtual worlds are persistent, online spaces in which people interact with one another via some kind of symbolic representation, called an avatar (Castronova, 2006). There are some key terms here. *Persistence* means that the world is always-on: even if every player logs off, the world can continue to evolve and change on a server according to whatever rules are set by the developer. In a persistent world every player's actions can have consequences for the experiences that all players have over the short, medium, and long term. This is to be distinguished from, for example, a racing game, where the track disappears and resets every time we turn the game off and on again.

A virtual world is an online *space*. It is a representation of a place that, whether 2-D or 3-D, whether large or small, is experienced as a space with its own unique geography and features. The space almost always has resources of some sort that players can gather, produce, and trade. It has other players' characters moving around in it, as well as computer-controlled characters, creatures, and environments. Thus, virtual worlds are online spaces that players can interact with.

Finally, avatars are symbolic representations of the players inside the online space. The avatar can take humanoid shape, or it can be a vehicle, or something else entirely, but is the thing on the screen through which players interact with the world and with one another. The extent to which players do interact with one another can vary widely, from fighting and gesturing to engaging in trade. Every virtual world places different limits on the extent and type of player-to-player and player-to-environment interactions that are allowed.

Virtual worlds have actually been around for quite some time, beginning with the text-based multi-user dungeons, or MUDs, of the early 1970s. Players – usually drawn from a pool of tech-savvy computer scientists on a university campus – interacted with the world and with one another entirely through text. Players could change the world, and the game was run on a server so it was persistent. In the mid-1980s, MUDs began to mix graphical and text-based elements, but because of technological and financial limitations, MUDs often limited the number of concurrent users to 20 or fewer. Then in 1991, internet service providers began to include access to graphical MUDs as an add-on to their subscription services. America Online's *Neverwinter Nights* and Sierra Online's *Shadows of Yserbius* were quite popular and allowed a larger number of concurrent users. The games were incredibly expensive, with players charged as much as $120 a month for unlimited play.

By 1996, both PCs and internet service were much faster, cheaper, and more widely available. There had also been significant developments in technologies that allowed PCs and video game consoles to render 3D graphics.[2] In the wake of this progress, the first fully graphical virtual worlds were developed and released. The 3DO Company's *Meridian 59* was released in June 1996, followed by Electronic Arts' *Ultima Online* in 1997. Turbine's *Asheron's Call* and Sony Online Entertainment's *Everquest* were both released in 1999. In South Korea, NCSoft's *Lineage*, released in 1998, was quite popular.

These games and their progeny are known as massively multiplayer online role-playing games, or MMORPGs, which is often shortened to MMO. The early MMO business model usually required the player to purchase a copy of the client software from the company at a cost of $50 to $70. The client, which is installed on the user's PC, contains everything static about the virtual world: its physical characteristics and the rules that govern it. In order to actually enter the world, players pay a monthly subscription fee, ranging from $10 to $15 a month. The user logs onto a server that contains and distributes information about the state of the world: locations of players and creatures, player inventories, and so on. Companies usually host several such servers, which contain replica versions of the world. The reasons for this distribution are twofold. One is strictly technological: Servers cannot handle hundreds of thousands of concurrent users without experiencing performance issues. The second reason is that in virtual worlds, space is scarce. A virtual world is built with a given population size in mind. In order to avoid congestion a new world is instantiated when available worlds approach the allocated size.

Not all virtual worlds are built explicitly to be games. Sulake's *Habbo* (released in 2000), Electronic Arts' *The Sims Online* (2002), and Linden Lab's *Second Life* (2003) are all examples of virtual worlds that are intended to be online social hangouts. The primary focus of these worlds is socialization with others, and although some people do play games in them, the worlds are not thought of as games in the way that MMOs often are. These virtual worlds also use a client-server system, but in most cases the client is free and there is no subscription. Instead, companies obtain revenues by selling virtual goods, services, or currencies directly to players. Occasionally, the companies also make money using in-game advertising, such as virtual billboards or through text messages.

Subscription-based virtual worlds are becoming increasingly rare, and many new MMOs use a "free to play" revenue model. In this model, players can enter the virtual world for free, but certain items and currencies can only be obtained by purchasing them directly from the developer. Some games, like Nexon's *MapleStory*, have always used this model. Others, like Turbine's *Lord of the Rings Online* and Electronic Arts' *Star Wars: The Old Republic*, began as subscription games and later converted to a free-to-play model.

The most recent additions to the landscape of virtual worlds are social games, which, by revenue, are the fastest growing sub-sector of the online game industry.[3] The social-gaming industry exists primarily as an appendage to major social networking websites like Facebook and Google+ in the United States and RenRen in China; however, they are also becoming more prevalent on mobile phones and tablets. Many, but not all social games, allow players to interact with one another within a fairly simple virtual world. Social games are so-called because they are built around the premise that players will use them to keep in touch with one another. Developers hope that this will incentivize players to buy low-priced virtual goods and currencies for themselves and for others. Well-known examples of social games are Zynga's *FarmVille* and Electronic Arts' *The Sims Social.*

Virtual Economies

Apart from the obscure MUD genre, games up to the mid-1990s had very simple, simulated economies. Most games, even those that were multiplayer, lacked both persistence and a means to trade with other players. If a game had an economy, it existed only as a "gating mechanism" – a term in game development that refers to any rule that forces players to experience content in stages, rather than all at once. In order to advance in some games, a player must amass a certain amount of wealth – gold coins, for instance – before they can buy the equipment they need to experience new areas and face new challenges. Alternatively, introducing markets into games is a way to force players to make choices that are (the game designer hopes) interesting. Role-playing games, like Enix's classic *Dragon Warrior* for the Nintendo Entertainment System, are examples of single-player games that use a simple economy to gate content. Players gained virtual wealth from killing monsters and, eventually, could afford to upgrade their weaponry by purchasing items from a computer-controlled non-player character (NPC). Simulation and strategy games, such as Electronic Arts' *SimCity* and Blizzard's *Starcraft II*, require players to gather scarce resources and carefully plan expenditures to shepherd their settlements or armies to prosperity and/or victory. Content gating and forcing interesting decisions remain important motivations for introducing markets into games.[4]

For MUD developers, a third motivation for having an economy existed: the desire to introduce realism into the virtual world. This led naturally to the decision to allow players to trade virtual items and money with one another. Just like in single-player role-playing games, there was almost no player activity that didn't result in more money and items being introduced into the world. Unlike single-player games, however, MUDs had persistence and dozens of economic agents entering and exiting the game over its entire product cycle. Thus, a common series of events went as follows: When the game was released, the first players entered the world and faced a very challenging game because they had no wealth at all. As time passed, these more experienced players amassed wealth and new players entered. The newer players could use the virtual money they collected to buy used, advanced weapons from more experienced players. This reduced the challenge of the game, and the cycle continued. The entire process was often likened to a faucet flowing continuously into a plugged sink. In MUDs, the glut of both money and items in the game became so enormous that the game challenges were trivialized. This was the phenomenon known colloquially as *MUDflation*, and by far the most common solution to the problem was to simply hit the reset button every once in a while. The inventories of all players were wiped clean, and players returned to the world and started the cycle over again.

But while MUD fans seemed to begrudgingly accept MUDflation as a necessary evil, mainstream software developers weren't so sure that consumers in larger markets would be so forgiving. Thus, as MMOs were introduced to wider audiences, more subtle solutions to the MUDflation problem were devised. One ambitious solution was developed by the makers of *Ultima Online* (UO) and is described in detail by Simpson (2000). The developers placed limits on the total amount of resources that could exist in the game at any one time by having a fixed (per player) stock of abstract "material" that could exist in the game. As items and units of currency were sourced from the virtual world, the amount of substance that was available to obtain directly from that world was diminished. As items depreciated or were sold to NPCs, their constituent parts returned to the æther to be mined again in some other way.

Although ingenious, this system created huge economic management issues for UO. One commonly cited problem was that such a system required the developers to impose a model of NPC vendor demand for items that players collected from the world (Castronova, 2005; Simpson, 2000). As players sold more to the vendors, the price that the vendors were willing to pay for the items diminished, eventually reaching zero. Without that system, an enterprising player could horde vast quantities of game currency, removing both liquidity and abstract substance from the system, and essentially stalling all trade. The problem was that players found the algorithm of vendor demand and absolute resource limits to be unenjoyable, and so they started leaving the game. These problems were also exacerbated by technical issues (Simpson, 2000).

In response to these problems, UO's developers dispensed with the limited resource paradigm and switched to the faucet system of MUDs. To fix the MUDflation problem, they took the analogy one step further and added several drains. So-called money and item "sinks" were introduced to balance the influx of money and items from their various faucets. Players still received most of their items and money from completing activities in the game. But mechanisms were put in place that forced items out of player-to-player trade, or out of the virtual world altogether. For example, some items could only be purchased from NPC merchants who were placed within the game world, which withdrew money from the economy. Item depreciation was introduced so that many valuable virtual items wore out and could only be repaired with money, if they could be repaired at all. Finally, virtual items were often bound to the players who used them, keeping them off the player-to-player market altogether. Ultimately, players seemed to find the game experience to be more enjoyable (Simpson, 2000).

This so-called *faucet-drain system* is the fundamental paradigm underlying all virtual economic design. To our knowledge, there is no MMO, virtual world, or social game that does not employ the faucet-drain system in its economy. By explicitly designing flows of items and currency so that they are subject to manual control, companies are able to carefully calibrate the economic difficulty of the game at a variety of stages. They are also able to fine-tune the scarcity of items and currency in the game, which is an immensely important tool for free-to-play and social games. While there are myriad other strategies employed to reduce the complexity of economic management, all of them work through the manipulation, creation, or removal of faucets and drains. The importance of the system and its implications for the management, analysis, and profitability of a virtual economy cannot be overstated.

Some readers may have noticed that the faucet-drain system is a direct appeal to the Quantity Theory of Money. Over any given time interval, exactly x units of currency are exchanged for y number of goods.[5] The amount of currency (M) that is in the system is known at any point in time, as is the price level (P) and the velocity of money (V). Thus one interesting (and so far unanswered) question is how well the familiar equation of exchange, $MV = PQ$, actually holds in these economies.

Virtual Asset Markets

As we have discussed, in most virtual worlds, players acquire virtual stuff – goods and currencies that exist only within that particular world. These items remain with a player's avatar until the player chooses to dispense with them by giving or throwing them away, trading them with other players or NPCs, losing them somehow, or by simply erasing the avatar in whose inventory the items exist.[6] That players have the ability to acquire, dispose of, and trade these assets means that they can have value that is explicitly denominated in real-world currency. In fact, current estimates place the total value of the worldwide market in virtual assets between two and six billion dollars, and the total value of existing virtual assets is many times that amount.[7]

Before we proceed further, it is useful to have some terminology under our belts. Real money transactions, or RMT, is the overarching term for any activities in which players, virtual world developers, or third parties buy and sell virtual items, currency, and/or entire user accounts in real-world markets using real-world currencies.[8] Such markets for virtual assets are of two types: primary and secondary (Lehdonvirta and Ernkvist, 2011). Primary virtual asset markets are those in which the virtual world developers sell virtual assets directly to players, while secondary markets are those in which players and third parties sell to one another. Secondary markets can be further split into two types – sanctioned and unsanctioned – as determined by the game developer. Third parties in this case are firms that buy assets from players and so-called "gold farms" and then sell the assets on to other players. Gold farms are firms that employ people to spend several hours a day inside of a virtual world gathering currency and items, or developing avatars on a particular game account, for the specific purpose of selling the assets or the accounts to players or retailers (Lehdonvirta and Ernkvist, 2011; Heeks, 2008).

RMT came into existence with the early graphical MUDs, but it did not attract much attention until virtual worlds entered popular culture. When UO was released, players began selling virtual goods, currency, and even entire game accounts on eBay or other websites. In the case of goods and currency sales, once the trade was executed and real money exchanged hands, the parties to the transaction would enter the world and exchange the relevant assets. One thousand virtual gold coins might cost $50; a powerful sword might sell for $100; and in the case of game accounts, the final price could reach $2,000 or more (Castronova, 2001, 2005).

Early on, developers of *Ultima Online*, *Lineage*, *Everquest*, *Asheron's Call*, and other subscription-based virtual worlds were all strictly opposed to secondary virtual asset markets, primarily because they believed that sales on such markets infringed their intellectual property rights, reduced their revenues, and increased their costs.[9] They deployed many strategies to identify and punish players who bought and sold virtual assets. Then starting around the year 2000, different revenue models were created for gaming and non-gaming virtual worlds alike. Rather than charging for subscriptions, some market entrants adopted a free-to-play model. Sulake and Nexon, Inc. – makers of *Habbo* and *MapleStory*, respectively – did not charge for players to enter their worlds. Instead, they sold low-priced virtual goods directly to players, while still specifically prohibiting RMT in secondary markets. Typically, though not always, secondary RMT was and remains unsanctioned by free-to-play companies. Part of the reason for choosing this business model is that in developing countries, a $50 up-front cost and $10 to $15 monthly subscriptions, such as required for an MMO, can inhibit uptake. Allowing free entry with the option to buy additional goods and services for one or two dollars each was a viable strategy for participating in game markets where the demand was characterized by lower-income players. It is at this point in the development of virtual worlds when the size and volume of the virtual asset markets really began to take off (Heeks, 2008).

One of the few companies that creates and distributes virtual assets and sanctions their trade on secondary markets is Linden Lab, maker of *Second Life*. Upon its release in 2003, Linden Lab decided to sell their world's currency, the Linden, on the primary market. The developer also sanctioned sales of the currency in secondary markets, and provided a retail channel through which sales could take place. It would also buy the currency back from users at a fixed rate of conversion. In *Second Life*, everyone populated the same world, and there was finite space. Thus, Linden Lab sold virtual real estate to users at various rates per unit area. Upon purchase, the area was added to the world. Users could also buy land from each other. Another innovative feature of *Second Life* was that Linden Lab provided a powerful toolkit that allowed users to construct virtual goods from basic building blocks and a scripting language. What users created could then be bought and sold using virtual and real currencies. Users could create, buy, and sell anything from virtual t-shirts that their avatars could wear to enormous mansions on private islands. Less known in the United States, but just as remarkable is MindArk's *Entropia Universe* (formerly *Project Entropia*), where virtual property deals are common.[10] *Entropia Universe*, *Second Life*, and a few other virtual worlds are unique in the degree of freedom they afford users to create new items and engage in RMT. They are also comparatively small firms in the virtual world and MMO industry.

The most recent development in virtual asset markets is the rise of social gaming and the so-called micro-transactions business model. The micro-transactions model is differentiated from free-to-play systems by the simplicity of the economic system and the restrictions on what players can do with the assets they purchase. Typically, players are limited to buying virtual currency, the use of which is restricted to purchasing virtual items for the player's own use or for gifting to others. Secondary markets are almost always unsanctioned, and in any event it can be very difficult to trade assets with others (by necessity, a robust secondary market requires that users be able to trade freely within the virtual economy). Nevertheless, the social and mobile gaming industries use this as their primary model and host the largest primary market for virtual assets.

2. THE EFFECT OF ASSET MARKETS ON VIRTUAL ECONOMICS

Game operators and developers expend a great deal of resources trying to manage the effects of virtual asset markets on their economies, and vice versa. As we discussed above, early MMO operators were ardently opposed to the sale of any virtual goods. This was an attitude held by most subscription-based MMO developers for a decade after their inception in 1997. The prohibition on these markets extended not only to secondary markets, but also primary markets: game developers had standing policies to never sell virtual items to players. The primary reason for this was that they believed that players would revolt and leave the game for a competitor who maintained the economic wall between the real and the virtual worlds (Simpson, 2000). A second reason may have been that there was significant uncertainty about the effects of a primary market on the virtual economy. *Ultima Online*'s early economic troubles were a cautionary tale that game economies were best left isolated from the real world as much as possible.

The secondary markets were universally unsanctioned. The terms of use for every virtual world at that time (and many to this day), to which every player had to agree, stated that all virtual items and currencies – and even player accounts – were the property of the respective developer. As far as developers were concerned, sellers were using the company's assets to make money while simultaneously diluting their value, for which the developer received no compensation.

Developers were also opposed to secondary markets because they increased the costs of economic management and customer service. To understand why this is the case, we need to go back to the faucet-drain system outlined above. Recall that the developer manages the stock of items and currency in the world at any time by adjusting a series of faucets and drains for those assets. Successful management of the system relies on the assumption that every activity that results in the creation of economic wealth has diminishing marginal utility. A player will create money from finding treasure chests or fight a dragon for a rare shield for only so long until other (usually non-productive) activities become relatively more attractive. Players then trade with one another or engage in activities that cause assets to leave the economy. The system relies upon the assumptions of a simple model of player utility; specifically, that any one activity will eventually get boring, incentivizing a player to do something else (Castronova, 2003).

So what happens if, instead of having to split between productive and consumptive activities, players can pay someone else to do all the production? Then players who can pay others with real money to produce virtual goods for them will have a competitive advantage in the game world, because they will not have to spend time engaging in productive activities. They can simply buy the virtual sword or currency from a gold farmer and move on to the next fun task (killing an even bigger dragon, for example) (Heeks, 2008; Castronova, 2006).

A single player with such a competitive advantage will usually not be much of a disruption. However, if dozens of players are buying virtual assets from gold farmers using real money, a number of difficulties begin to arise. The first is that players who don't buy virtual assets feel that those who do buy them are cheating, which creates customer service problems for a game developer. Second, the existence of gold farming raises prices overall. This happens because suppliers recognize that the average virtual income of other players has risen, and because the existence of gold farming means that the total amount of circulating currency rises. The resulting inflation disadvantages players who don't buy assets. Third, gold farmers tend to be very skilled players. They are able to exploit game resources and find ways to prevent other players from enjoying content, which also reduces player satisfaction. Fourth, because gold farming typically introduces more virtual items into the system, it may serve to reduce the overall challenge of the entire game, a problem that harkens back to MUDflation. Finally, gold farming brings real-world economic considerations into a game that was, ostensibly, an alternate reality where one's real life did not determine one's success and notoriety. Gold farming tends to poke holes in that feeling (Castronova, 2006; Bartle, 2003). Thus, whether by interfering with the faucet-drain system, or by angering players, secondary markets can create difficulties for MMO developers.

Still, these problems proved to be relatively minor. Then, in the early 2000s, industrialized gold farming arose, which threatened the existence of many virtual worlds. Early gold farms were comprised of one- or two-man teams, usually confined to Western nations where internet access was affordable and reliable and online transactions were secure (Castronova, 2006). This changed with the rapid development of eastern Asian nations like China, South Korea, and Vietnam, giving firms and residents access to Western goods and Western markets (Lehdonvirta and Ernkvist, 2011). Soon, the number of "players" in the game that engaged in virtual asset collection (rather than game-playing) skyrocketed, causing real-world prices for virtual goods and currencies to fall precipitously. Consequently, the number of players buying goods on secondary markets jumped, both because of the price effect and because of the perceived necessity to pay for virtual goods to "keep up with the virtual Joneses" (Castronova, 2006). Hyperinflation in many MMOs became a common problem. Economic management was untenable, and the normal routes of adjusting faucets and drains were closed off because of the negative effects such adjustments would have on players that did not buy assets on the secondary market. To make matters worse, gold farms began to turn to phishing schemes, credit card and game account theft, and other methods to obtain virtual assets, resulting in severe customer service issues.

The early debate over how best to tackle the gold farming problem led to a variety of solutions. Blizzard Entertainment engaged in regular bans of massive numbers of suspected gold farmer accounts in its game *World of Warcraft*, as well as all the assets tied to those accounts. It publicly announced those bans from 2005 to 2007, and there is some evidence that it was effective in eliminating inflationary problems (Knowles, 2007). It later moved to more covert operations, apparently to create greater uncertainty for gold farmers (Heeks, 2008).

Sony Online Entertainment took a different tack with *Everquest II*, the sequel to 1999's *Everquest*. It designated certain game servers on which players could actively and securely transact with one another in secondary asset markets. Station Exchange, as it was known, was considered a marginal success in that it did help reduce demand in secondary markets on some servers, but gold farming was still an issue on other servers (Robischon, 2007). In their game *EVE Online*, CCP games use, or have used, several interesting tactics. In an attempt to get excess currency out of the system, CCP now sells monthly subscription codes, called PLEX, to players in exchange for a substantial quantity of in-game currency. PLEX is also traded by players freely within the game in what is effectively a derivatives market.

The fight against secondary markets continues in earnest. However, most virtual worlds now offer some kind of virtual asset to players on primary markets. How this is perceived by players remains an open question. However, it does mean that most game developers now compete directly with third party virtual asset resellers (Heeks, 2008). This allows the companies to capture previously lost revenue while reducing the appeal of secondary markets.

3. VIRTUAL WORLDS, VIDEOGAMES, AND ECONOMICS

So far, we have discussed the origins of virtual worlds and their economies, outlined what is known about virtual asset markets, and explained how the asset markets relate to virtual economies. We are now in a position to discuss the economic literature in video games. It probably comes as no surprise that the economic study of video games coincided with the rise of virtual asset markets. The relationships between the virtual world, the real world, and virtual asset markets are the primary focus of almost all economic research in video games and virtual worlds. This is probably due to two major factors.

First, there is a great deal of interest within industry about how to generate and harness demand for virtual goods, grow the installed base, and maintain economic stability. Game developers must strike a balance between vague notions of fun (or "engagement"), management costs, and the encroachment of real economic concerns on what are, ostensibly, diversions from real life. The importance of fun, and the challenge of modelling it, is particularly interesting and deserves further attention.

Second, amongst the small group of academics who actively pursue research in the field, there is an interest in virtual worlds as laboratories for large-scale economic experiments (Giles, 2007). Virtual worlds may also offer real time clues about the state of the real world economy *vis à vis* virtual asset markets. Part of the work in videogame economics is progressing towards ways to make such analyses possible.

Castronova (2001) is commonly credited with bringing virtual economies and asset markets to the attention of the academy and the public at large. The paper provided a broad introduction to the virtual economy in Norrath, the virtual world in which the game *Everquest* is based. Using data gleaned from account sales on the secondary market, the value of total production per capita in Norrath was estimated to be somewhere between that of Russia and Bulgaria. The paper also estimated that *Everquest* players earned about $3.42 per hour in the course of their normal play, and revealed that one platinum piece – the virtual currency used in Norrath – exchanged at a rate of $0.0107 per unit.[11]

In the decade since then, the literature has sorted itself into three major areas. The first is largely theoretical, and deals with the question of why players enter games and how much time they spend there. The second literature deals specifically with virtual assets markets, their effect on the player experience, the determinants of player demand, and the nature of supply on the secondary markets. This area is by far the broadest, and has both empirical and theoretical elements. The third deals specifically with the idea that virtual economies can inform us about the real economy. This literature is small, empirical, and largely speculative. However, it represents the "holy grail" of virtual economic research.

Why Do People Play? An Economic Model

Castronova (2003) was the first attempt at providing a theoretical framework within which the decision to enter and exit a game or virtual world was analysed. Players in a game are assumed to be working on a puzzle with a particular level of challenge, C, and which provides a reward, R. Note that R could include psychic and monetary awards when virtual assets are a by-product of gameplay. There is also some ideal challenge level, given by Ω. Let M represent the level of immersion provided by the game; this will represent the effectiveness of a game at diverting player attention away from the "real" world. Then a player's satisfaction with the "puzzle" is given by Cox (2012):

$$S = f\left(\alpha R - \beta\left(C - \Omega\right)^2, M\right)$$

Now assume there are N games and that the *i*-th game provides S_i units of satisfaction. Denote the hours of play in a game by H_i and the price per hour of play by p_i. Let **p** and **h** represent vectors of prices and hours played. Normalize the prize of all other goods to 1 and let Y represent income. Then player utility could be represented in logarithmic form by:

$$U\left(\boldsymbol{h}, Y - \boldsymbol{ph}\right) = \gamma \ln\left(Y - \boldsymbol{ph}\right) + \sum_{i=1}^{N} S_i \ln h_i$$

From this model, we can draw several conclusions. First, because leisure is a normal good, and assuming that game time is leisure time, a change in the real-life wage of a player has opposing substitution and income effects on in-game time: An increase in wages will increase demand for game time, but it may also reduce demand for game time since more income can be obtained from work. Second, because virtual assets have value, time spent in a virtual world pays – or can pay – a wage. This means that changes in the in-world wage can and will affect the real-life labour supply decision.

Third, and perhaps most interesting, game players are willing to pay to be constrained. This follows from the idea that individual demand for a game, *ceteris paribus*, is not linear in the challenge of the game. For example, extremely easy games will be demanded less than moderately difficult games, which will be demanded more than extremely challenging games. This theoretical result becomes very important when attempting to understand player demand for virtual assets.

This model is yet to be tested empirically. Also, it does not account for network effects on demand, since a higher installed base is likely to positively affect demand for a virtual world (Huhh, 2008). Meanwhile, the literature on two-sided markets and video game consoles does address the network effect problem, but not the game entry decision (Lee, 2012).

Virtual Asset Demand

Researchers in both the academy and in industry have shown great interest in understanding the determination of the supply and demand for virtual assets and, to a lesser extent, their effects on virtual economies. Castronova (2001) examined the effect of avatar level – a measure of a player-character's advancement in the game – on an *Everquest* account's value on eBay. A linear spline regression of avatar level on account price reveals that between levels 20 and 50 (the maximum), each level was worth \$5.33, and at level 50, the value of each level was \$37.37. Castronova (2004) used a full vector of avatar characteristics in a hedonic pricing model of avatars in *Everquest*. He found evidence that in 2002, female avatars were valued \$40.94, or 8.8 percent to 9.6 percent less than male avatars (this despite the fact that gender was a strictly cosmetic characteristic of the avatars). The effect of entrance of competitors into the MMO market on the price of *Everquest*'s virtual assets were also analysed, and found to be negative (as expected).

By 2006, Blizzard's popular MMO *World of Warcraft* had generated significant buzz about virtual assets and gold-farming, and there was a great deal of debate about its effects on player experience and firm performance. As we have discussed, there was significant opposition to tolerance of secondary virtual asset markets because of their perceived negative effects. Castronova (2006) uses a conceptual model to argue that gold farming imposes a purely negative externality on both players and game firms, resulting in inefficient supply of virtual worlds. Back-of-the-envelope calculations suggest that the magnitude of that externality was \$1.8 million per 100,000 users in the game *World of Warcraft*. Although no confirmation from Blizzard was available, it is known that Blizzard's staff rose from some 400 in 2004 to 1,800 by 2006, mostly due to the need for a small army of customer service representatives.[12] Moreover, Blizzard's actions against gold farming during this time represented substantial costs on the part of the firm to correctly identify and eliminate gold-farming accounts.

Heeks (2009) argues for more subtle consideration of the effect of RMT on game demand and supply. One intriguing point Heeks makes is that virtual assets are complements for virtual worlds, so that the prices of assets are negatively correlated with hours of game play, a claim which is borne out by the model by Castronova (2003). Castronova (2001) noted that players with higher real-world wages played less time than players with lower real-world wages. Thus, there is good theoretical reason to suspect that players with higher wages use that extra income to buy virtual assets to keep up with the in-game progress of lower-income friends. This observation also suggests that there are conflicting incentives for game companies who want to keep higher income players, but also keep down customer service costs and prevent player defection due to RMT.

The complex interactions between players, game developers, and gold farmers have prompted several valuable contributions to the literature on video game economics. Huhh (2008, 2009) was the first to model the effect of the network externality of a game's installed base on demand for virtual assets, and to account for the interaction between asset demand and game demand. Installed base in MMOs is important because they are intrinsically social games. In Huhh's model, which does not include negative effects from RMT, the existence of secondary markets serves to push a game's installed based to critical mass more quickly, thus improving welfare. This model serves to demonstrate that the effect of RMT is to increase the supply of games, thus providing a counter-balance to the opposite conclusion reached by Castronova (2006).

Two other recent empirical studies bear mention. Wang et al. (forthcoming) develops an empirical model of the effect of MMO characteristics on the value of virtual goods across different games. One interesting finding from this study is that when games do not have robust virtual economies where players can trade virtual assets for one another, virtual asset prices are higher. This is because, all other things equal, it is harder for players to get the items they need inside the virtual world, thus increasing demand for virtual assets from outside sources. This provides a basic rationale for why most micro-transaction-based games only allow trade via barter and do not provide central markets for player-to-player trade. The authors also find that if a game requires more inter-player cooperation and interaction in order for players to complete challenges, the price of virtual assets is reduced. The reasoning here is that the return to productivity due to a virtual asset purchase that improves a player's avatar may be small compared to the return on an equivalent investment in social networking. What is most interesting about this finding is that it stands in contradiction to the idea that social games induce players to buy more by incorporating their social networks into the game. In fact, it seems players would pay higher prices for goods if they did not have as many friends in the game with them.

The other study (Jung et al., 2011), looks at the performance of a game developer given the level of RMT. The authors accept the argument in Castronova (2003) that players draw satisfaction from a game depending on the challenge it presents relative to their ideal level. They then argue that a player can use virtual asset purchases to adjust the challenge level of a game downward so that it is closer to their ideal. Their panel data analysis suggests that both the prices charged by a game company and the number of hours spent by players in a game are positively related to the volume of transactions in the secondary asset market. They also drive home the point that some players might be willing to pay a game developer to make the game more difficult.

These two papers have raised the expectations bar for future theoretical and empirical models. New research should seek to more explicitly integrate the play decision model in Castronova (2003) with the network effect arguments of Jung et al. (2011), Wang et al. (forthcoming), and Huhh (2009). Though data has been difficult to find, it is not impossible to obtain and the promise of large and useful advances in the field may prompt game companies to be more willing to share data with economists.

Video Games As Laboratories

The final category of studies in game economics concerns the use of virtual economies as laboratories for the study of complex policy issues. Castronova (2001) first suggested that virtual economies provided a unique venue to study economics because game developers could control every variable (except the player) and observe player's activity with remarkable detail. This argument has been reiterated by multiple economists working in industry, but so far there has not been much progress in the area.[13]

The primary reason for this slow development is a dearth of good data. Several studies, published or otherwise, are the result of the hard work and data collection of undergraduates (Kosminsky, 2009; Marks, 2009). But because most data that can be collected using automatic scraping programs are incomplete, scholars must either produce it on their own, as in Castronova et al. (2009a), or obtain it from a willing game company

(Williams et al., 2008). Thus, Castronova et al. (2009a, 2009b) are the only two papers that have made empirical progress in this respect.

Castronova et al. (2009a) documents an explicit test of the law of demand in virtual worlds. The researchers created their own MMO based in a virtual world and randomly assigned players to a control and a treatment group. The treatment group faced a higher price than the control group for a particular virtual item inside the game; otherwise, conditions were the same. The study showed that, in fact, players did respond to higher prices by purchasing a smaller quantity of this item. Further work in this area should probably deal with questions of willingness-to-pay for virtual world entry in the face of differential costs for virtual goods. This would address some of the questions raised in Castronova (2003).

Castronova et al. (2009b) used data from Sony Online Entertainment's *Everquest II* to measure the game equivalent of gross national product (called gross user product, or GUP), inflation, and money supply.[14] The major contributions of this paper were twofold. First, the paper developed some basic characteristics of virtual economies that we can use to contrast games with one another and with the real world. For example, the authors found that only 7 percent of transactions in the game, which include player-to-player, player-to-self, and player-to-NPC transactions, are analogically equivalent to transactions that are counted in a typical measure of GDP. This suggests that, by and large, game worlds have more in common with less-developed economies. The observation that the *Everquest II* economy was subject to severe swings in aggregate production serves to reinforce this point.

Second, the paper demonstrated that, in fact, the economy behaves in expected ways, given what we know about how the real economy functions. For example, the price level was found to move in the same direction as the money supply, a prediction that supports the Quantity Theory of Money. Or, as another example, changes in the population moved in the opposite direction of the price level, holding the money supply fixed. Taken as a whole, the results suggest that the relationships between aggregate virtual economic measures are the same as those predicted by theory and observed in real economies.

With respect to the study of economics by using virtual worlds as laboratories and exemplars, the field remains wide open. Some interesting questions are: How do games respond to the exchange rates between their currency and those in real life? Are virtual economies' savings rates relatively constant, or are they variable? Because at any time there is a possibility that a player will leave the economy, overlapping-generations models of growth and consumption are particularly apt and worth examining in the context of virtual worlds. Obtaining interesting hypotheses in this regard would also require further development of the play decision and the production decision in the game (see Castronova, 2005, Chapter 8). Much of the initial excitement and interest amongst academics in virtual worlds comes from their potential as laboratories for the study of policy. Elaborating on this possibility should remain a primary research goal in the economic study of video games and virtual worlds.

4. CONCLUSION

Although the field of study is now 15 years old, the economics of video games and virtual worlds has only recently emerged from its inchoate beginnings. In this chapter, we have traced the origins of virtual economies and virtual asset markets, and we have provided a basic review of the economic literature in the field. Because the business of virtual world creation is evolving, the field has tended to change with it. The focus of most game and virtual world developers on the sale of virtual goods and currencies directly to players is no doubt a driving force behind the field's recent coverage of virtual asset markets and their effects on virtual economies and virtual world demand (Hamari and Lehdonvirta, 2010).

It is worth emphasizing that the results of work in this field are not merely consequential for developers and the game-playing public. Indeed, the real-world economic fortunes of millions of people rise and fall on the performance of virtual economies. In a study commissioned by the World Bank, Lehdonvirta and Ernkvist (2011) write that in 2009, some 100,000 people in China and Korea earned income from collecting and selling virtual assets. This number has increased with the size of the virtual asset market, which has nearly doubled in size since then. Moreover, governments have shown increasing interest in virtual economic phenomena. For example, China's central bank restricted trading of Tencent's QQ coin in 2009, as many Chinese were beginning to use it not just to trade virtual assets, but real products, as well. In the United States, the IRS has shown interest in determining the tax status of virtual assets. And in the United States, Korea, and elsewhere, questions of who owns virtual assets are increasingly salient. Real-world economic policies are butting up against activities in virtual worlds. Sooner or later, policy-makers will require input on how best to address these issues. Much more work is required in the field of virtual world and video game economics to ensure that any policy interventions are well-informed and well-executed.

NOTES

1. See "The US virtual economy is set to make billions", http://news.bbc.co.uk/2/hi/technology/8425623.stm, predicting $5bn in virtual item sales by 2015. Such reports usually concern only the money made from selling virtual items for dollars, yen, and euros. This is a small fraction of the economic value of items created within virtual environments but not sold for real money. Like stock shares that are not traded, items that remain in virtual form and are not traded for real money still have economic value. The total value of such items is orders of magnitude larger than the value of virtual items traded for real money.
2. This development is also considered to be the primary reason why videogame arcades lost popularity and began to close down *en masse* in that same time period.
3. http://www.economist.com/node/21541164
4. Note that these are not unique to video games. *Monopoly* is a great example of a game in which the rules of the "economy" introduce pacing. As players become wealthier, the game moves from one focused purely on strategic acquisitions to one of strategic real-estate development and asset trading.
5. There is, to our knowledge, no such thing as high-powered money in any virtual economy because there nothing like fractional reserve banking is allowed. Sophisticated debt markets do exist, however, in games like CCP's *EVE Online*.
6. In some cases, virtual goods are designed to simply expire and disappear from the world.
7. See http://www.economist.com/node/21541163 and http://www.gamesbrief.com/2011/12/how-large-is-the-online-and-mobile-games-market/. Note also that since these estimates do not include the value of transfers on the secondary market (which is usually unsanctioned), they could be quite low.
8. Depending on the source, RMT may also mean "Real Money Trade" or "Real Money Transfers". Though we prefer real money transactions, the choice is essentially arbitrary.
9. While the former concern is a matter of some debate in law and policy circles, the latter has merit, and we will return to it shortly.
10. http://www.csmonitor.com/Innovation/Horizons/2010/1113/Man-makes-record-335-000-in-Entropia-Universe-virtual-real-estate-deal
11. Exchange rate data are now readily observed on any website that sells virtual currencies in the primary or secondary market.
12. 'An Online Game, Made in America, Seizes the Globe', *New York Times*: September 5, 2006.
13. See http://blogs.valvesoftware.com/economics/it-all-began-with-a-strange-email/ for the opinions of Valve's economist Yanis Varoufakis. http://blogs.wsj.com/economics/2010/06/21/real-economist-takes-lessons-from-virtual-world/ discusses the thoughts of CCP's Eyjolfur Gudmundsson.
14. See http://virtual-economy.org/2008/02/22/gross_user_product_of_a_virtua/ for a discussion of the definition of GUP.

REFERENCES

Bartle, R. (2003) *Designing Virtual Worlds*, Indianapolis: New Riders Publishers.

Castronova, E. et al. (2009a) 'A Test of the Law of Demand in a Virtual World: Exploring the Petri Dish Approach to Social Science', *International Journal of Gaming and Computer-Mediated Simulations*, **1**(2), 1–16.

Castronova, E. et al. (2009b) 'As real as real? Macroeconomic behaviour in a large-scale virtual world', *New Media and Society*, **11**(5), 685–707.

Castronova, E. (2006) 'A Cost-Benefit Analysis of Real-Money Trade in the Products of Synthetic Economies', *Info*, **8**(6), 56–68.

Castronova, E. (2005) *Synthetic Worlds: The Business and Culture of Online Games*, Chicago: The University of Chicago Press.

Castronova, E. (2004) 'The Price of Bodies: A Hedonic Analysis of Avatar Attributes in a Synthetic World', *Kyklos,* **57**(2), 173–196.

Castronova, E. (2003) 'On Virtual Economies', *Game Studies*, **3**(2), Online only: http://www.gamestudies.org/0302/castronova/

Castronova, E. (2001) 'Virtual Worlds: A First-Hand Account of Market and Society on the Cyberian Frontier', Working Paper. Online only: http://www.gamestudies.org/0302/castronova/

Cox, J. (2012) 'The Economics of the Video-gaming Leisure Market', in Cameron, Samuel (ed.), *Handbook On The Economics Of Leisure*, Cheltenham, UK and Northampton, MA, USA: Edward Elgar, pp. 407–427.

Ducheneaut, N., Yee, N., Nickell, E., and Moore, R.J. (2006) '"Alone Together?": Exploring the Social Dynamics of Massively Multiplayer Online Games', in *Proceedings of the SIGCHI Conference on Human Factors in Computing Systems*, pp. 406–417.

Giles, J. (2007) 'Social Sciences: Life's a Game,' *Nature*, 445, 18–20.

Hamari, J., and Lehdonvirta, V. (2010) 'Game Design as Marketing: How Game Mechanics Create Demand for Virtual Goods', *International Journal of Business Science and Applied Management*, **5**(1), 14–29.

Heeks, R. (2009) 'Understanding "Gold Farming" and Real-Money Trading as the Intersection of Real and Virtual Economies', *Journal of Virtual Worlds Research*, **2**(4), Online only: http://journals.tdl.org/jvwr/article/view/868

Heeks, R. (2008) 'Current Analysis and Future Research Agenda on "Gold Farming": Real-world Production in Developing Countries for the Virtual Economies of Online Games', IDPM Working papers, http://www.sed.manchester.ac.uk/idpm/research/publications/wp/di/documents/di_wp32.pdf

Huhh, J. (2009) 'An Economic Analysis on Online Game Service', Unublished manuscript, available at: http://ssrn.com/abstract=1335120

Huhh, J. (2008) 'Simple Economics of Real-Money Trading in Online games', Unpublished manuscript, available at: http://ssrn.com/abstract=1089307

Jung, G., Lee, B., Yoo, B., and Brynjolffson, E. (2011) 'Analysis of the Relationship between Virtual Goods Trading and Performance of Virtual Worlds', Working paper, available at: http://ssrn.com/abstract=1938313

Knowles, I. (2007) 'Medieval Fantasy, Modern Economy: The Interplay of Virtual Worlds and the Real Economy in Modern Online Games', Unpublished Manuscript.

Kosminsky, E. (2009) 'World of Warcraft: The Viability of Massively Multiplayer Online Role-Playing Games as Platforms for Modelling and Evaluating Perfect Competition', *Journal of Virtual Worlds Research*, **2**(4), Online only: http://journals.tdl.org/jvwr/article/view/869

Lee, R. (2012) 'Home Videogame Platforms', in M. Peitz and J. Waldfogel, *Oxford Handbook of the Digital Economy*, Oxford University Press.

Lehdonvirta, V. and Ernkvist, M. (2011) *Knowledge Map of the Virtual Economy*, Washington DC: World Bank.

Marks, E. (2009) 'Price Dynamics in Virtual World Auctions', Unpublished manuscript, available at http://econ-new.stanford.edu/files/Honors_Theses/Theses_2009/Marks,%20E.%202009.pdf

Robischon, N. (2007) 'Station Exchange, Year One', Industry white paper, available at: http://www.fredshouse.net/images/SOE%20Station%20Exchange%20White%20Paper%201.19.pdf

Ross, T.L., Castronova, E., and Wagner, G.G. (2012) 'Empirical Methods in Virtual Worlds', in C.N. Silva (eds), *Online Research Methods in Urban and Planning Studies: Design and Outcomes*, IGI-Global.

Simpson, Z.B. (2000) 'The In-Game Economics of Ultima Online,' presented at *Computer Game Developers Conference,* San Jose, CA. http://www.mine-control.com/zack/uoecon/uoecon.html

Wang, Q., Mayer-Schönberger, V., and Yang, X. (forthcoming) 'The Determinants of Monetary Value of Virtual Goods: An Empirical Study for a Cross-section of MMORPGs', *Information Systems Frontiers*.

Williams, D., Yee, N., and Caplan, S. (2008) 'Who Plays, How Much, and Why? Debunking the Stereotypical Gamer Profile', *Journal of Computer Mediated Communication*, **13**(4), 993–1018.

12. Digital technology, disruption and the market for news

Lisa George

> We need to hew very closely to traditional journalistic values and totally disregard traditional forms.[1]
>
> Ben Smith, Editor-in-Chief, BuzzFeed

The purpose of this chapter is to consider how digitization has shaped the industrial organization of media markets, with a focus on the market for news. In doing so, I will consider how the current literature has tackled these topics and highlight areas lacking in theory and evidence.

The first generation of economic research in technology and media owes much to important work by Shapiro and Varian (1999).[2] A central idea in that work was the transformative effects of low cost replication, customization and distribution made possible by digital technology. The insights of that work and the literature that followed are still relevant today.

This chapter shares the focus of Shapiro and Varian in considering the implications of technology shocks to costs. But in this chapter I consider how digitization altered transaction costs in media markets and the consequences of those changes for media firms and media markets. Relying on fundamentals of the economic theory of the firm outlined by Oliver Williamson (1985), I argue that shocks to transaction costs are an especially important factor in the changing industrial organization of media markets generally, and in the market for news in particular. Deeper understanding of the nature and impact of transaction costs in digital markets offers a key to understanding the future of media industries.

What is the nature of transaction costs in media markets? The internet unified geographic markets and content platforms, exploding the amount of information and entertainment available to consumers. At the same time, the internet dramatically reduced the cost of connecting creators, consumers and intermediaries. In the context of the theory of the firm, these lower costs created incentives to move transactions out of integrated firms into the marketplace.

On the consumer side, a massive increase in available news, information and entertainment with no commensurate explosion in leisure hours raised the importance of taste and quality in consumer choices. Search and selection costs borne by consumers became important forces in market outcomes. While lower transaction costs on the supply side pushed toward less integration, these higher transaction costs on the consumption side created new forces for integration inside of firms. But the institutions that arose to organize transactions were focused not on traditional links in the supply chain, but on the consumption experience. The new media landscape has come to be defined not only by the institutions designed to create and distribute content, but by the ones designed to organize and deliver it.

The chapter is organized as follows. I begin by discussing the implications of market integration for content in news markets. The next section considers the impact of supply-side transaction costs on market structure. The subsequent section describes the rise of consumption costs and the market institutions that have arisen to tackle them. The conclusion links changes in demand and supply institutions together in considering implications for the future.

PROLOGUE: DISTRIBUTION COSTS, MARKET INTEGRATION AND THE MARKET FOR NEWS

Shapiro and Varian grounded their important work on the implications of zero cost replication and distribution in information industries. A large literature continues to explore the implications of this cost structure. A central focus has been the causes and consequences of piracy in an environment where high quality reproduction and low cost distribution makes theft a profitable undertaking. A second focus has been on network industries and competitive platforms in media industries.

One implication of low distribution costs in media that has received less attention is the integration of geographic markets. When information can be transmitted instantaneously at zero cost, geography loses relevance in production and distribution choices. In most markets, geographic unification affects production choices only, not the design of the product. But in the case of perishable news, instantaneous transmission transformed the industry.

The geographic coverage boundaries in US news markets were inextricably linked to the economics of transporting heavy paper in trucks. A perishable newspaper loses value if not delivered before breakfast. Geography thus dictated the delivery range for a newspaper, which in turn influenced its coverage range. While some coverage of national affairs or events in large cities was provided by distant bureaus, the high cost of dispersed reporting networks ensured that the share of news outside the local market was ultimately small. With a large area and dispersed population, local content and local production was by necessity the norm for US daily newspapers.[3]

Broadcast media, especially television, created the market for national news in the United States. But scarce broadcast capacity and high demand for entertainment meant that the amount of TV time allocated to national news by television networks was low. Broadcast media were also imperfect substitutes for newspapers in terms of mobility, convenience and size. Newspapers, with their market boundaries driven by trucks, remained an important source of news and information for US households.

Satellite technology offered consumers the first real alternative to locally produced newspapers. *USA Today* was the first newspaper to use satellite technology to deliver formatted news content to local printers, from which point papers could be delivered to outlets by truck. The *New York Times* followed with local printing and local delivery outside of New York in the 1990s. The entry enabled by satellite transmission altered competition in newspaper markets. No empirical research studies the effect of *USA Today*, but George and Waldfogel (2006) documented that the *New York Times* reduced local newspaper circulation among college-educated readers. The shift of elites to more targeted media foreshadows larger consumption effects in the internet era.

Entry of the *New York Times* in local markets across the US triggered supply-side shifts in local newspaper coverage aimed at more closely matching the preferences of remaining readers. George (2008) documents more extensive shifts in coverage triggered by audience migration to the internet. As yet no economic research has tackled supply-side coverage shifts within digital media markets, but this evidence from local newspapers again suggest the possibility of changes triggered by the new media institutions discussed later in this chapter.

Because even national newspapers before the internet era remained constrained by physical delivery costs, changes to local newspapers brought about by entry of national papers were ultimately limited. Expansion of the internet and migration of consumers from page to screen represented a much more substantial shock to news markets, allowing news of the day on national topics or in any location to be accessed everywhere. For consumers, the consequence of market integration on the internet was a massive increase in the supply of news, information and entertainment available. Not only was news available from all geographic areas, but content from television, radio and magazines competed with newspapers for reader attention. News and commentary from individual experts, bloggers and citizens further added to supply.

With some exceptions, news on the internet was essentially free.[4] Given the chance to personalize news consumption, the result was a large shift to national news. National news outlets such as CNN, MSNBC and Fox News have been top news outlets online throughout the internet era, and national papers such as *USA Today*, the *New York Times* and *Wall Street Journal* the most frequently visited newspaper sites.[5] The success of national outlets suggests that the local structure of media markets was the most efficient market organization in an era where the cost of distributing and accessing national news was high relative to local news, but is not the optimal allocation under more equal costs. I argue in the sections that follow that relative costs in news consumption continue to play a role in the industrial organization of news markets.

For media outlets, a consequence of integration was new competitors across geography and across platforms. But at the same time, the cost to media firms of interacting in the marketplace with content providers fell, opening a door to new types of relationships and contracts. For consumers, the content explosion brought new costs of sifting and sorting content to find quality and match preferences. The institutions that emerged to handle these costs are the subject of the next sections.

THE CAUSES AND CONSEQUENCES OF DISINTERMEDIATION

The potential for technology to trigger disintermediation in media markets has been recognized for close to a decade, and today the term appears regularly in current academic and popular coverage. But the forces pushing away from integration and toward market relationships in media markets are not uniform, and not universal. This section considers the nature of costs and transactions to consider the nature of markets for content and coverage.

The most dramatic result of digitization was a large drop in the cost of connecting content producers, consumers and intermediaries. One effect was entry of new authors, journalists and musical artists into the market without mediation through a traditional book publisher, newspaper or record labels. Blogs, self-published authors, online magazines and independent musicians testify to entry effects. At the same time, direct access to consumers created incentives for individual creators affiliated with integrated media firms through employment or contracts to develop relationships outside the bounds of those traditional roles. Individual journalists and media personalities began to host blogs, web sites and social network pages, all of which allowed them to interact with consumers in ways not available in the print era.[6]

Direct connections between writers and readers pushed for less integrated media firms in several ways. Because the time available to read did not increase nearly as much as supply, the role of quality rose. Direct consumer access to news stories meant that quality choice could be based more strongly on writers and less on media brands. Quality competition when demand at zero price is low and marginal cost is zero are ingredients for formation of superstar markets, where consumption and earnings concentrate among the few top producers and fall for others.[7]

Superstar markets have long been important in markets with low distribution costs relative to fixed investment such as movies and books. Contracts were traditionally written so that up-front investment in authors by media firms ensured future returns from superstars that covered up-front costs and subsidized failures. Direct access to consumers created outside options for superstars, and the business model of intermediated books and music began to collapse.

Although long a part of music and book markets, there is clear evidence of growing superstar markets in news. News visits online are highly concentrated, with visits to top news sites such as CNN, Fox News, MSNBC and the *New York Times* dominating consumer attention.[8] For individual writers, the number of experts without a journalism background has increased relative to staff writers. For example, at the *New York Times*, reporting relationships with outside experts have multiplied in economics (for example Paul Krugman and Alan Gruber), food (for example Mark Bittman) and technology (for example David Pogue). Salaries for top journalists are very high, with "rock star" writers such as David Mossberg earning salaries comparable to television personalities.[9] Books and speaking fees by popular journalists have increased, having become prevalent enough to engender public controversy.[10] Some reporters have used their media platforms to launch lucrative ventures outside of writing and speaking, such as technology writer Michael Arrington's 2011 founding of a venture capital fund.[11]

Along with the rise of superstar journalists has come a change in the market for undifferentiated staff writing that does little to attract readers. The theory of the firm predicts shorter reporting contracts, more freelance articles, and new forms of "outsourced" content written by specialists rather than staff writers. Salary data from the Bureau of Labor Statistics reports steady or slightly declining nominal earnings for full-time journalists over the past five years, but surveys of news editors indicate that the use of part-time journalists and freelance reporting is rising.[12] Freelance job sites such as Elance, Halogen and Demand Media have emerged to organize the supply of written news and information to media firms and directly to the public.[13] Prices for work on these sites is below rates paid by urban daily papers, and market participants claim that rates are falling. Inside firms, short-term contracts for reporting have spread. The terms of these contracts are looser than traditional journalism employment arrangements, allowing wider scope for writers to produce and sell material through other channels.[14]

Lower transaction costs in connecting readers and writers pushes media markets toward disintermediation and superstar markets. But the pressure is not uniform, and the theory of the firm also suggests the types of content most likely to remain integrated inside newspapers and other traditional media firms. Specifically, the greater the uncertainty over the popularity of a story in terms of the link between effort and results, the larger the role for integrated firms. Investigative reporting is a good example of output uncertainty, as a journalist might spend weeks or months researching political corruption or shady business dealings only to find the allegations unfounded or exposed by other sources.[15] Topics for which uncertainty in the relationship between effort and quality is low, such as cultural or technology reviews, can more easily drift into the freelance market, or move toward short-term reporting contracts. A differential trend toward a looser vertical structure in areas of low contracting costs is already apparent at the nation's largest newspapers. At the *New York Times*, reporting relationships with outside experts noted above have multiplied. These trends are not so apparent in business coverage or investigative reporting, where staff writing remains the norm. These anecdotes are suggestive, but indicate a trend warranting more comprehensive research.

Theory also predicts that integration within firms is related to asset specificity. The concept of "relationship-specific investments" has a quite literal interpretation in journalism, where successful reporting can depend on the personal relationships between reporters and their sources in business, politics and the community. The greater the importance of relationships in the quality and value of the product, the more likely coverage will remain organized inside firms. Local political coverage is a good example, as this type of coverage requires building relationships with politicians and bureaucrats able to offer tips and scoops. These personal connections have their greatest value in the reporting context, so workers will tend to under-invest in them without the security that they will be compensated for the investment over the long term. In contrast, topics requiring more subject-matter knowledge, such as health or economics, depend less on relationships and more on specialized expertise. These topics are thus more readily contracted in markets. The importance of personal relationships in access to information is likely to play a growing role in determining the types of coverage residing inside media firms.

The focus above has been on news media, particularly newspapers. This is because market integration led to the largest increases in supply in this industry and because news firms have long been more tightly integrated than books or music. But the pressures of disintermediation operate in many media markets. In music, piracy helped break apart the album model, unbundling music into individual songs demanded by most consumers. Entry of iTunes and a model for purchasing individual songs is the music analogy of the newspaper disintegration.[16] The book market, with its reliance on contracts rather than integration, has seen less dramatic change.

What are the limits of disintermediation? Lower costs and consumer access to quality generally raise welfare. It is possible today to conceive of a world where there are no media firms, and writers and readers connect exclusively through individual articles. But at the same time that direct connections between readers and writers reduce supply-side costs, decentralization imposes new types of costs associated with the consumption of news and information. These new costs are all associated with finding and choosing what to read. The next section considers how markets and institutions arise to manage these costs.

CONSUMPTION COSTS, TECHNOLOGY AND NEW MEDIA INSTITUTIONS

In markets to allocate limited attention, search and selection waste time that would otherwise be available for media consumption. Since most media goods on the internet are free, even small transaction costs can shift markets.[17]

Media markets are increasingly shaped by the firms and institutions that have arisen to manage consumption costs. George and Hogendorn (2012) report that as of 2010, over 50 percent of visits to news outlets online were directed through search, aggregators and other intermediaries. For the most part these institutions create real value and enhance welfare. Search engines reduce the time needed to find desired content. Aggregators such as Google News offer access to new content popular with readers. Social media connect readers with news consumed by peers. But at the same time, these institutions can shift relative costs of consuming different types of content, so can have substantial market impacts. On the supply side, writers and media firms respond to these shifts with new content, altering coverage in ways not yet fully understood.

Google, Yahoo! and other search engines were the first institutions that emerged to reduce transaction costs associated with content proliferation. Search engine improvements have successfully reduced consumption costs in media markets over time. Consumption of disaggregated content would be very difficult without this technology. But search has limitations. For example, search is most effective for identifying "searchable" topics well-formed in the minds of readers – and is of little use in introducing new issues and topics which the reader may not know to search. Since search cannot readily expand the reader's information horizon but only deepen knowledge of familiar topics, it only captures part of the potential value of decentralized information markets.

Because of this limitation, search engines reduce the cost of finding "searchable" information relative to "unsearchable" news. On the margin, consumer attention might be expected to shift away from news toward information and commentary. Similarly, on the supply side, media outlets seeking to attract readers have incentives to write "searchable" material. Newspapers and other content providers maximizing readership might also be expected to shift on the margin away from news to informational content. This idea remains essentially untested in a research context, though the book of business for Demand Media, EHow and other search engine optimizers suggests that entrants are heavily focused on informational content.[18]

The search process itself consumes scarce time and attention, suggesting a role for firms that anticipate the desires of different types of consumers. On the internet, the process of linking stories and topics on a single site has come to be called "aggregation." Aggregators are vilified by traditional media executives as pirates, but when content is free and abundant, institutions that reduce the time needed to find good matches create substantial surplus. As the supply of news and information expands, so does the relative value of editorial section compared to content production.

Where does the value in aggregation come from? Two clear avenues are horizontal matching and quality sorting. Economists call the process of designing products to appeal to distinct consumer groups targeting. A good deal of empirical evidence suggests that product characteristics matter substantially in consumption across media.[19] Because consumers differ so much in their tastes for topics, style, ideology and depth, potentially many firms can co-exist in the emerging editorial/aggregator role, assembling overlapping bundles catering to different tastes. And because entry in the editorial function is free, many firms may ultimately emerge in this role.

Newspapers, in their editorial function, compete directly with Yahoo News, Google News and other aggregators' sites. A crucial question for the future of newspapers is how effective they will ultimately be in identifying and organizing content desired by heterogeneous consumer groups. Some newspapers appear to be highly skilled at targeting: the *New York Times* routinely touts surveys of its highly educated, high income demographic to advertisers.[20] High readership in print and online suggest this identity will allow the company to thrive in the internet age. Fox News and the *Wall Street Journal* are also highly targeted products commanding high online and offline ratings. In contrast, geographically targeted media such as daily newspapers have much lower electronic readership and eroding readership in print.[21]

What would it take for newspapers to compete effectively with Google News in the aggregator market? One important ingredient might be separation of content production from editorial choice. This does not mean that newspapers will produce no content, but rather that the editorial selection of articles will be focused on satisfying readers regardless of whether the content was best produced inside the firm. This likely means a move toward some non-exclusive content that can be bought in the marketplace as demand emerges. The growth of university media centers that contribute or collaborate with newspapers on specialized topics reflects this trend.[22] Collaboration by media firms in local news gathering is another example of the growth of non-exclusive content.[23]

There is also evidence that aggregators have moved toward supplementing aggregated content with original reporting. The Huffington Post has maintained a model of aggregated content supplemented by expert analysis from an early date. Even BuzzFeed, the media firm most closely allied to social media, has a business model grounded in professional journalists producing original content.[24] The Huffington Post, with its blend of curated and produced content, now surpasses Google News in site visits.[25]

But just as search lowered the cost of accessing information relative to news, aggregators can reduce cost of access to some types of information relative to others. The algorithms that underlie Google News and other aggregators emphasize popularity, so they might facilitate access to national or mass-market sites relative to local or niche content. The algorithms also focus on speed, potentially driving consumers to the faster rather than higher quality reporting. While the equilibrium readership shifts triggered by differential changes in transaction costs are generally efficient, these relative shifts can move markets.

A particular concern has been that aggregators over time have reduced the costs of obtaining national relative to local news. Recent technological advances have allowed aggregators to geo-target consumers and supplement general content with local links. Evidence suggests that reduction in transaction costs has resulted in some shifts toward local news, though the effect is small.[26]

The proliferation of news and information on the internet creates another new role for firms in signaling the quality of information to readers. Vast new supply of written information on every conceivable topic means readers have access to higher quality coverage. But just as transaction costs are important in formulating bundles to satisfy tastes, verifying the validity of information is also a costly process. So consumers are likely to have some willingness to pay for institutions that can credibly signal information quality. This creates an important role for brands, and another incentive to organize the production of news and information inside media firms.

The difficulty distinguishing informed analysis from uninformed opinion on the internet suggests that enterprises which establish a reputation for quality can earn returns on these investments. But as with editorial selection, the process of validating quality is separable from news production and subject to marketplace competition. Many organizations endorse quality, and writers with outside credentials help establish the reputation of the media firm just as much as affiliation with a media firm enhances the career of a writer. For example, Paul Krugman is under contract to write economics opinion articles for the *New York Times.* Since Krugman has a Nobel Prize, the *Times* does little substantively to endorse his credentials. A similar argument holds for writers with specialized expertise in medicine, politics or economics at aggregator sites such as Huffington Post.

Basic economics indicates that if media firms benefit from the reputation of outside writers, the firm will have to pay for that benefit. Hence the profitability of media firms will crucially depend on the organizational ability to "make" rather than "buy" talent, in other words to identify unknown writers, invest in their skills, and promote their work. Contracts will need to ensure that media firms capture some of the value of writers' output, broadly defined. Not all writers will ultimately earn high returns, but if the few superstars generate enough value under contract to firms to cover losses on others, the media firm can succeed.

Practically, the success of this model depends on creativity and innovation in contracts between media firms and writers. If firms cannot be sure of capturing returns from top writers, they will under-invest in developing and promoting talent. If firms seek too much, promising writers will pursue independent channels for developing their skills. While achieving the right balance might take time and experimentation, the end result of this process might well be both higher quality coverage and higher pay for writers than seen before the internet age. But at the same time, unknown writers can benefit greatly from the reputational effects of affiliation with a popular newspaper and would be expected to compete more aggressively for these positions. It is therefore quite likely that compensation for unproven talent will fall. It is perhaps even possible to imagine a media model where payments *from* writers to firms become a future revenue stream for firms.[27]

The relative importance of horizontal matching versus vertical sorting will also play a role in the media institutions that survive in the digital marketplace. In areas like investigative reporting where accuracy, insight and analysis are important, traditional media brands can play a continuing and strong role. When demand is based in greater share of taste and trends, even aggregators such as Google News may not be able to compete with firms that aggregate directly from social networks such as BuzzFeed.

To this point, little has been said about the role of advertising or pricing models in digital media markets. While a full discussion of pricing is beyond the scope of this chapter, a few summary points are in order. Transaction costs on the advertising have fallen with digital technology, creating incentives for disintermediation and new institutions akin to those on the content side. Specifically, the internet has lowered the costs to advertisers of identifying potential buyers for products, either through search engines or direct connection with topical web sites. For some advertisers, the opportunity to connect to narrowly defined content reduces the costs of connecting with customers, and these advertisers migrate away from media firms to specialized sites. Examples abound, as evidenced by the preponderance of camera ads on photography web sites, golf equipment on golf web sites and beauty product advertisements on fashion sites.

But for other advertisers, only a small fraction of potential buyers are to be found on sites that are closely linked to products. For these advertisers, demographically targeted news media will likely continue to offer a viable alternative. Success for media firms again becomes an issue of successful targeting through editorial selection rather than content itself. The ultimate share of advertising revenue to aggregators versus writers will likely very much depend on this targeting balance.

CONCLUSIONS

This chapter considers the impact of technology in the market for news, focusing on the changing nature of transaction costs and the implications for media firms and market structure. The analyses considered how changing relationships between writers, media firms and advertisers create incentives for disintermediation in traditional media, while at the same time growing transaction costs in consumption lead to tighter integration with new media institutions. Horizontal matching, quality sorting, and relative shifts in transaction costs all play a role.

An important unresolved question is the role existing newspapers and other traditional news firms will play as new institutional arrangements emerge. The ability of existing firms to innovate in reporting contracts and relationships will play an important role, as will the ability to develop journalistic talent in a national, integrated market. The willingness of media firms to break apart and reconstruct new relationships between content production and editorial selection will also likely be central. A barrier to this process has been a reluctance to adopt micropayment or other mechanisms that would allow media firms to buy and sell non-exclusive rights to content at prices that reflect its marketplace value. Technology for "pennies per click" payments is well developed, but media firms resist its implementation in favor of fixed-price bundles. While firms believe that selling unbundled content will lower the value of their output, the current model also likely prevents established firms from realizing the full value of their editorial resources and brands. The ultimate outcome for these firms thus remains uncertain. But the relevance of the economic theory of the firm will remain.

NOTES

1. Ben Smith commenting in the AtlanticWire.com how BuzzFeed sees competition in the digital media environment: http://www.theatlanticwire.com/business/2012/01/future-buzzfeed-looks-newsier-facebook-news-feed/47790/.
2. Carl Shapiro and Hal R. Varian, 1999.
3. The preponderance of local newspapers stands in contrast to most European countries, where many newspapers have long been distributed nationally.
4. Many national newspapers have experimented with paywalls, and some such as the *Wall Street Journal* have maintained hard paywalls through most of their digital history. From 2009 to 2011 paywalls were rare, but have since expanded rapidly and

about 25% of newspapers today have some form of paywall in place. Broadcast sites such as CNN and Fox News have not relied on paywall models. Wikipedia provides a useful history: http://en.wikipedia.org/wiki/Paywall.

5. The annual *State of the News Media* reports from the Pew Project for Excellence in Journalism site provide useful annual summaries and highlights. See http://www.journalism.org/.
6. In books, self-publishing has changed the market in both directions, with published authors foregoing contracts to self-publish, and self-published authors taking representation. Several major book publishers have also bought or taken partnerships with self-publishing platforms (Greenfield, 2012).
7. The economic theory of superstar markets was developed by Rosen (1981). The theory has wide-ranging applications in entertainment markets such as books and movies, where a large number of individuals can consume the same product. However to date, economic research can offer only limited insight into the factors that will shape superstar markets for news and information. More work in this area is warranted.
8. Latest Nielsen statistics for news sites available here: http://blog.nielsen.com/nielsenwire/online_mobile/may-2012-top-u-s-web-brands-and-news-websites/.
9. The trend away from journalists to politicians and public intellectuals is even more pronounced on television. Phil Griffen, president of MSNBC, commented in an interview on the trend away from journalists in broadcast news commentary in the Tampa Bay Times: "I'm sorry, I don't care about journalists. ... I want fair-minded, smart people who understand the world and can interpret it," and "If they're journalists, great. This notion that somehow you have to have done something to earn so-called journalists' credentials? Stop." The interview is reported at http://www.tampabay.com/features/media/article1214749.ece.
10. Some salary information is reported in this *New Yorker* profile of David Mossberg: http://www.newyorker.com/reporting/2007/05/14/070514fa_fact_auletta. *Slate* raised potential conflicts created by speaking fees of *New Yorker* journalists in 2004 (Shafer, 2004). The public editor at the *New York Times* has taken up the issue on multiple occasions (Hoyt, 2009a, b).
11. CNN Money reports on the announcement, highlighting the tradeoff between Arrington's expertise and financial conflicts, see http://finance.fortune.cnn.com/2011/09/01/michael-arrington-venture-capital-fund/?iid=SF_F_River.
12. BLS salary data for reporters is available here: http://www.bls.gov/oes/current/oes273022.htm. See Pew Project for Excellence in Journalism (2010) for more on the changing composition of the newsroom at both local television stations and daily newspapers.
13. A useful summary of Demand Media and its role in supplying information markets is covered in Carr (2010). Elance is a global freelance writing job site.
14. The changing relationship between newspaper firms and journalists was highlighted in recent reporting at the *New York Times*, where violations of newsroom ethics rules by contributing writers resulted in public controversy and debate (Hoyt, 2010).
15. There are other reasons why investigative reporting might be under-provided regardless of whether writing is organized inside firms or in markets. The reasons have less to do with contracts or technological innovation than the fact that the full social benefits of investigative efforts are never captured by the media firm. This is because firms or writers benefit only when corruption is uncovered and a salable story produced, while society benefits from the deterrence effect of investigative research. For more on the external effects of media markets in different contexts, see George and Waldfogel (2008), Snyder and Stromberg (2010) and Gentzkow (2006).
16. Waldfogel (2012) considers the impact of industry disintermediation on the supply of recorded music.

17. The role of "microcosts" in television has long been recognized, with lead-in effects an important strategic variable in programming. Transaction costs have been studied directly by Esteves-Sorenson and Perretti (2012).
18. The media firm's tradeoff between continuing analysis of popular topics and introduction of new material is explored in Ho and Liu (2010). and George and Oberholzer-Gee (2012).
19. Evidence abounds: Waldfogel (2003) studies the effect of product variety on radio listening, and George and Waldfogel (2003) and George (2007) document the effect of variety on newspaper readership. George and Waldfogel (2006) and George (2008) illustrate ways that new media affect targeting and readership in daily newspapers.
20. See past reports on audience demographics available at http://www.accessabc.com/products/freereports.htm. The advertising sales portal at the *Times* says this of *Times* readers: "NYTimes.com readers are educated, affluent and influential. Reach a highly qualified audience that has a spiral of influence – they get and spread ideas." See http://www.nytimes.com/marketing/selfservice/audience.html.
21. George (2013) and George and Hogendorn (2013).
22. The partnership between Drexel University in Philadelphia and the Philadelphia Daily News in expanding arts coverage is a recent example. See http://www.drexel.edu/now/news-media/releases/archive/2011/October/Drexel-Wins-Knight-Foundation-NEA-Grant/.
23. Cooperation across competitors in collecting news footage and covering stories has become a controversial topic in media regulation. News firms argue that shared content reduces costs but can still be customized to the audience. Opponents argue that newsroom collaboration undermines anti-trust laws and local ownership regulations. See *Outsourcing The News: How Covert Consolidation is Destroying Newsrooms and Circumventing Media Ownership Rules,* available at www.freepress.net/sites/default/…/Outsourcing%20the%20News.pdf.
24. The *New York Times* reports on the BuzzFeed business model here: http://www.nytimes.com/2012/02/06/business/media/at-buzzfeed-the-significant-and-the-silly.html?pagewanted=all&_r=0. Wikipedia provides a useful history of the Huffington Post: http://en.wikipedia.org/wiki/The_Huffington_Post.
25. Data from Alexa News category: http://www.alexa.com/topsites/category/Top/News.
26. George (2013) and George and Hogendorn (2013).
27. This model operates today in the trade press, where magazines such as *Financier Worldwide* charge fees to contributors yet remain widely respected and read. The model also has parallels with scientific journals that charge submission fees.

REFERENCES

Carr, David (2010) "Plentiful Content, So Cheap," *The New York Times* February 7.

Esteves-Sorenson, Constança and Fabrizio Perretti (2012) "Micro-costs: Inertia in Television Viewing," *Economic Journal* 122(563), 867–902.

Gentzkow, Matthew (2006) "Television and Voter Turnout," *Quarterly Journal of Economics* 121(3), 931–72.

George, Lisa (2007) "What's Fit to Print: The Effect of Ownership Concentration on Product Variety in Daily Newspaper Markets," *Information Economics and Policy* 19(3–4), 285–303.

George, Lisa M. (2008) "The Internet and the Market for Daily Newspapers," *B.E. Journal of Economic Analysis and Policy: Advances in Economic Analysis and Policy* 8(1).

George, Lisa M. (2013) "Local News Online," *Time Warner Cable Research Program on Digital Communications,* Washington, DC, Winter.

George, Lisa M. and Christiaan Hogendorn (2012) "Aggregators Search and the Economics of New Media Institutions," *Information Economics and Policy* 22(1), 40–51.
George, Lisa Megargle and Christiaan Hogendorn (2013) "Local News Online: Aggregators, Geo-Targeting and the Market for Local News" (November 1). Available at SSRN: http://ssrn.com/abstract=2357586 orhttp://dx.doi.org/10.2139/ssrn.2357586
George, Lisa M. and Felix Oberholzer-Gee (2011) "Diversity in Local Television News," *US Federal Communications Commission Quadrennial Review*, Washington, DC, July.
George, Lisa, and Joel Waldfogel (2003) "Who Affects Whom in Daily Newspaper Markets?" *Journal of Political Economy* 111(4), 765–84.
George, Lisa M. and Joel Waldfogel (2006) "The *New York Times* and the Market for Local Newspapers," *American Economic Review* 96(1), 435–477.
George, Lisa M., and Joel Waldfogel (2008) "National Media and Local Political Participation: The Case of the New York Times," In *Information and Public Choice: From Media Markets to Policy Making*, edited by Roumeen Islam, 33–48. Washington, DC: World Bank.
Greenfield, Jeremy (2012) "When Self-Published Ebooks Become Best-Sellers," *Forbes*, December 3. Available at http://www.forbes.com/sites/jeremygreenfield/2012/12/03/when-self-published-ebooks-become-best-sellers/
Ho, B. and P. Liu (2010) "Novelty and Popularity in the Market for News," Cornell University Working Paper.
Hoyt, Clark (2009a) "The Writers Make News. Unfortunately," *The New York Times*, May 23.
Hoyt, Clark (2009b) "He Works for The Times, Too," *The New York Times*, September 5.
Hoyt, Clark (2010) "Times Staffers, Standards or Not," *The New York Times*, January 10.
Pew Project for Excellence in Journalism (2010) *State of the News Media, 2010*, March 15.
Rosen, Sherwin (1981) "The Economics of Superstars," In *Cultural Economics: The Arts, the Heritage and the Media Industries. Volume 2*, edited by Ruth Towse, 187–200, International Library of Critical Writings in Economics, vol. 80. Cheltenham UK and Lyme, NH, USA: Edward Elgar.
Shafer, Jack (2004) "Money Talks: How Closely Should The New Yorker Police Its Writers' Speaking Engagements?" *Slate*, Dec. 3.
Shapiro, Carl, and Hal R. Varian (1999) *Information Rules: A Strategic Guide to the Network Economy*. Boston: Harvard Business School Press.
Snyder, James M., Jr., and David Stromberg (2010) "Press Coverage and Political Accountability," *Journal of Political Economy* 118(2), 355–408.
Waldfogel, Joel (2003) "Preference Externalities: An Empirical Study of Who Benefits Whom in Differentiated-Product Markets," *RAND Journal of Economics* 34(3), 557–68.
Waldfogel, Joel (2012) "And the Band Played On: Digital Disintermediation and the Quality of Recorded Music." Available at SSRN: http://ssrn.com/abstract=2117372 or http://dx.doi.org/10.2139/ssrn.2117372
Williamson, Oliver E. (1985) *The Economic Institutions of Capitalism: Firms, Markets, Relational Contracting*. New York: The Free Press.

PART III

ECONOMICS AND POLICY

13. Economic analysis in media policy making

*Jonathan D. Levy**

INTRODUCTION AND CONCEPTUAL FRAMEWORK

Because this volume examines the economics of media from multiple perspectives, it is important to begin this chapter with a clear understanding of the specific media economics issues to be addressed herein. Media policy means a goal or series of goals, set by society, in this case taken to mean a national government, together with a series of policy instruments that can be implemented and adjusted to foster the goals. The goals may vary from country to country and, due, *inter alia*, to differences in the national legal system, the menu of policy instruments is also likely to vary across countries. This chapter will focus on the US and the UK, although the discussion of goals and the review of relevant literature will certainly be applicable to other areas as well. The focus will be on electronic media, both free-to-air (television) and pay (cable television, satellite television, and to some extent, Internet-delivered content). Some attention will be paid to newspapers as well. As it happens, much of the theoretical work is not tied to any distribution technology. Moreover, much of the empirical work on media content analysis focuses on newspapers, due to the availability of data (that is, the actual text of newspaper stories is relatively easy to find, whereas recordings or transcripts of, say, television news programs are far less widely available). Due to space limitations, coverage will be selective. In addition to the other chapters of this volume, there are several valuable survey works available.[1]

At least two characteristics distinguish the media sector from many other economic goods and services. First, particularly with respect to free-to-air broadcasting, the service is a public good (non-excludable and also non-rival in consumption). Second, society normally assigns non-economic goals to the media sector and these are hard to quantify. For example, the Federal Communications Commission (FCC) sees its media policy goals as competition, diversity, and localism. Economic competition, both in the provision of programming and in the sale of advertising, is important for promoting efficiency and innovation. The FCC has employed multiple concepts of diversity, but a core meaning is diversity of political viewpoints (known in UK parlance as "plurality"). This goal is also instrumental, in the sense that it is designed to provide citizens with the information they need to discharge the obligations of citizenship. This could include various types of political participation, for example voting, attending public meetings, signing petitions, communicating with public officials, monitoring their performance, or holding them accountable for that performance. Localism refers to program content that is produced or selected specifically to cater to the needs of local populations. It may or may not be locally produced. These non-economic goals can also fit into the framework of economic analysis under the heading of externalities – a better informed citizen generally confers benefits on her fellow citizens.

In addition to the three policy goals cited above (which were articulated by the FCC), the US also has an implicit "universal service" goal for broadcasting. Without using that precise term, the Communications Act of 1934 directs the FCC to make a "distribution of licenses … among the several States and communities as to provide a fair, efficient, and equitable distribution of radio services to each of the same."[2] More recently, as formerly separate voice and video transmission technologies have converged, the FCC has broadened the traditional telecommunications concept of universal service to include some level of broadband.[3]

As distribution technology has developed over the past 30 years or so, it has become possible to provide video content on a paid basis. This goes a long way toward solving the public good problem with regard to media content; in particular, more narrowly targeted programming that may be intensely valued by a small share of the population has become profitable to provide.[4] On the other hand, even in the wealthiest countries, free-to-air distribution still plays an important role.[5] To the extent that society is concerned with non-economic goals or addressing externalities or universal service, there may still be a case for some intervention in the market. As a matter of principle, society could achieve this goal in more than one way – universal free-to-air service with some degree of government subsidy is the traditional route, but one could also imagine subsidizing access to pay television. The form and magnitude of intervention would differ across countries based on the legal system and political culture, although, to the extent that one of the goals of media policy is to permit citizens to monitor the performance of the government, state-owned media would be less desirable.

There are significant differences between the US and the UK with regard to the three categories of government policy that are applied specifically to media: subsidy (including direct government provision), structural regulation (media ownership rules, merger review), and behavioural (content regulation). The US government provides a rather small annual subsidy to public media programming via the Corporation for Public Broadcasting; another program in the past has provided a very small subsidy for public media infrastructure. The BBC's license fee revenues are at least ten times larger than the CPB subsidy and, of course, are deployed to a smaller population.

In the US, the media ownership rules are mostly at the local level (for example, limits on the number of television stations or radio stations one entity can own in a local market, prohibition on common ownership of a daily newspaper and a radio or television station in a local market). In the UK the remaining cross-media rule is national (limiting common ownership of newspapers and ITV licensees). Within the television sector, there is, for example, a prohibition on common ownership of Channel 4 and either ITV licensees or Channel 5.

This contrast between more local media markets in the US and more national media markets in the UK has implications for the application of empirical economic analysis to media ownership regulation. As a threshold matter, it is important to note that the techniques of economic analysis can and are applied to policies designed to promote non-economic goals, for example by studying the impact of media market structure on those goals. As discussed in more detail below, one of the big challenges is finding measurable performance metrics for non-economic goals. But here the point is more mechanical – in order to examine the impact of media market structure on policy goals, economic or non-economic, there must be some source of market structure variation. In the US there are over 200 distinct local geographic television markets, with significant variation in the number of stations per market, so there is at least the possibility of cross-section analysis. It is also possible to use panel data (as in Erb 2011), although this is only fruitful if there is sufficient variation in ownership structure across panel years. In the UK, with a more national media market structure, one is limited primarily to time series analysis.

The FCC reviews media mergers based on a public interest standard that includes both traditional competition law criteria and consideration of non-economic goals.[6] UK authorities also consider both categories of goal in merger review. With regard to UK review of proposed mergers for plurality concerns, a recent OFCOM statement defines plurality as "ensuring that there is a diversity of viewpoints available, *and consumed*, across and within media enterprises; and preventing any one media owner or voice from having too much influence over public opinion and the political agenda" (OFCOM 2012b, p. 1, emphasis added). Note that

OFCOM stressed both "internal" and "external" (that is, within a media outlet and across media outlets in a market) plurality and referenced both availability and consumption of media content; the same document later states that "consumption metrics … form the foundation of a plurality assessment."[7] The OFCOM statement also highlights the necessity "to consider what level of plurality is sufficient," noting that this is "challenging, as it requires a subjective judgment." This statement is a reminder of the challenges of applying economic (or other systematic modes of) analysis to plurality/diversity concerns. First, defining a performance metric is hard; second, deciding what level is acceptable involves judgment; third, at least part of what actually affects citizens is *consumption* of media content, something that generally cannot be regulated.

The discussion of plurality invites attention to content, the third category of regulation. The First Amendment to the US Constitution stringently limits content regulation. Even for free-to-air (FTA) broadcasting, where the scope for regulation is greatest, it is limited primarily to measures to protect children and provide politicians access to purchased advertising time. For pay media, there is even less content regulation. In the UK the degree of content regulation differs to some extent across classes of licensee, but overall it is more stringent than in the US. Thus, while US policy focuses primarily on structural regulation as an indirect way of affecting the range of content provided, in the UK, both the BBC and OFCOM (which has oversight over the other television providers) have developed explicit content-based performance criteria. The approach of the two organizations is similar; a brief description of the OFCOM procedures is provided here (OFCOM 2011).

OFCOM's four purposes of public service broadcasting are to "inform ourselves and others and to increase our understanding of the world," to "stimulate our interest in and knowledge of arts, science, history and other topics," to "reflect and strengthen our cultural identity through original programming at UK, national and regional level," and to "make us aware of different cultures and alternative viewpoints." OFCOM measures performance by collecting data on inputs (such as spending on programming), outputs (such as hours of programming output, viewing levels), and via extensive audience research. OFCOM surveys are designed to elicit audience evaluation of performance with respect to each of the four purposes and to assess the importance that audience members place on each purpose or indicator of purpose. Good performance/high importance is taken to be the fraction of respondents giving a rating of 7–10. OFCOM can then compare importance and performance measures. This type of evaluation works best for monitoring performance over time rather than across different media market structures and it does not provide a clear and principled standard for determining good performance. Nevertheless, data of this nature can certainly inform decisions about broadcaster priorities.

Thus, the US has more limited tools than the UK to influence internal plurality. If promotion of external plurality is to meet the social goal of enabling an informed citizenry, it will be important for citizens to be "conscientious readers" in the sense of Mullainathan and Shleifer (2005), referenced below. Even with regard to programming that does exhibit "internal plurality", the proliferation of media outlets over the past 20 years or so, coupled with the advent of devices from the remote control to the mute button to the digital video recorder make it easier, even within the program of a particular outlet, for viewers/consumers to tune out dissonant material, even if it is presented in the same program as confirmatory material. Policy makers may need to reconcile themselves to the reality that, while they may be able to affect the range of content transmitted, they have less ability than before to affect what is actually received.

This chapter focuses primarily on advertiser-supported media, but pay services (such as cable and satellite television distributors) raise some additional policy issues. The following are addressed briefly: rate regulation, competition among pay television providers, channel bundling, and vertical relationships between content providers and pay television distributors.

The balance of this chapter is organized as follows. The next section takes up some "big picture" issues regarding the organization of the media and international comparisons. Because the presumed purpose of media diversity/plurality goals is to enhance political participation, the following section addresses the impact of media availability on political participation and outcomes. The impact of media ownership regulation on viewpoint diversity will depend on the extent to which media content is driven by citizen demand as opposed to determined by media owner preferences. Hence the subsequent section reviews theoretical and empirical work on media slant. The next section addresses other theoretical and empirical work on non-economic objectives and additional topics including market definition and research that explicitly introduces the two-sided market framework into media policy analysis, including the merger simulation context. Next is a brief section on pay television regulatory issues, followed by conclusions.

HIGH-LEVEL ANALYSIS OF MEDIA POLICY AND MARKET STRUCTURE

Besley and Prat (2006) examine the relationship of media market structure to effective monitoring of the performance of government. They show that media pluralism, that is, a larger number of outlets, makes it more expensive and hence less likely that the government will be able to "capture" the media (suppress information), because to suppress information the government would need to pay off all media outlets as if each were a monopoly provider. In order to pay off media outlets, the government needs to have some mechanism to pay them. The crudest example is direct payments, such as happened in Peru during the Fujimori years, as documented by McMillan and Zoido (2004). More subtle and less visible techniques include government policy decisions that benefit the media, perhaps through direct expenditures on advertising or actions that benefit the non-media interests of media companies. In any event, the model suggests the importance of independent media, that is, those with high transactions costs of transferring resources from government to media. In the Besley and Prat model, the sole function of media is to report (or not) on the quality of the incumbent politician. One could imagine extending the process to incorporate monitoring rival media (and the transfers that they get from government) as part of the competitive function of the media market. Besley and Prat also link their model to political outcomes, showing that media capture reduces voter utility and is reflected by reduced political turnover.

Djankov et al. (2003) examine media ownership patterns in 97 countries as of 1999 and find that, in many countries, state ownership is substantial in all three media (newspaper, television, radio) examined. The other widely significant form of ownership is "family." Using a subjective index of autocracy, they find that more autocratic regimes are associated with higher levels of state ownership. The authors also examine the association of state media ownership with various constructed indices of press, political, and economic freedom holding constant various country characteristics thought to influence media ownership. State ownership generally has a negative impact (sometimes statistically significant) on these indicators. Besley and Prat (2006) compile data for 88 countries on the years in office of the chief executive and an index of corruption and examine variations with respect to levels of state ownership of newspapers and newspaper ownership concentration, based on data from Djankov et al. For both chief executive tenure and corruption, they find a positive association with both ownership measures.

MEDIA AVAILABILITY AND POLITICAL PARTICIPATION

The diversity/plurality goal is instrumental in the sense that it is designed to ensure that citizens can participate productively in the political process. There is a significant strain of literature that examines the impact of media availability on various political activities or outcomes. These include voter turnout, participation in other civic activities, knowledge of candidates and their positions, actual voter choices by political party, and outcomes such as the behaviour of elected representatives and provision of public services to particular geographic areas.

Gentzkow et al. (2011) use historical data from 1869 to 2004 to examine the impact of newspapers on political participation and find that newspaper availability has a statistically significant positive effect on voting. However, they find that most of the impact comes from the first newspaper. Moreover, they find that newspaper impact on average presidential turnout declines with the introduction of radio and television, while the impact on Congressional turnout does not. This is consistent with earlier work (Gentzkow 2006), which uses exogenous variation across US markets in the timing of television's introduction in the 1940s and 1950s to examine the impact of television on voter turnout and political knowledge. He found that the introduction of television "crowded out" consumption of radio and newspaper content, reducing voter turnout and political knowledge.

Snyder and Stromberg (2010) find that media availability, particularly newspapers, is associated with a chain of events from greater voter participation to members of Congress taking more procedural actions that directly benefit their constituents to a greater incidence of government spending in the Congressional district. Snyder and Stromberg find that "congruence" between the circulation area of a newspaper and the boundaries of Congressional districts is an important determinant of how effective the political process is in enabling citizens to act to increase the benefits they get from government activity. They find a smaller impact for television congruence and note that television provides less information about local members of Congress than newspapers and that television stations generally have larger service areas than newspaper circulation areas, which is likely to reduce local congruence. This work suggests that having media outlets targeted to local markets/jurisdictions has some value.[8]

There are several other articles that address these issues using similar techniques; to wit, taking advantage of plausibly exogenous variations in the introduction or availability of media to study media impact on behaviour. The variations studied include the differential arrival of radio in the Midwestern United States during the 1930s (Stromberg 2004), the differential availability of Spanish-language local television news (Oberholzer-Gee and Waldfogel 2009), the differential availability of a Russian national television channel independent from the government (Enikolopov et al. 2011), and the differential availability of Serbian radio stations in neighbouring Croatia (DellaVigna et al. 2012).

Schulhofer-Wohl and Garrido (2012) examine the consequences of the closure of one of the two major newspapers in the Cincinnati, Ohio market, focusing on election indicators in suburban counties in Kentucky that had been particularly reliant on the paper that closed. Oberholzer-Gee and Waldfogel (2005) examine variations across US markets in availability of African-American targeted radio stations and weekly newspapers, finding a positive effect of targeted media on voter turnout.[9]

DellaVigna and Kaplan (2007) examine not only voter turnout but also party voting shares, as a function of the availability of the cable channel Fox News. They found that the availability of Fox News increased voter turnout and the Republican share of the vote. Their persuasion rate calculations suggest that between 3 and 28 percent of Fox News viewers were persuaded by exposure to the network to vote Republican.

Some researchers have examined the impact of media availability on other social outcomes. For example, Jensen and Oster (2009) use the differential arrival of cable television in areas of India to find a positive impact of media on school enrolment by girls and other indicators of well-being. Olken (2009) uses variations across Indonesian villages in television signal reception to determine that increased television channel availability is associated with increased time spent watching television and with reductions in the number of and participation in social groups within the village. On the other hand, Olken does not find that these changes result in a lower quality of village governance.

There is a certain irony in the fact that the studies summarized above depend on exogenous variation in the availability of media to make their empirical analysis valid. The studies generally show that media availability or consumption does have a positive impact on political participation, but since the policy goal is in fact political participation, the main policy takeaway is support for the universal service goal of media policy and, to some extent, for having at least some locally targeted media outlets since they are more likely to cover local political events. The results also offer some support for the idea of multiple independent media outlets.

One thing that none of the studies reviewed did is relate political participation or knowledge directly to something that regulatory agencies can directly control. As noted above, aside from merger review, the major structural policy lever available to regulatory agencies (such as the US FCC) is ownership regulation. Pursuant to a mandate from the US Congress, the FCC conducts a Quadrennial Review of media ownership regulations.[10] Each of the last three reviews has included a group of academic studies, some of which are specifically referenced herein.[11] One recent study, Vavreck et al. (2011), examined the impact of local variations in US media market structure on various measures of knowledge regarding local Congressional candidates, Presidential candidates, and voter turnout, focusing on the 2006 and 2008 US elections. The study did not find a statistically significant relationship between any of these measures and market structure.

MEDIA SLANT

Slant refers to the practice of a media outlet not to report information accurately, either refraining from reporting true information or distorting that information. The question of slant is important for media policy because, if media content is demand determined, then policy measures aimed at media ownership are less likely to have an impact. Of course, even if owner preferences do play a role, it is not clear what the policy implications are for media ownership regulation. Countries that practice content regulation may have more scope for action here.[12]

Theoretical Models

Mullainathan and Shleifer (2005) present a model in which media outlets are profit maximizers without political positions, but they can slant the news in order to attract readers. Readers' utility is a function of the distance between their beliefs and the news as reported. When readers are rational, there is no slant. If readers have biased but homogeneous preferences, then the news is slanted towards consumers' beliefs and the degree of slant is the same for each media outlet, monopoly and duopoly. If preferences are heterogeneous (along a linear interval), the monopolist slants toward an interior point in the distribution of beliefs, while duopolists slant toward the extremes of the preference distribution with the result that "competition tends to polarize the news." Nevertheless, if a "conscientious reader" peruses both newspapers, she can, by cross-checking, assemble a more accurate picture than would have been available under monopoly.

Gentzkow and Shapiro (2006) present a model in which firms do not have ideological preferences but slant their news reports toward the prior expectations of readers in order to develop a reputation for quality which in turn increases their profits. Consumers value accurate information but also update their prior assessment of a media outlet's quality based on the information it reports regarding the state of the world. There are two possible firm types – a high quality firm always receives and reports accurate information on the state of the world; a "normal" firm receives a signal about the state of the world that may or may not be accurate and it has discretion over the content of its report. In a subsequent time period, the firm receives a "continuation payoff" that is an increasing function of its estimated quality. When consumers receive feedback regarding the state of the world, the likelihood of truthful reporting is increased. When there are two categories of consumer (say, R and L), among the equilibria is a "segmented" one with paper biased towards R and read by the R people and one biased toward L and read by the L people. If the firms are independently owned, then equilibrium bias is (weakly) decreasing with the number of firms; if the firms are all commonly owned, equilibrium bias is independent of the number of firms. This provides some theoretical underpinning for media ownership policies that limit ownership consolidation.

Gentzkow and Shapiro (2008) present a less technical review of research on how competition in media can limit bias or distortion. When the incentives to distort originate on the supply side, competition can provide effective discipline. When the incentives originate on the demand side (citizen/consumers prefer inaccurate information that confirms their prior beliefs), competition has an ambiguous effect (depending on whether the preference for confirming information is based on a desire to avoid cognitive dissonance or on the belief that sources conforming to their priors are actually more accurate; if the latter is true, then competition can limit biased reporting). With respect to the supply side, competition, that is, the presence of multiple independent outlets, can reduce the likelihood of government capture of the media through bribery. If different outlets have different ideological preferences and distort their news coverage accordingly, a "conscientious reader" can discover the truth. Moreover, knowing that the truth will come out anyway may blunt a partisan media outlet's incentives to distort the news. This can amount to a case for diversity of media ownership, provided that one assumes that owners have a range of ideological preferences. If all media were owned separately by people with identical ideologies, this mechanism would not work.

Anderson and McLaren (2012) build a model with two firms and each has two possibly conflicting goals – profits and advancing a political agenda. Unlike Gentzkow and Shapiro (2006), theirs is a one-period model with no reputation effects. Consumers are assumed to be rational, to have identical tastes, and to know the bias of the firms. Firms can either report information (regarding a policy variable that in turn informs citizen and media owner preferences regarding a policy decision) truthfully or report nothing. The authors compare competition and monopoly structures, finding that welfare is higher under competition. From a public policy point of view, the key result is that prohibiting mergers either has no effect on welfare or improves it. In cases where welfare is improved, the merger ban results in increased viewpoint diversity. One important caveat is that the model assumes zero production costs for the news product, so mergers cannot improve productive efficiency.

Balan et al. (2009) present a model in which outlet owners have preferred ideologies and derive utility from the amount of "effective persuasion" in the market and from economic profits. Their model includes two firms; firm owners (actual and prospective) can have one of two types of ideology (A and B). Each owner's utility is a linear function of economic profits and ideological utility, which in turn is a function of effective persuasion. The form of the ideological utility function and the parameter that describes the divergence of the two ideologies are crucial for the model results with respect to diversity, which Balan et al. define as ownership of one outlet by an A-type owner and one by a B-type owner. If common ownership is prohibited, there may or may not be diversity. Of particular interest is the finding that, for some parameter values, permitting common ownership is actually a requirement for diversity (this is because a merger between outlets whose owners have the same ideology will increase the level of persuasion; a market structure with two separate type A owners leaves a potential type B owner unwilling to enter, but the prospect of a type A monopoly owner changes the potential type B owner's utility calculation and it will outbid the potential type A monopolist).

Empirical Studies

Perhaps the biggest challenge for an empirical study of media slant is characterizing the position of a particular media outlet through examination and calibration of its content. In most cases, the assumption is that ideological positions are distributed along a line, for example from liberal to conservative, Republican to Democrat, or right to left. Thus, the standards are generally relative rather than absolute. A notable early example is Groseclose and Milyo (2005). They placed 20 major media outlets on a liberal-conservative continuum by counting the times that each quoted a finding from any of 50 "think tanks." They searched the *Congressional Record* for the years 1993–2002 to determine the number of times each member of Congress quoted from those sources and assigned ideological scores to each member based on ratings from the lobbying group Americans for Democratic Action (ADA). Their statistical analysis essentially treated each media outlet as equivalent to an additional member of Congress and used the pattern of quotations to locate them along the ADA continuum. They found that 18 of 20 outlets were left of center and some were substantially left of center, relative to their placement of the average US voter, but they also found that 19 of the 20 were located in between the average Democratic and the average Republican member of Congress.

Gentzkow and Shapiro (2010) also look to the *Congressional Record* for a measure of media slant, apply it to a large sample of newspapers, and then take the next step of trying to determine the impact of market forces on slant. The authors use an automated procedure to study the 2005 *Congressional Record*, creating a database of policy-related phrases that are used differentially by Democrats and Republicans. Using the Republican share of the 2004 presidential vote in a Congressperson's district as a measure of ideology, they create an "ideology estimator" which is a function of the phrase frequencies. Next, they determine phrase frequencies for "over 400" daily newspapers in 2005. Gentzkow and Shapiro treat each newspaper as if it were a member of Congress and proceed to calculate the ideology of the hypothetical Congressperson's "district." The authors then estimate "ideal slant", that is, the profit maximizing level, for each Congressional district based on the assumption that the demand for slant in each district is a function of the share of campaign contributions directed to Republicans. They find that the actual calculated slant is close to the ideal slant and, based on additional analysis, conclude that consumer demand has a significant impact on slant. By contrast, they find little evidence that newspaper owners play a significant role in determining their papers' slant (for example, they do not find a statistical relationship between the slant of a newspaper and that of other papers with the same owner).

Ho and Quinn (2008, 2009) take a broadly similar approach to measuring newspaper slant, but they rely on the positions of US Supreme Court Justices in non-unanimous decisions and look at explicit positions of newspapers, as reflected in editorials on Supreme Court decisions (examining all non-unanimous decisions from 1994 to 2004), rather than recovering implicit slant through analysis of phrases used or authorities quoted as above. They place the Justices on a liberal-conservative continuum, assuming that Justice Thomas is on the right end of the spectrum and Justice Stevens on the left. Treating each newspaper as an additional "Justice," they characterize the papers' ideology. They examine five newspaper mergers, analyzing the impact on the editorial positions of the papers with varying results. The analysis is complicated by idiosyncratic institutional features of the newspapers, but they did not find clear evidence that mergers brought editorial position convergence.

Gans and Leigh (2012) use a variety of techniques to examine media slant in Australia. They make use of data from Media Monitors Australia (http://www.mediamonitors.com.au/), which provides data on media content, and from *Hansard*, the Australian equivalent of the US *Congressional Record*. For positioning, the authors use mentions of "public intellectuals" by members of the two major political groupings in Parliament. They examine 27 media outlets (newspapers, radio stations, and television networks). The measured difference between their slant and the centre position is not statistically significant in any case other than the major public television broadcaster ABC, which is slanted toward the ideology of the party in power. There is some evidence of divergence across the two public television networks and some dispersion among the six public (Australian Broadcasting Corporation) radio stations, with the nationally targeted one being precisely centrist and the five in major metropolitan areas all being slightly to the right.

Brian Knight and two colleagues have also examined media slant using techniques similar to those described. Durante and Knight (2012) investigate viewer response to partisan bias in Italian television news, utilizing television content data (collected by the Italian Communications Regulatory Authority) and viewing data. The authors compare a time period when the government was controlled by a "centre-left" coalition and one during which the government was controlled by a "centre-right" coalition. They examine coverage of the "right" when it is in power with coverage of the "left" when it is in power, measured by speaking time for members of each political coalition; deviations from symmetry are interpreted as bias. They find that the private channels (which during this period were controlled by Silvio Berlusconi, who was Prime Minister for part of the period) are more biased to the right than the public channels. They find some evidence of dispersion across the three commonly owned private channels and across the three public channels. The authors' examination of survey data suggests that viewers have a preference for content that matches their personal bias.

Chiang and Knight (2011) examine the impact of newspaper endorsements on intention to vote, based on survey data during the run-up to the

2000 and 2004 US Presidential elections. They find that endorsements do influence voting intentions and that "credible" endorsements have the biggest impact. A credible endorsement is one that is unexpected relative to the estimated ideology of the newspaper (for example, a Democratic-leaning paper endorses the Republican candidate). Ideology (essentially the probability that a newspaper will endorse the Democratic candidate) is estimated as a function of both demand side (reader preferences) and supply side (newspaper group owner fixed effects) factors.

Milyo (2007), in a report commissioned by the FCC, attempts to relate media slant to cross-ownership of newspapers and television stations in the same market, something that is regulated by the FCC. Milyo assembled recordings of three days of late evening newscasts in November of 2006, coded their content manually,[13] and developed quantity measures of news content, partisan slant (based on differences in speaking time and in total coverage for candidates of the two major political parties, differences in "partisan issue coverage," and differences in coverage of opinion polls favouring each of the two major political parties). He finds that cross-owned television stations provide more total news coverage and more coverage in various local news categories. He also finds "little consistent and significant difference in the partisan slant" among cross-owned stations and others in the market. This could be construed as evidence that cross-ownership of a television station and a daily newspaper in the same market does not affect viewpoint diversity.

OTHER THEORETICAL AND EMPIRICAL WORK ON NON-ECONOMIC OBJECTIVES

Diversity and Localism

One metric used by the FCC to examine performance with respect to the localism goal is the quantity of local television news provided. Erb (2011) undertook a study of the impact of local media market structure (including two features subject to FCC regulation – common ownership of television and radio stations in a market and common ownership of a daily newspaper and a television or radio station in the market) on the minutes of local television news provided (based on television program guide scheduling information). Erb conducts his analysis at the station level and at the market level. At the station level, he finds that television stations commonly-owned with newspapers or radio stations in the market provide more news than other television stations in the market. However, in neither case does this result hold at the market level. The total amount of news provided, other things equal, is not higher in markets with cross-owned stations.[14]

George and Oberholzer-Gee (2011) employ a novel data set to investigate the impact of local media market structure on viewpoint diversity in television news. They obtain transcripts of local television news programs (from the closed captioning feed provided for viewers who are hard of hearing) of major US television stations across 40 markets and several years. They construct performance metrics, based on keyword shares, to reflect issue diversity, political diversity, and geographic diversity (of localities mentioned within a larger market). The authors "find little evidence for a robust influence of market structure on diversity."

Brocas et al. (2011), in an FCC-commissioned study, provide a theoretical model of local media market competition that relates market structure, in this case the number of independent outlets, and firm viewpoint to the amount of information disclosed to viewers. In the most policy-relevant version of their analysis ("Model III"), firms can withhold information, "garble" the information transmitted by another firm, or reveal true information. Firms incur reputation costs if they garble information. In order for viewpoint information to be revealed, there must be competition among firms with the same viewpoint. Hence, in the case of a single issue on which there are two possible viewpoints, the model shows that four firms, two holding each viewpoint, are necessary for full information transmission.

Minority Ownership

As part of its diversity goal, the FCC has long considered it important to encourage some minority ownership of broadcast facilities. This issue arises in various contexts, including the Quadrennial Review of media ownership regulations (FCC 2011d, paragraphs 152, 158, 167, and 170). One reason that minority ownership might be important is if it were to increase the diversity of program offerings by increasing the amount of minority-targeted programming.

Siegelman and Waldfogel (2001) apply the preference externality (see note 9) framework to radio programming, for which it is possible to identify "minority-targeted" programming (with respect to African Americans and Hispanics), based on radio station formats. They show that minority group radio listening is higher in markets with larger minority populations and that different population groups have distinct radio programming preferences. In general, they find a positive relationship between minority group population in a market and the number of minority-targeted radio stations. Most minority-targeted radio stations are not owned by members of minority groups, but some are. If the quantity of minority programming available in a market were strictly driven by demand, the identity of the owner would not be significant. Using an exogenous change in the extent of minority radio station ownership (triggered by Congress's relaxation of the US local radio station ownership rules in 1996), the authors show that an increase in the number of minority-owned stations in a market results in a net increase in the total minority-targeted stations. In a study for the FCC's 2010 Quadrennial Review, using data from 2005 and 2007, Waldfogel (2011) finds some evidence of the same result, although he is unable strictly to repeat the 2001 analysis, because of the lack of an exogenous shock to minority ownership.

MARKET DEFINITION, TWO-SIDED MARKETS, AND MERGER SIMULATION

Market Definition

Keeping up with technical change is an important challenge for the media policy maker. Technological progress may require a change in the definition of the relevant product market and perhaps a change in the definition of the relevant geographic market, either for merger analysis or for structural ownership rules review. The concept of relevant market is most relevant for economic goals but the "marketplace of ideas" is sometimes a useful concept for examining alternative goals such as diversity/pluralism.

The migration of media content from analogue to digital media and the increasing use of the Internet to distribute media content raise the questions of whether and how to incorporate new media into analysis of these issues. The FCC faced this issue in the Comcast-NBCU merger transaction. The agency concluded "that most consumers *today* do not see online video distributor ('OVD') service as a substitute for their multichannel video programming distributor ('MVPD') service, but as an additional method of viewing programming." However, it also found that "as a vertically integrated company, Comcast will have the incentive and ability to hinder competition from other OVDs, both traditional MVPDs and standalone OVDs." This led the FCC to impose certain conditions on the merged entity.[15]

The impact of the Internet on the availability of media content addressing the FCC's diversity and localism goals has also been the subject of research. On behalf of the FCC, Waldfogel (2002) examined consumer substitution among media, including broadcast and cable television, radio, newspapers, and the Internet. He found evidence of consumer substitution between Internet and broadcast television with respect to news (and also overall). The data available for this study did not permit examination of the origin of news accessed via the Internet, in particular whether it consisted of the online version of a television station or newspaper. In another FCC-commissioned study, Hindman (2011) examined the largest 100 television markets in the United States, employing Internet usage and classification data from comScore and customized directed search to identify additional relevant websites. He found that the net effect of Internet sites on local news availability was quite small. First, there are few such sites, and second, many of them (including the most frequently visited ones) are associated with either local newspapers or local television stations.

Two-sided Markets and Merger Simulation

Gentzkow et al. (2012) calibrate a model of the supply of and demand for daily newspapers in the United States as of 1924. They have data on the sequence of entry of daily newspapers leading up to 1924; moreover, at that time most newspapers explicitly declared a political affiliation. Unlike today, many markets had multiple daily newspapers (even in the city size range of 3,000–100,000 population on which they focus). The model explains newspaper affiliation choices and explicitly includes both advertising and circulation prices. The authors find that citizens have a taste for news consistent with their ideology (proxied here by the Republican vote share) and they show that newspapers respond to citizen "demand" as well as to differentiate themselves from rival newspapers in the market. Competition among newspapers increases diversity of political affiliation in the model. One assumption that is important both for the analysis of advertising competition and for assessing diversity is that citizens can read more than one newspaper; model results and data from readership surveys suggest that 16–20 percent of citizens do this. The authors conduct a number of policy simulations, concluding that joint ownership of newspapers in the same market reduces diversity and consumer welfare.

Fan (2012) also constructs a structural model of US newspaper markets, using 1997–2005 data. She considers both the advertising and circulation side of the newspaper market and uses the model to simulate the results of a newspaper merger that had been blocked by US antitrust authorities. An important innovation of her paper is the explicit account it takes of product characteristics (for example the quality of news) and the impact of post-merger adjustments in quality as well as price. She shows that ignoring product characteristic adjustments results in an underestimate of the welfare loss from the merger simulated.

PAY TELEVISION REGULATORY ISSUES

The initial (and still most prevalent) pay television platform in the US is cable television. Congress imposed rate regulation on cable in 1992; it relaxed regulation as of 1999 except for the basic tier of service (which can be regulated at the local level in the absence of effective competition). Widespread direct-to-home satellite service became available starting in 1994. In order to implement rate regulation, the FCC undertook a cross-section econometric analysis of cable rates, taking advantage of the fact that there were a limited number of markets with more than one cable system offering service to the same households (FCC 1994).

Economists have studied both the impact of rate regulation and the impact of competition on consumer welfare. Hazlett and Spitzer (1997) examine US cable rate regulation and conclude that it was ineffective in constraining quality-adjusted cable rates. They find that regulation did keep monthly cable rates lower than they otherwise would have been post-1992 but they suggest that this was accompanied by a decline in the quality of programming offered (presumably reflecting lower investment in cable content). As evidence, they cite a drop in ratings for the basic cable services subject to regulation. This analysis points to the important methodological challenge of defining/measuring the quality of cable or other media content.

Although a pay television market consisting of (usually) one cable operator and two satellite operators available in each local market cannot be considered perfectly competitive, the work of Goolsbee and Petrin (2004) suggests that, at least in the US context, satellite service appears to significantly constrain cable prices and promote increased cable quality. Hence competition benefits both satellite and cable subscribers. Wise and Duwadi (2005) find broadly similar results with an analysis that emphasizes the importance of switching costs.

Seabright and Weeds (2007, pp. 63–69), in their analysis of how the advent of pay television is affecting the broadcasting sector, highlight two developments – that "Exclusivity over premium content may be anticompetitive" and that "Bundling is essential to broadcasting." Both issues have in fact come up in the policy debate and research context.

In the US, retransmission of local broadcast channels by pay television platforms is of great competitive importance, and the local channels may require a commercial agreement to permit it. The FCC has an open proceeding examining the negotiation process between broadcast channels and pay television distributors (FCC 2011b). Moreover, at least since the 1992 Cable Act, Congress and the FCC have recognized the possibility that vertically integrated satellite cable programmers (that is, companies that own program networks and cable distribution plant) may have incentives to act anticompetitively by signing exclusive contracts that shut out rival platforms from access to content; for example, a cable-owned program service might be made available to cable systems in areas not covered by the program service's cable affiliate but not made available to the satellite platform. Until recently, the FCC had program access regulations prohibiting such contracts; in 2012 the agency switched to a case-by-case analysis (FCC 2012c).

These issues can also come up in the merger context. One example is the Comcast-NBC Universal merger, which brought together a major cable company and a firm with various content assets. The FCC's economic analysis included evaluation of the profitability of a foreclosure strategy by the merged entity and also the profitability that the merged entity would raise prices of its programming to rival distributors. The analysis of (temporary or permanent) foreclosure involved a "critical value" analysis that compared the increased profits from customers who switched to the merged entity with the loss of profits from (former) programming customers who remained with their previous distributor. Staff determined the departure rate of customers from other distributors and the fraction of them that switched to the merged entity. To determine if the critical value was likely to be exceeded should the merger be consummated, staff performed an empirical analysis of departure rates based on an instance in which a pay television platform temporarily lost access to local broadcast signals. The critical value analysis assumed that programming prices would remain constant. FCC staff also analyzed the possibility that the merged entity would raise prices using a Nash bargaining model and found that the merged entity was likely to raise programming prices. The FCC ended up imposing conditions on the merger regarding rival platforms' access to programming and programming prices.[16]

The FCC's 2007 order extending the prohibition on exclusive programming contracts by vertically integrated satellite cable programmers also included a critical value analysis similar to that of the Comcast-NBCU merger order (FCC 2007, Appendix C). In the UK context, OFCOM found that Sky (the British satellite pay television platform) had market power with respect to the wholesale distribution of certain sports programming and required Sky to offer that programming to rival platforms at regulated prices (OFCOM 2010). This action was later overturned, not on jurisdictional but on substantive grounds (Competition Appeal Tribunal 2012, paragraph 5 *et seq.*).

Both cable television and satellite platforms generally offer their content in channel bundles; although currently some content is available "over the top" via the open Internet, bundling is likely to be practiced by the industry for the foreseeable future. Prompted in part by a policy debate in the US on the impact of a requirement that pay television platforms offer channels on an a la carte basis, Crawford and Yurukoglu (2012) have investigated the welfare effects of channel bundling. Their model predicts that a la carte pricing would cause an increase in the cost of channels that would roughly offset the benefits to consumers from being able to purchase only the channels of specific interest. On balance, they conclude that consumer welfare would decrease in the presence of a la carte pricing.

CONCLUSIONS

Economic analysis is an important component of media policy making and policy analysis. This is true for the economic goals of media policy, such as competition and innovation, which are not specific to the sector and for the non-economic goals as well, which may sometimes usefully be thought of as externalities (for example, the goal of diversity or plurality, which is instrumental for good citizenship, which presumably benefits all). With respect to the non-economic goals, perhaps the biggest challenge is coming up with reasonable performance indicators to which the quantitative techniques of economic analysis may be applied. Often these indicators require gathering data on actual media content and then characterizing that content either via human coders or some automatic text analysis software. This is a labour-intensive process; a database of media content, perhaps collected consistently over time, would be a wonderful research resource. A second empirical challenge is salient in countries, such as the US, in which direct content regulation is not a significant policy option (for legal reasons). When the primary policy lever is ownership regulation, in order to do good empirical work it is necessary to have some variation in media market structure. This is particularly challenging in countries such as the UK, where the media are primarily national, but the problem arises even in the US, with its hundreds of local media markets. These challenges, and the technological dynamism (currently manifested by the growing use of the Internet as a delivery platform, both wireline and wireless, for media content) of the media sector mean that there is plenty of interesting and important economic media policy analysis to be done in the 21st century.

NOTES

* The opinions expressed herein are those of the author and do not necessarily represent the views of the Federal Communications Commission or any other member of its staff.

1. Seabright and Von Hagen (2007) is an anthology of 10 articles on the economics of broadcast regulation. Besley and Prat (2011) is an article-length literature review. A less technical discussion of some issues is found in Gentzkow and Shapiro (2008).
2. 47 U.S.C. §307(b).
3. See FCC (2011c).
4. Some, e.g. Seabright and Weeds (2007), have argued that, with the advent of pay television and the replacement of the advertising market with the "viewer market", the case for government intervention dissipates. However, even a competitive pay television industry is not unambiguously superior to an advertiser-supported in terms of social welfare (Owen and Wildman 1992).
5. In the US, roughly 10 percent of television households rely solely on FTA television; in the UK the figure is 42 percent.
6. Whether it be a merger or an analysis of structural ownership rules, it is necessary to take account of the possibility that there may be tradeoffs across goals. See Alexander and Brown (2007).
7. See also Polo (2007).
8. One could speculate that this is one of the considerations behind the recent decision of the UK regulator OFCOM to license some local television services (OFCOM 2012a).
9. Waldfogel and colleagues employ the concept of "preference externalities," the idea that for differentiated products with high fixed costs and varying consumer preferences, the number of consumers sharing a particular preference will be an important determinant of the product characteristics actually offered in the market. George and Waldfogel (2003) demonstrate that African Americans are more likely to purchase daily newspapers in markets with larger African American populations. Oberholzer-Gee and Waldfogel (2005) find that a demographic group's voter turnout increases with that group's share of the area's population and also (more weakly) with the group's total population. The population size effect is stronger at the county level than at the state level, suggesting the county may be a better approximation of the service area of these media outlets than the state.
10. See, e.g., FCC (2011c).
11. See http://transition.fcc.gov/ownership/ for links to the full set of studies associated with the 2006 and 2010 media ownership reviews. The studies associated with the 2002 media ownership review are among those archived at http://www.fcc.gov/working-papers (all are dated Sept. 1, 2002, but some additional papers also have that date).
12. Until 1987, the FCC enforced a regime known as the "Fairness Doctrine," under which broadcast stations were required to provide coverage of controversial issues of public importance and to provide a reasonable opportunity for presentation of contrasting views. This provided interested parties with an opportunity to complain

to the FCC if they did not consider a station's coverage of issues adequate. The FCC's decision to eliminate the doctrine drew on Constitutional principles and also on a finding that it imposed substantial burdens on broadcasters without compensating benefits. Indeed, the decision ending the doctrine grew out of an extended administrative proceeding in which a station's coverage decisions were contested by interested parties. It appeared that one (unintended) effect of the doctrine was to cause stations to shy away from coverage of certain issues to avoid "litigation." See FCC (1987). Hazlett and Sosa (1997) conclude that elimination of the doctrine actually increased the supply of informational programming (news, news/talk, talk, and public affairs formats).

13. In terms of manually coded content data, a major study of local media coverage of city government activities in the United States is noteworthy, even though it did not relate coverage variations to variations in media market structure. Baldwin et al. (2010) collected content data from newspapers, radio, television, cable television and "citizen journalism" sources across 98 markets, finding that daily and weekly newspapers are the most significant sources of coverage.
14. See Shiman et al. (2007) for a series of studies that address similar issues.
15. See FCC (2011a). An OVD is an entity that offers video content by means of the Internet or other Internet Protocol (IP)-based transmission path provided by a person or entity other than the OVD. MVPDs include cable television and satellite television systems. See also FCC (2012a).
16. See FCC (2011a, Appendix B) for a description of the staff analysis of these and other issues.

REFERENCES

Alexander, P. and Brown, K. (2007) "Policymaking and policy trade-offs: broadcast media regulation in the United States", in Seabright, P. and Von Hagen, J. (eds) *The Economic Regulation of Broadcasting Markets: Evolving Technology and Challenges for Policy*, Cambridge, UK: Cambridge University Press, pp. 50–188.

Anderson, S. and McLaren, J. (2012) "Media Mergers and Media Bias with Rational Consumers", *Journal of the European Economic Association* 10(4), 831–859.

Balan, D., DeGraba, P., and Wickelgreen, A. (2009) "Ideological Persuasion in the Media", available at http://works.bepress.com/cgi/viewcontent.cgi?article=1001&context=david_balan

Baldwin, T., Bergan, D., Fico, F., Lacy, S., and Wildman, S. (2010) "News Media Coverage of City Governments in 2009", available at http://quello.msu.edu/sites/default/files/pdf/PEJ_City_Govt_report-final.pdf

Besley, T. and Prat, A. (2011) "The Political Economy of Mass Media", available at http://econ.lse.ac.uk/staff/prat/papers/mediasurvey11.pdf

Besley, T. and Prat, A. (2006) "Handcuffs for the Grabbing Hand? Media Capture and Government Accountability", *American Economic Review* 96(3), 720–736.

Brocas, I., Carrillo, J., and Wilkie, S. (2011) "A Theoretical Analysis of the Impact of Local Market Structure on the Range of Viewpoints Supplied", FCC Media Study No. 9, available at http://hraunfoss.fcc.gov/edocs_public/attachmatch/DOC-307525A1.pdf

Chiang, C. and Knight, B. (2011) "Media Bias and Influence: Evidence from Newspaper Endorsements", *Review of Economic Studies* 78(3), 795–820.

Competition Appeal Tribunal (2012) *In the Competition Appeal Tribunal; British Sky Broadcasting Limited et al. v. Office of Communications* (8 August 2012), available at http://www.catribunal.org.uk/238-7780/Judgment-Non-confidential-version.html

Crawford, G. and Yurukoglu, A. (2012) "The Welfare Effects of Bundling in Multichannel Television Markets", *American Economic Review* 102(2), 643–685.

DellaVigna, S. and Kaplan, E. (2007) "The Fox News Effect: Media Bias and Voting", *Quarterly Journal of Economics* 122(3), 1187–1233.

DellaVigna, S., Enikolopov, R., Mironova, V., Petrova, M., and Zhuravskaya, E. (2012) "Cross-border media and nationalism: Evidence from Serbian radio in Croatia", available at http://elsa.berkeley.edu/~sdellavi/wp/Croatian_paper_12_10_12V2.pdf

Djankov, S., McLiesh, C., Nenova, T., and Shleifer, A. (2003) "Who Owns the Media?", *Journal of Law and Economics* 46(2), 341–382.

Durante, R. and Knight, B. (2012) "Partisan Control, Media Bias, and Viewer Responses: Evidence from Berlusconi's Italy", *Journal of the European Economic Association* 10(3), 451–481.

Enikolopov, R., Petrova, M., and Zhuravskaya, E. (2011) "Media and Political Persuasion: Evidence from Russia", *American Economic Review* 101(7), 3253–3285.

Erb, J. (2011) "Local Information Programming and the Structure of Television Markets", FCC Media Study No. 4, available at http://hraunfoss.fcc.gov/edocs_public/attachmatch/DOC-308508A1.pdf and http://hraunfoss.fcc.gov/edocs_public/attachmatch/DOC-308507A1.pdf

Fan, Y. (2012) "Ownership Consolidation and Product Characteristics: A Study of the U.S. Daily Newspaper Market", *American Economic Review* (forthcoming), available at http://www-personal.umich.edu/~yingfan/DailyNewspaper_Fan.pdf

FCC (2012a) *Notice of Inquiry* in MB Docket No. 12-203, available at http://hraunfoss.fcc.gov/edocs_public/attachmatch/FCC-12-80A1.pdf

FCC (2012b) *Report on Cable Industry Prices*, MM Docket No. 92-266, available at http://hraunfoss.fcc.gov/edocs_public/attachmatch/DA-12-1322A1.pdf

FCC (2012c) *Report and Order* in MB Docket Nos. 12-68, 07-18, 05-192*; Further Notice of Proposed Rulemaking* in MB Docket No. 12-68*; Order on Reconsideration* in MB Docket No. 07-29, available at http://hraunfoss.fcc.gov/edocs_public/attachmatch/FCC-12-123A1.pdf

FCC (2011a) *Memorandum Opinion and Order* in MB Docket No. 10-56, available at http://hraunfoss.fcc.gov/edocs_public/attachmatch/FCC-11-4A1.doc

FCC (2011b) *Notice of Proposed Rulemaking* in MB Docket No. 10-71, available at http://hraunfoss.fcc.gov/edocs_public/attachmatch/FCC-11-31A1.pdf

FCC (2011c) *Report and Order and Further Notice of Proposed Rulemaking* in WC Docket No. 10-90; available at http://hraunfoss.fcc.gov/edocs_public/attachmatch/FCC-11-161A1.pdf

FCC (2011d) *Notice of Proposed Rulemaking* in MB Docket No. 09-182; available at http://hraunfoss.fcc.gov/edocs_public/attachmatch/FCC-11-186A1.pdf

FCC (2007) *Report and Order and Notice of Proposed Rulemaking* in MB Docket No. 07-198, available at http://hraunfoss.fcc.gov/edocs_public/attachmatch/FCC-07-169A1.pdf

FCC (1994) *Second Order on Reconsideration, Fourth Report and Order, and Fifth Notice of Proposed Rulemaking* in MM Docket 92-266, 8 FCC Rcd 5361 (1994).

FCC (1987) *Syracuse Peace Council*, 2 FCC Rcd 5043 (1987), *recon. denied*, 3 FCC Rcd 2035 (1988).

Gans, J. and Leigh, A. (2012) "How Partisan is the Press? Multiple Measures of Media Slant", *Economic Record* 88(280), 127–147.

Gentzkow, M. (2006) "Television and Voter Turnout", *Quarterly Journal of Economics* 121(3), 931–972.

Gentzkow, M. and Shapiro, J. (2010) "What Drives Media Slant? Evidence from U.S. Daily Newspapers", *Econometrica* 78(1), 35–71.

Gentzkow, M. and Shapiro, J. (2008) "Competition and Truth in the Market for News", *Journal of Economic Perspectives* 22(2), 133–154.

Gentzkow, M. and Shapiro, J. (2006) "Media Bias and Reputation", *Journal of Political Economy* 114(2), 280–316.
Gentzkow, M., Shapiro, J., and Sinkinson, M. (2012) "Competition and Ideological Diversity: Historical Evidence from US Newspapers", available at http://faculty.chicagobooth.edu/jesse.shapiro/research/competition.pdf
Gentzkow, M., Shapiro, J., and Sinkinson, M. (2011) "The Effect of Newspaper Entry and Exit on Electoral Politics", *American Economic Review* 101(7), 2980–3018.
George, L. and Oberholzer-Gee, F. (2011) "Diversity in Local Television News", FCC Media Study No. 8B, available at http://hraunfoss.fcc.gov/edocs_public/attachmatch/DOC-308602A1.pdf
George, L. and Waldfogel, J. (2006) "The New York Times and the Market for Local Newspapers", *American Economic Review* 96(1), 435–447.
George, L. and Waldfogel, J. (2003) "Who Affects Whom in Daily Newspaper Markets?", *Journal of Political Economy* 111(4), 765–784.
Goolsbee, A. and Petrin, A. (2004) "The Consumer Gains from Direct Broadcast Satellites and the Competition with Cable TV", *Econometrica* 72(2), 351–381.
Groseclose, T. and Milyo, J. (2005) "A Measure of Media Bias", *Quarterly Journal of Economics* 120(4), 1191–1237.
Hazlett, T. and Sosa, D. (1997) "Was the Fairness Doctrine a 'Chilling Effect'? Evidence from the Postderegulation Radio Market", *Journal of Legal Studies* 26(1), 279–301.
Hazlett, T. and Spitzer, M. (1997) *Public Policy Toward Cable Television*, Cambridge, MA: The MIT Press.
Hindman, M. (2011) "Less of the Same: The Lack of Local News on the Internet", FCC Media Study No. 6, available at http://hraunfoss.fcc.gov/edocs_public/attachmatch/DOC-307524A1.pdf
Ho, D. and Quinn, K. (2009) "Viewpoint Diversity and Media Consolidation: An Empirical Study", *Stanford Law Review* 61(4), 781–868.
Ho, D. and Quinn, K. (2008) "Measuring Explicit Political Positions of Media", *Quarterly Journal of Political Science* 3(4), 353–377.
Jensen, R. and Oster, E. (2009) "The Power of TV: Cable Television and Women's Status in India", *Quarterly Journal of Economics* 124(3), 1057–1094.
McMillan, J. and Zoido, P. (2004) "How to Subvert Democracy: Montesinos in Peru", *Journal of Economic Perspectives* 18(4), 69–82.
Milyo, J. (2007) "The Effects of Cross-Ownership on the Local Content and Political Slant of Local Television News", FCC Media Study 6, available at http://hraunfoss.fcc.gov/edocs_public/attachmatch/DA-07-3470A7.pdf
Mullainathan, S. and Shleifer, A. (2005) "The Market for News", *American Economic Review* 95(4), 1031–1053.
Oberholzer-Gee, F. and Waldfogel, J. (2009) "Media Markets and Localism: Does Local News en Espanol Boost Hispanic Voter Turnout?", *American Economic Review* 99(5), 2120–2128.
Oberholzer-Gee, F. and Waldfogel, J. (2005) "Strength in Numbers: Group Size and Political Mobilization", *Journal of Law and Economics* 48(1), 73–91.
OFCOM (2012a) "Licensing Local Television," available at http://stakeholders.ofcom.org.uk/binaries/consultations/localtv/statement/local-tv-statement.pdf
OFCOM (2012b) "Measuring Media Plurality: Supplementary advice to the Secretary of State for Culture, Media and Sport and the Leveson Inquiry," available at http://stakeholders.ofcom.org.uk/binaries/consultations/measuring-plurality/letters/advice.pdf
OFCOM (2011) *Public Service Broadcasting: Annual Report 2011*, available at http://stakeholders.ofcom.org.uk/binaries/broadcast/reviews-investigations/psb-review/psb2011/psb-summary-A.pdf
OFCOM (2010) "Pay TV statement," available at http://stakeholders.ofcom.org.uk/binaries/consultations/third_paytv/statement/paytv_statement.pdf

Olken, B. (2009) "Do Television and Radio Destroy Social Capital? Evidence from Indonesian Villages", *American Economic Journal: Applied Economics* 1(4), 1–33.
Owen, B. and Wildman, S. (1992) *Video Economics*, Cambridge, MA: Harvard University Press.
Polo, M. (2007) "Regulation for pluralism in media markets", in Seabright, P. and Von Hagen, J. (eds) *The Economic Regulation of Broadcasting Markets: Evolving Technology and Challenges for Policy*, Cambridge, UK: Cambridge University Press, pp. 50–188.
Schulhofer-Wohl, S. and Garrido, M. (2012) "Do Newspapers Matter? Short-Run and Long-Run Evidence from the Closure of the *Cincinnati Post*", available at http://www.minneapolisfed.org/research/sr/sr474.pdf
Seabright, P. and Von Hagen, J. (eds) (2007) *The Economic Regulation of Broadcasting Markets: Evolving Technology and Challenges for Policy*, Cambridge, UK: Cambridge University Press.
Seabright, P. and Weeds, H. (2007) "Competition and Market Power in Broadcasting: Where Are the Rents?", in Seabright, P. and Von Hagen, J. (eds) *The Economic Regulation of Broadcasting Markets: Evolving Technology and Challenges for Policy*, Cambridge: Cambridge University Press, pp. 47–80.
Shiman, D., Lynch, K., Stroup, C. and Almoguera, P. (2007) "News Operations", FCC Media Study No. 4, available at http://hraunfoss.fcc.gov/edocs_public/attachmatch/DA-07-3470A5.pdf
Siegelman, P. and Waldfogel, J. (2001) "Race and Radio: Preference Externalities, Minority Ownership, and the Provision of Programming to Minorities", in Baye, M. and Nelson, J. *Advances in Applied Microeconomics, Vol. 10*, Bingley, UK: Emerald Group, pp. 73–107.
Snyder, J. and Stromberg, D. (2010) "Press Coverage and Political Accountability", *Journal of Political Economy* 118(2), 355–408.
Stromberg, D. (2004) "Radio's Impact on Public Spending", *Quarterly Journal of Economics* 119(1), 189–221.
Vavreck, L., Jackman, S., and Lewis, J. (2011) "How the Ownership Structure of Media Markets Affects Civic Engagement and Political Knowledge, 2006-2008", FCC Media Study No. 3, available at http://hraunfoss.fcc.gov/edocs_public/attachmatch/DOC-307466A1.pdf
Waldfogel, J. (2011) "Radio Station Ownership Structure and the Provision of Programming to Minority Audiences: Evidence from 2005–2009", FCC Media Study No. 7, available at http://hraunfoss.fcc.gov/edocs_public/attachmatch/DOC-308591A1.pdf
Waldfogel, J. (2002) "Consumer Substitution Among Media", FCC Media Ownership Working Group Study 3, available at http://transition.fcc.gov/ownership/materials/already-released/consumer090002.pdf
Wise, A. and Duwadi, K. (2005) "Competition between Cable Television and Direct Broadcast Satellite – It's More Complicated than You Think", FCC Media Bureau Staff Research Paper 1, available at http:// hraunfoss.fcc.gov/edocs_public/attachmatch/DOC-255869A1.pdf

14. Media economics in competition law

Tom Björkroth and Mikko Grönlund

Economic reasoning has always been an integral part of antitrust analysis. This is natural as competition law is essentially founded on results derived from economic theory and addresses questions that have economic characteristics. Economics has, as many sciences do, different schools of thought, or doctrines, which may influence the approach to and assessment of a particular economic phenomenon both over time and across jurisdictions. Consequently, the implementation of competition law and policy may be significantly affected by influences from contemporary schools of thought.[1]

According to Owers et al. (1998) the term "media economics" refers to the business operations and activities of firms producing and selling output into various media industries. For the purpose of this chapter we may be a bit more specific and refer to media economics as a branch of economics that applies prevalent theories and methods of economic sciences on media sectors.[2] Therefore, this chapter wants rather to highlight the importance of the special features of media markets and of the field of research for antitrust analysis, rather than the importance of approaches that have sprung off the traditional industrial organization. This is in fact to underline the notion by Shapiro and Varian (1998) that the fundamental principles of economic theory do hold irrespective of the sector they are applied to.[3] However, for the purpose of this chapter it is useful to let the concept of antitrust define the relevant features, phenomena and issues to consider from the viewpoint of media economics.

ANTITRUST LAW AND ECONOMICS

What we refer to as antitrust is in fact a part of the broader implementation of competition policy and therein also of competition law. National competition authorities (NCAs) are responsible for the implementation of competition law at the national level. The competition law in European Union Member States must not be in conflict with the competition rules set out in the Treaty on the Functioning of the European Union (TFEU) and the national laws are to a high degree harmonized with the relevant articles in the TFEU. On one hand this, together with the cooperation between the NCAs, strives to ensure a uniform application of competition rules throughout the Member States in a way that is in line with the decision practices of the European Commission and adheres to the case law (judgements of Court of First Instance, CFI and European Court of Justice, ECJ) and the guidelines issued by the European Commission.

Consequently, the principles and methods of economic analysis of alleged infringements of competition law tend to converge, although the pace of development and sophistication varies across jurisdictions.

As a result, a natural focus of this chapter is to compile the European experiences of the use of media economics or economics of industrial organization applied to the media sector.

ON EUROPEAN COMPETITION LAW

To review the entire EU, US or any national competition law is beyond scope of this chapter. One should however note that the main constituents of EU competition law are Articles 101, 102 of TFEU. Legislation also includes the case law, that is, the decisions of Courts (Court of First Instance and European Court of Justice). The guidelines of the European Commission on how to interpret Articles 101 and 102, for example, can also be seen as a part of the legislation, whereas guidance or discussions are not as binding in a legal or economic assessment.[4] At the national level, the NCAs' decisions and practices should comply with the national competition laws. The interpretations and matters of procedure are in addition to EU law, guided by the preparatory documents (government propositions to the Parliament of the enacted legislation), and by the guidelines provided by the NCAs.[5]

An overarching principle in the EU competition law is the principle of a single market. Agreements or conducts that threaten this principle are likely to be in conflict with competition law. An excellent example that illustrates the case of this principle is the case where the Court ruled in favour of a UK pub owner, defending her right to show satellite broadcasting using equipment purchased outside the UK, but within the EU.[6]

European competition law differs from competition law in the United States, which makes it worthwhile to highlight the transatlantic differences and competition law relevant for media sectors.

ANTITRUST LAWS IN THE US

Competition law is known in the United States as "antitrust law", which consists of a number of federal Acts. The first antitrust law, the Sherman Act, was passed by the Congress as early as 1890 as a "comprehensive charter of economic liberty aimed at preserving free and unfettered competition as the rule of trade." In 1914, the Congress passed two additional antitrust laws: the Federal Trade Commission Act, which created the Federal Trade Commission (FTC), and the Clayton Act. These three Acts, with the subsequent amendments, constitute the core federal antitrust laws still in effect today.[7]

The Sherman Act (Sherman Act, July 2, 1890, ch. 647, 26 Stat. 209, 15 U.S.C. § 1–7) outlaws "every contract, combination, or conspiracy in restraint of trade," and any "monopolization, attempted monopolization, or conspiracy or combination to monopolize." Subsequent court decisions have meant that the Sherman Act does not prohibit all restraints of trade, but only those that do this in an unreasonable fashion. The competitive harm of some restraints is considered so serious and universal, that they constitute a per se violation of the Sherman Act (for example, arrangements among competing individuals or businesses to fix prices, divide markets, or to rig bids).[8]

The Federal Trade Commission Act (15 U.S.C §§ 41–58, as amended) bans "unfair methods of competition" and "unfair or deceptive acts or practices." According to the Supreme Court all violations of the Sherman Act also violate the FTC Act. This is of practical importance as it can bring cases under the FTC Act against the same kinds of activities that violate the Sherman Act. The FTC Act also reaches other practices that harm competition, but that may not fit precisely into categories of conduct formally prohibited by the Sherman Act.

The Clayton Act is a civil statute, carrying no criminal penalties. It addresses those specific practices that the Sherman Act does not clearly prohibit, such as mergers and interlocking directorates (that is, competing firms having the same persons in the decision making bodies). Mergers that may lessen or distort competition, or create monopolies are prohibited by (Section 7 of) the Clayton Act. Moreover, the Robinson-Patman Act of 1936 (or Anti-Price Discrimination Act, Pub. L. No. 74-692, 49 Stat. 1526 (codified at 15 U.S.C. § 13)) amended the Clayton Act to include bans of certain discriminatory prices, services, and allowances in dealings between merchants.[9] The Clayton Act also authorizes private parties to sue for triple damages when they have been harmed by conduct that violates either the Sherman or Clayton Act and to obtain a court order prohibiting the anticompetitive practice in the future.[10] The US Department of Justice and the Federal Trade Commission have also issued guidelines on the assessment of horizontal mergers.[11]

DISTINCTIVE FEATURES OF MEDIA SECTORS COMPARED WITH TRADITIONAL INDUSTRIES

Many media products or services, especially those that bring together audience and advertisers, are usually referred to as platforms that form a basis for two-sided markets. In two-sided markets, successful media get both readers and advertisers "on board".[12] The two-sidedness poses challenges to antitrust analysis which, if not addressed properly, might lead to serious difference of opinion in the market definition phase. The interrelatedness of the two sides cannot be disregarded in the other parts of the analysis either.

Another of the numerous special features of the media sector is the role of public sector and public interest. National broadcasting services have traditionally been regulated and to a large extent controlled by publicly owned enterprises. Technological development and deregulation has contributed to shape these markets into mixed oligopolies, where public service and commercial broadcasting coexist. Due to the differences in the rationale of operation, this constellation can raise issues regarding competition neutrality, or the existence of a level playing field between the firms in the marketplace. Government financed public services may raise doubts that state aid can be used to distort competition neutrality in these markets. However, from an EU perspective, the Member States are provided with relatively large discretion defining the scale, scope and ways of financing the public service provision.[13] However, once the scope of public service has been well defined, the scope for competition is determined by the scarcity of bandwidth or the availability of licences. A related question concerns how the policies associated with the allocation of licenses can be managed in a fair and efficient manner from a competition point of view. Issues like democracy, voice and pluralism are important when considering the configuration of media landscape, or "the marketplace of ideas".

APPLICATION OF MEDIA ECONOMICS IN ANTITRUST

In principle, antitrust cases can be divided into restrictions of competition by object and by effect.[14] The former refer to cases or conduct that are assessed to be harmful as such (or per se), and no analysis of effects is required. Naked cartels are a good example of pure by object cases. However, once an alleged infringement of competition law is not a clear-cut by object case, the evaluation of the infringement has to be based on an assessment of the effects of the alleged infringement on competition.[15] This is where qualitative or quantitative economic analysis steps in. In practice this assessment shares a number of features with the assessment performed in merger cases, that is, definition of the relevant market and the theory of harm, backed up by empirical evidence whenever needed.

It is fair to say that the role of economic theory and empirical methods has increased during the last decades. This has been clearly visible in the "more economic approach" of the European Commission, which underlines the importance of a by effect approach or a case by case economic analysis.[16]

Abuse of dominance is another topical issue in antitrust. In addition to the need to define the relevant markets, establishing dominance requires a solid theory and evidence that a firm has market power. In law, dominance is defined as a firm's ability to act independently (enough) of its competitors and consumers. In economics market power manifests itself as a possibility to price above costs. As empirical modelling to assess market power often provides a fragile ground for decision making, a shortcut has been to assess dominance in terms of market shares. Although there is no single universal threshold for dominance, literature reports this being located somewhere between 40 and 60 per cent. This is of course highly dependent on the particular market configuration and the prevailing institutional setting. In the UK, the Competition Commission has indicated the threshold being as low as 8 per cent in some markets.[17]

In addition to the issues of dominance and abuse of dominant position, antitrust enforcement also covers detection and prosecution of cartels or practices that facilitate collusion between undertakings. Moreover, the merger control is to be regarded as a proactive implementation of competition policy, because the goal is to assess the effects of mergers on competition and, if necessary, block the merger or require commitments that remove the existing concerns.

Competition advocacy involves both proactive and reactive elements, as it can try to influence the law drafting process, where required, to give proper consideration to competition issues. The reactive element stems from initiatives taken to change existing regulation to better respond to or enable workable competition.

MARKET DEFINITION – A KEYSTONE OF THE ARGUMENTATION CONSTRUCT

There is hardly an antitrust case which does not at some stage require the definition of what in competition law jargon are called the relevant product market and the relevant geographic market.[18] This is a common bone of contention in antitrust analysis and many intellectual constructs of the parties stand or fall by their market definition efforts. Therefore it deserves special attention in this chapter. The European Commission has published extensive reports on market definition in the media sector,[19] including a comparative legal analysis.[20]

The Relevant Product Market

In the definition of product market, and in the competition law operating environment in general, for a relatively long time we have been accustomed to the SSNIP test way of thinking – in other words, the product market has been very well defined when such a group of commodities has been found where individual commodities substitute one another, and the prices for them can be raised profitably by 5–10 per cent without consumers looking for alternatives outside this group to any greater extent.[21] The principle sounds easy, but its practical implementation may well lead to considerable differences of opinion between the parties involved: for example, whether current price levels are too high or even too low to carry out the SSNIP test. An unbiased estimate of the demand function in the broad product space is a demanding task for trained scientists, but the spirit of the SSNIP test may come into its own in other less arduous or inconsistent analyses.

But let us return for a moment to the purpose of defining a market. In 1985 George Stigler and Robert Sherwin summarized this as follows (p. 558):

> The purpose of the market definition is to identify the sellers and buyers who establish the price for the product in the area. It is not a purpose of the market definition to determine whether the market is competitive or monopolistic, although the determination of the market is usually an essential step in that investigation.

This summarized view covers the product market definition as well as its regional dimension. A number of Commission decisions may illustrate the points mentioned above. For printed media the market delineation is affected by the substitution between different printed media according to the characteristics such as content, frequency and not least the quality of the product (*Recoletos/UNEDISA*[22]).

Wegener/PCM[23] is a good example of the Commission's approach to product market definition. Although the definition is left open due to assumed negligible impact of the concentration, it provides an idea of substitutability between different newspapers. The Commission concludes (Section 19) that, although free newspapers influence the degree of penetration of paid for newspapers and can constitute a competitive constraint, paid for newspapers do not belong to the same product market as free newspapers. Furthermore the decision identifies the subcategories of the paid newspapers as these can be divided into: "a market for regional newspapers which are in competition with regional editions of national newspapers, and a market for national newspapers which includes national newspapers with regional editions and national newspapers without regional editions." It is also recognized that the market could be further subdivided into specialized newspapers and general information newspapers.

The extent of the product market can also be affected by factors such as periodicity, style, presentation, and price.[24]

Regarding the substitution between different media, attention has to be paid to what extent the market is characterized by inter-media competition. These points are illustrated in the Commission decisions in cases *Grüner+JAHR/Financial Times*[25] and in *Newspaper Publishing*.[26]

However, the Commission decision in *Recoletos/UNEDISA* implies that TV and radio broadcasting should not be regarded as substitutes for printed media concerning the range and depth of the information provided. This highlights the distinction between the two sides of a market as these conclusions need not hold regarding the substitutability between different media as advertising channels.

Regarding demand substitution, it is not uncommon that the relevant product markets are quite narrow and scattered according to characteristics such as frequency, content and their scope on local service.

Looking at the advertising side of the market the Commission's past decisions[27] reveal two possible ways to delineate it. The first way is on the basis of the topic of the relevant magazines in relation to the reader market and the second way is the so called 25 per cent test (according to this test, two magazines can be regarded as belonging to the same advertising market when they have at least 25 per cent of advertisers in common). In this respect, the Commission has recently declined to use the 25 per cent test as the sole criterion for delineating advertising markets for magazines.[28]

In the United States, case law provides an example of employing well-established principles of market delineation; see Community Publishers, Inc. v. Donrey Corp., 892 F. Supp. 1146, 1153-55 (W.D. Ark. 1995). In this case too however, the correct market definition seems to be a matter of disagreement.[29]

In electronic advertising the European Commission has established a distinction between online and offline advertising. See Commission decisions in cases IV/JV.1 – Telia/Telenor/Schibstedt of 27 May 1998, IV/M.1439 Telia/Telenor of 3 October 1999 and IV/M.0048 Vodafone/Vivendi/Canal Plus of 20 July 2000 and Case No COMP/M.5051 – APW/ GMG/ Emap.[30]

Printing Industry

Printing of magazines represents a more traditional industry and is not associated with the multisidedness present in other parts of the media markets. In the decision in Bertelsmann/Springer/JV,[31] the Commission states that market investigation has shown that rotogravure printing can generally not be substituted by offset printing. Rotogravure printing is mainly used for large-volume print orders, that is, print orders with a big number of copies and pages, while the use of the offset method is largely restricted to smaller volumes.[32]

QUANTITATIVE METHODS

The idea of the hypothetical monopolist test or the SSNIP test rests upon own and cross price elasticities, which both determine the sensitivity of demand to price changes.[33] Once we have identified a set of products that are substitutable and whose price can profitably be increased 5 to 10 per cent, we have probably defined the relevant product market.

Estimating elasticities usually requires econometric estimation, which is not too frequently used when considering media markets. Argentesi and Ivaldi (2005) refer to a French case *SOCPRESSE/ Groupe Expresse-Expansion* as one of the rare occasions when elasticities have been obtained using econometric techniques. Estimates from econometric models are sensitive to specification errors in the models, which require thorough consideration in the modelling phase. Moreover, traditional modelling is argued to omit the simultaneous two-sidedness in media markets. Argentesi and Ivaldi (2005) suggest relieving this problem by estimating the following equation for newspaper demand with s denoting the market share:

$$\ln\left(s_j^N\right)-\ln\left(s_0^N\right)=x_j^N\beta^N-\alpha^N p_j^N+\gamma^N y_j^A+\varepsilon_j^N$$

where x_j^N is a vector including characteristics that affect the loyalty of the readers (longevity of publication, number of content pages and so on). The cover price is denoted by p_j^N. The quantity of advertising in the newspaper is represented by y_j^A while the ε represents the fixed effect. The advertising demand can be written as

$$\ln\left(s_j^A\right)-\ln\left(s_0^A\right)=x_j^A\beta^A-\alpha^A p_j^A+\gamma^A y_j^N+\varepsilon_j^N$$

where the vector x comprises variables related to the composition of the audience, variables concerning descriptive features of the newspaper. y_j^N stands for the newspaper *j*'s circulation, which may affect advertising demand. The idea is that the parameters γ capture the link between these two markets. According to Argentesi and Ivaldi, estimating the system above should overcome the problem with simultaneity and yield more correctly identified price sensitivity parameters. These parameters play a key role in proper market definition.

One less technical analysis to support the market definition which bears a close relationship with the own and cross price elasticities, is the use of diversion ratios.[34] Diversion ratios measure the substitutability between different products. This analysis is rather convenient as it can be based on surveys, although sensitive to proper interviewing techniques being used. Diversion ratios are used in merger analysis in order to estimate the unilateral effects of proposed mergers, but can contribute to definition of both product and geographic market definition. In case of differentiated products, which are usually the case in the media sector, the substitutability has to be determined from a consumer perspective.[35] The initial question for a consumer to answer is in principle: "How would your consumption change if the price level of this service (or product) increased by 5 to 10 per cent?" As percentage calculation is not always straightforward the question can be modified to monetary terms or even be formulated as: "How would your consumption change if this service (product) ceased to exist?" From the sample of answers it is fairly easy to infer which products are considered as substitutes to the product of interest and to what extent. From the background information of the respondents (how much do you spend annually on this service), one can estimate the diversion of purchasing power or total consumption between two products. It may also indicate differences in preferences of different consumer groups. Moreover, analysis of diversion ratios may reveal how many consumers (or how much purchasing power) will actually abandon the market altogether.

Suppose that the price of product A, which is supplied in Region I, increases by 5 per cent, with all other things being equal. The price increase results in a part of the sales (a quantity of 1000) being diverted to substitutes according to Figure 14.1.

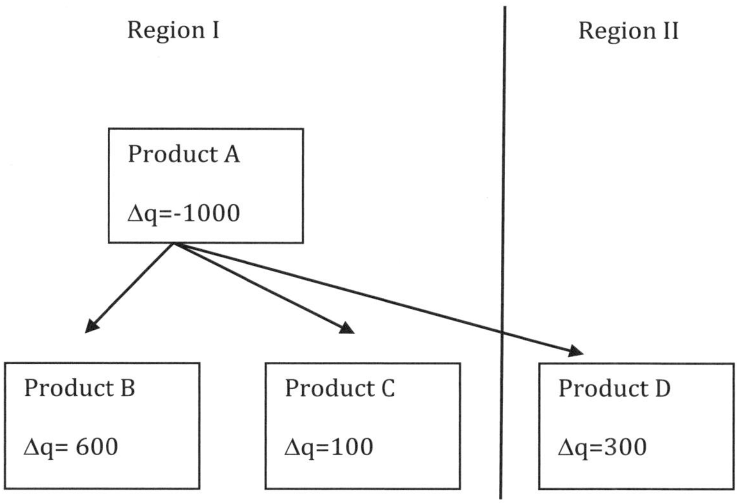

Figure 14.1 Diversion of sales as a result of price increase on product A

From this illustration we can see that the diversion ratio from product A to B, C and D is 60 per cent, 10 per cent and 30 per cent respectively. This would imply that the candidate market consists at least of products A and B, and possibly also product D. Note that we have let product D be supplied in or from Region II, so if product D is considered to impose a competitive constraint on product A, the geographic market should include the adjacent Regions I and II. The definition of the relevant geographic market will be considered in detail below.

Diversion ratios have a nice property in that they are defined as the quota between the cross price elasticity and own price elasticity of a product.[36] Therefore, if one knows two of these magnitudes, the third can be derived, although the confidence intervals may be considerable. The method of diversion ratios has recently been extended by Filistrucchi et al. (2014) to take into account two-sided markets. However, the interpretation of the diversion ratio requires thorough consideration, as is shown by Kate and Niels (2014).

Examples of Relevant Product Markets

As mentioned above, the nature of a media as a platform that in fact combines a number of markets can make an assessment very complicated if one is required to assess the broad range of dynamics and interactions simultaneously. Therefore market definition can be used to structure the assessment. In its decision on *Wegener-PCM* joint venture, the European Commission identified the following markets: the geographic market for the readers' market, the market for advertisement space, the market for printing newspapers and the market for distributing newspapers.[37]

It is possible that competition authorities distinguish between three different programme categories, that is to say news and current affairs programmes, special events and finally sports programmes according to the standards, practices and prohibitions relating to sponsorship of broadcasting services. Consequently, different markets may be assumed for TV productions based on the commercial relationship between the producers of TV programmes and the TV stations. There are examples of definitions of a separate product market for the licensing of sports programmes covering widely popular sports or major international events.[38]

In Ireland the Competition Authority delineated a general market for newspapers to be distinguished from radio and TV broadcasting. According to chapter 7 in the European Commission's report on market definition, analysis was conducted as follows: Newspapers comprising in principle three classes with regard to their quality, (i) up-market, (ii) middle-market and (iii) down-market had to be distinguished from both (iv) regional/provincial newspapers including so-called free sheets and from (v) magazines. The Authority distinguished between low-market or so-called tabloid on the one hand, and quality newspapers on the other hand. With regard shown to the similarity or homogeneity that still existed between the three categories originally mentioned, that is, up-market, middle- and down-market in the small Republic of Ireland, it cut the general newspaper market into just two and not into three individual sub-markets. Second, it drew a distinction between Sunday newspapers and daily papers despite the fact that some Saturday editions of dailies comprised many of the features typical of Sunday papers. Third, a distinction was drawn between morning and evening papers.

Relevant Geographic Market

The definition of the geographic market is an essential part of the overall definition of market, but, as illustrated above, it is not always totally separate from the product market definition.

The scope of a geographic market may have crucial importance, for example, for any conclusions drawn on the position of a company undergoing assessment or the effects of a merger or acquisition. Being assessed are, in principle, the same factors as in a product market definition: demand- and supply-side substitutability. Now, however, the matter is to be conceived as a mapping exercise in the spirit of the SSNIP test referred to earlier. In such a case, the question to be put is more or less this: can the price levels for a given group of commodities (products that can substitute one another) be profitably raised in a certain area or region by 5–10 per cent? We therefore want to discover whether there are any suggestions that, when prices go up, demand is not significantly targeted at local areas (or that the supply from local areas to the area or region in question does not significantly increase as a result of the price rise). If no significant price differentials have resulted, but they have not generated major trade flows, we have defined a relevant geographic market.

The extent of a geographic market also depends on the size of that area in which customers are able to make their purchases on the same terms and conditions. The most obvious example of such a case is the situation where companies buy their products, for example, on the basis of an invitation to tender that extends to the European Union.

For newspapers the question of geographic market definition relates to local or regional newspapers. In the UK the Office of Fair Trading addressed this question in its decision *Regional Independent Media Ltd and Gannett UK Ltd / Johnston Press Plc/Guardian Media Group*. In this decision the OFT distinguished so called "overlap areas", where one or several competing newspapers had a share of circulation equal to or greater than 10 per cent.

Overlapping is also an issue in the competition between national newspapers and local newspapers. This is because the former do have "core areas" of distribution (such as large cities), which overlap with the area of circulation of the local papers. This was illustrated in the Italian case.

Methods

Diversion ratios can be of substantial help in defining the relevant geographic market. The question about what a consumer would do if the price of the product or service he is currently consuming increased, can also reveal a geographical pattern of substitution. Figure 14.1 could summarize the answers to such a survey. The rather large switching from product A to product D, indicates that these products are in the same relevant product market, and consequently Regions I and II can be thought of as belonging to the same geographic market. This conclusion is strengthened if a similar survey is performed in Region II, and the result indicates that consumers of product D (or some imaginary products E, F …) would respond to a price increase of these products by increasing their purchases of product A to C.

Shipment tests

A study of trade flows, which, according to economic theory, tend to erase any price differences in a given geographic market, can be a good indication of the extent of the geographic market. The ratio of exports to production in an area and the ratio of imports to the consumption in an area can be good indicators of the openness of a region. Openness is usually interpreted to mean that the region is part of a wider geographic market.

The extent of the geographic market can be affected by the time sensitiveness of the product printed.[39] In 2005 Pönni et al. conducted a comprehensive study that examined the competitiveness of the printing industry in Finland. Based on expert interviews and wider online-questionnaire responses[40] competition in the printing industry spreads out wider, the less time critical the product is. In book printing, especially in bigger print runs, the competition is very international and even global. In magazine printing the competition can be international within the transportation time of approximately 48 hours. On the other hand printing of daily newspapers is mainly local/regional, and competition in daily newspaper printing is at its widest scope national.

Indeed, although helpful, the shipments tests and actual trade flows are not always decisive in delineating the geographic market. This was shown in *Bertelsmann/Springer/JV*, where consideration was given to the possibility or ease with which customers could turn to supply from other areas. To quote (Point 15): "Advertisement printing for German customers is apparently to a large extent done in Germany. However, in spite of a lower import ratio for advertisement printing than for catalogue printing, German customers can easily turn to credible foreign printers."

As suggested by Pönni et al. (2006), time sensitiveness can indeed affect the geographic reach of supply substitution, and has therefore to be taken into account in the overall assessment of market definition. Such an overall assessment includes an analysis of the trade flows. Trade flows can be used to perform so called shipment tests.

Price tests

The competition authorities or involved parties rarely rely on a thorough SSNIP test for defining the geographic market. One reason for this may be that there are simpler methods available that are equally reliable in terms of the weight of evidence, and which are appropriate from the perspective of economy of procedure. One such is the critical loss analysis. On the other hand, the existence of some analyses that differ from the SSNIP test is due to the equally powerful notion that there is clear competitive interaction between two different areas. This has an obvious connection with the fact that, in a uniform geographic market area, the homogeneous conditions of competition can be said to prevail.

This idea has been put to use in the application of price tests in both the product market and geographic market definition. Traditionally, the aim has been to demonstrate that two regions lie in the same relevant market by means of price correlation tests, although the weight of evidence is often fairly unimpressive, mainly owing to the interpretative weaknesses associated with the test. Additional support is derived from methods that are closer to the analysis of homogeneous conditions of competition. The principle is simpler than practical analysis: you test the assumption that the relationship between prices in two separate geographical areas significantly deviates over time and in absolute terms from one standard value. If this assumption cannot be rejected, it is hard to accept the argument that there is a competitive link between some areas and that these areas are in the same relevant geographic market. In statistical terms, we speak about the non-stationary assumption in price relationships between regions. But at this point we need to be careful, because a rejection of the non-stationary assumption does not mean that the assumption of stationarity is to be accepted. This latter option calls for its very own test, of which the article written in 2002 by Mario Forni on the Italian milk market is a splendid example.

The notion of "uniform conditions of competition" should not be considered to be a sudden whim of economists or statisticians. They are also mentioned in the European Commission's Notice on the definition of relevant market (point 91), which also reflects earlier case law:

> The relevant geographic market comprises the area in which the undertakings concerned are involved in the supply and demand of products or services, in which the conditions of competition are sufficiently homogeneous and which can be distinguished from neighbouring areas because the conditions of competition are appreciably different in those area.

This is very well illustrated in the memorandum by Charles River Associates (CRA), which describes how price relationships were used to show that the geographic market for farmed salmon actually covers the European Community. This was the conclusion arrived at through an examination of the price relationship between salmon farmed in Scotland and Norway, which proved to be relatively constant. In addition, an analysis was conducted of the price in France and elsewhere in Europe of salmon farmed in Scotland, compared to its price in the UK, and these were also fairly constant, that is stationary. The analysis related to a merger or acquisition being considered by the Office of Fair Trading and the Competition Commission, which, in the end, was prohibited because of the impact on the fish feed market. The Competition Commission actually adopted the market definition. This approach is clearly linked to the notion of the "law of one price" and to a fairly easily comprehensible visualization of technical analysis, both of which speak in favour of it.

The idea that prices in two areas in the same market can move in parallel has also been tested from the perspective of what is known as co-integration. The thinking here is that, if areas are in the same geographic market, there must be long-term equilibrium between the prices for the same or substitute products sold in these areas. These analyses are somewhat more demanding to carry out as tests, because it is difficult to have access to sufficiently long time series and reliable data. Moreover, the test's probative value is weak, unless it is supplemented with other evaluations. Such a separately performed evaluation will lack any direct cause and effect assessment, which is also one of the drawbacks with correlation analysis. A classic example of confusing correlation and cause and effect might be the observation that there is a correlation between the stork population and the birth rate in an area.

Price tests based on notions of cause and effect are an excellent way to boost the credibility of the arguments put forward in the market definition. The fundamental idea with these tests to determine causality is that, first of all, an explanation has to be given, for example, of price Y in a given area with a certain number of background variables. Then it can be tested as to whether an increase in prices X in another area and their delays over time improve the performance of the explanatory model. The test is, and should be, conducted the other way round also. In this way it can be concluded whether X causes a change in Y, or if a change in Y is behind the changes in X. It is also possible that causality flows in both directions or that there is no link to be found.[41]

Examples of Relevant Geographic Market

In the European Commission decision practice, the geographic scope of TV broadcasting markets was often assessed to be national. This was due to differences in regulatory regimes, language barriers, cultural factors and copyright restrictions, with language clearly being the dominant factor. In its more recent decisions, the Commission has stuck to these market definitions with the exception of the Nordic member states.[42]

ASSESSMENT OF MARKET POWER OR DOMINANCE

Market Power and Dominance

A constellation like Figure 14.1 serves perhaps best in the definition of the relevant product and geographic market. It can be tempting to use such a framework in order to assess the market power or dominance of, say the firm that produces product A. This would however require knowledge of whether the unilateral price increase of product A is profitable. This, again, requires knowledge of the total production and the profit margin of product A. This is intuitively plausible, as a profit maximizing firm has no power or incentive to increase its profits, if increasing prices means losing money.

The two- or many-sidedness of the media sector complicates the assessment. Suppose that product A is only one side of the media market, circulation of a newspaper for example. A small significant non transitory increase in price of subscription or single copy could imply a loss of sales as depicted in Figure 14.1, but how do advertisers respond to this? Advertisers care about the household or reader penetration and therefore possible gains in revenue from a price increase on subscriptions can be (more than) offset by reductions in advertising revenues. This is a part of the bias that Argentesi and Ivaldi (2005) claim to follow from a too simplistic treatment of media markets.

A strong position in a narrowly defined market is tempting to define as a dominant position. In the context of newspaper circulation, for example, one should try to elaborate on the differences in conclusions that arise between relating the circulation growth to overall circulation of newspapers and setting the growth in circulation in relation to what seems to be the potential audience within a well-defined geographical area. If one takes a traditional way of analysing the market share of the leading newspaper in the narrowly defined newspaper market, the conclusion can be somewhat misleading. For example based on the circulation figures of the leading newspapers and the total circulation of all newspapers in that particular region, one might argue that the market share of the number one newspaper is increasing even if its circulation is declining. If we take a broader approach and take into account the total number of possible audience (for example number of households) the overall picture might be significantly different. For example if the number of potential audience is increasing but circulation of the leading newspaper is declining the household coverage of that newspaper is declining even though its market share in the narrowly defined market is still growing.

Abuse of Dominance

A firm may abuse its dominant position in a number of ways. The allegation may concern below cost pricing, rebate schemes or bundling of services, for example. The main point is that the behaviour of the dominant firm has as its intention or effect to foreclose rivals. When the allegation concerns predatory pricing, the antitrust analysis focuses on whether an "as efficient" firm as the dominant one, could survive in the market. The relevant cost benchmark used as reference may vary depending on the nature of the product or service in question. The standard approach has been to compare whether a price exceeds average variable cost. If not, a firm is thought to be making losses in the short run and failing to cover the variable costs of its operations. This test is referred to as the Areeda-Turner test. Once a dominant firm does not cover its variable cost, it is not necessary for the competition authorities to show proof of foreclosing intent of the predator. However, suppose that the price charged by the dominant firm covers the average variable cost, but still remains below average total cost. This does not necessarily provide a safe harbour for the dominant firm, if such a strategy can be shown to include a clear intent to foreclose rivals. Alternative cost benchmarks are long run average incremental cost, that is, the additions to costs from producing the services alleged to be priced in a predatory manner. A more novel approach than the above, builds on comparing the price charged with average avoidable cost (AAC). AAC is the unit cost that could have been avoided by not managing to sell the output subject to the predatory pricing. AAC includes the average variable cost for producing this output, but also any fixed costs that the firm incurred from this. The idea behind this test is to show that the dominant firm exposed itself to losses that it could have avoided. Pricing below the AAC benchmark is assumed to entail the intention of foreclosing the dominant firm's rivals.

In the UK, the OFT's BSkyB decisions[43] regarding alleged abuse of dominance show that the behaviour of a dominant firm should be considered abusive only when it actually has an anti-competitive effect or where such an effect is likely to occur.

Essential facilities, such as the delivery system, can raise allegations of the abuse of dominant position. A milestone decision in this regard is the preliminary ruling by ECJ (ECR I-7791) in the case *Oscar Bronner* (C-7/97). The judgment was a preliminary ruling requested by an Austrian court in a dispute between Oscar Bronner, the publisher of a newspaper, and Mediaprint, a large newspaper publisher and operator of a home delivery scheme. Oscar Bronner wished to be able to use Mediaprint's distribution scheme. Mediaprint did not consider that it had a duty to provide such access. The judgment was in Mediaprint's favour, on the principal grounds that the distribution network was not an essential facility. This was because it was not considered necessary for the companies like Oscar Bronner to have access to a home delivery network in order to be able to offer their product on the market.[44]

Exclusivity

A famous case from a media perspective was the battle between a British pub landlady Karen Murphy and the English Premier League over her use of a foreign satellite TV decoder to show live Premier League football games in her pub in Portsmouth. She had imported the satellite card from the Greek broadcaster NOVA, and paid only around a tenth of the fee normally charged by Sky.

Being fined almost £8,000, she brought the case to the European Court of Justice, which overthrew the decision. The judgement[45] of the ECJ reflects the weight given to the principle of a single market, in that it held that (to quote):

> national legislation which prohibits the import, sale or use of foreign decoder cards is contrary to the freedom to provide services and cannot be justified either in light of the objective of protecting intellectual property rights or by the objective of encouraging the public to attend football stadiums.

The judgement touches upon what one can claim copyright on and what can be considered to construct one's intellectual creation. The restriction was not justified in light of the objective of protecting intellectual property rights. According to the judgement the FAPL cannot claim copyright in the Premier League matches themselves, as those sporting events cannot be considered to be an author's own intellectual creation and, therefore, to be "works" for the purposes of copyright in the European Union.

The motivation behind the existing exclusivity may have been to confer comparable protection upon sporting events, but a prohibition on using foreign decoder cards was considered beyond what is necessary to ensure appropriate remuneration for the holders of the rights concerned.[46]

For similar reasons, a system of exclusive licences is also contrary to European Union competition law if the licence agreements prohibit the supply of decoder cards to television viewers who wish to watch the broadcasts outside the Member State for which the licence is granted.

It is true that European Union competition law does not, in principle, preclude a right holder from granting to a sole licensee the exclusive right to broadcast protected subject-matter by satellite, during a specified period, from a single Member State of broadcast or from a number of Member States of broadcast.

However, the licence agreements must not prohibit the broadcasters from effecting any cross-border provision of services that relates to the sporting events concerned, because such an agreement would enable each broadcaster to be granted absolute territorial exclusivity in the area covered by its licence, would therefore eliminate all competition between broadcasters in the field of those services and would thus partition the markets in accordance with national borders, which would be in conflict with the single market imperative.

ON DOMINANCE IN MERGER CONTROL

Merger control is usually based on either the so called dominance test or on the SLC (substantial lessening of competition),[47] or SIEC (significant impediment of effective competition). Blocking a merger under a dominance standard requires evidence of a creation or a strengthening of a dominant position of the merged entity. The other two tests take also into account the effect of a merger in "softening" the competition in the market following a merger. This softening can arise as a natural result of the decreasing number of firms, without any form of coordination. The SIEC and SLC standards devote much attention to the so called unilateral effects of mergers. According to Shapiro (1996), "The 1992 DOJ and FTC Merger Guidelines have placed important attention on the 'unilateral effects' of a merger", that is, the tendency of a horizontal merger to lead to higher prices simply by virtue of the fact that the merger will eliminate the direct competition between the two merging firms, even if all other firms in the market continue to compete independently.

The antitrust authorities nowadays apply tests for upward pricing pressure (UPP-test) or illustrative price rise (IPR-test), in order to intervene in mergers with high probability of substantial price rises.[48] Filistrucchi et al. (2012) show how the assessment of unilateral effects can be performed for two-sided markets.

Collusion Facilitating Practices

Multimarket contact

In emphasizing the regional character of newspapers in competition and market definition Argentesi and Ivaldi (2005) recognize an overlap between national and local papers at least in the core areas of national newspapers.[49] National newspapers have progressively increased the coverage of local events by introducing dedicated sections in the newspaper or, more recently, by bundling the national newspapers with local ones. The degree to which this intensifies the competition may ultimately depend on the ownership of newspapers and other media in the relevant geographical market. Focusing on the aspects of multimarket contact and on the configuration of the regional markets, may help us to see more clearly the competitive landscape of media markets. Multimarket contact may, for example, facilitate (tacit) collusion and lead to higher prices.[50] Fu (2003) showed that multimarket contacts in the newspaper industry may affect competition in both advertising and circulation.[51]

> The newspaper ownership consolidation, purposively or unintentionally, widens interaction amid the limited number of remaining market players. Extended market interdependence is conducive to collusion between firms. Paper firms which become acquainted this way are induced to avoid or reduce intrusion into each other's otherwise exclusive terrain.

Fu (2003) finds advertising prices to be significantly higher in newspapers with multimarket contacts. These results are in some contrast to results obtained from broadcasting markets. Using a panel data set on 248 geographic US radio broadcast markets, Waldfogel and Wulf (2006) find that multimarket contact has little effect on advertising prices.

Exchange of information

The horizontal guidelines[52] provide a basis for how to assess information exchanged between competitors. The economic reasoning rests on the application of dynamic game theory (Ivaldi et al. 2003), which has been developed to take into account the type of information exchanged (granularity and time perspective) (Overgaard and Møllgaard 2005)[53] as well as how it relates to markets with consumer switching costs (Björkroth 2010).[54]

In the Commission decision on the *Wegener-PCM* joint venture, the parties had to sign to a commitment that (Annex II section 2):

> The supervisory board shall ensure that the managing board does not share the information of the company relating to the composition of its turnover, particularly but not limited to the pricing of advertising space, special offers, etc., with its shareholders, except for the customary half year and annual figures.

CONCLUDING REMARKS

Antitrust and competition issues in media industries are exceedingly multidimensional and more complex than one might at first think.

Solid market definition, either relevant product or geographic, is crucial in competition and antitrust analysis. Both the quantitative and qualitative analysis applied in media economics provide foundation for that. Due to its versatile approaches, media economics works well in this context, irrespective of how one strikes the balance between quantitative and qualitative evidence. In the end, market definition can be thought of as a foundation of any argumentation construct in antitrust claims, which makes it an utterly critical and important exercise.

The characteristics of the two-sided markets combined with aspects of time sensitiveness increase the complexity of the analysis even more, and consequently accentuates the importance of thorough expertise in assessment of antitrust cases. Indeed, in the present complex media environment narrow market definitions and traditional ways of analysis are increasingly a source of disagreement.

New technologies (online) create new challenges in that they contribute to further increase the dynamics in an already swiftly changing sector. Consequently, an antitrust assessment calls for a weighing between the allocative inefficiencies in a static sense and the prospective dynamic efficiencies which can be obtained through product or process innovations. Moreover, the development and application of online technologies, for example, are apt to on their own part complicate the definition of relevant markets.

Summing up, the media sector serves as a good example of an area, where antitrust and competition analysis is required to swiftly understand and adopt state of the art analyses, be they qualitative or quantitative. Advances in media economics illustrates well the need for antitrust analysis to continue to precede beyond the traditional approach of market shares and ownership to take into account sector specific characteristics, such as the two-sided markets presence or joint ventures, for example.

NOTES

1. See Kovacic and Shapiro (2000).
2. This is in line with the attempts that have been made to formalize a definition of media economics. A traditional definition of economics is that it studies how people make choices to cope with scarcity (Parkin et al., 1997: 8). Accordingly, Picard (1989) argues media economics to be "concerned with how media operators meet the informational and entertainment wants and needs of audiences, advertisers and society with available resources" (1989: 7). Albarran's (1996) definition of media economics focuses on "how media industries use scarce resources to produce content… to satisfy various wants and needs" (1996: 5).
3. For example, "Ignore basic economic principles at your own risk. Technology changes. Economic laws do not" (Shapiro and Varian, 1998).
4. Examples of guidelines are: Guidelines on the assessment of horizontal mergers under the Council Regulation on the control of concentrations between undertakings, *Official Journal C 031 , 05/02/2004 p. 5–18;* Communication from the Commission – Guidelines on the applicability of Article 101 of the Treaty on the Functioning of the European Union to horizontal co-operation agreements, *Official Journal C 011, 14/01/2011 p. 1–72*; and Guidelines on vertical restraints: http://ec.europa.eu/competition/antitrust/legislation/guidelines_vertical_en.pdf.
5. For extensive presentation of European competition law see Jones and Sufrin (2004) and Whish (2009).
6. We will return to the case of the pub owner Karen Murphy in the text below.
7. The US antitrust laws proscribe unlawful mergers and business practices in general terms, leaving courts to decide which ones are illegal based on the facts of each case. The general applicability of these laws is illustrated by the FTC in that "… Courts have applied the antitrust laws to changing markets, from a time of horse and buggies to the present digital age." The unchanged basic objectives, to protect the process of competition for the benefit of consumers (low prices, high quality), and to provide for incentives for efficient operation of firms, have remained unchanged.
8. The penalties for violating the Sherman Act can be severe. Although most enforcement actions are civil, the Sherman Act is also a criminal law, and individuals and businesses that violate it may be prosecuted by the Department of Justice. Criminal prosecutions are typically limited to intentional and clear violations such as when competitors fix prices or rig bids. The Sherman Act imposes criminal penalties of up to $100 million for a corporation and $1 million for an individual, along with up to 10 years in prison. Under federal law, the maximum fine may be increased to twice

the amount the conspirators gained from the illegal acts or twice the money lost by the victims of the crime, if either of those amounts is over $100 million.

9. The Clayton Act was amended again in 1976 by the Hart-Scott-Rodino Antitrust Improvements Act to require companies planning large mergers or acquisitions to notify the government of their plans in advance.
10. In addition to these federal statutes, most states have antitrust laws that are enforced by state attorneys general or private plaintiffs. Many of these statutes are based on the federal antitrust laws.
11. Horizontal Merger Guidelines August 19th 2010. U.S. Department of Justice and Federal Trade Commission (http://www.ftc.gov/os/2010/08/100819hmg.pdf).
12. Evans (2003). For seminal contributions in the theory of two-sided markets see Rochet and Tirole (2003) and Armstrong (2006).
13. For an example of a Court decision regarding ways of financing public service broadcasting and state aid, see Case T-309/04 Commission v. Denmark's TV2.
14. See Whish (2009).
15. It would be an exaggeration to say that every case can easily be allocated into a "by object" or "by effect" box. Moreover, there may be differences between legal systems in what is considered a by object or per se infringement. This seems to be the case concerning resale price maintenance, for example, where EU competition law takes a much stricter stance than US Courts.
16. Gual, J., Hellwig, M., Perrot, A., Polo, M., Rey, P., Schmidt, K., Stenbacka, R. (2005) *Report by the EAGCP. An economic approach to Article 82*. Munich Discussion Paper No. 2005-26, Department of Economics, University of Munich.
17. The groceries and supermarkets code of practice concerns all supermarkets in the UK with a market share above 8 per cent (see OFT). In fact all UK retailers with groceries turnover in excess of £1 billion per year are included within its scope (Competition Commission, news release February 26, 2009).
18. ABA Section of Antitrust Law (2012) provides for an excellent compilation of examples from United States on market definition in newspaper and radio markets and in two-sided markets.
19. For a general view of and list of cases concerning market definition in media sectors see European Commission's Reports on market definitions in the media sector: Chapter 1, Media Market Definitions in EC Competition Law – Recent Developments, available at: http://ec.europa.eu/competition/sectors/media/documents/chapter_1_ec_final.pdf
20. European Commission (2003) Media Market Definitions. Comparative Legal Analysis Final Report (July/October 2003). Available at: http://ec.europa.eu/competition/sectors/media/documents/
21. A more detailed presentation on the principles of market definition is provided in Commission notice on the definition of relevant market for the purposes of Community competition law [Official Journal C 372 of 9.12.1997].
22. Case IV/M 1041 RECOLETOS / UNEDISA 09/02 1999.
23. Case No COMP/M.3817 – Wegener / PCM / JV 7.7.2005. Reference is made to cases Case N° IV/M.423 – Newspaper Publishing, Commission decision dated 14.03.1994; Case N° IV/M.665 – CEP/Groupe de la Cité, Commission decision dated 29/11/1995; Case N° IV/M.1455 – Gruner + Jahr/Financial Times, Commission decision dated 20/04/1999.
24. Commission decisions in Case COMP/M.3178 Bertelsmann/Springer and COMP/M.3197 Candover/Cinven/Bertelsmann-Springer.
25. Case IV/M 1455GRUNER+JAHR/FINANCIAL TIMES /JV 20.4.1999.
26. Case IV/M 423-NEWSPAPER PUBLISHING 14.3.1994.
27. Case COMP M. 3420 GIMD/Socpresse.

28. See the decision on joint venture *Case No COMP/M.4122-BURDA/HACHETTE/ JV26.4.2006*. http://ec.europa.eu/competition/mergers/cases/decisions/m4122_20060426_20310_en.pdf
29. http://caselaw.findlaw.com/us-8th-circuit/1097566.html. Section IV.
30. http://eur-lex.europa.eu/LexUriServ/LexUriServ.do?uri=CELEX:32008M5051:EN:HTML
31. Case COMP/M.3178 – Bertelsmann/Springer/JV.
32. http://eur-lex.europa.eu/LexUriServ/LexUriServ.do?uri=CELEX:32006D0171:EN:HTML
33. It can be useful to think of own price elasticity as the movement along the product's demand curve when its price changes. The cross price elasticity refers to shifts in this demand curve when the prices of substitutes or complementary goods are altered.
34. For a comprehensive treatment of the concept and use of diversion ratios, see Oxera (2009).
35. In the case of perfectly homogeneous goods, the diversion ratio can also be approximated with the help of firms' market shares. This is however not possible in the market definition exercise itself.
36. Shapiro (1996) notes that "If the unit sales of the merging brands are equal prior to the merger, the Diversion Ratio from Brand A to Brand B is equal to the cross elasticity of demand from Brand A to Brand B, divided by the own-price elasticity of demand for Brand A."
37. See http://eurlex.europa.eu/LexUriServ/LexUriServ.do?uri=CELEX:32005M3817:EN:HTML
38. Commission Decision of 11 June 1993, Case IV/32.150, [1993] OJ L179/23, EBU/Eurovision System and Commission Decision of 13 October 2000, Case COMP/M.2050, paragraph 17 Vivendi/Canal+/Seagram.
39. Picard and Grönlund (2003).
40. Eleven national and seven international expert interviews and 92 internet questionnaire responses from industry representatives.
41. Design as well as interpretation of causality test needs to be performed carefully. The example provided here is actually one of precedence or predictability, which should not be confused with it being a solid theory of cause and effect. Without proper care taken, one could end up stating that the massive purchase of Christmas presents causes Christmas.
42. Commission Decision, Case COMP/M.3411, 17 May 2004.
43. The decision of 2002 concerned bundling of channels and the rebates given on the rates charged to distributors of its premium television channels (OFT decision, 17 December 2002). See Whish (2009: 729).
44. http://eur-lex.europa.eu/LexUriServ/LexUriServ.do?uri=CELEX:61997J0007:EN:HTML
45. Judgment in Cases C-403/08 and C-429/08 Football Association Premier League and Others v QC Leisure and Others Karen Murphy v Media Protection Services Ltd.
46. In this regard, the Court observes, first, that when calculating such appropriate remuneration it is possible to take account of the actual and potential audience both in the Member State of broadcast and in any other Member State where the broadcasts are received, and that it is thus not necessary to limit the free movement of services within the European Union. Second, payment by the television stations of a premium in order to ensure themselves absolute territorial exclusivity goes beyond what is necessary to ensure the right holders appropriate remuneration, because such a practice may result in artificial price differences between the partitioned national markets. Such partitioning and such an artificial price difference are irreconcilable with the fundamental aim of the Treaty, which is completion of the internal market.

47. On the application of SLC see e.g. the OFT decision Completed acquisition by Johnston Press plc of Local Press Ltd. http://www.oft.gov.uk/OFTwork/mergers/decisions/2006/johnston2
48. For a comprehensive illustration of the unilateral effects see for example Oxera (2010).
49. To quote (p. 5): "Therefore, at least from a demand-side perspective, printed media markets are usually segmented in relatively tiny sub-markets according to their frequency, content, and local characterization."
50. C.f. Bernheim and Whinston (1990) and Parker and Röller (1997).
51. On effects of multimarket contact on prices in other industries, see for example Jans and Rosenbaum (1997) and Busse (2000). Prince and Simon (2009) find evidence that multimarket contact facilitates collusion not only in prices, but in quality of service as well.
52. Guidelines on the applicability of Article 101 of the Treaty on the Functioning of the European Union to horizontal co-operation agreements [Official Journal C 11 of 14.1.2011].
53. Overgaard and Møllgaard (2005).
54. Björkroth (2010).

REFERENCES

ABA Section of Antitrust Law (2012). *Market Definition in Antitrust-Theory and Case Studies.* American Bar Association.

Albarran, A. (1996). *Media Economics: Understanding Markets, Industries and Concepts.* Ames: Iowa State University Press.

Argentesi, E. & Ivaldi, M. (2005). Market definition in printed media industries. Lessons from Broadcasting. University of Bologna and University of Toulouse (IDEI) and CEPR.

Armstrong, M. (2006). Competition in two-sided markets. *RAND Journal of Economics* 37(3), 668–691.

Bernheim, B. & Whinston, M. (1990). Multimarket contact and collusive behavior. *RAND Journal of Economics* (21), Spring, 1–26.

Björkroth, T. (2010). Exchange of information and collusion – do consumer switching costs matter? *European Competition Journal* 6(1), 179–196.

Busse, M. (2000). Multimarket contract and price coordination in the cellular telephone industry. *Journal of Economics & Management Strategy* 9(3), 287–320.

Evans, D.S. (2003). The Antitrust Economics of Multi-Sided Platform Markets. *Yale Journal on Regulation* 20, 325–382.

Filistrucchi, L., Gerardin, D., van Damme, E. & Affeldt, P. (2014). Market definition in two-sided markets: theory and practice. *Journal of Competition Law & Economics* 10(2).

Filistrucchi, L., Klein, T.J. & Michielsen, T.O. (2012). Assessing unilateral merger effects in a two-sided market: An application to the Dutch daily newspaper market. *Journal of Competition Law and Economics* 1–33.

Forni, M. & Paba, S. (2002). Spillovers and the growth of local industries. *The Journal of Industrial Economics* 50(2), 151–171.

Fu, W.W. (2003). Multimarket contact of US newspaper chains: Circulation competition and market coordination. *Information Economics and Policy* 15(4), 501–519.

Ivaldi, M., Jullien, B., Rey, P., Seabright, P. & Tirole, J. (2003). The economics of tacit collusion. Final Report for DG Competition, European Commission. March.

Jans, I. and Rosenbaum, D.I. (1997). Multimarket contact and pricing: Evidence from the US cement industry. *International Journal of Industrial Organization* 15, 391–412.
Jones, A. and Sufrin, B. (2004). *EC Competition Law – Text, Cases, and Materials* (2nd ed.). Oxford University Press.
Kate, A. & Niels, G. (2014). The diversion story: resolving the ambiguities surrounding the concept of diversion ratio. *Journal of Competition Law & Economics* 10(2), 361–374.
Kovacic, W.E. & Shapiro, C. (2000). Antitrust policy: a century of economic and legal thinking. *Journal of Economic Perspectives* 14 (1), 43–60.
Overgaard, P.B. & Møllgaard, H.P. (2005). Information exchange, market transparency and dynamic oligopoly. Centre for Industrial Economics Discussion Papers 11-2005.
Owers, J., Carveth, R. & Alexander, A. (1998). An introduction to media economics theory and practice. In Alexander, A., Owers, J. & Carveth, R. (ed.) *Media Economics – Theory and Practice* (2nd ed.). Mahwah, NJ: Lawrence Erlbaum Associates, 1–44.
Oxera (2009). Diversion ratios: Why does it matter where customers go if a shop is closed? *Agenda Advancing Economics in Business*, February.
Oxera (2010). Best of both worlds? Innovative approaches to modeling merger price rises. *Agenda*, May.
Parker, P.M., & Röller, L.-H. (1997). Collusive conduct in duopolies: Multimarket contact and cross-ownership in the mobile telephone industry. *RAND Journal of Economics* 28 (2), 304–322.
Parkin, M., King, D.N., Powell, M., Matthews, K. & Matthews K.G.P. (1997). *Economics* (3rd ed.). Addison Wesley.
Picard, R.G. (1989). *Media Economics: Concepts and Issues*. Beverly Hills, CA: Sage.
Picard, R. & Grönlund, M. (2003). Temporal aspects of media distribution. In Albarran, A.B. & Arrese, A. (eds) *Time and Media Markets*. Mahwah, NJ: Lawrence Erlbaum Associates, 49–60.
Pönni, Veijo et al. (2006). *Suomalaisen painamisen kilpailukyky.* Turku School of Economics. Business Research and Development Centre. Media Group. Series B Research Reports. B 3/2006. Tampere.
Prince, J.T. & Simon, D.H. (2009). Multimarket contact and service quality: Evidence from on-time performance in the US airline industry. *Academy of Management Journal* 52, 336–354.
Rochet, J.-C., & Tirole, J. (2003). Platform competition in two-sided markets. *Journal of European Economic Association* 1, 990–1029.
Shapiro, C. (1996). Mergers with differentiated products. *Antitrust*, Spring, 23–40.
Shapiro, C. & Varian, H. (1998). *Information Rules*. Harvard Business School Press.
Stigler, G.J. & Sherwin, R.A. (1985). The extent of the market. *Journal of Law and Economics* 28(3), October, 555–585.
Waldfogel, J. & Wulf, J. (2006). Measuring the effect of multimarket contact on competition: Evidence from mergers following radio broadcast ownership deregulation. *Contributions to Economic Analysis and Policy* 5(1), Article 17.
Whish, R. (2009). *Competition Law* (6th ed.). Oxford University Press.

15. Economics and economic impact of copyright

Ruth Towse

With one or two notable exceptions, interest in the economics of copyright developed in the last quarter of the twentieth century, the period in which copying devices became widely used in various media – photocopying for printed material, cassettes then CD burners for music, video machines and time-shifting for TV and camcorders for filming films in cinemas. As newer and more powerful copying and distribution technologies developed so did large scale unlawful copying ('piracy') and that stimulated interest in the economic aspects of copyright. Subsequently, digitization has led to questioning of the role and feasibility of copyright as an economic incentive for creativity and to a search for business models that can promote markets for digital media products. These developments have proceeded hand in hand with the recognition of the contribution of the creative industries (cultural and media industries) to GDP in both developed and developing countries and the impact of copyright on economic growth.[1]

There are essentially three aspects to the economics of copyright: one, the application of economic theories to copyright; two, empirical measurement of the contribution to GDP and employment (the 'positive' side) of so-called copyright-based industries and of the impact of illegal uses or 'piracy' (the negative side) in those industries, reflecting a shift from purely legal concerns towards the recognition of the economic, social and political effects of copyright on the part of policy and policy-makers who look to economists for evidence. Third, the political economy aspects involved in changing copyright law and the international dimension.

ECONOMIC THEORY OF COPYRIGHT

Getting Copyright Works to Market

The general economic setting in which copyright operates is that an author creates an original work using her accumulated human capital and skill and in order to get it disseminated, she contracts with a publisher who turns the work into a marketable product. The underlying work is protected by copyright if it falls within the scope of the law (that is, a literary, dramatic, artistic, musical or other such work, including original databases); musical and audiovisual performances, broadcasts and sound recording are also part of the scope of copyright law as having a neighbouring right related to copyright and in some jurisdictions, design rights are part of copyright law. Thus the term 'author' covers a wide range of creators and the 'publisher' may be one of a host of intermediaries in the arts and media industries. The exclusive right to control the use of the work resides in the first place with the author who then contracts with the publisher in one way or another to use the work. Copyright is a bundle of rights covering reproduction, distribution, communication to the public by electronic means, public performance, rental and lending, and the various rights may be traded individually depending on the circumstances. Copyright protection in most developed countries now lasts for 70 years after the death of the author and 70 or more years from the date of fixation for sound recordings. The term of protection for any given work by an author depends on when in her lifetime it was created, so if a work was created when the author was 25 and she lived to be 75, the work is protected for 120 years.

Many copyright works have to be turned into a product to be sold or licensed by the publisher: a book is printed and bound before it can be sold and/or it is formatted for electronic delivery; a sound recording such as a CD or DVD requires a more complex process involving other rights holders – composers and lyricists, performers, sound recording makers, artists – and the publisher must obtain all the necessary rights for the product and bundle them together along with the physical materials to form the product. When it is sold on the market, the buyer is thus assured that the rights have been cleared and use of the underlying works is legal. In digital form, products are licensed in a variety of ways for legal use, depending on the business model (subscription, flat fee and so on) and on the limitations placed on the licensee's further use of the item, such as the number of downloads, ability to copy to several platforms, and so on.

Payment for the use of these rights is the reward to the author and is intended to provide an incentive for creating the work. The size of the reward is determined by the revenue it generates on the market and the type of contract that is made between author and publisher. The reward is an *ex post* payment causing the author to share the risk of success or otherwise on the market with the publisher; an advance of future royalties may be obtained as an *ex ante* payment that, however, does not reduce the risk.

Incentives and Disincentives

Before digitization and the spread of the Internet, copying of both the legal and illegal variety was limited in its economic effects. It is fair to say that the very few economists who considered it at all were on balance more worried about the anti-competitive aspects of copyright than anything else. Widely quoted is the dictum of the nineteenth century English lawyer and politician, Thomas Babington Macaulay who saw copyright as a necessary evil, though a 'tax on readers for the benefit of authors'. Plant (1934) was the first economist to analyze copyright law using modern economics and his conclusions make interesting reading today, even though the technical ability to copy about which he wrote was essentially reprinting by typesetting; that may strike modern readers as quaint but there had been wholesale copying of books and other printed material throughout the eighteenth and nineteenth centuries, first in Scotland and later in a major country sponsoring piracy, the USA! There was also widespread unauthorized copying of printed music. Even with the technological necessity to virtually start all over again to copy these works, piracy was an economic problem for authors and publishers and economic loss was not the only concern about unauthorized copying; the debasement of works and the author's reputation due to poor quality copying was also a major complaint.

Plant held the now unorthodox view that copyright encouraged over-production of works – too many books, too many authors and too many publishers – because by enabling the publisher to charge a monopoly price, copyright encouraged greater risk-taking. He acknowledged that the publishing business pooled risk by financing losers with successes – something widely recognized in the creative industries (Caves, 2000) – but turned it on its head by showing that the protection of copyright law merely led to more output of titles than the market would bear, though fewer copies of each. In contemporary economics this is moral hazard. In contemporary economics, though, the rationale for copyright is precisely the opposite – that a sub-optimal number of works would be produced without the incentive of the higher than competitive price that copyright makes possible. Plant thought that the monopoly afforded by 'lead time' of being first to market was sufficient incentive, a view that is reiterated even in the digital era by some economists for whom business models are the preferred incentive to copyright (for instance, Varian, 2005).

Successors to Plant, writing 50 years later, saw things differently: the publisher of the 'original', who was contracted to pay the author a royalty and bore other fixed costs, such as the cost of advertising the book or other copyrightable work, was vulnerable to competition by a 'copier' who would have to finance only the marginal cost of supplying copies and so could undercut the price of the original. Copyright was therefore required to protect the original publisher from losses which would force her out of the market, leading to under-production of copyright works (Novos and Waldman, 1984: Johnson, 1985). This view reflected Arrow's analysis of information goods in general, that having the characteristics of public goods, being non-rival and non-excludable, they were open to free-riding and only enforcement of copyright would provide excludability (Arrow, 1962). Copying technologies before digitization were not perfect, however, and the inferior quality of copies meant the original publisher had the advantage over the copier. Prior to the spread of the Internet, the copier would also have some expenses of marketing. Both have now radically changed.

Not all economists took that line, however. Landes and Posner (1989) focused not on the monopoly aspects of copyright but on its impact on what they called the 'cost of creation' – the transaction and search costs of creating new works since copyright makes it necessary for authors to ensure that they are not copying an existing work in creating a new one and that permission be obtained from the author and publisher for transformative use (a new edition, an arrangement of a musical work and so on). Their analysis reflected the view that cultural production is an evolutionary process in which new works reflect some element of the old. Landes and Posner adopted this approach to analyze the various features of copyright law – its scope, duration of the term and doctrines, such as fair use – as a way of providing a rationale for the law in terms of the balance between the incentive to create and the disincentive of transaction costs. This seminal article and Posner's book now in its eighth edition (Posner, 2010) became the cornerstone of the law and economics approach to copyright.

One thing most economists agree on is that copyright is a trade-off between the opposing forces of the incentive of reward offered by the exclusive right and the disincentive of the costs to which it gives rise. Put another way, copyright law is a second best solution to market failure in the market for information goods and as such, the case for changing it must be made on empirical evidence of net benefit. Still, not all economists agree that there is a case for copyright at all: Plant's view that copyright was mostly unnecessary or damaging and that as an alternative, grants could be made to high quality literary authors has been repeated in variations by Hurt and Schuchman (1966), Agarwal and Gort (2001) and Boldrin and Levine (2005).

Appropriability

In the 1980s, another line of argument against copyright was introduced by Liebowitz (1985), namely, that rewards could be obtained through the market without it. He applied this theory of 'indirect appropriability' to academic publishing, showing that publishers used price discrimination as a means of compensating for loss of sales due to photocopying: their ability to charge libraries a higher price than individual subscribers meant that revenues could be maintained. Besen (1986) utilized the same idea. Varian (2000) applied indirect appropriability to file-sharing showing that sharing could lead to an increase in the producer's profit if the transaction costs of sharing were less than the marginal costs of production, both of which would now be recognized as almost zero; besides practising price discrimination, consumers with differing tastes and budget have the option to share or buy; sharing allows the supplier to serve an otherwise neglected market segment.

Indirect appropriability was also taken up and applied to discussions about the impact of digital piracy on revenues, suggesting that in some fields, unauthorized use was beneficial as it acted as a form of advertising; this is still held to be the case for games and music (Peitz and Waelbroeck, 2006). Other writers have come to the same conclusion: Gayer and Shy (2006) demonstrate that unauthorized file-sharing in music may raise artists' incomes by increasing demand for their live performances (though publishers would not benefit unless they contracted to manage concerts). Takeyama (1994) applied the concept to network externalities from unauthorized copying of software, arguing that since consumers benefit from network externalities, they are willing to pay a higher price, encouraging producers to tolerate unauthorized use that increases the size of the network; thus unauthorized copying could both raise a firm's profit and improve social welfare. Liebowitz and Margolis (1995) rejected the interpretation, however, and ten years later in a symposium devoted to the appraisal of indirect appropriability, Liebowitz (2005) stated the view that while the concept had limited application in its day, it had been taken too far by some authors. Its main contribution had been to demonstrate that in some cases, copyright was not needed to protect revenues and market solutions could be found.[2]

The Royalty Contract

One of the institutional arrangements that often puzzle economists when they first confront copyright is the system of royalties. Given that copyright is supposed to be an incentive to create, is it rational that the author (or other creator or performer) has to wait, often some considerable time, for the publisher to collect revenues from sales before paying the royalty, on top of having already invested considerable time and other resources in creating the work before it is published? Moreover, the author is sharing the risk with the publisher who may not even be careful with the production and marketing of the work. After all, there is no requirement in copyright law that a royalty be paid – a flat fee could be paid upfront for the whole bundle of rights embodied in the work. Towse (1999) showed that a 'buy-out' contract offered different incentives and transaction costs than does a royalty contract; with the latter, the copyright holder – in this case musical performers – had the incentive to maintain quality of work over time and to co-operate with the publisher on publicity; however, royalty contracts are associated with higher transaction costs. By contrast, a buy-out has no such incentives (though it has low transaction costs) but it would only suit routine work for which the author or performer has no incentive to maintain quality; buy-outs are also to be found in situations where there is jointly produced work, such as happens in a chorus for a musical or opera, in which case the employment contract would then stipulate compensation for copyrightable work, such as public performances of sound recordings. This is not to be confused with the 'work-for-hire' situation analyzed by Landes and Posner (1989) which is familiar in some media industries, particularly the movie industry, whereby the copyright of employed workers belongs in the first instance to the producer or other employer who directs the work – obviously a way of lessening hold-ups (Chisholm, 1997; Caves, 2000).

In economic terms, a spot price would, in ideal circumstances, be equal to the discounted present value of the expected future earnings. Several factors make this unrealistic: first and foremost is the uncertainty surrounding any new creative product or venture in the media and creative industries. That alone would be sufficient to make the calculation difficult but another factor also comes into play, which is the asymmetric information between the author and the publisher: most authors seem to over-estimate their chances of success while the publisher has more knowledge of market conditions. Moreover, publishers are able to pool risk over a stable of authors while the author has a more limited repertoire or 'back catalogue' ('all her eggs in one basket', as the colloquial phrase has it) and time preference rates are likely to differ too, with the author likely to have a shorter and the publisher a longer perspective.[3] These factors apparently explain the preference authors and performers have for royalty over buy-out deals.[4]

In practice, royalty contracts depend upon the bargaining power of the author with the publisher, with the former typically being in the weaker position. That is because in general there are more authors and performers looking for an outlet for their work than there are publishers willing to take them on, a situation that has been analyzed by cultural economists working on artists' labour markets as one of excess supply. Though economists like to characterize contracting in principal agent terms – the creator as principal and the publisher as agent – this seems realistic only in the case of the relatively few superstar authors and performers; the rest are typically presented with a take it or leave it offer, which may well in fact 'take' too much in terms of rights (often requiring all rights, not just the relevant ones, to be transferred) in a standard contract. This is a familiar situation to academic authors for whom publishers, especially the journal publishers, demand all rights with no possibility of bargaining.[5] Standard royalty deals are a fixed (linear) percentage of the sale price, which is set by the publisher, often of 10–15 per cent depending on the medium, paid once or twice a year; established authors and performers may get a higher rate on a high sales volume and an advance on royalties. Caves (2000) explains these arrangements in terms of contract theory and provides many examples from a range of the creative industries.[6] Needless to say, the more complex the terms of a contract, the greater are the costs of transacting and enforcing it.

Administration of Copyright

In addition to studying copyright in general terms, a few economists have analyzed the operation of copyright collecting societies (Hollander, 1984; Besen et al., 1992; Towse, 2013a).[7] While the primary use of copyright material is controlled by contract between author and publisher, collecting societies (also called copyright management organizations) deal with secondary use situations in which it would be either impossible or too costly for the rights holder to contract with or even know the user. Typical situations are public performance of sound recordings, reuse of broadcasts, syndicated articles and photographs.

Collecting societies are membership organizations to which both authors and publishers working in a specific medium belong, and they manage a specific bundle of rights assigned to them by members. Due to the multiplicity of rights and media, and the fact that copyright is territorial (that is, it relates to a particular nation and is national law), every country has a number of such organizations. The functions they perform include the licensing of rights to various users, setting licence fees in accordance with the type and extent of the uses made (for instance, according to the capacity of a restaurant or sports hall playing music), distributing licence fee revenues and other sources of income, such as remuneration from statutory licences, monitoring use and enforcing rights. In addition to licensing domestic repertoire, collecting societies make international agreements with counterpart societies, and that allows the national society to license foreign repertoire as well.

By requiring rights holders to assign their rights to them, the collecting society typically offers a blanket licence to users, which it negotiates with trade bodies representing users. This system reduces transaction costs for both rights holder and user. It is therefore administratively efficient but it is not economically efficient since the same rate is paid to all members, with only the amount of use made of their works (which is reported in detail for large-scale users but estimated for others) determining the value of the reward distributed. Pricing does not reflect the greater value to users of individual works and authors; some commentators argue that collecting societies could license individually (Hollander, 1984; Katz, 2005); others have argued that the blanket licence is regarded as essential to the operations of collecting societies.[8]

The main economic feature of this system of administration is that the societies have monopoly power as sole suppliers of administration services. The monopoly is due to the considerable economies of scale and scope in joint management which are the basis of the natural monopoly. The high sunk costs of setting up the databases of works, rights owners and licensees act as a barrier to entry for a competitor and the assignment of exclusive rights to the society makes competition impossible without some form of compulsory licensing or similar statutory intervention. Average fixed costs fall without limit as more works and rights holders join and the marginal cost of administering one more work or membership are negligible, especially since this is now done by the member online. These advantages combined with the society's blanket licence seem to make them incontestable (Towse, 2012).

Needless to say, the societies' monopolies have attracted the attention of competition authorities in a number of countries and of the EU too. Where there have been formal enquiries and court cases, the natural monopoly is almost always accepted as being beneficial to rights holders and users as it reduces transaction costs of the copyright system (Gallini, 2011). Moreover, some form of state regulation is in place to curb excessive exercise of monopoly power in each jurisdiction, ranging in strength from a tribunal or ombudsman to oversight by a board, court or government department of the rates charged as licence fees.

MEASUREMENT OF THE CONTRIBUTION OF THE COPYRIGHT-BASED INDUSTRIES AND UNAUTHORIZED COPYING

We now switch from the microeconomic analysis of copyright to macroeconomic studies of the contribution of the copyright-based industries to GDP. In the 1980s and 1990s, interest developed in viewing industries in which copyright plays a significant role as a 'sector' of the economy and empirical estimates of its size and growth began to be measured. It was also claimed that these studies put a value on copyright. As unauthorized copying grew, especially after the development of P2P then MP3 technologies, measures of lost revenue began to be made, especially in the music industry as one of the first media industries to experience large scale file-sharing. Initially, many of these studies were undertaken at the behest of industry and other interest groups; later, measurement of the contribution of the creative industries came to be done by official statistical services. In this section, I discuss the main issues involved in making these estimates, the problems and how some of them have been resolved.

Nomenclature

There has been a certain amount of confusion about what to call this 'sector'. I use inverted commas here to indicate that (to my knowledge) no country has yet made this an official sector in its national income accounts; the creative industries form part of the service sector. Terms used vary from 'cultural' industries to 'copyright', 'copyright-based' or 'creative industries'. The significance is not so much in the name as in the output that is included according to one listing or another (Towse, 2010).

One of the first of these studies in the early 1980s appears to have been done in the Netherlands on behalf of a consortium of collecting societies. It specifically adopted the term 'copyright' industries and the purpose was to demonstrate to the government the economic importance of copyright. Its list of industries was press and literature, design, software, research, music and theatre, broadcasting, film and video, photography, multi-media, visual arts, and copyright and administration (van Asselt et al., 1997). Similarly, Siwek and Furchgott-Roth (1990) produced the first of 13 reports *Copyright Industries in the US Economy* (Siwek, 2011) for the International Intellectual Property Alliance (IIPA) of America, a lobbying organization whose role is to fight copyright theft. Though these reports purport to measure the value of copyright, in fact they simply assume that copyright is necessary for the generation of the GDP of these industries.

UNESCO, however, still retained the term used earlier, 'cultural' industries:

> The notion of cultural industries generally includes printing, publishing and multimedia, audio-visual, phonographic and cinematographic productions, as well as crafts and design. For some countries, this concept also embraces architecture, visual and performing arts, sports, manufacturing of musical instruments, advertising and cultural tourism. (UNESCO, 2000; 11)

The UK's short-lived 'Cool Britannia' branding exercise in the 1990s resulted in the *Creative Industries Mapping Document* published in 1998 by the Department of Culture, Media and Sport (DCMS), using as its definition 'those industries which have their origin in individual creativity, skill and talent and which have a potential for wealth and job creation through the generation and exploitation of intellectual property'. The DCMS list consisted of 13 industries – advertising, architecture, art and antiques, craft, design, designer fashion, film and video, interactive leisure software, music, performing arts, publishing, software, television and radio. The purpose of this exercise was to highlight the economic importance of the arts and culture in the UK in terms of its contribution to GDP and employment rather than (at the time) to stress the importance of copyright; however, it distinguished in 'layers' a hierarchy of creativity with a core consisting of primary creative activities, fanning out to the edges where manufactured products necessary for the creative activities in the other layers were included in the creative industries (Towse, 2001: 36). This list became the standard one for further work in the UK and the basis for such work elsewhere.

The distinction of 'core' and 'dependent' activities and products with the focus on copyright was solidified in the World Intellectual Property Organization (WIPO) *Guide on Surveying the Economic Contribution of the Copyright-Based Industries* (WIPO, 2003). In doing so, it followed the Siwek and Furchgott-Roth (1990) report which divided the copyright industries into four groups: core, partial, distribution and copyright related (these terms were changed after 2003 for compatibility with the WIPO *Guide*). The *Guide* identifies four categories: core copyright industries, interdependent industries, partial copyright industries and non-dedicated support industries. The distinction is based on the notion of a chain of production that starts with a core of creative content that then supports subsequent activities. The core can be readily entirely connected to copyright works but for the other categories it is necessary to estimate what proportion of their production is 'dependent' upon the core and so on along the chain of production to avoid double-counting and to correctly measure the gross value-added (GVA).

These variations in nomenclature and their implications are reviewed in the *Creative Economy Report 2008* jointly authored by UNESCO, WIPO and UNCTAD (UNCTAD, 2008). By 2008, the various terms used by different organizations – 'knowledge' economy, information age/ economy and so on had centred on the word 'creative'. None of this matters greatly to economists, however: the crucial issue is to adopt a 'reasonable' list of products and activities and use standard statistical measures to value them.

Measurement Issues

Though all economists understand the importance of using GVA in national income accounting, some of the early measures did not comply with this requirement, mostly due to the lack of available data. Instead turnover data were used, often supplied by industry bodies with little or no explanation of what exactly they represented. And though the purpose of national income accounts is simply to measure national income consistently without double-counting, the industry to which a particular set of goods and services is designated is what determines its 'economic impact' on GDP. The WIPO *Guide* recommended using the ISIC (International Standard Industrial Classification) for measuring the contribution of the copyright-based industries. That used to be very cumbersome but it has recently been revised with a new Section J 'Information and Communication'. The ISIC has ascending levels of detail (one-digit, two-digit, and so on) with four-digit as the most detailed in the ISIC Revision 4.[9] So, for example, Division 58, Publishing, includes: 581, Publishing of books, periodicals and other publishing activities; 5813, Publishing of newspapers, journals and periodicals. Division 59 is Motion picture, video and television programme production, sound recording and music publishing activities, including: 591, Motion picture, video and television programme activities; 5914, Motion picture projection activities. Renting of video tapes and disks, however, is far off in 7722; so, there is still room for manoeuvre, meaning that if aggrandizing the figures were the order of the day, that is where it would happen. What can be seen from these examples is that the 'core copyright' would be generously interpreted even using the four-digit level since these activities clearly include more than just content creation and copyright works.

A report commissioned by the UK Department of Culture, Media and Sport looked at a finer five-digit breakdown, which allowed a more detailed view of the 'creative core', that is, 'Writing, Acting, Filming, Performing, Composition, and Programming'. But value-added data are not available at the five-digit level in the UK and therefore, turnover data had to be used instead (Frontier Economics, 2007). However, applying the five-digit level data reduced the previously calculated contribution to GDP of 'core creative activities' in the same list of creative industries from 3.4 per cent to 2.7 per cent (and showed that over 40 per cent of that was in the software and games industries).

The new UN ISIC is a considerable improvement as a classification and as a guide to which items to include in measurements of the creative or copyright-based industries but the more difficult question is how many countries are able to adopt it and to do so with value-added figures. Data on 'employment' are even more difficult to obtain since many creators have multiple jobs, are self-employed and may not fit into one particular occupational category (see Towse, 2010: 472–3). But the system does not avoid the problem inherent in the WIPO *Guide* that industry data has to be manipulated by weights in order to isolate out the non-copyright element in interdependent, partial copyright and non-dedicated support industries, which is essentially a subjective exercise.

Moreover, changing the system of measurement risks losing consistent year on year comparisons that are needed for measuring the growth of the sector, a metric that is made much of politically: the higher growth rates of the creative industries are held to be the saviour of failing post-industrial economies that justifies increasing copyright protection. So, for example, the Siwek reports on the US referred to above used the North American Industrial Classification (NAIC) in preference to the ISIC, making international comparisons difficult between countries that operate other systems of measurement, something that the WIPO *Guide* set out to avert.[10]

Comparing Different Systems of Measurement

An interesting comparison between the earlier measures and the WIPO *Guide* system is an exercise that was undertaken in the Netherlands (where the SEO had consistently measured the growth of its classification of industries since the 1980s). In 2008, the SEO team was commissioned by the Ministry of Economic Affairs to follow the WIPO *Guide* methods and make the comparison with those of the 2003 study by SEO. Using the WIPO *Guide* methodology required a new configuration of National Income data and affected the results as follows: GVA as a percentage of

GDP in 2008 was 6.8 per cent, while the WIPO *Guide*-style figure was 5.9 per cent. For employment the comparison between the 2003 and 2008 methods was 6.2 per cent and 8.8 per cent respectively (Leenheer et al., 2008). Overall, therefore, the value of output was lower but employment was higher. Were these differences due to the different measurement system or to real changes in the cultural sector? That is precisely the issue!

Copyright Measured as Investment in Assets

In the last few years, a new paradigm of measurement of the economic importance of copyright has been developed, treating the creation of copyright works as investment in intangible capital assets in the National Income Accounts, rather than as income or output (Soloveichik, 2010; Goodridge and Haskel, 2011). Intangible capital consists of the original work of a film, television programme, musical and literary composition and so on that is the basis of the production of copies and other output, such as derivative works. These are labelled 'artistic originals' in the UK national accounts. This method is said to have the advantage of being consistent with measurement of other intangible capital, such as software and mineral exploration, that is already measured in GDP. It also avoids the issue of designating an activity to one industry and avoids the need to use a weighting to remove the non-copyright elements in output and therefore the risk of double-counting. Once the activities have been identified using cost of production as the measure of investment, the discounted future revenue can be calculated from income data. Goodridge and Haskel compare results from the standard national income accounting method of GVA and the intangibles method for the UK and find that 'artistic originals' were significantly underestimated in the national accounts although by the income method, DCMS over-estimated the contribution of the creative industries.[11] Whatever the improvement in accuracy of measurement, the economic effect of copyright as an incentive still is not established as a causal factor, as the authors point out.

Results of Measuring of the Contribution of Copyright to GDP

I have concentrated here on the problems of measurement rather than results because generally speaking, the interest for economists lies in the effect the system of measurement and the listing of industries has on the figures that are so gleefully bandied about rather than in the figures themselves. And it is worth noting that there is a political element to all this (Towse, 2004). Moreover, what the above demonstrates all too clearly is that without understanding the basis of the measurement, the resulting data cannot be correctly interpreted.

In general, the copyright or creative industries' contribution to GDP measured in GVA is substantial and has had growth rates above the national average, though these have been falling and even were in recession, reflecting the worldwide recession. In the US in 2010, the 'core' copyright industries produced 6.4 per cent of GDP in current dollar terms and the 'total' copyright industries 11 per cent (Siwek, 2011). The core copyright industries' real value-added grew at over 3 per cent in 2009/10 but had declined by 3 per cent in 2008/9; 'total' copyright industries grew at over 4 per cent in 2009/10 but had minus 2 per cent real growth in 2008/9. These industries employed 4 per cent of the total workforce in 2007 but that also fell with the recession. Some industries experienced sustained growth; the real annual growth rate of the US computer and video game software industry was 10.6 per cent for the period 2005–09. The picture in the UK was not dissimilar: in 2009, the creative industries' GVA represented 2.9 per cent of UK GDP with negative growth of 1 per cent over the previous year; employment was just over 5 per cent of total UK employment; however, by 2012 growth had returned at 9.4 percent from 2011/12 (DCMS, Key Findings, 2011, 2014).[12] In both countries, these industries make a significant contribution to exports. Of course, as explained in detail earlier, these figures are based on different ways of selecting the list of industries and their classification; they are not directly comparable and the figures can only be fully understood in terms of how they were measured. Nevertheless, they offer ballpark numbers to illustrate the effect of these industries on the US and UK economies.

WIPO (2012) provides an overview of 30 country studies using its 2003 *Guide* (WIPO, 2003). Though each attempts to use the same classification, it is unlikely that all had access to equally detailed data sources from the national income accounts and they probably are not strictly comparable. The data also apply to somewhat different years. According to the study, in 16 countries, the 'total' copyright industries contribute 5 per cent or more to GDP, with the USA and Australia exceeding 10 per cent. As to the 'core' industries, Australia, the USA and Panama exceed 5 per cent, nearly all being the more developed countries. There seems to be little pattern to other aspects studied, including that between GDP and employment; a labour productivity index does little to illuminate. In terms of the dominant industries, almost two-thirds of the combined contribution to GDP of the core copyright industries is due to Press and Publishing (40 per cent) and Software and Databases (23 per cent).

Measuring Piracy

Unauthorized use of copyright works, widely known as piracy, has also been subject to a multitude of measurement exercises by industry bodies, such as the International Federation of Phonographic Industries (IFPI) which produces raw data for sound recordings, by professional economists who are commissioned to make the case for such bodies and by academics who have sought to present an independent picture and also to explain causal effects. It hardly bears saying that all these measures are liable to one sort of bias or another since data sources on illegal use are difficult to research, so that results vary quite considerably. Handke (2012) has compiled a detailed review of this research, which mostly relates to the music industry. That said, there is a general consensus by economists that piracy has had an overall negative impact on revenues in the music industry and in other industries, such as software, which have, however, been less studied in the academic literature.

THE POLITICAL ECONOMY OF COPYRIGHT

Copyright has become a highly controversial and politicized topic. Lobby groups of all persuasions, many with powerful business interests and large purses, constantly lobby national governments, organizations such as the European Commission and international organizations with an interest in copyright (WIPO, UNCTAD, UNESCO) for stronger copyright protection and enforcement. There is a pro-piracy political party in Europe representing the other view and there are moderate pressure groups, such as those advocating open source, representing a range of interests seeking legal alternatives to stronger protection. Governments have become aware that the development of Internet and the widespread use of social media call for understanding the economic and social effects of copyright law, not just its purely legal aspects, and economists and other social scientists are increasingly consulted on changes to copyright law.

Digitization and the Internet have upset the economic effects of copyright; incumbent businesses in the creative industries have fought to retain their existing business models based on effective copyright enforcement, while new entrants claim that innovative business opportunities are being held back by outdated legal provisions and administration of copyright, particularly by collecting societies. Collecting societies, however, are regulated in various ways with pricing often subject to legal scrutiny. Governments scramble to adjudicate between opposing stakeholder interests and also to reconcile national interests with the terms of international copyright agreements, such as TRIPS, that have become indispensable for the globalization of trade in creative goods and services. One aspect of the adjudication process is the proliferation of enquiries into various aspects of reforming and implementing changes to copyright law; another is the commissioning of independent reports from economists in the hope that evidence will show a clear path through the thicket. Indeed, the WIPO *Guide*, discussed above, was intended to provide clear cut data for use as evidence in this process.

The UK has had three independent enquiries into the role of copyright as part of the wider intellectual property (IP) framework of patents, trademarks and design rights – Gowers (2006), Hargreaves (2011) and Hooper (2012a, b). Each had a somewhat different thrust: Gowers was set up to consider if the whole IP system was fit for purpose in an era of globalization, digitization and increasing economic specialization; Hargreaves was asked to consider whether the IP framework was sufficiently well designed to promote innovation and growth in the UK economy. One of the Hargreaves recommendations was that a Digital Copyright Exchange be set up and that was then investigated by Hooper. Similar enquiries are afoot elsewhere. The European Union has a proposed Directive on collective management of copyright and related rights and multi-territorial licensing of rights in musical works for online uses in the internal market (EC, 2012). Similar enquiries are underway elsewhere in the world and no doubt more will follow. Each involves calls for evidence, stakeholder submissions and lobbying, independent evaluations and so on as part of the business of making and changing the law. Needless to say, these enquiries are costly in terms of both the expenditure on the exercise itself and the time taken by stakeholders and other organizations in responding, and as a result, the better funded and more voluble are more effective in making their claims. They encourage rent-seeking over research, something that Hargreaves labelled 'lobbynomics'. Nor, in my view, do these enquiries get at the question at the heart of the economics of copyright, namely the incentive to create novel content without which the cultural and media industries would simply end up regurgitating back catalogue (Towse, 2011). The Intellectual Property Office (IPO) that had the task of dealing with the submissions to the Hargreaves Report later issued guidelines to set a standard for what they are prepared to consider as evidence; evidence must be clearly stated, must be independently verifiable and capable of being peer reviewed (Mitra-Khan, 2011; Towse, 2013b).

Another feature of the politicization of copyright is the effect of international harmonization of copyright on national law. A notable example is the 2007 EC proposal that the 50 year term of protection for sound recordings and performers' rights in sound recordings should be extended to 95 years. The Gowers Report recommended the UK government should resist; it did so on the basis of strong economic evidence that the move would not achieve the claims made for it, namely that it would benefit performers great and small (Gowers, 2006, pp. 52–57). Indeed a group of prominent economists (Akerlof et al., 2002) had tried (but failed) to resist the US government's own Copyright Term Extension Act (CTEA) extending copyright in sound recordings to 95 years, which undoubtedly led to pressure on the EU to conform. The EC eventually settled for a 70 year extension from the previous 50 years from the date of fixation of a work, to which the UK government eventually consented and which has to be implemented by every member state. It is worth pointing out that extending the term of copyright is equated in the minds of many interest groups as 'increasing protection'; the result is the terms are always increased, never reduced, though most economists believe present day terms to be excessive (Gowers, 2006).

CONCLUSION

This chapter demonstrated that the economic theory of copyright and its administration is well developed; with the overall conclusion that copyright is a trade-off between the economic incentive and transaction costs, however, the burden falls to empirical evidence as a guide to policy-making. It has been shown that attempting to measure the economic benefits of copyright is complex and frequently unsatisfactory and that even where evidence does exist, political considerations in policy-making may override economic evidence. That is no reason to give up on empirical research on the economics of copyright but it has proved a challenge, among other reasons because copyright is ubiquitous. In my view, microeconomic analysis such as that outlined earlier is far more fruitful than macro studies; more empirical microeconomic studies of copyright are needed, however.

The Internet and digitization have had a fundamental effect on copyright, even calling into question its role in the creative economy of the future. Copyright law has already been reformed to take into account some of the effects of new technologies and the uses to which they have given rise, and businesses are looking for new models that enable copyright to yield revenue. New sources of revenue are sought to replace lost royalties from unauthorized use of copyright, in particular, levies on hardware; they are blunt instruments from the point of view of economic efficiency, though. It is likely that copyright law will be further modified to make it more workable in the digital economy, enabling creative works to be exploited more profitably. Other, 'exogenous' changes impinge on copyright, for example, the speed of broadband and regulation of communications. Copyright law is likely to survive in one form or another but the future economic effects of copyright are very hard to predict.

NOTES

1. Towse et al. (2008) survey the development of economic analysis of copyright. Handke (2012) is an excellent survey of the empirical research in the economics of copyright. This chapter draws on both.
2. The *Review of Economic Research in Copyright Issues* (RERCI) (2005) has all the symposium papers and comments.
3. The term of copyright is set according to the age of the author and the expected lifetime of her successors, propounding the view that authors have a strong bequest motive. In view of what we know about authors' earnings, namely that they are below the national average, this seems paternalistic and unrealistic.
4. Watt (2000) contains a detailed and definitive formal analysis of this and related topics. See also Watt (2006, 2010, 2011, 2014), Kretschmer (2006) and Michel (2006) in a Symposium on Economics of Copyright Contracts in RERCI (2006).
5. For the fate of other authors, see the findings of a Symposium on Copyright and Contracts available on http://www.cippm.org.uk/symposia/symposium-2009.html
6. See also Moothoo (2006) for a non-technical explanation of bargaining theory.
7. For a survey of this literature, see Handke and Towse (2007).
8. There is an interesting literature on pricing of licences which I do not cover here. See Watt (2000), Watt (2010) and Snow and Watt (2005).
9. UN *International Standard Industrial Classification of All Economic Activities (206 ISIC), Revision 4* available via http://unstats.un.org/unsd/cr/registry/isic-4.asp. These classifications were correct at the time of writing but are subject to periodic update.
10. Siwek (2011) states that his estimates are consistent with the WIPO *Guide*.
11. The DCMS estimated the creative industries contributed 2.89 per cent of UK GVA in 2009; using the intangibles method that contribution falls to 2.6 per cent. Including investment in software, however, those estimates increase to 5.5 and 4.5 per cent respectively.
12. The story is complex as classifications changed over this period.

REFERENCES

Agarwal, R. and Gort, M. (2001), 'First-mover advantage and the speed of competitive entry, 1887–1986', *Journal of Law and Economics*, 44, 161–177.

Akerlof, G., Arrow, K., Bresnahan, T., Buchanan, J., Coase, R., Cohen, L., Friedman, M., Green, J., Hahn, R., Hazlett, T., Hemphill, C., Litan, R., Noll, R., Schmalensee, R., Shavell, S., Varian, H. and Zeckhauser, H. (2002), *Brief as Amici Curiae in Support of Petitioners, Eric Eldred et al. v. John D. Ashcroft, Attorney General, the Supreme Court of the United States of America*, No. 01-618.

Arrow, K. (1962), 'Economic welfare and the allocation of resources for invention', in National Bureau of Economic Research (ed.), *The Rate and Direction of Inventive Activity*, Princeton: Princeton University Press, pp. 609–625.

van Asselt, E., Hakfoort, J. and Minkman, M. (1997), *De Economische betekehis van het auteursrecht in* 1994, SEO Report 432, Sdu Uitgevers, Den Haag. English Version, *The Economic Importance of Copyright in the Netherlands in 1994*, Amstelveen, Stichting Auteursrechtbelangen.

Besen, Stanley (1986), 'Private copying, reproduction costs, and the supply of intellectual property', *Information Economics and Policy*, 2 (1), 5–22.

Besen, S., Kirby, S. and Salop, S. (1992), 'An economic analysis of copyright collectives', *Virginia Law Review*, 78 (38), 383–411.

Boldrin, Michele and David Levine (2005), 'Intellectual property and the efficient allocation of social surplus from creation', *Review of Economic Research in Copyright Issues*, 2 (1), 45–67.

Caves, R. (2000), *Creative Industries Contracts Between Art and Commerce*, Cambridge MA: Harvard University Press.

Chisholm, D. (1997), 'Profit-sharing versus fixed-payment contracts: evidence from the motion pictures industry', *Journal of Law, Economics, & Organization*, 13 (1), 169–201.

DCMS (2011), *Key Findings*. Available on http://www.culture.gov.uk/what_we_do/research_and_statistics/4848.aspx

DCMS (2014), *Creative Industries Economic Estimates*, London: DCMS. Available on https://www.gov.uk/government/uploads/system/uploads/attachment_data/file/271008/Creative_Industries_Economic_Estimates_-_January_2014.pdf

European Commission (EC) (2012), *Proposal for a Directive on collective management of copyright and related rights and multi-territorial licensing of rights in musical works for online uses in the internal market*. Available on http://ec.europa.eu/internal_market/copyright/docs/management/com-2012-3722_en.pdf http://www.ceriba.org.uk/bin/view/CERIBA/IPRsGrowth

Frontier Economics (2007), *Creative Industry Performance: A Statistical Analysis for the DCMS*, London: DCMS.

Gallini, N. (2011), 'Competition policy, patent policy and copyright collectives', *Review of Economic Research on Copyright Issues*, 8(2), 3–34.

Gayer, A. and Shy, O. (2006), 'Publishers, artists and copyright enforcement', *Information Economics and Policy*, 18, 374–384.

Goodridge, Peter and Haskel, Jonathan (2011), *Film, Television & Radio, Books, Music and Art: UK Investment in Artistic Originals*, London: Intellectual Property Office.

Gowers, A. (2006), *Gowers Review of Intellectual Property*, Norwich: HMSO.

Handke, C. (2012), 'A taxonomy of empirical research on copyright – how do we inform policy?' *Review of Economic Research on Copyright Issues*, 9 (1), 47–92.

Handke, C. and Towse, R. (2007), 'Economics of copyright collecting societies', *International Review of Intellectual Property and Competition Law*, 38 (8), 937–957.

Hargreaves, I. (2011), *Digital Opportunity. A Review of Intellectual Property and Growth*, Newport: IPO.

Hollander, Abraham (1984), 'Market structure and performance in intellectual property: the case of copyright collectives', *International Journal of Industrial Organization*, 2 (3), 199–216.
Hooper, R. (2012a), *Rights and Wrongs: Is Copyright Licensing Fit for Purpose for the Digital Age? The First Report of the Digital Copyright Exchange Feasibility Study*, Newport: Intellectual Property Office. Available on http://www.ipo.gov.uk/dce-report-phase1.pdf
Hooper, R. (2012b), *Copyright Works: Streamlining Copyright Licensing for the Digital Age*, Newport: Intellectual Property Office. Available on http://www.ipo.gov.uk/dce-report-phase2.pdf
Hurt, R. and Schuchman, R. (1966), 'The economic rationale of copyright', *American Economic Review Papers and Proceedings*, 56 (2), 421–432.
Johnson, W. (1985), 'The economics of copying', *Journal of Political Economy*, 93 (1), 158–174.
Katz, A. (2005), 'The potential demise of another natural monopoly: Rethinking collective administration of rights', *Journal of Competition Law and Economics*, 1 (3), 541–593.
Kretschmer, M. (2006), 'Copyright and contracts: a brief introduction', *RERCI*, 3 (1), 75–81.
Landes, William M. and Richard A. Posner (1989), 'An economic analysis of copyright law', *Journal of Legal Studies*, 18 (2), 325–363.
Leenheer, J., Bremer, S. and Theeuwes, J. (2008), *The Economic Contribution of Copyright-Based Industries in the Netherlands*, SEO, University of Amsterdam.
Liebowitz, S. (1985), 'Copying and indirect appropriability', *Journal of Political Economy*, 93 (5), 945–957.
Liebowitz, S. (2005), 'Economists' topsy-turvy view of piracy', *Review of Economic Research on Copyright Issues*, 2 (1), 5–17.
Liebowitz, Stan J. and Steven E. Margolis (1995), 'Are network externalities a new source of market failure?', *Research in Law and Economics*, 17, 1–22.
Liebowitz, S. and Watt, R. (2006), 'How best to ensure the remuneration of creators in the market for music? Copyright and its alternatives', *Journal of Economic Surveys*, 20 (4), 513–545.
Michel, Norbert J. (2006), 'Digital file sharing and the music industry: Was there a substitution effect?', *Review of Economic Research on Copyright Issues*, 2 (2), 41–52.
Mitra-Khan, B. (2011), 'Copyright, evidence and lobbynomics: the world after the UK's Hargreaves review', *Review of Economic Research on Copyright Issues*, 8 (2), 65–100.
Moothoo, A. (2006), 'Bargaining theory and royalty contract negotiations', *Review of Economic Research on Copyright Issues*, 3 (1), 19–28.
Novos, I., and Waldman, M. (1984), 'The effects of increased copyright protection: an analytic approach', *Journal of Political Economy*, 92 (2), 236–246.
Peitz, M., and Waelbroeck, P. (2006), 'Why the music industry may gain from free downloading: the role of sampling', *International Journal of Industrial Organization*, 24 (5), 907–913.
Plant, Arnold (1934), 'The economic aspects of copyright in books', *Economica*, 1 (2), 167–195.
Posner, R. (2010), *Economic Analysis of Law* (8th ed.), Boston, Toronto and London: Little, Brown and Co.
Review of Economic Research on Copyright Issues (*RERCI*) (2005), *Symposium: Indirect Appropriability 20 Years On*, 2 (1).
Review of Economic Research on Copyright Issues (*RERCI*) (2006), *Symposium on Economics of Copyright Contracts*, 3 (1).
Siwek, S. (2004), 'The measurement of "copyright" industries: the US experience', *RERCI*, 1 (1), 12–25.

Siwek, S. (2011), *Copyright Industries in the U.S. Economy: The 2011 Report*, Prepared for the International Intellectual Property Alliance (IIPA), Washington DC: Economists Incorporated.
Siwek, S. and Furchgott-Roth, H. (1990), *Copyright Industries in the U.S. Economy,* Prepared for the International Intellectual Property Alliance (IIPA), Washington DC: Economists Incorporated.
Snow, A. and Watt, R. (2005), 'Risk-sharing and the Distribution of Copyright Collective Income', in Takeyama, L., W. Gordon and R. Towse (eds), *Developments in the Economics of Copyright*, Cheltenham UK and Northampton, MA, USA: Edward Elgar, pp. 23–36.
Soloveichik, R. (2010), 'Artistic originals as a capital asset', *American Economic Review*, 100 (2), 110–114.
Takeyama, L. (1994), 'The welfare implications of unauthorized reproduction of intellectual property in the presence of demand network externalities', *Journal of Industrial Economics*, 42, 155–166.
Towse, R. (1999), 'Copyright, incentives and performers' earnings', *Kyklos*, 5 (3), 369–390.
Towse, R. (2001), *Creativity, Incentive and Reward*, Cheltenham UK and Northampton, MA, USA: Edward Elgar.
Towse, R. (2004), 'Comment: Number-crunching is not just a "neutral" activity', R*eview of Economic Research on Copyright Issues*, 1 (1), 79–82.
Towse, R. (2010), 'Creativity, copyright and the creative industries paradigm', *Kyklos*, 3, 483–500.
Towse, R. (2011), 'What we know, what we don't know and what policy-makers would like us to know about the economics of copyright', *Review of Economic Research on Copyright Issues*, 8 (2), 101–120.
Towse, R. (2012), 'Economics of copyright collecting societies and digital rights: is there a case for a centralised Digital Copyright Exchange?' *Review of Economic Research on Copyright Issues*, 9(2); 31–58.
Towse. R. (2013a), 'The Economic Effects of Digitization on the Administration of Musical Copyrights', *Review of Economic Research on Copyright Issues*, 10(2), 55–67.
Towse, R. (2013b), 'The Quest for Evidence on the Economic Effects of Copyright Law', *Cambridge Journal of Economics*, 37 (5), 1187–1202.
Towse, R., Handke, C. and Stepan, P. (2008), 'The economics of copyright law: a stocktake of the literature', *Review of Economic Research on Copyright Issues*, 5 (1), 1–22.
UNCTAD (2008), *Creative Economy Report 2008: The Challenge of Assessing the Creative Economy: Towards Informed Policy-making*, Geneva: UNCTAD.
UNESCO (2000), *Culture, Trade and Globalization: Questions and Answers*, Paris: UNESCO http://unesdoc.unesco.org/images/0012/001213/121360E.pdf
Varian, Hal (2000), 'Buying, sharing and renting information goods', *Journal of Industrial Economics*, 48 (4), 473–488.
Varian, Hal (2005), 'Copying and copyright', *Journal of Economic Perspectives*, 19 (2), 121–138.
Watt, Richard (2000), *Copyright and Economic Theory: Friends or Foes?* Cheltenham, UK and Northampton, MA, USA: Edward Elgar.
Watt, Richard (2006), 'Licensing and royalty contracts for copyright', *Review of Economic Research on Copyright Issues*, 3 (1), 1–17.
Watt, Richard (2010), 'Fair copyright remuneration: The case of music radio', *Review of Economic Research on Copyright Issues*, 7 (2), 21–37.
Watt, Richard (2011), 'Revenue sharing as compensation for copyright holders', *Review of Economic Research on Copyright Issues*, 8 (1), 51–97.

Watt, Richard (ed.) (2014), *Handbook on the Economics of Copyright*. Cheltenham, UK and Northampton, MA, USA: Edward Elgar.

WIPO (2003), *WIPO Guide on Surveying the Economic Contribution of the Copyright-Based Industries*, Geneva: WIPO.

WIPO (2012), *WIPO Studies on the Economic Contribution of the Copyright Industries*, Geneva: WIPO. Available on http://www.wipo.int/ip-development/en/creative_industry/pdf/economic_contribution_analysis_2012.pdf

16. Effects of taxes and subsidies on media services

Hans Jarle Kind and Jarle Møen

Controversies over the role of the press are almost as old as the press itself (Sánchez-Tabernero, 2006). Controversies over taxes also have a long history, and for the media industry it dates back to protests against the British stamp duty that was introduced on newspapers in the early 1700s. *The Examiner*, started in 1808, consistently labeled the duty a "tax on knowledge", and this slogan is still used by the media industry today. Some publishers refused to pay the stamp duty, claiming that the tax restricted circulation of journals to people of high income. Incidentally, there is some evidence that the tax was used at least partly to obstruct the radical press, and thus to reduce newspaper circulation (Simkin, 2012). Modern press policies typically have the opposite objectives. A major aim is to increase circulation and educate the people.

After World War II, a large number of countries started to subsidize domestic newspapers. In particular, press subsidies have been used to halt newspaper mortality since the 1960s and 1970s (see for example Picard, 2006). According to Krumsvik (2011, p. 69), government support to media is perceived as a prerequisite for a free press in social democratic countries, while it is perceived as an obstacle for a free press in more market oriented countries. The background for Krumsvik's claim is an early study by Picard (1985) and more recent studies such as Hallin and Mancini (2004). The latter analysed public policies towards the media sector in 18 countries in Western Europe and North America. Countries like France, Italy, Belgium, Norway and Sweden were found to have highly interventionist policies, while market forces dominate the newspaper industry in for instance the US and the UK. That being said, also in these countries, newspapers receive substantial subsidies (Nielsen and Linnebank, 2011).

Ideologically driven differences in intervention levels may help to explain why media policies very seldom undergo cost-benefit analysis. Actually, in an evaluation of the Norwegian media support system, Statskonsult (1998) maintained that the Norwegian Ministry of Culture "in respect of the free press" deliberately avoided formulating measures that would make it possible to evaluate the efficiency of its media policy.[1]

It is not immediately clear that the ideal of an independent and critical press is a good argument for not analysing whether policies work or not. However, it does give support to Picard's (2007) claim that "The Nordic model appears to be based more on rhetoric and good intentions than actually producing and operating a system of support that leads to the desired outcomes." Unfortunately, there is reason to believe that this is true for media support systems in most countries. Sánchez-Tabernero (2006, p. 24), for instance, argues that France leads the way in using a protectionist media policy "for reasons of cultural tradition".

It is customary to distinguish between direct and indirect media support (Picard and Grönlund, 2003). In contrast to direct aid, indirect aid does not enter as observable items in a firm's financial statement. Earlier, reduced postal and telecommunications rates used to be important forms of indirect support, but at present the dominant vehicle is reduction of, or even exemption from, value-added taxes (VAT). Support which is given to all firms within some broad guidelines is labeled general, while selective aid is targeted to specific recipients.

It is widely believed that indirect general aid (like reduced value-added taxes on newspaper sales) is less likely to be subject to political capture than direct aid; in particular, one might expect that newspapers that depend on selective direct aid would hesitate to bite the hand that feeds them, the government. However, there is no consensus as to how serious this problem is in practice. De Bens and Østbye (1998, p. 14), for instance, argue that there are no indications that subsidies make the press less critical. On the contrary, they argue that some of the most critical voices against governments depend on press subsidies to survive. Others are much more sceptical (see Sánchez-Tabernero, 2006, for a good discussion), and in an evaluation of Norwegian press subsidies Skogerbø (1997, p. 102) notes that "... the close relationship between the press and the political parties is one reason why it was possible to muster widespread support in favor of a system that has continuously been criticized for undermining both press freedom and freedom of competition".[2] In a recent review of the literature on the political economy of mass media, Prat and Strömberg (2011) argue that "different sources of evidence provide support for the idea that ownership plurality is the most effective defence against capture".

The rest of this chapter is organized as follows. In section 1 we summarize some common welfare economics arguments for why it may be optimal to subsidize media firms. We limit our attention to newspaper support though many of the arguments also hold for television and radio (public broadcasters are the biggest recipients of media support in many countries). In section 2 we present a theoretical framework for analysing the effects of taxes and subsidies on newspapers' pricing behavior, quality investments and differentiation incentives. We also discuss their usefulness in ensuring newspaper survival. Our main focus is on literature which considers indirect media support, as this is more demanding to analyse than direct support (such as pure money transfers). In section 3 we present some empirical work on the effect of subsidies. Most of this literature discusses direct subsidies. As pointed out by Humphreys (2006, p. 39) indirect subsidies often involve "impressively large sums", but they have nonetheless tended to be uncontroversial. This is presumably a main reason why there exist only a few studies on the effects of indirect subsidies. In section 4 we sum up and discuss some avenues for future research that seem particularly promising and important.

1. AN ECONOMIC JUSTIFICATION FOR MEDIA SUPPORT

Traditionally, media support has been justified by the claim that widespread reading of newspapers promotes the national language and culture, and that a diversity of newspapers is important for freedom of speech and democracy. There is a lot of truth in these arguments, but it is not self-explanatory why they call for government interventions.

In a market economy, subsidies are used to correct market failure. A modern media support scheme should be based on this principle. Economic theory suggests that one should start the analysis with an accurate description of the market failure. When the market failure is identified, one should design schemes that directly address the inefficiency. However, one should be aware that not all market failures can be corrected, and that one usually faces a trade-off between market failure and various forms of government failures. In particular, one may worry that media support appear preservative, as emphasized for example by Picard (2007) and that it leads to media capture.

Market failure in the media industry can take many forms. The most obvious can be identified from economic theory of knowledge and information, hereunder economies of scale in knowledge production, pure and pecuniary knowledge externalities, public good aspects of investigative journalism and network externalities associated with small language communities. Another important source of market failure is associated with the theory of imperfections in two-sided markets. Newspapers are platforms that internalize externalities between readers and advertisers, but there is no guarantee that they will do this in an optimal way from a welfare theoretical point of view. The structure of the newspaper market is such that one cannot expect that a free market will produce the right amount of journalism, nor that the quality and editorial choices will be optimally adapted to the demand.

Pure Knowledge Externalities

Externalities between newspapers

Journalists are knowledge workers. The main reason for subsidizing production of knowledge, for example through support for R&D, is that those who generate knowledge rarely reap the full benefit of their work. One reason for this is that it is expensive to generate new knowledge, but relatively easy to copy, distribute and build on others' knowledge once it is made available (Arrow, 1962; Romer, 1990). In the media world this is illustrated by the fact that many online newspapers and free of charge newspapers more or less live off copying material from others. It is not completely free to make a newspaper this way and news decreases in value when it is no longer fresh and exclusive, but there is little doubt that the reuse of material generates large values that do not accrue to the editorial staff that originally produced it. Another variant of the same mechanism is that editors build on each other's stories. When editorial staff are considering whether to look into an issue, they do not take into account that they also create value for other editors who with moderate additional investments can continue to pursue the case with their own approach. These are examples of what economists call "pure knowledge externalities".[3] The extent of externalities between different media is illustrated in Lund (2001), Lund et al. (2009) and Erdal (2010). Lund studies the national news flow in Denmark – which he coins the "journalistic food chain" – during one week in 1999 and again during the same week in 2008. The detailed empirical analysis is based on more than 100 000 news items from traditional newspapers, internet newspapers, magazines, news agencies, radio and TV, and it documents that news spread across different media to a large and increasing extent. In 1999 42 percent of about 32 000 news items were categorized as "recycled, borrowed or stolen" while in 2008 this category accounted for 64 percent of about 75 000 news items. The low cost of disseminating news online is probably a contributing factor to the growth. In a similar study, Erdal (2010) maps the flow of news in Norway and finds that about half of the articles in the national newspapers were produced by in-house editorial staff, while the other half was redistribution of material from other newsrooms.

Externalities between citizens

Readers buy newspapers to keep up to date. In part, this is consumption, not very different from other types of entertainment, but newspaper reading also helps to maintain people's literacy and strengthen their knowledge base. This may be considered an investment in human capital. A person who never reads newspapers or otherwise stays updated on what happens in society is likely to be inhibited both within and outside of the workplace, and is likely to be vulnerable in restructuring processes. In a welfare society, this will have negative effects on other taxpayers. Moreover, such persons will not be able to manage their democratic rights in a satisfactory way. Informed citizens make better decisions, not only for themselves but also for their children and in politics. Hence, the whole community benefits to some extent from high levels of newspaper circulation. If the price of newspapers is initially high and newspaper consumption low, the social return on newspaper subsidies that increases consumption among groups with low purchasing power may be positive. It may also be desirable to subsidize certain types of newspaper contents that are little in demand because of low consumption value, but which have high information value. This is analogous to advertising. The government pays newspapers to give column space to important and useful information which is added to the material that the readers want (Bruns and Himmler, 2011, p. 472).

Investigative Journalism as a Public Good

At the outset, public goods must be provided collectively because the benefits they generate cannot be easily confined to those who pay for them. Not only are they non-excludable, but they are also non-rivalrous, meaning that one person's use does not reduce the availability to others. Classical examples of public goods are flood control systems, street lighting and national defence. These are only to a small extent produced in private markets because it is expensive or impossible to charge anyone for them.

Critical and investigative journalism is expensive to produce and has properties of being a public good because it promotes efficient use of resources in the public sector. Good journalism ensures the quality of many large and small decisions that civil servants and local government employees make on behalf of society every day. All citizens benefit from this, not only those who pay for and read newspapers. In most developed countries, government expenditures are in the order of 30–50 percent of GDP. It is also common that governments manage large public funds, and have significant ownership stakes in private sector companies. One can hardly overestimate the value to society of having the enormous cash flows generated by government consumption, transfers and investments monitored and debated constantly. Good journalism also contributes to building of institutions and inhibits negligence, unethical behavior and crime. Bhattacharyya and Hodler (2010) find that countries with valuable natural resources more frequently face problems with corruption than other countries, but that high quality of the democratic institutions counters the problem. In extreme cases, the economic consequences of a weak media can be very dramatic. The financial crisis in Iceland in 2008 was no natural disaster, but a result of poor political handling and economic wrongdoings that could have been uncovered by the media. Much the same can be said about the financial problems that have developed in Greece.

The importance of the media for local democracy has recently been empirically documented by the German economists Bruns and Himmler (2011). They emphasize that radio, television and the internet are alternative sources of information about national politics, but local newspapers dominate when it comes to monitoring local decision making. Their data material covers 150 Norwegian newspapers and more than 400 municipalities in the years 2001 to 2005. They view Norway as an interesting laboratory because the country has both high newspaper coverage and a decentralized management structure with many small municipalities. After having controlled for observable differences between the municipalities such as size, population density, income and education level, as well as possible unobserved permanent differences in efficiency, Bruns and Himmler find a positive correlation between the distribution of local newspapers and efficiency in the municipal sector. Their municipal efficiency indexes take into account both quantitative and qualitative aspects of 17 types of municipal services. The measured effect is reinforced when they weight the newspaper distribution in each municipality with a measurement of how much municipality-specific information the various newspapers contain. Moreover, they find that the effect is particularly strong in small municipalities, defined as municipalities with fewer than 10 000 inhabitants.

Consumer Surplus

Another form of market failure relates to the concept of consumer surplus. Even if newspapers were perfect monopolies and could charge for all re-use of material, they would not be able to extract the individual reader's full willingness to pay without requiring a different payment from each reader. Such perfect price discrimination is impossible to achieve in practice. Simply put, there may be one or more buyers who think the product is just worth its price and who will not buy the newspaper if it costs more. Most readers, however, will tolerate a moderate price increase. For these customers, the value of the product is higher than the price. This implies that there will exist journalistic projects that are not undertaken despite the fact that the total value for readers is higher than the cost of producing the material.

If we look at a possible newspaper article as a product of knowledge, it is easy to imagine that the value for some readers may be far higher than the Euro or so that it costs. An example might be so-called consumer journalism that provides guidelines on major purchases. The consumer surplus that newspapers generate for private individuals, however, may not be very different from the consumer surplus generated by other products. For business customers, on the other hand, the value of newspapers may be much higher compared to the price. Through the media, businesses obtain information on trends, business partners, customers, competitors and new markets. Moreover, when business journalists follow companies with employed management, they produce valuable governance information for the owners.

Economies of Scale and Scope

The cost structure in the media industry gives rise to significant economies of scale and scope. As with many informational goods, the bulk of the cost is associated with producing the first copy (hence there are high fixed costs) while it is relatively cheap to distribute additional copies to new readers on the same or different platforms (that is, there are low marginal costs). For digital media, the marginal cost – the cost of serving the marginal reader – is equal to zero. For printed newspapers, the marginal cost is greater than zero, but fixed costs such as rent, salaries, and so on, are clearly more important than costs associated with printing and distribution of extra copies. This type of cost structure creates some challenges.

First of all, the fixed costs mean that it is not possible for a newspaper to survive without reaching a critical level of revenue from advertising and readers. This implies that in small markets, it may not be possible to operate even one newspaper at a profit, and in medium size markets, it is difficult to establish competitors to an incumbent player. More generally, large fixed costs act as a barrier to entry. This problem is arguably particularly severe in the media sector, since newspapers with much smaller circulations than their rivals may find it difficult to attract advertisers (which in turn could make the newspapers even less attractive for the readers).[4] The result can be monopoly formation and little diversity. This may justify support for small local newspapers, start-ups and so-called No. 2 newspapers, that is, newspapers that are second in circulation in their market.

A second and related challenge caused by large fixed costs is that in order to survive, even idealistically run newspapers must charge a price that is higher than marginal cost (unless advertising revenue is very high). This implies that there will be readers who have a willingness to pay that exceeds the cost of producing an extra copy, but who nonetheless will be excluded. This leads to a welfare loss in the form of reduced newspaper reading and is an argument for using subsidies to reduce the actual price of the printed newspaper. In this respect, zero pricing is a positive aspect of free newspapers online.[5] Online newspapers are in reality public goods, and they have most likely increased total newspaper consumption even though the effect on the printed newspaper circulation has been negative. From a democratic and income distribution perspective, it is especially valuable that online newspapers reach out to groups with low purchasing power. The problem with free newspapers is that both the quality and the diversity will be badly affected. We return to this issue later.

Economies of scale are used to justify subsidies also to other media products than newspapers. Examples include books, films and music. The argument is that the high fixed costs associated with producing the first issue provide little width and cultural diversity. On the other hand, it must be noted that there are many markets where economies of scale are significant without the producers receiving subsidies, and one can imagine situations where the market conditions are such that too many different varieties are produced so that economies of scale are utilized to an insufficient extent. This can happen because some of the profits that new products generate do not represent a welfare gain to society, but are simply a transfer of income from competitors who lose customers.

Although economic theory does not provide an unambiguous basis for determining whether a free market produces too much or too little diversity of newspapers, we observe that increased diversity is a common political goal used to justify press subsidies. If this goal is interpreted as an outcome of a democratic process, it indicates that citizens want more diversity than the free markets can offer.

Language as Network Externality

Press subsidies may also be used for linguistic policy reasons, for example to promote minority languages or local languages in small language areas. This may be justified on the grounds that the use of a particular language represents a so-called network externality that benefits other users of the same language. The classic example of a good that creates network externalities is the telephone. No-one benefits from having access to a phone unless there are other people who also have phones. Moreover, when new users connect to the network, the value of having a phone increases for all existing and potential users. Similarly, a language is not useful unless it is understood and used by others. This may create evil and good circles of use. If few people use a particular language today, even fewer will use it in the future – and if many people use a particular language even more people will use it. A large language area also provides a greater market and better opportunities for the exploitation of economies of scale. When a "linguistic network" is in place with sufficiently many users, however, there is no need for subsidies.

Credit Market Imperfections

During periods of rapid changes in technologies and market conditions, it is commonly argued that governments should provide funds to help firms adjust to new environments (for example helping traditional newspapers to transform to the digital era). In the absence of market failure, this is not a valid argument. Financial markets would then provide funds if and only if such an adjustment is profitable (in expectation). However, credit market imperfections create inefficiencies that might call for public interventions and subsidization. A problem, though, known both from micro- and macro analyses, is that such aid has strong tendencies to become permanent. This may prevent modernization and productivity. The media industry is not very different from other industries with respect to arguments in favor of, and against, infant industry support and support for restructuring of incumbent firms. We do not therefore pursue this topic any further from a theoretical point of view. Some empirical evidence is discussed in section 3.

Externalities in Two-sided Markets

Media economic research has accelerated in recent decades, and this is partly due to the development of theories on two-sided markets. There are numerous examples of important two-sided markets, such as credit cards, software and browsers.[6] None of these markets can be understood without explicitly taking the two-sidedness into account, and it has been claimed that one reason why Apple nearly went bankrupt before the company was revitalized was their lack of knowledge about the mechanisms of two-sided markets. Similarly, it may be argued that knowledge on two-sided markets is necessary in order to understand the impact of various media political initiatives.

Somewhat informally, we have a two-sided market if there are (a) two or more customer groups for a given product, (b) positive network externalities from at least one customer group to another, and (c) there is a platform that internalizes the externalities.[7] Newspapers obviously operate in a two-sided market, since they sell their products to both readers and advertisers. The gain from advertising in a newspaper will typically be higher the greater the number of readers, but this is an effect that no single reader takes into account when buying a newspaper. Hence, we have a positive externality from the reader side of the market to the advertiser side. We might have positive externalities also from the advertiser side to the reader side. This is true if a reader's valuation of a newspaper is increasing in the advertising volume, for instance because the ads provide information on local offers and activities. If readers in general dislike advertising, on the other hand, we have negative externalities. In any case, the newspaper is a platform that must find a business model which internalizes the externalities between the advertisers and the readers. A newspaper will, for instance, typically choose lower subscription prices than those that would maximize revenues from the reader side of the market, since they thus increase advertising revenues by attracting more readers. This is a simple and straightforward mechanism. However, the interrelationship between the two sides of the market makes it challenging to see what the effects of, for example, reduced-rate value-added taxes really are, as they affect prices, profiles and quality choices. Since the formal literature which analyses these issues is new, we shall use the next section to develop a theoretical framework that allows a unified analysis of some stylized press support schemes.

2. THE EFFECTS OF TAXES AND SUBSIDIES: A THEORETICAL FRAMEWORK

Based on the discussion of market failures in the previous section, we take as a premise for the rest of this chapter that the newspaper market with no policy interventions gives:

1. Too small circulation of existing newspapers
2. Too few titles

3. Too small investments in journalism and other factors that increase the quality of the newspaper
4. Too little media diversity.

We start out by reviewing theoretical findings on the effects of VAT reduction, which most likely is the largest component of worldwide press subsidies. It also seems to be the component of press subsidies whose effects are least understood.

Value-added Taxation in Two-sided Markets

Price and quantity effects of value-added taxes

The traditional argument for levying low indirect taxes (VAT in Europe) on newspapers is that this reduces the cover price and thus increases newspaper circulation. To see the argument formally in an intuitive way, let us abstract from the two-sidedness of the market and consider a media firm which sells *N* copies of a newspaper at price p^N. The inverse demand curve for the newspaper is downward-sloping in own quantity, such that we have $p_n^N(n) \overset{\text{def}}{=} \frac{\partial p^N}{\partial n} < 0$ (subscripts henceforth denote partial derivatives). Labeling the ad valorem tax rate by *t*, this implies that the media firm receives the price $p^N/(1+t)$ per copy it sells of the newspaper.

The newspaper's profit level is given by

$$\pi = \frac{np^N(n)}{1+t} + R(a) - C(°), \tag{16.1}$$

where *a* is the newspaper's advertising volume, $R(a)$ advertising revenue and $C(°)$ is the cost function. We assume that the cost and demand functions are well behaved, and that the second-order conditions for profit-maximization hold.

The media firm maximizes profits with respect to the advertising volume (*a*) and newspaper circulation (*n*). Starting with the former, we find that $\partial\pi/\partial a = 0$ implies

$$R'(a) = C_a. \tag{16.2}$$

This simply says that marginal revenue of selling ads is equal to marginal costs in optimum. The first-order condition for newspaper sales ($\partial\pi/\partial n = 0$) is likewise given by

$$\frac{p^N + np_n^N}{1+t} = C_n \tag{16.3}$$

A positive VAT on newspapers ($t > 0$) reduces the marginal revenue of selling newspapers but does not affect the marginal revenue of selling ads. Differentiating equations (16.2) and (16.3) with respect to t therefore shows that the advertising volume is independent of t ($\partial a/\partial t = 0$). However, the higher the VAT rate, the higher is the price that the readers have to pay, and the smaller therefore newspaper circulation will be:[8]

$$\frac{dn}{dt} = \frac{-C_n}{-\pi_{nn}(1+t)} < 0 \text{ and } \frac{dp^N}{dt} = p_n^N \frac{dn}{dt} > 0. \tag{16.4}$$

The signs in (16.4) follow from the fact that the second-order conditions require that $\pi_{nn} < 0$ and support the conventional view that newspaper prices will fall and the circulation increase if the VAT is reduced. Equation (16.4) further makes it clear that the smaller the marginal costs of producing (and distributing) newspapers, the less the circulation will fall. If marginal costs are negligible ($C_n \approx 0$), then the VAT rate has almost no effect on price and output. In this case the VAT rate is equivalent to a surplus tax. This is of particular importance if we consider electronic newspapers, where marginal costs are very close to zero. Other things equal, this says that the price of electronic newspapers is independent of the VAT rate (making VAT act as a surplus tax, see below).

The problem with the above analysis is that it does not take into account the two-sidedness of the market. To incorporate this as simply as possible, we hold on to the assumption that newspaper readers are indifferent to the ad level in the newspaper (this is not a critical assumption; see Kind et al. 2008).[9] However, we assume that demand for ads is increasing in newspaper circulation ($\partial a/\partial n > 0$). This means that $R(°)$ is a function of n, such that the solution to $\partial \pi/\partial a = 0$ is given by $\frac{p^N + np_n^N}{1+t} + R'(a)\frac{da}{dn} = C_n$. To clearly see the implication of this, assume that we have a downward-sloping inverse demand curve also for ads, such that we can write $R(a) = ap^A(a)$ with $p_a^A < 0$. Then the equivalent of (16.3) becomes

$$\frac{p^N + np_n^N}{1+t} + ap_n^A = C_n, \tag{16.5}$$

which shows that the marginal revenue of selling newspapers is greater in a two-sided market than in a one-sided market. This is true since the externality term ap^A on the left hand side of equation (16.5) is positive. The intuition is that the advertisers' willingness to pay for an ad increases with p_n^A units if one more reader buys the newspaper, and this creates a gain equal to ap_n^A for the newspaper when it sells a units of ads. This formalizes the claim that newspaper circulation is higher the more important it is for the advertisers to reach a large audience.

Now, differentiating (16.2) and (16.5) with respect to t we find

$$\frac{dn}{dt} = S\frac{ap_n^A - C_n}{-\pi_{nn}(1+t)} \quad \text{and} \quad \frac{dp^N}{dt} = p_n^N \frac{dn}{dt}, \tag{16.6}$$

where the second-order conditions require that $S > 0$.[10] This means that $dn/dt > 0$ and $dp^N/dt < 0$ if $ap_n^A - C_n > 0$. We may thus get the seemingly paradoxical result that a higher VAT on newspapers increases sales and reduces the price that the readers have to pay. The intuition is that if the value on the advertising side of the market of capturing one extra reader, ap_n^A, is greater than the marginal costs of serving that reader, C_n, then it is profitable to reduce the newspaper price marginally. Thereby the readership increases, allowing the media firm to sell more advertising and make a higher profit than if it increased the price and reduced the output of newspapers. Total profits for the newspaper certainly fall subsequent to the tax increase, but it makes higher profits on the advertising side.[11]

What happens to the advertising level and advertising price depends on the exact shape of the demand and cost function, which we will not discuss here (see Kind et al., 2008, for an analysis). However, it can be shown that both the advertising level and newspaper sales might increase under reasonable assumptions. If this happens, it is welfare improving to have a positive VAT rate on newspapers. The media firms will lose, but both the readers and the advertisers gain, because the media firm reduces the newspaper price in order to attract more readers and more advertisers. Such positive welfare effects of taxation could never be observed in a one-sided market, unless we consider goods which impose negative externalities such as pollution.

To see that the results above are not just theoretical curiosities, assume that t approaches infinity. Obviously, the newspaper would then have no reason to charge a positive consumer price. However, the newspaper might still be profitable, since it has the option of raising revenue through the advertising market and giving the newspaper away for free. This, obviously, is another fundamental difference between the effects of taxation in one-sided and two-sided markets; a higher VAT in a one-sided market can never increase sales, and profits can never be positive if the VAT rate becomes sufficiently high. Contrary to a firm operating in a one-sided market, firms operating on a two-sided platform can reduce their tax burden by shifting revenue to the side of the market where the tax rate is unchanged.[12]

Whether the condition $ap_n^A - C_n > 0$ holds, implying that increased VAT *reduces* the price of newspapers, is an empirical question. There are high fixed costs in the media sector, but the marginal cost of a newspaper copy is relatively low (and zero on the internet). It should further be noted that advertising is the primary or only source of income for some media outlets, indicating that ap_n^A is relatively high. Hence, it is not inconceivable that $p_n^A - C_n > 0$. The main takeaway from the above analysis, however, is that reduced-rate VAT-regimes are not likely to be an effective means of reducing newspaper prices. Another important takeaway is that the VAT rate affects to what extent newspapers have to rely on advertising revenue. This has implications for media pluralism as we show in the next section.

Value-added taxes and differentiation incentives

The workhorse for analysing differentiation incentives in economics is the Hotelling model. Let us briefly go through the main ingredients in the standard set-up; details can be found in most text books on industrial organization (for example Tirole, 1988). First, consumers are heterogeneous along one dimension. To be specific, assume that they differ in political opinion, and that their preferences are uniformly distributed along a line with length equal to one. This "Hotelling line" is illustrated in Figure 16.1. Extremely left-wing readers are at or close to point 0 on this line, extremely right-wing readers at or close to point 1, while those with more moderate views are located somewhere in between. Suppose that there are two newspapers, $i = 1,2$, and that each consumer buys one and only one of them. The location of newspaper 1 is given by point X_1 (such that it is relatively, but not extremely, left-wing), while its more right-wing competitor is located at point X_2. For the moment we shall let the newspapers be advertising-free, such that they raise profits only through the price p_i that they charge the readers (meaning that it operates in a one-sided market). Following the standard set-up, let the utility of a consumer who is located at some point x on the line and who buys newspaper i be given by

$$U_i = v + q_i - p_i - w(d_i - x)^2, \qquad (16.7)$$

where $d_1 = x_1$ and $d_2 = 1 - x_2$. The parameter $v > 0$ is a positive constant which we assume is sufficiently large to ensure that all readers buy one (and only one) newspaper, w is a measure of the intensity of the consumers' preferences, and q_i is the perceived quality of newspaper i.

The newspapers can increase the perceived quality by investing in journalism, and the profit function of newspaper i equals $\pi_i = (p_i - c)D_i - \varphi q_1^2/2$, where $\varphi q_1^2/2$ is the cost of investing in journalism ($\varphi > 0$) and D_i is demand. Now, consider a two-stage game where the newspapers first choose locations non-cooperatively and then compete in prices. With this formulation it is well known from the literature (for example Tirole, 1988) that there will be maximal differentiation, such that the firms will locate at each end-point on the line ($x_1 = 0$, $x_2 = 1$). The reason is that each newspaper will have a strategic incentive to move away from its rival; by doing this, the competitive pressure falls. Thereby the firms can charge higher prices, and make higher profits. From a policy point of view, it is important to note that since value-added taxes do not affect the strategic interactions between the newspapers, the locations (newspaper profiles) are independent of the tax rate. However, as is always the case in one-sided markets, the price that the readers have to pay is strictly increasing in the tax rate if marginal production costs are positive ($p_i = w + c(1 + t)$). It can further be shown that investment in journalism is strictly decreasing in the tax rate $q_i = \frac{1}{3\varphi(1+t)}$. The reason for this is that taxes reduce the newspaper's profit margin on each copy it sells, and therefore the incentive to capture new readers by investing more in journalism falls.

Figure 16.1 Differentiation along the Hotelling line

The model in Figure 16.1 does not tell us much about how firms that receive revenues both from advertisers and readers will locate. It is challenging to analyse the choice of location in two-sided markets formally, but among the first to succeed with this were Gabszewicz et al. (2001, 2002). An important innovation in their work is to add a third stage to the game, where the newspapers set the price of ad insets.[13] The advertisers are assumed to be heterogeneous, and might buy ads in one, both or none of the newspapers. Gabszewicz et al. abstract from investment issues and assume that the readers are indifferent to the ad level. The analysis is nonetheless algebraically complex, and they arrive at two corner solutions; either maximum or minimum differentiation. If the readers have strong political preferences and/or the advertising market is small, the newspapers will be maximally differentiated. Otherwise, they will be minimally differentiated (that is, locate at the midpoint of the line), and only rely on advertising revenue. The intuition for their result is most easily grasped by noting that since the readers are indifferent to the ad level in a newspaper, there are no strategic reasons to differentiate with regard to the advertising market. On the contrary, if the newspapers are located at points x_1 and x_2, newspaper 1 will steal readers from its rival and thus increase advertising revenue if it moves just to the left of newspaper 2. A similar argument applies for newspaper 2, and therefore they end up being located at the centre of the line if the advertising market is sufficiently large. This highlights the potentially important aspect that we might expect media pluralism to be small if newspapers to a large extent have to rely on advertising revenue.

Gabszewicz et al. did not consider tax issues; this is the topic in Kind et al. (2012). Using insight from Anderson and Coate (2005) they simplify the advertising side of the market. They also differ from Gabszewicz et al. in that they set up a game where the newspapers determine quality investments and locations at stage 1, advertising prices at stage 2, and cover prices at stage 3.[14] The newspapers' profit functions are given by

$$\pi_i = \left(\frac{p_i}{1+t} - c\right)D_i + R(a) - \frac{\varphi}{2}q_i^2 , \tag{16.8}$$

where advertising revenue is given by $R(a) = p^A(a_i)a_iD_i$, and the inverse demand curve for ads is specified as $p^A(a_i) = \alpha - a_i$. The greater is α, the greater is thus the advertisers' willingness to pay for ad insets, and the higher will the newspapers' advertising revenue be in equilibrium.

In contrast to Gabszewicz et al., this model generates interior solutions with respect to location (unless the advertising market is too large or too small), and the more important the advertising market is, the closer to the mid-point of the line the newspapers will locate. The effects of increasing the tax rate is as follows:

$$\frac{dx_i}{dt} = \frac{\alpha^2}{16t} > 0, \quad \frac{dp_i}{dt} = c - \frac{\alpha^2}{8} \geq\leq 0 \text{ and } \frac{dqi}{dt} = \sigma\left(\frac{8}{3}\frac{dx_i}{dt} - \frac{1}{1+t}\right) \geq\leq 0. \tag{16.9}$$

In equation (16.9) σ is a positive parameter. A higher VAT rate increases the relative importance of the advertising market, bringing the newspapers closer to the centre of the line. A higher tax rate thus implies that both newspapers will focus more on the mass market and become less differentiated. However, the fact that they become less differentiated also means that the competitive pressure increases, and if the advertising market is sufficiently large, the newspaper price will fall subsequent to the tax increase. The same is true if marginal costs are sufficiently small (and if $c = 0$ we always have $\frac{dp_i}{dt} < 0$). Note that these competitive reasons for reducing the newspaper price come in addition to the effect discussed in the monopoly model above. Another interesting finding in equation (16.9) is that a higher tax rate might increase quality investments, in sharp contrast to what we find in one-sided markets. This happens if $\frac{dx_i}{dt}$ is sufficiently large. The intuition is that if newspapers become less differentiated, then each of them will have an incentive to invest more in quality (and charge a lower price) in order to steal business from their rival. If this business-stealing effect is strong, then we cannot disregard the possibility that it dominates over the effect discussed above, namely that the newspapers will invest less since the profit margin falls.

Summing up, the sparse literature that exists on indirect taxation in two-sided markets suggests that the price-reducing and quantity-increasing effects of the low-rate tax regimes on newspapers are at best weak. At the outset this might seem surprising, but it is important to bear in mind that, other things equal, a change in the VAT rate in one-sided markets will have no effect on price or quantity if marginal production costs are equal to zero (as shown above). Bearing this in mind, it is perhaps not too surprising that once we bring the two-sidedness into the analysis, the advertising market might make it optimal to reduce the prices.

Tax Credit for Editorial Costs

Although VAT exemption and reduction is by far the most important type of indirect media support, it is not difficult to envisage alternative tax reliefs that could correct for the market failures we discussed in section 1. We have argued that a free market is likely to underinvest in journalism. It then follows directly from optimal tax theory that journalism should be taxed at a lower rate than other activities without such positive externalities. This is exactly what McChesney and Nichols (2010) suggest in a recent book discussing the need for press subsidies in the United States. They propose a "journalist tax credit". A similar proposal was put forward by a committee commissioned to design a new media support model for Norway (NOU, 2010). The committee was unable to reach a consensus, but the committee's chairman and his faction proposed to partly replace VAT exemption for printed newspapers with a tax credit for editorial costs. The idea was to create a "platform neutral" subsidy scheme, where newspapers and news magazines were eligible regardless of whether their editorial product is distributed on paper or in digital form. The Norwegian committee was inspired by R&D tax credits schemes which have gained popularity in OECD countries over the last decades. The justification for R&D tax credits is positive knowledge externalities of the same type as those created by journalism. The Norwegian government has not yet decided whether they will go for the new model, but in France journalists already benefit from a tax deduction.[15] Even though the tax rebate is given directly to the journalists, it will have much the same effect because it lowers the cost of hiring journalists.

To capture the idea of having a tax deduction for the salary of journalists and other editorial expenses, let us reformulate equation (16.8) to

$$\pi_i = \left(\frac{p_i}{1+t} - c\right)D_i + r(a)D_i - (1-T)\frac{\varphi}{2}q_i^2 \tag{16.10}$$

The newspaper can deduct a greater share of their investment costs the larger is $T\,(0 \leq T < 1)$.

Denoting the equilibrium price, quantity and quality by p_i^*, D_i^* and q_i^*, respectively, we find that the profitability effect of investing in journalism can be written as

$$\frac{d\pi_i}{dq_i} = \left[\left(\frac{p_i^*}{1+t} - c\right) + r(a)\right]\frac{dD_i^*}{dq_i} + \frac{D_i^*}{1+t}\frac{dp_i^*}{dq_i} - (1-T)\varphi q_i^* \tag{16.11}$$

The number of readers increases if the newspaper invests more in journalism, $\frac{dD_i^*}{dq_i} > 0$. The first term on the right-hand side of equation (16.11) thus shows that the larger is the profit margin of selling the newspaper, $\left(\frac{p_i^*}{1+t} - c\right)$, and the value of a new reader in the advertising market, $r(a)$, the greater is the marginal profit of investing in journalism. We further have that $\frac{dp_i^*}{dq_i} > 0$, since the willingness to pay for the newspaper is increasing in its perceived quality level. Therefore the second term in (16.11) is positive, and more so the larger the number of subscribers, D_i.

The last term in (16.11) shows that a higher T reduces the marginal costs of investing in journalism. In equilibrium, where marginal revenue of investing in journalism is equal to marginal costs, it must thus be true that q_i is increasing in T. The newspaper will consequently employ a larger number of journalists the greater the marginal tax deduction rate, T.

Other things equal, a tax deduction for editorial expenses will not affect the competitive pressure between newspapers, nor the relative importance of the advertising market compared to the reader market. This means that the newspapers' differentiation incentives will be independent of T. To gain some further insight into the effects of tax deduction for editorial expenses in an easy way we can therefore abstract from competition, and consider a monopoly newspaper. We further simplify utility function (16.7) to $U_i = v + q_i - p_i - wx_i$ and set $t = 0$ (no value-added taxes). It can then be shown that in equilibrium we have $q_i = [(4(v-c)+\alpha^2]/\{4[2w\varphi(1-T)-1]\}$, with

$$\frac{dq_i}{dT} = \frac{D_i}{\varphi(1-T)^2} + \frac{1}{\varphi(1-T)}\frac{dD_i}{dT} \tag{16.12}$$

A tax deduction for editorial expenses thus increases investments in journalism directly because it reduces the marginal investment costs as captured by the first term in (16.12), and indirectly because the higher investments in turn increase newspaper circulation – as captured by the second term.

It is a general rule that policy makers need at least as many instruments as goals. The theories presented in this section indicate that tax deduction for editorial expenses is a well suited instrument for increasing journalistic investments, while a preferential VAT regime for newspaper sales provides higher differentiation incentives between existing newspapers.

Direct Subsidies

Direct media support is usually given as cash transfers or payment for government advertisement, to targeted newspapers, that is, newspapers with a small advertising base, minority language newspapers, ideological newspapers and so on. Such transfers are easily incorporated in the framework presented above by including a fixed transfer (lump-sum subsidy) from the government to the newspaper, $F_i \geq 0$. The profit function is then

$$\pi_i = \left(\frac{p_i}{1+t} - c\right)D_i + r(a)D_i - (1-T)\frac{\varphi}{2}q_i^2 + F_i \tag{16.13}$$

As long as the transfer is not a function of circulation or editorial costs in general, it is easy to show that such transfers will only affect entry and exit decisions of newspapers that would otherwise have negative profit. Hence, direct subsidies are an efficient instrument to reduce entry barriers or avoid newspaper mortality, but will not affect editorial choices. Formally, this follows from the fact that the firms' first-order condition for optimal investments, equation (16.11), is independent of whether a fixed term F_i enters the profit functions. The reason is simply that neither marginal revenue nor marginal costs depend on the size of the fixed transfer from the government. This is an important point which is often overlooked in public debates. A transfer that improves the profitability of newspapers will not make profit-maximizing newspapers invest more in journalism, but rather be passed on to the owners.

In theory it is easy to distinguish fixed transfers from other subsidization schemes. In practice it might be more difficult. In the tax deduction scheme recently put forward in Norway (NOU, 2010), for instance, the governmental commission proposed a 40 million NOK cap for the maximum tax credit given to any single firm. This cap will be a binding restriction for the largest newspapers, and thus reduces the total cost of the scheme significantly. However, for the newspapers where the cap is binding, the subsidy will have no effect on marginal costs. Rather, the subsidy will have the same effects as a direct transfer. It makes the owners wealthier, but does not increase investments.[16] Another example is a special program put in place by the Dutch government to foster employment and training of young journalists. The Ministry for Education, Culture and Science is paying the salary of about 60 newly trained journalists for two years to be hired by approximately 30 newspapers. The selection of journalists, how they are utilized and how their output is published, are left entirely to the newspapers (OECD, 2010; Nielsen and Linnebank, 2011). Since there are "no strings attached", this support scheme comes very close to being a pure cash transfer. Commercial newspapers would prefer to let one of their previously employed journalists go, and instead hire a journalist with wages paid by the government. Aside from an adjustment period, the newspapers will have no incentive to expand the number of journalists.

According to Picard (2006, p. 213) "most types of support simply help pay variable costs rather than fixed costs". Let us therefore consider the possibility that each media firm receives a direct subsidy of s Euro per copy it sells of its newspaper. The profit function can then be written as $\pi_i = \left(\frac{p_i}{1+t} - c - s\right) D_i + r(a) D_i - (1-T)\frac{\varphi}{2} q_i^2 + F_i$. Evidently, an increase in s is equivalent to a reduction of marginal production costs. For this kind of subsidy there are no qualitative differences between one-sided and two-sided markets; lower marginal costs reduce the optimal price and increase output.[17] Hence, a subsidy per copy sold will directly address a policy goal of increasing circulation for existing newspapers. In this respect it complements the direct transfer, F_i, which increases the number of newspaper titles.

Note that neither the unit subsidy s nor the direct transfer F_i affect strategic choices or the relative importance of the advertising market relative to the consumer market. Compared to reduced VAT rates, unit subsidies are therefore more likely to be an efficient tool for increasing circulation, but will at the outset not affect newspaper differentiation. To take a historically relevant example: previously many countries subsidized the postal rates that the newspapers had to pay. Whether we think within the context of a one-sided or two-sided market, we should expect this to lower newspaper prices but not to affect media pluralism.[18]

3. THE EFFECTS OF TAXES AND SUBSIDIES: EMPIRICAL ANALYSES

Below, we give an overview over some of the empirical literature on the effects of taxing and subsidizing media products. Since the design of media policies is highly non-uniform both over time and across countries (see the discussion on Finland below), we will not provide a detailed description of the policy tools that are actually used. It should also be stressed that media firms in many countries have become substantially more market oriented than they used to be. This is important to bear in mind, since for instance lump-sum subsidies might be expected to increase quality investments if newspapers primarily are run for political reasons, but not if they can best be described as being profit maximizing. In the same manner, newspapers might "afford" to reduce subscription prices if the VAT rates are low. This could be an important factor for ideologically driven publishers, while what is important for commercial publishers is not which price is "affordable" but which price maximizes profits. A given set of policy tools could thus be efficient in the 1970s but not today, and vice versa.

Empirical Analyses of Direct Media Support

Apart from political considerations, which clearly are important, the qualitative arguments for and against direct subsidies build to a large extent on the same underlying theories in the media sector as in more traditional industries.

In an interesting article, Murschetz (1998) provides a comparative study of state support to the daily press in Austria, France, Norway and Sweden. All these countries have over a long period of time employed extensive interventionist policies, direct as well as indirect. At the time of Murschetz's study, the support consisted of, for example, postal and telecommunication rate advantages, support of journalistic training and education, and exemption from VAT. Murschetz discusses these subsidization schemes in some detail, and argues that Sweden commonly is held as a "shining example of a country which has a politically neutral allocation of subsidies to its press". More specifically, the country had a fixed rule which granted general selective production subsidies if and only if a newspaper had 40 percent or less household coverage in the relevant area (p. 303).[19] Norway had a somewhat similar system. Murschetz argues that in France and Austria, on the other hand, the support system was much more vulnerable to and governed by political factors. In both these countries he found that the media support system harmed competition and froze the market power of the big, established newspapers. Arguably, this lends support to the minimalist approach taken in Anglo-Saxon countries.

A major challenge for the newspapers in the period investigated by Murschetz was competition in the advertising market from evolving commercial broadcasters (already in place for all countries in the study except for Austria). This is somewhat similar to the growing competition from internet firms like Facebook and Google that newspapers face today. Market imperfections might then call for temporary adjustment aid. However, findings in the literature are quite disappointing in this respect. Indeed, Picard and Grönlund (2003, p. 4) argue that "most subsidies in Europe have had little effect on financial situations of newspapers and do not provide a mechanism for real long-term viability of subsidies for newspapers". They argue that a main reason for this is that the existing subsidies typically attack variable costs rather than fixed costs. Consistent with this, Picard and Grönlund (2003) find that instead of promoting a variety of viewpoints, Finnish press subsidies have primarily benefited the press of the dominant political parties, thus resembling the results found for France and Austria in Murschetz (1998). It is noteworthy that Finland has subsequently abolished almost all direct press subsidies, down from Euro 14.2 million in 2007 to Euro 0.5 million in 2008 (NOU, 2010, p. 50). Now the subsidies go directly to political parties, which in turn might reallocate the funds to the party press.

There are very few studies of how press subsidies affect company performance. One exception is Picard (2003), who combines data on Swedish press subsidies and newspapers' accounting figures. The investigated subsidies were provided to financially weak newspapers. An important insight from this study is the clear indication that the funding authorities perceive the subsidies as operating aid (though such subsidies are at odds with EU laws). If this is also the view of the newspapers, then there is clearly a danger that they will have small incentives to restructure and adjust to market conditions so as to become economically viable on their own. In the words of Picard (2003, p. 106), the net result might be that the subsidy scheme creates a dependency culture where "the needs of the audience are ignored, and inefficiency is subsidized". This is a well-known effect which is found in many international studies of other industries; see the discussion above on the infant industry literature. The subsidies help low-coverage newspapers to survive, but do little to solve the structural problems in the industry. Even worse, a large share of the subsidies might end up in the pockets of commercial media firms that do not serve any specific social purposes. According to Picard (2006, p. 213) this problem has been particularly severe in Sweden, "where publishers often make operational and strategic choices to ensure their continued subsidization rather than improvement of their papers."

Gustafsson (2007), whose views partly contradict those of Picard, provides an overview of the evolution of Swedish press subsidies. A direct press subsidy – given to subscription newspapers in financial distress – was proposed in 1963, though not implemented until 1971. Importantly, this aid was intended as ongoing production support (as found by Picard, 2003) and not investment funding. Gustafsson describes the support system in some detail, and argues (p. 13) that it was the first and only government funding scheme with roots in competition theory. He further argues that the subsidies created healthy competition between high- and low-coverage newspapers, resulting in higher quality also in the newspapers that did not receive any subsidies. In stark contrast to non-interventionists, Gustafsson claims that the press subsidies increased media pluralism by giving mouthpieces to new political movements, and he dismisses the idea that the subsidies should be given on a "help-people-to-help-themselves" basis. The reason why this would not work, he argues, is that there are strong barriers to growth in the newspaper industry, not least because it is difficult for low-coverage newspapers to compete on the advertising market. Yearly subsidies may therefore be necessary. Gustafsson (p. 56) actually praises the subsidy system, stating that "The fact that there is still a diverse range of Swedish daily newspapers in 2007 is due to the production support that the government introduced in 1971 to assist daily papers in a weak competitive position." He then concludes by forcefully claiming that only a selective support system can work; such a system weakens market forces and benefits low-coverage newspapers, while a general support system strengthens market forces and thus also high-coverage newspapers at the expense of low-coverage newspapers.

In a broader survey of the development of the newspaper market in Europe since the 1970s, Gustafsson (2004) likewise argues that the Swedish subsidy system was the "main power" behind the relatively large number of newspaper start-ups in Sweden between 1975 and 2000.[20] However, it should be noted that Gustafsson does not provide any cost-benefit analysis, making it difficult to assess whether the policy really is worth its price even if it works. This is by no means unique for Gustafsson's studies; there barely exists any thorough cost-benefit analysis of either direct or indirect press subsidies in any country (see Sánchez-Tabernero, 2006, for a short discussion of some elements to consider in such an analysis).

Empirical Analyses of Indirect Media Support

While direct media support is hotly debated in most countries, indirect media support is rarely subject to scrutiny. In many cases indirect support has a long history embedded in law, and the instruments have modest visibility as they, more or less by definition, are not allocated over government budgets. This also makes it difficult to calculate their exact value. Nevertheless, several attempts to estimate the importance of indirect media subsidies have been made. Nielsen and Linnebank (2011), for example, present estimates showing that the value of indirect press support far outweighs the value of direct press support in all the six countries they review: Finland, France, Germany, Italy, United Kingdom and the United States.

The most important form of indirect support is VAT reductions and exemptions. According to OECD (2010, Table 6), Belgium, Denmark, Finland, Korea, Luxembourg, Mexico, Norway and United Kingdom have full VAT exemption for newspapers, while Austria, Czech Republic, France, Germany, Hungary, Iceland, Italy, Netherlands, Poland, Portugal, Spain, Sweden, Switzerland and Turkey have a reduced rate. This implies that the newspaper industry is heavily subsidized, and one can only wonder why there is so little academic interest in evaluating the effect of the subsidies. In comparison, there is a vast and highly advanced industrial economics literature on, for example, R&D subsidies and agricultural subsidies.

Although the literature on indirect media support is small, interest in the topic is increasing. A strong technological push for restructuring of the media industry has put media support on the political agenda in many countries. The size of the indirect subsidies makes it likely that these policy instruments, in particular low VAT rates, will come under pressure. First, committees considering reforms are typically asked to present at least one alternative that does not increase the total support. Second, fiscal difficulties faced by many countries suggest that all VAT exemptions are likely to be re-examined, as VAT is a very important source of tax revenue.

Finnish politicians have already taken action. In late 2011, the Finnish parliament passed an act introducing a new value-added tax on newspaper and magazine subscriptions valid from 1 January 2012. The new 9 percent tax on newspaper and magazine subscriptions took the media industry by surprise. Previously, the printed press was subject to a 23 percent tax on advertisements and single copy selling, but enjoyed full VAT exemption on subscriptions (Hyvönen, 2012).

In Denmark the Ministry of Culture in 2009 published a report which discusses the consequences of increasing the VAT rate on newspapers (Rambøll Management Consulting, 2009). A similar report was published by the Norwegian Ministry of Culture one year later (NOU, 2010). The Danish Report points out two main consequences of abolishing the VAT exemption for newspapers. First, it will improve the competitiveness of, for example, electronic newspapers, because the price of paper-based newspapers will increase. Second, and as a direct consequence of the price increase, the consumers who buy paper-based newspapers will be harmed. The Danish Report neglects the fact that newspapers serve both advertisers and readers, and thus that they operate in two-sided markets. This neglect means, for example, that the Report's estimation of demand elasticities on the reader side of the market says very little about the consequences of higher newspaper taxes. The interdependence between the reader and the advertising market seems to be missing in public debates also in other countries that consider the possibility of increasing the VAT rate on newspapers. Even if the two-sidedness of the newspaper market is acknowledged, as for example in the Norwegian report on media support, little can be said about the full effect since it has not been studied empirically.

There exist a few empirical assessments of the effect of VAT exemption, but they disregard the two-sidedness of the market. Both De Bens and Østbye (1998, p. 13) and McQuail and Siume (1998, p. 13) cite an analysis by Price Waterhouse which argues that if the VAT on newspapers in the UK in the 1990s had been increased from 0 percent to 6 percent, then most UK regional dailies would disappear, and the circulation of the national dailies would fall by 10 percent. Similarly, Wilberg (2010), commissioned by the Norwegian Media Businesses' Association, paints a very gloomy picture of the consequences of VAT on newspapers using informed judgment based on detailed industry knowledge, company performance data and forecasting techniques.

The only study we are aware of that utilizes an exogenous shift in the VAT rate is Gustafsson (2007, pp. 29–30). Unfortunately, this is neither an econometric analysis nor an analysis of VAT as such. Gustafsson describes the development in aggregate circulation for Swedish subscription newspapers. The average annual decrease in circulation from 1989 to 2007 was about 1 percent. In 1996, however, the drop in circulation was more than 4 percent. He explains this drop by the introduction of a 6 percent VAT on newspapers that year, causing a price increase of 10–11 percent. This was twice as much as the normal price increase.

Another Swedish policy change towards the publishing industry is discussed by Copenhagen Economics (2007, p. 82) and NOU (2010, p. 94) building mostly on Ahlmark (2004). In December 2002 the Swedish parliament decided to reduce the VAT on books from 25 percent to 6 percent in response to increasing competition from internet bookstores located in low-VAT countries. The VAT reduction was immediately reflected in lower prices, and even the long-run pass-through was close to full. However, since book publishers operate in one-sided markets, the transfer value of this study to the newspaper market is limited. It should also be noted that Ahlmark (2004) is written for the Swedish booksellers' and publishers' associations in response to a more negative assessment by the Council for Official Statistics. It is obviously a weakness that much analysis in this area is both industry financed, and not published in peer reviewed channels.

We are aware of only one relevant analysis of VAT that is published in a scientific journal. That is Depken (2004), who analyses the effect of VAT on the market structure in the magazine industry, utilizing cross sectional variation in VAT rates between 23 countries. He finds that "a one-unit increase in an ad valorem tax (e.g., from 6 percent to 7 percent) correlates with a reduction in 21 consumer magazine titles, on average, and 52 business titles". In a country with an average number of consumer and business magazines, these numbers correspond to a 2.1 percent and 3.9 percent decrease in magazine titles, respectively. These numbers are arguably surprisingly high, and underline the need for further studies.

Taken together, the scant evidence reviewed above suggests that an increase in the VAT rate for newspapers will negatively affect circulation and survival. This, however, is only a partial input to a cost-benefit analysis. Direct transfers will be a more efficient way to help newspapers that are threatened by a shutdown.

4. CONCLUDING REMARKS AND PATHS FOR FUTURE RESEARCH

The media industry has for decades received substantial subsidies. While other types of industry support are frequently evaluated, media support has received little attention from economists. This is unfortunate. The media industry is important economically, politically and culturally. It is rapidly changing and has characteristics that require specialized models.

The literature has identified several types of market failure in the media industry. Knowledge externalities, public good characteristics of investigative journalism and non-appropriability of consumer surplus all suggest that the social value of journalism is much larger than what the newspapers are able to extract. This indicates that a free market will underinvest in journalism. Problems related to economies of scale and scope may further imply that newspaper prices are too high (too small circulations) and the number of newspapers too small. The presence of an advertising market may give newspapers too strong incentives to aim for the mass market, resulting in too little media diversity. Low VAT rates may reduce this latter problem, since it makes the advertising market relatively less important for newspaper profits.

Tax credits or other indirect subsidy schemes that directly reduce the marginal cost of investing in journalism are the most efficient scheme to increase the quality and quantity of journalism and stimulate investigative journalism. Tax credit schemes are widely used in OECD countries to promote R&D investments, but not much used as a media policy instrument. We believe they deserve far more attention from both academics and policy makers who reflect on how to secure high quality journalism when the traditional business model of the media industry is eroded by the internet and more or less free distribution of news.

Identifying a market failure is not in itself an argument for policy intervention, however. It is also important to keep an eye on potential government failure and how lobbyism may distort the implementation of efficient policy measures. Press associations dominated by large and profitable newspapers may, for example, push for further VAT breaks or zero-VAT regimes, rather than potentially more efficient subsidy regimes that they themselves will not benefit from. In terms of political economy, one should also notice that entrants to digital platforms may have very different interests from incumbent media firms. Typically, entrants also command less resources and have smaller incentives to invest in lobbyism since the gains they obtain will stimulate further entry and competition, as noted by Baldwin and Robert-Nicoud (2007). Finally, it is important to bear in mind that there are large welfare losses associated with tax payments because taxes lead to inefficient adjustments in goods- and labour-markets. Some studies argue that the effective cost for each one million of subsidies can be as high as two million (as measured by the marginal cost of public funds, MCF). This is the major reason why very few sectors of society are subsidized, even in cases where large market imperfections can be proven.

In order to evaluate the effect of direct and indirect press subsidies, both formal modelling skills and modern econometric tools are needed to identify the full causal effects. One can hope that economists will take up the challenge. This needs to be done in cooperation with media scientists as some of the effects that should be evaluated demand methodologies for content analysis. We believe two issues are particularly pressing and achievable. One is panel data analyses utilizing the significant variation in VAT rates that the publishing industry faces within and between countries. This might help to assess the effects of VAT reduction schemes on newspaper circulation and diversity. Another is to analyse the effect of monopolized regional newspaper markets. The extensive subsidy regimes that were introduced in many European countries after World War II were largely motivated by newspaper mortality, but increasing concentration in the newspaper industry has nonetheless been a striking trend (Picard, 2006). Every exit of a secondary newspaper is an experiment that allows media scientists to explore how newspaper competition matters for the profile and quality of primary newspapers. These events have not been explored to the extent one would expect given the emphasis newspaper mortality has in the policy debate.[21] In particular, there seems to be little work on the effect of media competition by European media scientists. More work on the importance of local newspapers, similar to the innovative study by Bruns and Himmler (2011), is also called for.

NOTES

1. See Krumsvik (2011, p. 93).
2. Quotation from Humphreys (2006, p. 42).
3. Normally one thinks of knowledge externalities as positive. For the sake of completeness it should be mentioned that one can also think of negative externalities

that result in overinvestment in knowledge development in a free market. For example two companies can invest in the same research in the hope of becoming the first to patent or copyright the product. A parallel in the media world would be newspapers chasing the same news. The parallel is not perfect, however. Two journalists who write about the same case control one another. In the absence of the second journalist, one journalist would easily be able to distort the truth. Gentzkow and Shapiro (2008) give an overview of the literature on "truth-telling" and the importance of competition in the news market.

4. See Gustafsson (1978) and Gabszewicz et al. (2007) for a discussion of the so-called circulation spiral.
5. In general, there is a trade-off between "static" and "dynamic" efficiency. Simple economic analysis suggests that the price of knowledge already developed should be close to zero, so that everyone that can benefit from the knowledge will have access to it. From this perspective, online newspapers are correctly priced. The problem is that such pricing leads to dynamic or long-term inefficiency. Who will invest in developing material if they do not get paid? This is the problem newspapers face today. They are not able to charge readers as much as before, and they have also lost a lot of the advertising market to the internet. This undermines the journalistic production, and is an argument for increased public support. For radio and television the development has gone in the opposite direction. From the start it was not possible to charge user fees, and with insufficient advertising revenue, public funding of public broadcasters was essential. Paternalistic and democratic considerations also played a role when many countries chose to run broadcasters in the public sector, e.g. the BBC in Britain.
6. Evans (2003a, b) provides a useful and interesting classification and discussion on different types of two-sided markets.
7. See Rochet and Tirole (2003) for a more precise and formal definition.
8. Here we have implicitly assumed that C_{an} (which means that the newspaper's marginal costs of inserting an ad are independent of the circulation). This simplifies the analysis, but is an innocent assumption in our context.
9. Empirical analysis does not give a definite answer as to whether readers perceive ads as a good or a bad (this is in sharp contrast to commercials on TV, which generally are perceived as a nuisance). See, for instance, Ferguson (1983), Blair and Romano (1993), Sonnac (2000), and Wilbur (2008).
10. The variable S is equal to $\pi_{aa}\,\pi_{nn}/H$, where H is the Hessian matrix.
11. Differentiating the equilibrium value of eq. (16.1) with respect to t, and using the envelope theorem, we find $d\pi/dt = -p^N(n, a)\,n\,(1 + t)^{-2} < 0$ so the profit level is strictly decreasing in the tax rate. However, the marginal change in profits earned in the ad market is $(ap_a^A + p^A)da/dt + p_n^A dn/dt$ which is positive if quantity responses are positive (i.e., $ap_n^A - C_n > 0$).
12. See Fullerton and Metcalf (2002) for an overview over the tax incidence literature in one-sided markets.
13. It can be shown that within the Hotelling framework, it is irrelevant for the location of the firms and their profits whether there is an advertising market (and how large it is) if newspaper prices and advertising prices are determined at the same stage. This is due to some peculiarities of the Hotelling model. See Gabszewicz et al. (2001, 2002), Anderson and Coate (2005) and Peitz and Valletti (2008) for discussions.
14. Kind et al. (2010) use the original timing of Gabszewicz et al. (2001, 2002) and show that the higher is the tax rate, the more likely it is that the newspapers will be minimally differentiated. Perhaps somewhat surprisingly, they show that this holds independent of whether readers consider ads as a good or a bad.
15. From the mid-1930s to 1998, journalists and some other newspaper employees in France could deduct 30% of their income as professional expenses. Through this

arrangement newspapers also saved 30% on their social insurance payments. The value of this deduction corresponded to about one month's pay (Thogmartin, 1998, p. 343). Since 1998 the automatic deduction for professional expenses has been fixed at €7650. (This is regulated in circular BOI 5 F-14-99 from the French Tax Administration.)

16. A better way to limit the costs may be to differentiate the tax credit so that large newspapers get a lower deduction rate. The R&D tax credit in the Netherlands has this structure.
17. See Kind et al. 2008 for a formal proof.
18. Subsidized postal rates might of course help smaller newspapers survive, but as discussed above this is most efficiently achieved through the fixed subsidy component *F*.
19. See also Murschetz (2009).
20. Exactly the same claim has been made for Norway, see NOU (2010, p. 89).
21. See Trim et al. (1983) for an early and interesting study of this kind. They report a significant decline in the quantity and quality of news in the aftermath of two Canadian cities going from being "two-newspaper towns" to "one-newspaper towns". In a very recent study, Drago et al. (2014) evaluate effects of newspaper entry and exit in Italian cities using data from 1993–2009. They find that newspaper entry increases turnout in municipal elections, the reelection probability of the incumbent mayor, and the efficiency of the municipal government.

REFERENCES

Ahlmark, D. (2004) 'Measuring the development of book prices', in *Cultural VAT on Books – An Evaluation of the Three First Years*, Stockholm: The Swedish Booksellers' Association and The Swedish Publishers' Association, 15–28.

Anderson, S.P. and S. Coate (2005) 'Market provision of broadcasting: A welfare analysis', *Review of Economic Studies*, 72 (4), 947–972.

Arrow, K.J. (1962) 'Economic welfare and the allocation of resources for invention', in Nelson, R.R. (ed.), *The Rate and Direction of Inventive Activity*, New Jersey: Princeton University Press, pp. 609–626.

Baldwin, R.E. and F. Robert-Nicoud (2007) 'Entry and asymmetric lobbying: Why governments pick losers', *Journal of the European Economic Association*, 5 (5), 1064–1093.

Bhattacharyya, S. and R. Hodler (2010) 'Natural resources, democracy and corruption', *European Economic Review*, 54 (4), 608–621.

Blair, R.D. and R.E. Romano (1993) 'Pricing decisions of the newspaper monopolist', *Southern Economic Journal*, 54 (9), 721–732.

Bruns, C. and O. Himmler (2011) 'Newspaper circulation and local government efficiency', *Scandinavian Journal of Economics*, 113 (2), 470–492.

Copenhagen Economics (2007) 'Study on reduced VAT applied to goods and services in the Member States of the European Union', Taxation papers WP 13/07, European Commission.

De Bens, E. and H. Østbye (1998) 'The European newspaper market', Ch. 2 in D. McQuail and K. Siune (eds), *Media Policy: Convergence, Concentration and Commerce*, London: Sage, pp. 7–22.

Depken II, Craig A. (2004) 'Market structure and ad valorem taxes: cross-country evidence from the magazine industry', *Applied Economics Letters*, 11 (8), 477–481.

Drago, F., T. Nannicini and F. Sobbrio (2014) 'Meet the Press: How Voters and Politicians Respond to Newspaper Entry and Exit', *American Economic Journal: Applied Economics*, 6 (3), 159–188.

Erdal, I.J. (2010) 'Hvor kommer nyhetene fra?' (Where does the news come from?), Appendix 1 to Official Norwegian Report, NOU 2010: 14 (Public Media Support Committee), 129–137.

Evans, D.S. (2003a) 'The antitrust economics of two-sided markets', *Yale Journal on Regulation*, 20 (2), 325–381.

Evans, D.S. (2003b) 'Some empirical aspects of multi-sided platform industries', *Review of Network Economics*, 2 (3), 191–209.

Ferguson, J.M. (1983) 'Daily newspaper advertising rates, local media cross-ownership, and media competition', *Journal of Law and Economics*, 26 (3), 635–654.

Fullerton, D. and G.E. Metcalf (2002) 'Tax incidence', Chapter 26 in A.J. Auerbach and M. Feldstein (eds), *Handbook of Public Economics*, vol. 4, Amsterdam: Elsevier, pp. 1787–1872.

Gabszewicz, J.J., D. Laussel and N. Sonnac (2001) 'Press advertising and the ascent of the "Pensee Unique"', *European Economic Review*, 45 (4–6), 645–651.

Gabszewicz, J.J., D. Laussel and N. Sonnac (2002) 'Press advertising and the political differentiation of newspapers', *Journal of Public Economic Theory*, 4 (3), 317–334.

Gabszewicz, J.J., Garella, P.G. and N. Sonnac (2007) 'Newspapers' market shares and the theory of the circulation spiral', *Information Economics and Policy*, 19 (3–4), 405–413.

Gentzkow, M. and J.M. Shapiro (2008) 'Competition and truth in the market for news', *Journal of Economic Perspectives*, 22 (2), 133–154.

Gustafsson, K.E. (1978) 'The circulation spiral and the principle of household coverage', *The Scandinavian Economic History Review*, 26 (1), 1–14.

Gustafsson, K.E. (2004) 'Stability and change: success and failure of new newspapers in Europe since the 1970s', in R.G. Picard (ed.), *Strategic Responses to Media Market Changes*, JIBS Research Report Series 2004-2, 121–131.

Gustafsson, K.E. (2007) 'Det svenska presstödets marknadskonsekvenser' (The Market Consequences of Swedish Press Subsidies). Analysis commissioned by the Swedish Ministry of Culture.

Hallin, D.C. and P. Mancini (2004) *Comparing Media Systems: Three Models of Media and Politics*, Cambridge, UK: Cambridge University Press.

Humphreys, P. (2006) 'Press subsidies in the context of the information society. Historical perspective, modalities, concept and justification', in I.F. Alonso, M. de Moragas, J.J. Blasco Gil and N. Almiron (eds), *Press Subsidies in Europe*, Institut de la Comunicació, Universitat Autònoma de Barcelona, pp. 38–55.

Hyvönen, H. (2012) 'New tax on subscriptions hits Finnish printed press sector', European Journalism Centre, published online January 30, 2012, www.ejc.net/magazine/.

Kind, H.J., M. Koethenbuerger and G. Schjelderup (2008) 'Efficiency-enhancing taxation in two-sided markets', *Journal of Public Economics*, 92 (5–6), 1531–1539.

Kind, H.J., M. Koethenbuerger and G. Schjelderup (2010) 'Tax responses in platform industries', *Oxford Economic Papers*, 62 (4), 764–783.

Kind, H.J., G. Schjelderup and F. Stähler (2012) 'Newspaper differentiation and investments in journalism: the role of tax policy', *Economica*, forthcoming.

Krumsvik, A.H. (2011) *Medienes privilegier – en innføring i mediepolitikk* (The Privileges of the Media – An Introduction to Media policy), Kristiansand: IJ-forlaget.

Lund, A.B. (2001) 'The genealogy of news researching journalistic food-chains', *Nordicom Review*, 22 (1), 37–43.

Lund, A.B, I. Willig and M. Blach-Ørsten (2009) *Hvor kommer nyhederne fra? Den journalistiske fødekæde i Danmark før og nu* (Where does the news come from? The Danish journalistic food-chains before and now), Århus: Forlaget Ajour.

McChesney, R. and J. Nichols (2010) *The Death and Life of American Journalism: The Media Revolution That Will Begin the World Again*, Philadelphia: Nation Books.

McQuail, D. and K. Siume (1998) *Media Policy: Convergence, Concentration and Commerce*, London: Sage.

Murschetz, P. (1998) 'State Support for the Daily Press in Europe: A Critical Appraisal. Austria, France, Sweden and Norway Compared', *European Journal of Communication*, 13 (3), 291–313.

Murschetz, P. (2009) 'Examining effects of public financial subsidies to daily newspapers in Europe – do they avoid market failure?' in *Die österreichische Medienlandschaft im Umbruch*, Wien: Austrian Academy of Sciences Press, pp. 295–319.

Nielsen, R.K. and G. Linnebank (2011) 'Public support for the media: A six-country overview of direct and indirect subsidies', Report from Reuters Institute for the Study of Journalism.

NOU (2010) 'Lett å komme til orde, vanskelig å bli hørt – en moderne mediestøtte' (Recommendations from the Public Media Support Committee), Official Norwegian Report 2010:14, Oslo: Ministry of Culture.

OECD (2010) *Working Party on the Information Economy: The Evolution of News and the Internet*, DSTI/ICCP/IE(2009)14/FINAL.

Peitz, M. and T. Valletti (2008) 'Content and advertising in the media: Pay-tv versus free-to-air', *International Journal of Industrial Organization*, 26 (4), 949–965.

Picard, R.G. (1985) 'Pattern of state intervention in Western press economics', *Journalism Quarterly*, 62 (Spring), 3–9.

Picard, R.G. (1988) 'The Nordic region' in A.B. Albarran and S.M. Chan-Olmsted (eds), *Global Media Economics: Commercialization, Concentration, and Integration of World Media Markets*, Ames: Iowa State University Press, pp. 150–163.

Picard, R.G. (2003) 'Press support and company performance', in U. Carlsson (ed.), *Penningen & Politiken: Medieföretag förr och nu*, Göteborg: Nordicom, pp. 96–107.

Picard, R.G. (2006) 'Issues and challenges in the provision of press subsidies' in I.F. Alonso, M. de Moragas, J.J. Blasco Gil and N. Almiron (eds), *Press Subsidies in Europe*, Institut de la Comunicació, Universitat Autònoma de Barcelona, pp. 211–223.

Picard, R.G. (2007) 'Subsidies for newspapers: Can the Nordic model remain viable?', in H. Bohrmann, E. Klaus and M. Machill (eds), *Media Industry, Journalism Culture, and Communication Policies in Europe*, Köln: Herbert von Halem Verlag, pp. 236–246.

Picard, R.G., and M. Grönlund (2003) 'Development and effects of Finnish press subsidies', *Journalism Studies,* 4 (1), 105–119.

Prat, A. and D. Strömberg (2011) 'The political economy of mass media', CEPR DP 8246.

Rambøll Management Consulting (2009) 'Utredning af Den Fremtidige Offentlige Mediestøtte' (Study on the future press support), Ebook ISBN 87-89227-52-2, Copenhagen: Rambøll Management Consulting.

Rochet, J.C. and J. Tirole (2003) 'Platform competition in two-sided markets', *Journal of the European Economic Association*, 1 (4), 990–1029.

Romer, P.M. (1990) 'Endogenous technological change', *Journal of Political Economy*, 98 (5), S71–S102.

Sánchez-Tabernero, A. (2006) 'The European press at the beginning of the 21st century. Defining characteristics and future trends', in I.F. Alonso, M. de Moragas, J.J. Blasco Gil and N. Almiron (eds), *Press Subsidies in Europe*, Institut de la Comunicació, Universitat Autònoma de Barcelona, pp. 18–37.

Simkin, J. (2012) 'Taxes on knowledge', www.spartacus.schoolnet.co.uk/PRknowledge.htm.

Skogerbø, E. (1997) 'The press subsidy system in Norway: Controversial past – unpredictable future?', *European Journal of Communication*, 12 (1), 99–118.

Sonnac, N. (2000) 'Readers' attitudes towards press advertising: Are they ad-lovers or ad-averse?', *Journal of Media Economics*, 13 (4), 249–259.

Statskonsult (1998) 'Om pressestøtten og statens annonseregelverk' (About the press subsidy and the regulation for governmental advertisements), Rapport 1998:2, Oslo: Statskonsult.

Thogmartin, C. (1998) *The National Daily Press of France*, Birmingham, AL: Summa.

Tirole, J. (1988) *The Theory of Industrial Organization*, Massachusetts: MIT Press.
Trim, K., G. Pizante and J. Yaraskavitch (1983) 'The effect of monopoly on the news: A before and after study of two Canadian one-newspaper towns', *Canadian Journal of Communication*, 9 (3), 33–56.
Wilberg, E. (2010) 'Økonomisk konsekvensanalyse for aviser 2010–2015 – Analyse og beregninger' (Economic consequences for newspapers 2010–2015), Appendix 7 in 'Helt i sin tid, en mediepolitikk for morgendagen' (A media policy for tomorrow), Oslo: Norwegian Media Businesses' Association.
Wilbur, K.C. (2008) 'A two-sided, empirical model of television advertising and viewing markets', *Marketing Science*, 27 (3), 356–378.

Index